You & Your Child

Photography by Anthea Sieveking

The specialist A–Z of child development and the ailments, diseases and problems of pregnant mothers and children from conception to adolescence was written by:

Richard Barry Jones BMBCh MRCP DCH DRCOG

Former lecturer in developmental medicine at the Wolfson Centre, Institute of Child Health, London, and now Consultant Paediatrician to the Hospital for Sick Children, London, and to Moorfields Eye Hospitals, London. Dr Jones is also Medical Director, Donald Winnicott Assessment Centre, Queen Elizabeth Hospital for Children, London; Honorary Consultant Paediatrician to The Royal National Institute for the Blind; and Editor of *Child: Care, Health and Development.*

John Coleman BA PhD ABPsS

trained as both an educational and clinical psychologist and is now Senior Lecturer in clinical psychology at The London Hospital Medical College. He has a wide knowledge of the stresses and problems encountered by children of all ages, but is particularly involved with his own research into adolescent development and the running of a special nursery and assessment centre for disturbed pre-school children.

Consultants

Dr Neville Bennett BEd PhD
Lecturer in research methods at the Department of Educational Research, University of Lancaster. Research Director of National Inquiry into Open-plan Primary Schools.

Dr John Coleman BA PhD ABPsS
Senior Lecturer in clinical psychology at The London Hospital Medical College. Specialist in pre-school children and adolescents.

Dr Margaret Harris BSc PhD
Lecturer in developmental psychology at Birkbeck College, University of London. Specialist in cognitive development and language.

Professor Peter Huntingford MD FRCOG
Professor of obstetrics and gynaecology at London Hospital and St Bartholomew's Hospital Medical Colleges (University of London).

Dr Peter Husband BMBCh MRCP DCH DRCOG
Consultant Paediatrician at West Middlesex Hospital and Ashford General Hospital, Middlesex.

Sheila Kitzinger
Anthropologist and childbirth educator, author of *The Experience of Childbirth* and other books on the subject. Member of the Advisory Board of the National Childbirth Trust.

Michael Roe BA ABPsS
Chief Educational Psychologist, Borough of Bexley, Kent. Specialist in school behaviour and learning.

This edition published in USA 1984
by Exeter Books
Distributed by Bookthrift
Exeter is a trademark of Simon & Schuster, Inc.
Bookthrift is a registered trademark of
Simon & Schuster, Inc. New York, New York.

ISBN 0 671 07230 7

You and Your Child was edited and designed by Mitchell Beazley Publishers Limited, Artists House, 14–15 Manette Street, London W1V 5LB

Typeset by Servis Filmsetting Limited, Manchester
Origination by Gilchrist Bros Limited, Leeds
Printed in Spain by Printer industria gráfica sa.,
Sant Vicenç dels Horts, Barcelona. 1980
Depósito Legal B—2093—1978.

YOU & YOUR CHILD

The complete guide to parenthood

SUSAN GOODMAN

Exeter Books ★ New York

CONTENTS

4 EARLY CHILDHOOD
An Individual Mind

5 SCHOOL YEARS
The Widening World

I have long felt, from my own experience, that a book was needed that dealt sensibly with the practicalities of daily child care and yet also gave insight into how children think and grow. A parent's need for knowledge and advice does not suddenly cease, as most baby books imply, at two or ten or when the child starts school. Bringing up a child is a continuous process; the parents' responsibility does not end until the child is able to assume that responsibility. This book, then, takes you all the way through to that time at which the law at least recognizes your child as an adult.

It also recognizes that parents have to take care of themselves as well as their children, and that the inevitable stresses and strains of family life cannot be considered in isolation from the upbringing of a child. Writing the book was both a challenge and a labor of love. *From the first, I believed in it.* I had lots of help, from colleagues and consultants; and I am convinced that we have produced a book that is unique in the scope and information it offers to mothers—and to fathers, whose expanding role in child raising is wholeheartedly acknowledged.

My apologies to mothers of girls for referring to the baby (and the doctor!) throughout as "he" not "she." As a mother of three sons this comes naturally to me, but this is not the only reason. It has been done principally to avoid confusion with the mother (also she), who is usually more involved in the daily care of a young child than the father.

If you are a young parent today, *you're lucky*! You have a baby because you choose to; because you and your husband feel that this is the right time to start, or add to, your family. So your baby begins life with the priceless advantage of being wanted; apart from health, this is the most precious gift you can give him. Your husband will probably be as thrilled as you to watch your expanding abdomen, and will want to take an active and loving part in the baby's

upbringing, doing practical things like bathing him, a pleasure that convention probably denied his own father.

It's worth pausing here, briefly, to count a few blessings. Unlike your grandmother there is almost no chance that you will die in childbirth. Having a baby is hard work—no mother who has opted for the natural methods of childbirth, as many do, would think otherwise; but it is not a horrifying experience. Afterward, you won't suffer because of breast or vaginal infections (common until the widespread use of antibiotics in the late 1940s)—and if you choose not to, you won't be pregnant again in three months or a year. A baby born now in this country has a life expectancy into his seventies. He has a far greater chance of surviving infancy than at the turn of the century; in the field of childhood illness great medical strides have been made— diphtheria, whooping cough, polio, meningitis, all killers until after the Second World War, are now eradicated or treatable.

However, it must also be said that in raising a child parents today must face problems that were unheard of years ago. Our society is highly industrialized and competitive; middle-class children may be burdened with many unrealistic expectations: they may face too much pressure from parents, teachers, and friends for high-powered jobs and places at universities. All too often young adults from minority groups in urban areas experience the bitterness of discrimination and unemployment. As your child grows toward adulthood in a more open society with its emphasis on the individual, parents must somehow find the wisdom to guide him through the pitfalls of schooling, drugs, and drink and too early, irresponsible sex. It is not easy; as a parent myself, I know we need all the help we can get. That is why I believe this book, which follows parents and child from conception through

INTRODUCTION

early adulthood, has so much valuable information and support to give parents who care vitally, as I do, about what happens to their child.

I know something about all this because, like most people of my age, around forty, I've been through it. *And it's still going on!* Marriage, children, divorce, remarriage, work—all mixed up between England and the United States. In fact, whenever I am asked a specific question about my family—why my son is at a university in America, for example—it occurs to me that my life is something of a transatlantic muddle, hopeless even to try to explain to a casual acquaintance. In simple terms, after leaving school in England I went straight to America on a scholarship to a college in the Midwest. Except for visits with my family, I did not live in England again for nearly twenty years.

I married an American. We had three sons and I worked at being their mother and, as they got older, as a journalist also. But unlike my youngest son's favorite bedtime reading—Grimms' fairy tales—this marriage did not have a happy ending. We were divorced several years ago, and I have since been married again, to an Englishman, and come back to live in England. My eldest son goes to school in America because, of course, he is an American. My youngest son, now ten, a life-enhancer despite the predictable weekly loss of his football boots, lives with me and his stepfather in London, and he visits America twice a year. My middle son is a brain-damaged child who inhabits some strange world of his own where we cannot reach him. Although the doctors could find nothing wrong physically, by four he was not speaking. We were told that he was slow, that he showed a peculiar pattern of behavior described as "autistic," but, with careful handling and exposure to other children, might improve. Despite our love and hopes, he did not. We despaired when he was seven and for all our sakes,

his particularly, we decided to place him in an institution. He seems calm and happy there, for which we are unendingly grateful—and he will stay there for the rest of his life. Our pain goes on.

After some twenty years of parenthood I find I can no longer clearly remember the time when I did not have a child. My most recent pleasure of parenthood has been watching trust and affection develop, as it surely has, between stepfather and stepson. And for myself, too, arriving at middle age has had its rewards. I now understand that a good man/woman relationship is an important human achievement which needs love and understanding and maturity. And work. Whoever thought of things like that at twenty?

So, emotional or not, having had these three sons and survived tragedy with one of them, I feel there is no life experience to equal the challenge—the sheer creativity—of raising a child. You need everything you've got to do it well, and more: guts and sensitivity, love and luck, and a sense of humor. Sometimes, you will think that you're a hopeless parent; I often do. But it's not true; you must be doing something right to care so much, and most of us do this with our children most of the time. You will have awful moments—disrupted nights when they are little, bad school experiences, bills, and heartaches. All our children are hostages to fortune; there are no guarantees, and pain may be unavoidable. But the sentiment, not sentimentality, is there also—first words, first steps, the wonder of watching a child reach out and grow and develop, a touching letter from a shy adolescent son. . . .

I'm sure you'll think it's all worth it. I do.

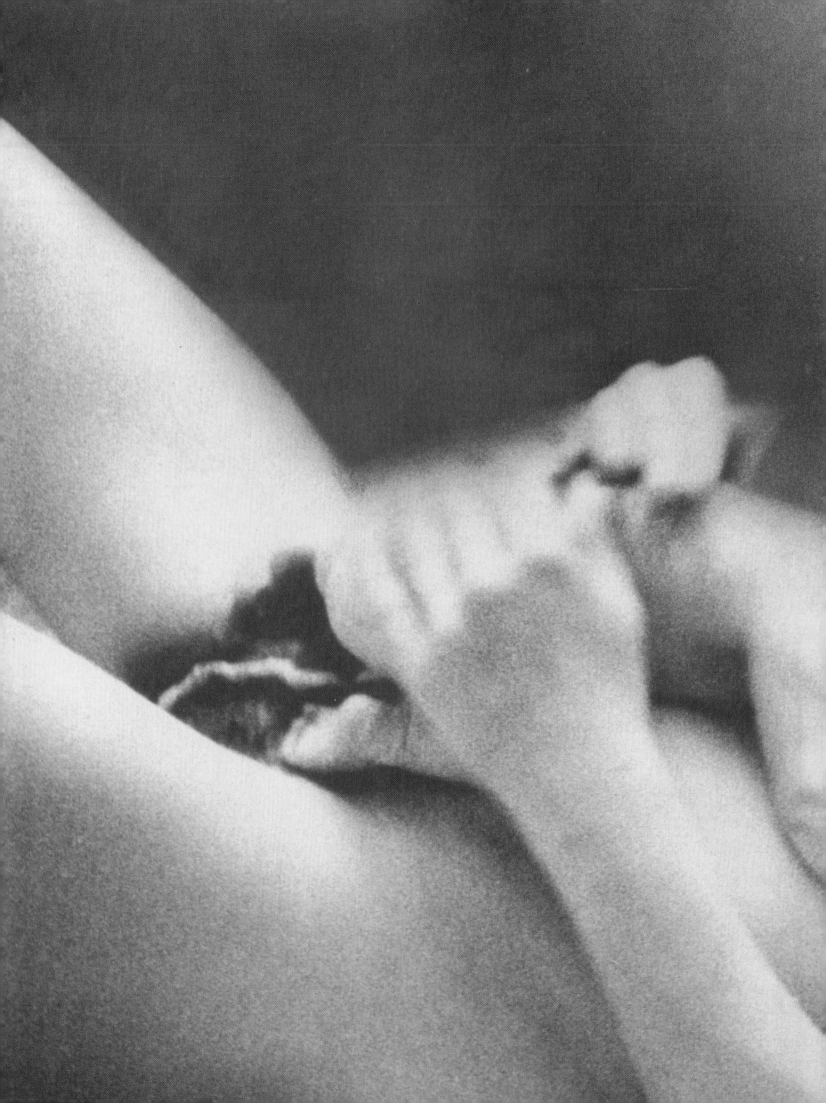

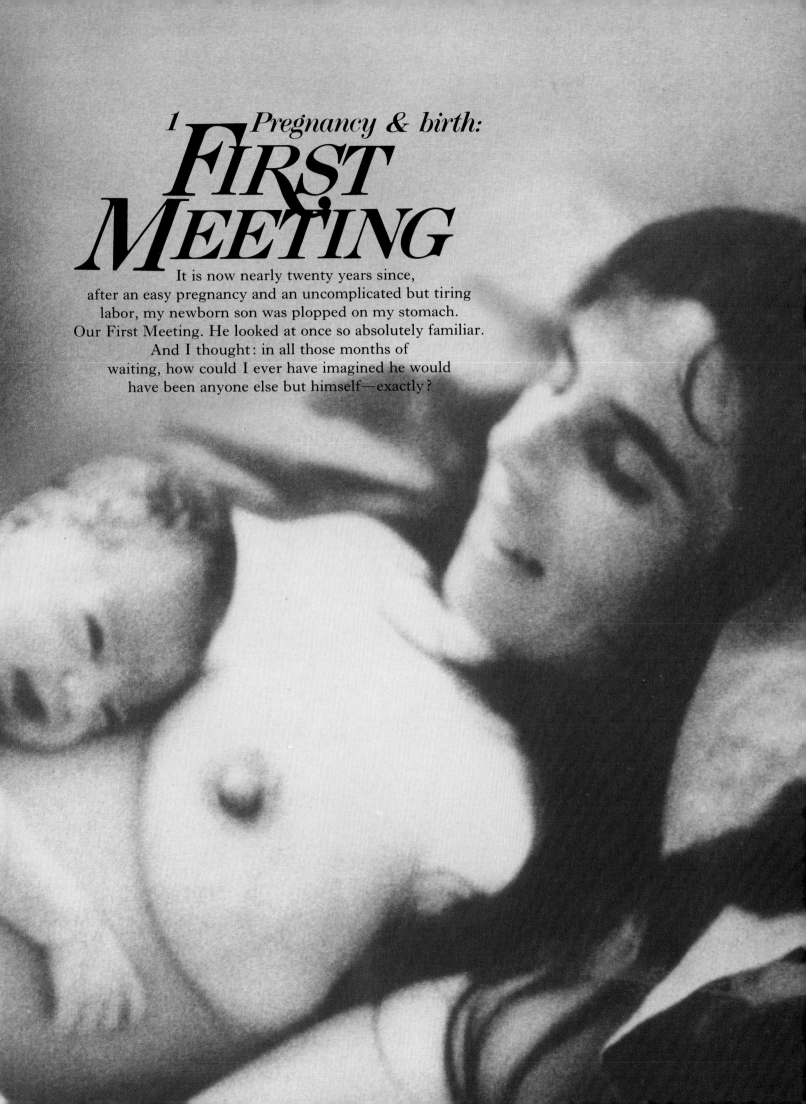

1 *Pregnancy & birth:*
FIRST MEETING

It is now nearly twenty years since,
after an easy pregnancy and an uncomplicated but tiring
labor, my newborn son was plopped on my stomach.
Our First Meeting. He looked at once so absolutely familiar.
And I thought: in all those months of
waiting, how could I ever have imagined he would
have been anyone else but himself—exactly?

Conception

It was once believed that the miniature individual—or preformed homunculus—was contained, whole, in the male sperm and that the womb was no more than a place in which the man's seed could grow like a plant in the earth. Now we know that about the fourteenth day of a woman's monthly cycle, ovulation takes place—an egg being released from a follicle in the ovary into the Fallopian tube. It is carried by a small amount of fluid along the tube, maturing on its way. All that is needed to fertilize this egg (or ovum) is a potent sperm, millions of which are deposited at the upper end of the vaginal passage during sexual intercourse.

From there the sperm must travel through the cervical mucus, across the uterus, and up into the Fallopian tube to meet and fertilize the egg. Each tiny sperm, which when magnified looks like a transparent tadpole, is propelled by the whiplash of its tail. Of the millions of ejaculated sperm only a few hundred will reach and seek to penetrate the waiting egg, which is like a crystal ball, just large enough to be visible to the naked eye. And of these hundreds, only a single sperm will burrow through the egg's outer covering—or zona pellucida—and effect fertilization.

At the instant when sperm and egg unite—that magical coming together of inherited characteristics in the male and female chromosomes, twenty-three from each parent—another human being begins.

In the six- or seven-day interval between fertilization and the beginning of pregnancy a minutely devised sequence of events takes place. Although the length of time an egg can be fertilized is short—about twenty-four hours of a twenty-eight-day cycle—sperm can survive for several days in the female reproductive tract. If chemical signals from a ripe and ready ovum beckon sperm on, they can move rapidly from the cervix into the Fallopian tube, covering a distance of about 8 in/200 mm, at an approximate rate of $\frac{1}{8}$ in/3 mm per minute, to reach the mature egg in just over an hour. Some sperm soon die, but others stay alive, so that fertilization can take place if intercourse occurs any time from a few days before ovulation to twenty-four or so hours after ovulation.

A few sperm cells, each with a head containing the chromosomes and a tail, swim together in the same direction, attracted by chemical signals from the egg. Photograph by courtesy of Dr. Landrum Shettles.

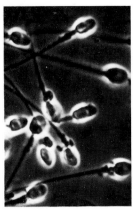

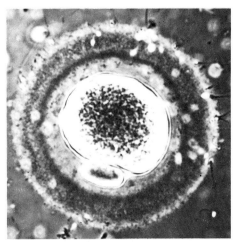

The egg is surrounded by a hundred or more sperms seeking entry. A digestive enzyme in their heads helps two or three to penetrate the egg's outer cover, but only one will be selected to unite with the egg's nucleus. The egg's volume is eighty-five thousand times that of the sperm. Photograph by courtesy of Dr. Landrum Shettles.

A time chart of the journey of the ovum from expulsion out of the follicle to implantation in the womb.
1 The mature ovum, a tiny speck surrounded by an entourage of some 6,000 nurse cells, gradually makes its way down the Fallopian tube.
2 Within twenty-four hours the ovum can be penetrated by the sperm. A further twelve to twenty-four hours sees the sperm and egg united to form the tiny, single cell.
3 This cell travels down the Fallopian tube, and after a further thirty hours begins to divide.
4 Four days after fertilization the cluster of ever-dividing cells reaches the uterine cavity.
5 During the next twenty-four hours some of the cells begin to congregate at one side to form the embryo, while the rest provide the membranes that will protect the fetus throughout pregnancy.
6 Within a week after fertilization the mass of cells will make contact with the lining of the womb and there embed themselves—the position from which the embryo will grow for the next nine months.

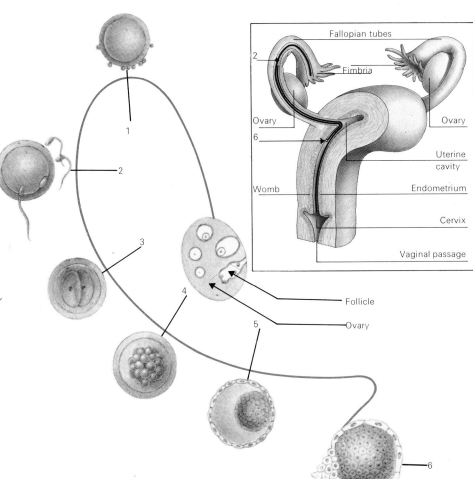

Fallopian tubes
Fimbria
Ovary
Ovary
Uterine cavity
Womb
Endometrium
Cervix
Vaginal passage
Follicle
Ovary

The womb, which is situated within the pelvic cavity, can be moved painlessly not only up and down but also sideways and from front to back. It is normally tilted forward with its upper part against the bladder. When the bladder fills the womb is pushed upward and backward so that it lies in direct line with the vagina.

Lining the uterine cavity is the endometrium, a highly specialized layer of glandular tissue which, when no fertilization takes place, is shed at menstruation. At the outer end of each Fallopian tube are the finger-like folds called the fimbria which sweep the ovum into the canal of the tube itself.

The black line traces the passage of the sperm up into the Fallopian tube where it can penetrate the ovum (at 2). The journey of the ovum descending from the ovary into the lining of the womb (at 6) is indicated by the red line.

The beginning of pregnancy

Then, some hours after the union of sperm and egg, the resulting cell begins to divide—into two . . . into four . . . into eight . . . into sixteen . . . doubling the number of cells with each successive division. This process transforms the egg into a ball-shaped cluster of rapidly dividing cells, which is called a morula. Under a microscope it looks rather like a mulberry. So, dividing all the while, the morula makes its way down the Fallopian tube toward the womb (the uterus)—a journey that will take four days. By the time the ever-dividing cluster reaches the womb, it has become a hollow fluid-filled ball of cells, the blastocyst. During the next two days the blastocyst attaches itself by sinking into the lining of the womb. The process of attachment is called implantation—and thus, six days after fertilization, pregnancy begins.

The first few weeks

In terms we all understand, a couple has made love, the woman has conceived, and another baby will be born. Somehow the obliviousness of its creators makes the happening all the more dramatic. For in that original fertilized cell—to divide again and again—the genetic code is all there: boy or girl, artistic or athletic, blue-eyed or brown. But all this will be revealed in the future; the following days for the parents-to-be will not be noticeably different from any others. It will be fourteen days or more before the woman realizes her period is late.

By this time the new person is well established, though no more than a small round disk, burrowing beneath the lining of the womb. Many women as early as this, and with no other obvious symptoms, "feel pregnant." I have myself—and been right each time—and I can only describe it as an inner awareness, and the sense of being just a little bit miraculous.

But even as the days go by and the certainty grows, to an onlooker the mother-to-be appears no different at all. The existence of this momentous and magically developing dot within remains hidden from the rest of the world.

The first signs

All women vary in their symptoms of pregnancy. All pregnancies are different, even for the same woman. Some women go for a couple of months before the new life growing within them produces any noticeable changes in their own lives, or indeed their own bodies. Others may show signs very early. The first indications are often a bloated feeling, caused by fluid retention, and a slight swelling of the breasts, which sometimes become tender, and the appearance round the edge of the areola, the pink or brownish skin surrounding the nipple, of small swellings like a ring of miniature nipples.

Diet and food fads

A pregnant woman does not need to increase the quantity of her normal varied daily diet, and the idea that a mother-to-be should "eat for two" is pure fallacy. She should be especially careful to have plenty of protein, calcium, iron, and vitamins C and D.

Food fads and dislikes, although exaggerated by folklore, may appear quite early, perhaps before pregnancy is recognized. A woman may experience a change in how things taste. She may go off foods she formerly liked and enjoy foods she formerly hated. This is not the legendary pica, which modern diet has almost eliminated. Pica is a craving for quite unusual things—earth and coal were quite common—which resulted from the body lacking certain vital substances, especially iron.

Morning sickness

The slight feelings of nausea and retching of fluid, popularly known as morning sickness—even though it can occur at any time of day—are quite common in the early stages of pregnancy as the mother adjusts to the changes in hormones coursing round her body. She is unlucky, however, if they persist or are severe. Actual vomiting is uncommon but is not a sign that there is something wrong with the baby, and unless it occurs three or four times a day it is seldom serious.

Mood swings

High hormone levels account for the traditional mood swings of pregnancy. The basic personality does not change, but a pregnant woman may become more temperamental. Small decisions may loom out of all proportion; intense pleasure may be followed by despair and despondency.

Confirming the pregnancy

About six weeks after conception, the mother-to-be misses her second period. Feeling both excited and a little apprehensive, she is now almost certain that she is pregnant. This is the time to visit her doctor for confirmation and examination. He will either do this himself, or refer her to the nearest prenatal clinic, which may be in the hospital where she will have her baby.

There the mother will be given a complete medical checkup, and her own medical history and that of her husband and family will be noted. The thorough and regular check on the health of the mother and the development of the baby-to-be has helped to reduce to a minimum all the risks that formerly were linked to childbirth. It is now quite rare for an unexpected emergency to occur in labor.

Doubts

If you have any doubts or any questions during pregnancy—ask. If you feel you do not fully understand the answer, do not be afraid to ask again. One of the common causes of worry in pregnancy is something the doctor, nurse, or someone else may have said which has not been properly understood. This may inadvertently upset the mother; during pregnancy a woman may be extra sensitive.

Calculating the date

When the mother-to-be leaves the clinic or doctor's office she will have been given her baby's estimated date of arrival. The average period of gestation is 266 days from conception, but pregnancy is calculated as 280 days (ten lunar months) from the first day of the last period. This is seven days over the nine calendar months normally thought of. It is only an average date. Should the mother's menstrual cycle normally be less than twenty-eight days, the pregnancy will probably be shorter and, if her cycle is longer, then the pregnancy is also likely to be longer. It is quite normal for babies to be born at any time between two weeks before and two weeks after the estimated date; first babies are more often "late" than not.

If conception follows immediately after stopping "the pill," calculating the estimated date of delivery may be less certain. This is because there may be a delay of two weeks or so before ovulation.

Things to avoid

The first four months are the baby's most vulnerable period. If she is not already immune it is crucial that the mother keeps clear of rubella (German measles), which can deform the developing child. She may know that she is immune because she has already had German measles herself. Or she can find out from the blood test at her first medical checkup. It is also best if she can keep off all drugs of any kind throughout pregnancy, particularly in the first two months, when the embryo is still forming.

How active?

Once she knows that she is pregnant, the mother-to-be is faced with all sorts of new problems, and often conflicting advice from well-wishers. The simplest advice is: do whatever you feel like doing and can cope with without strain. Old wives' tales that it is bad to climb stairs or stretch your arms above your head are absurd. Many women engage in tennis and other sports until quite late. However, should you find any of your usual activities tiring, give them up.

Sex during pregnancy

Many people still worry about sex during pregnancy. There is no reason at all why a couple should not continue making love just as long as they want to. The old idea that semen can damage the fetus is nonsense.

The fear that orgasm can cause a miscarriage can also be discounted, unless there is already a strong risk. In most instances this will be apparent either because of bleeding or from your history and you will have been warned of the dangers.

It is normal to feel contractions for a while after an orgasm. Rest until they fade away. Clearly in the last months making love can be awkward, but a change of position and less deep penetration can usually solve that problem. It is usually easiest with the man lying on his back and the woman sitting astride his hips. For some, entry from behind may be more comfortable.

Growing into parenthood

The joy of having a wished-for pregnancy confirmed is followed by the realization that nothing will ever again be the same and that the delights of irresponsibility and casual social arrangements are about to become a thing of the past. And it is this realization that sets off the process of maturing into a new role —parenthood.

Starting a new baby can also be like enjoying a second birth oneself, with all its enticing

implications of another youth. All the accepted perspectives of the parents-to-be must gradually change. A close couple must adjust to a new possibility, the intrusion of a third personality.

The young man has to face the fact that his wife is now on the way to becoming a mother. For the young mother-to-be the process can help to put her at last on an equal footing with her own mother. Very large responsibilities loom, and these, together with the change in status and the changing relationships both with each other and with each other's families, are bound to cause some inner turmoil. This is quite normal. Coping with it, being realistically aware of the challenges ahead as well as the loving rewards, and talking over the coming event together, are an important part of the parents' own growing up.

Often the pregnancy was not planned, or one or both of the parents feel unsure about the timing of the new baby. The American pediatrician Dr. Lee Salk has found that the way pregnancy comes about "contributes heavily to the way new parents behave after the birth of their child." A hesitant parent would do well to admit and talk about these inner doubts before the baby is born.

It also seems that despite—perhaps because of—all the physical changes, motherhood is accepted more naturally than fatherhood. Even though having a child was a mutual decision, when actually faced with pregnancy some fathers-to-be become increasingly uncomfortable. Parenthood is for adults; fatherhood may signal an end to the freedoms of young manhood even more decisively than the commitment of marriage. Unless this conflict is recognized and resolved, it may affect the relationship between both parents and their child.

The bloom of pregnancy

At twelve weeks the mother will probably have gained about 2.2 lb/1 kg. If she is gaining too much, the doctor may advise her to go on a diet. Her body is beginning to show definite changes. The top of the womb emerges from the pelvic girdle and at about sixteen weeks is about halfway up to her navel. Her bump is beginning to show, although probably not when she is dressed.

Any unpleasant symptoms, such as morning sickness, usually disappear after the third month and many women start to experience a heightened sense of well-being. Now is the time when most mothers-to-be begin to bloom in that characteristic glow of pregnancy. This may be partly psychological, for those women for whom motherhood is a fulfillment, and partly physiological. The hormones that the placenta produces usually clarify her skin and lend luster to her hair, her contours fill out, and her own excitement makes her eyes sparkle. A few women, however, are not so lucky, and occasionally the skin and hair become drier.

Coming to terms with motherhood

When the coming baby is public knowledge, the mother-to-be will find that all sorts of people are ready and eager to give her advice

Toward the end of pregnancy the mother's abdomen reaches magnificent proportions. It will return to its former size within a few weeks or months after the birth.

and a wish that everything could be as it was three months ago is also understandable: both are reassuring evidence that she is coming to terms with the new life within her.

The middle months

After four months the top of the mother's womb is only halfway up to her navel, and is not yet exerting real pressure on the rest of her insides. However, she may feel "stitches" or cramps in the lower abdomen as the muscles controlling the womb take up the strain. Now is the time to make the most of the precious months when movement is still unrestricted and she is neither too big nor too easily tired. Many mothers find a tremendous fund of energy at this stage, and set about buying the layette for the new baby and clearing out and decorating a room. There is no harm in such strenuous activity, provided it does not involve any undue straining. However, it is unwise to work in a room filled with paint or other chemical fumes, such as those given off by a powerful oven cleaner, because they can be absorbed through the lungs into the bloodstream and then passed on to the baby.

The importance of fitness

Physical fitness is important in pregnancy, because the business of producing the baby during labor is very hard work indeed. A young woman who normally leads a fairly inactive life should try to exercise more regularly. Many women worry that exertion will damage the unborn baby. Except in extreme cases this is simply not so. Listen to your body, respond to your baby. When you are tired—stop.

Which sports?

Highly strenuous sports should be avoided by those unused to them or out of training. Because of the dangers of vibration and falling, vigorous horseback riding, motorcycling, skiing, and waterskiing are unwise. Diving can be dangerous, but swimming exercises many of the muscles gently and is a very good form of exercise. Leisurely tennis and badminton and gentle dancing are fine. Walk as much as possible.

Driving

There is no special reason why a mother-to-be should not drive. In all normal situations there can be no direct effect on the baby. You may hear it said that a pregnant woman should not wear a seat belt. This is dangerous advice. If a mother-to-be is involved in an accident, the pressure of the belt may possibly cause a miscarriage. But if the crash is bad enough for this, she would almost certainly lose the baby without the belt, and possibly kill herself, too. A woman who is pregnant should drive carefully—just as she should if she is not pregnant.

The effects of drugs and smoking

Extreme care should be taken with all pre-'scription drugs during pregnancy, and *all* medications should be discussed with the doctor. Although there is still some dispute about the effects of smoking during pregnancy, more and more studies are pointing to evidence that smoking does have an impact on the fetus as well as on the mother.

and tell tales about their own experiences. And she will discover a curious paradox. Many women seem all too glad to tell of the terrible times they themselves had in pregnancy and childbirth. Somehow it seems expected that hard work and suffering are the right things to go through. Fortunately these old-fashioned attitudes are slowly but surely passing away.

Nonetheless, in some ways the young woman of today is not as well off as her forebears. Modern women have fewer babies and often have them in the hospital. So although prenatal care has made childbirth easier and safer than ever before, the reassurance that can come from an everyday acquaintance with the process is harder to come by. The newly pregnant young woman may find that she is not as prepared for her state as she expected. It is all too easy for a pregnant woman to feel isolated, someone unusual in a world apparently peopled by slim, active eighteen-year-olds and dauntingly experienced matrons.

Pregnancy is in the nature of things a period of change, a time when a woman adjusts to her new status. Feelings of impatience are natural,

Exercises to help your baby

A baby whose mother is fully aware of her body and has learned how to relax all or part of it during labor will have an easier birth than one whose mother has not prepared herself fully for the birth of her child. These exercises will reduce tension and anxiety during labor and may shorten the length of the birth.

A good one with which to begin is to lie on your back with your head and shoulders raised, propped up with cushions. Spread out your arms and legs in a relaxed position. Clench one fist as hard as you can, allowing the tension to spread up your arm to the shoulder. Then slowly relax until the hand and the whole arm feel loose. Do this three or four times and then repeat with the other hand and arm. Next, tense each foot and leg as though you were pushing against a door, and relax. (Do not curl your toes as this can cause cramp in the foot.)

Once your limbs are relaxed, start training your body. Tighten your belly as though you were expecting a punch, then relax. Breathe in deeply, then hold it for half a minute before slowly letting off the pressure by breathing out. Repeat both exercises several times.

Pull your legs toward you, keeping your feet on the floor. Place a hand on each leg just inside the knee, then push your knees inward against the hands until the knees are upright. Then relax and allow the legs to flop.

Finally, practice reaching a state of complete relaxation and then exerting one set of muscles at a time. End with your pelvic muscles: the two circles of muscle around the anus and the vagina, and other layers of this muscle farther up inside that support the bladder and the womb.

Practice tightening them by stopping in the middle when you are urinating. Also learn how to release these muscles in preparation for expelling the baby. Sitting on a hard chair, press them down without tensing the legs or buttocks. Finish with a firm tightening movement as you pull up the muscles again.

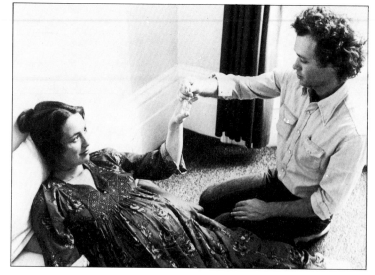

Clench your fist and relax it three or four times ; then ask your husband or a friend to lift your arm and then let it go. It should fall relaxed and loose to the ground.

Push your knees upward against your hands ; do this several times. Repeat, allowing the hands to win (not too easily), so that your knees are pushed out toward the floor. Then relax.
Right : As well as preparing her for the birth, the prenatal class can help a mother who may feel isolated. Fathers should go as well ; they will learn how best to support the mother-to-be throughout pregnancy and during birth.

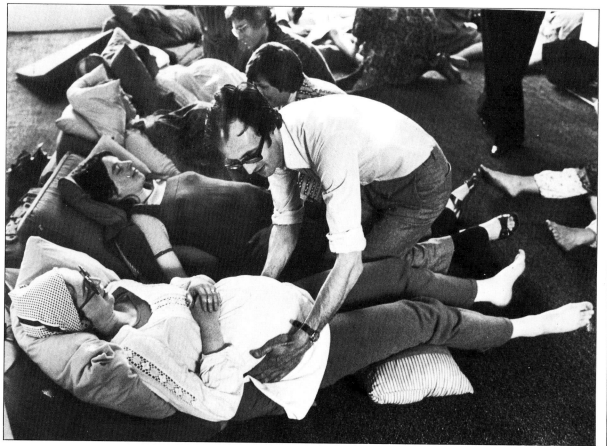

Women who smoke often find that pregnancy gives them a welcome and strong motivation to stop!

Smoking raises the mother's heart rate and adrenalin level, and nicotine can cross the placenta into the baby's bloodstream and have the same effects on him. Although a direct relationship has not been definitely established, statistics show that the babies of mothers who smoke heavily in pregnancy run a greater risk of being stillborn. They are more likely to be underweight at birth and to do less well at school later on.

What to wear

It was a great step forward for women when maternity clothes were introduced. Before then fashion dictated various artificial shapes for women, which could only be achieved by wearing tight corsets and carefully fitted dresses. In the past "confinement" meant literally that; the pregnant woman had to stay indoors and, as time drew on, in her bedroom. Changing fashions and the arrival of maternity clothes allowed women to get out and about in comfort.

If you like the idea of buying a new special outfit—pretty and loose fitting—then that is what you should get. If you prefer to stick to well-loved jeans and to let the front grow open, holding it together under a short top with a safety or diaper pin, then that is for you. Only do make sure that they are not too tight at the crotch and around your thighs, as good circulation in your legs is important. Your own comfort and well-being is what counts. Tight belts and corsets are better avoided, but the pressure of an ordinary belt will do no harm.

Low-heeled shoes are best. The weight of the baby tends to pull the mother's back forward, tilting her pelvis. High-heeled shoes exaggerate this, increasing the probability of backache. They also increase the likelihood of falling over.

Stretch marks

Many women worry about "stretch marks": lines, sometimes a faint pink, sometimes a vivid, angry-looking red. They can appear on the breasts, buttocks, and shoulders as well as on the belly. They have nothing to do with the skin, but are caused by changes in the elastic tissue below it due to hormone changes in pregnancy. This means that they cannot be prevented or treated by massage, oils, or creams, although it is good to keep your skin supple. Because stretch marks are much more likely to occur when a woman suddenly puts on a lot of weight, the likelihood of their appearing can be reduced by keeping your weight gain during pregnancy within bounds, not more than 20 lb/9 kg. After pregnancy stretch marks leave a very faint silvery scar, often only visible on a deeply tanned skin.

Hair loss

Some women find that they seem to be losing hair at an alarming rate. This is only an acceleration of the normal process by which we all lose up to one hundred hairs every day. The lost hair is all replaced. The mother-to-be will not go bald.

After about twenty-four weeks a mother-to-be should start prenatal classes, where she will be taught how to prepare herself for the birth. The father should also attend as he can give valuable support to his wife while learning about his role during pregnancy. They will be able to see films of how a baby develops up to and after birth and of the birth process itself. The mother will do exercises in the class to help her body prepare. She will be taught patterns of breathing to help her relax during the first stage of labor and to push to greatest effect in the second stage. The father can help her practice these breathing and relaxation exercises. A mother *should* go to classes of some sort because she is much more likely to have a relatively easy time in birth if she understands what is happening to her, and the baby will benefit accordingly.

Preparing for the birth

The links between the mother's emotions and the health of her unborn baby are still not completely clear. In China more than a thousand years ago prenatal clinics emphasized the mother's emotional tranquillity because it was thought that a tranquil mother gave birth to a tranquil baby. Popular tracts in the Middle Ages taught that "once having conceived, expectant mothers should think the thoughts, feel the emotions, and practice the virtues that would most felicitously shape the characters of their unborn children." It is known that if the mother experiences severe stress, if she is very anxious or unhappy, or if she lets herself become physically very tired, she may produce a more anxious or fretful infant. But the key word here is *severe*: ordinarily, unless the mother works in a very stressful job until late in her pregnancy, or unless she is severely disturbed, with proper rest and nutrition mother and baby should do well. A mother's illness does not normally infect her unborn child, except in the case of infections such as German measles. The placenta filters out most viruses and bacteria from the mother's bloodstream. A mother who is ill during pregnancy, however, should get a good deal of rest.

How a mother's health affects her unborn baby

A certain level of anxiety in the mother seems, perhaps surprisingly, to be a good thing. Many young women worry, especially in the last three months, about the baby inside them. Is he well? Does he kick enough? Does he kick too much? Will he be deformed? Will she be able to cope when he is born? It has been found that mothers who experience these fears to a moderate degree are most likely to be happy with their baby once he is born. It seems that these apparently irrational fears are signs of an essential process of adjustment to the coming child. However, if the mother-to-be is anxious to the point of panic, she should talk to her doctor or childbirth educator or, perhaps, to a marriage counselor. Mothers who say they feel totally unaffected and unconcerned by the coming baby may be storing up trouble for themselves by repressing fears and avoiding the process of adjustment.

Fears and worries

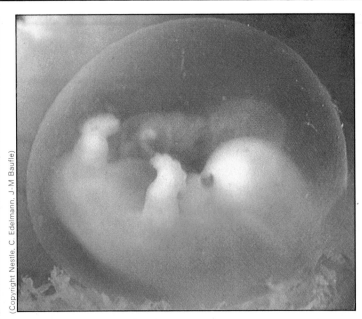

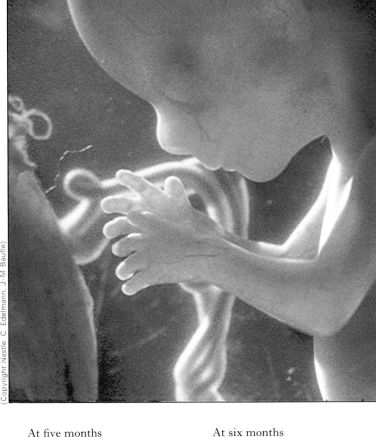

These photographs show what goes on inside the womb. Above : The seven-week-old fetus is $\frac{3}{4}$ in/19 mm long. Its face has rounded out and begun to look human. A distinct neck connects the huge head to the body. The limb buds are clearly distinguishable as arms and legs, with the beginnings of fingers and toes. The eyes are developing, although the skin over them (which will become the eyelids) is still intact.

Right : At twelve to sixteen weeks old the baby has a recognizable face with eyes behind closed eyelids, a small nose, lips and the beginnings of ears. The face looks more human as the eyes, formerly at the side of the head, have moved to the front. The baby can now register facial expressions such as grimaces and frowns. Although sex is fixed from conception, this is the time that the sex organs of the baby start to bud. In these four weeks the baby will grow from about $3\frac{1}{2}$ in/9 cm to 6 in/15 cm long.

At four weeks
The embryo is about $\frac{1}{5}$ in/5 mm long, ten thousand times larger than the fertilized egg. Its spinal column and the beginnings of nerves have been formed, blood vessels are appearing and, although incomplete, the primitive heart starts to beat for the first time.

At six weeks
The fetus is now $\frac{1}{2}$ in/13 mm long. The head, while still large, has well-shaped jaws. The arm buds have developed into upper and lower arms with hand plates ; the legs progress at a slower rate. The rudimentary brain is completed, and a spinal column and spinal cord are properly formed. The face has not yet taken its final shape, but small depressions are appearing where the eyes and ears will be.

At nine weeks
Although only $1\frac{1}{2}$ in/38 mm from head to buttocks, the fetus has now finished its most crucial stage of development, and all the forerunners of the major organ systems have been formed. It is instantly recognizable as a tiny baby, with delicate arms, legs, fingers, and toes, slit-like eyes, a nose, and a mouth.

At five months
Measuring 8–10 in/20–25 cm long, the baby is covered with a fine fuzz of hair, known as lanugo. He also has eyelashes, eyebrows, hair, and nails. During this month the skin glands produce the vernix caseosa, a white creamy paste that protects the delicate new skin.

At six months
The baby is 10–12 in/25–30 cm long and weighs about $1\frac{1}{2}$ lb/0.7 kg. He is able to open his eyes although he is not aware of light changes until the seventh month. As he drinks the amniotic fluid he may get hiccups, and his mother may be able to feel these.

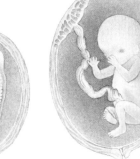

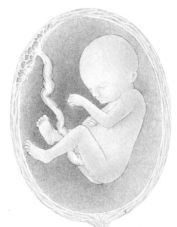

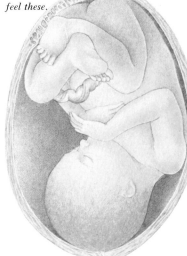

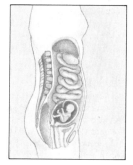

Left : Like a dreamer in the womb, the baby is about five months old and measures 8–10 in/20–25 cm long. The eyebrows and eyelashes have started to grow and hair is appearing on the head.

Below : Although the baby looks fully mature, he is only six months old and is not likely to survive if born now. The liver and lungs will not be ready to work efficiently until just before birth.

Below : The placenta passes nutrients and oxygen from the mother's blood to the baby's and waste products in the opposite direction. Sitting inside the wall of the womb (1), it is like a large pink sponge filled with the mother's blood (2). The baby's blood (3) passes through it in tubes (4). The walls are so fine that molecules of gases and solids can pass through while the two bloodstreams are kept apart.

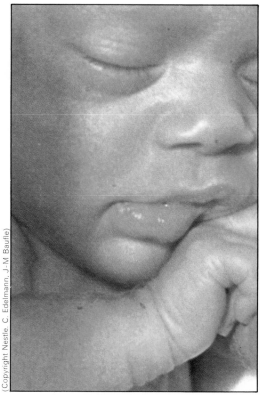

(Copyright Nestlé. C. Edelmann, J.-M. Baufle)

At nine months
The baby is no longer capable of his former weightless acrobatics, as he is about 20 in/50 cm long, weighs about 7 lb/3 kg, and occupies all the space in the womb. He has normally turned so that his head is able to settle into the pelvic cavity. This is a comfortable position for the baby and the easiest and safest position for delivery. He will probably be lying with his spine to the front of the mother's abdomen in the fetal position : his head is bent forward with the chin resting on the chest, his arms are crossed and his legs drawn up so that his feet cross over the genital area. Sometimes, if her baby is an energetic individual, the mother may feel strong kicks and thrusts just under the ribs ; alternatively he may become relaxed and passive, almost as if he is conserving his strength for the tremendous task ahead.

In the first twenty-two days after implantation in the womb lining, the fertilized ovum becomes an intricately organized cluster of cells surrounded by a fluid-filled bubble called the amnion, or bag of waters. The infant embryo draws nourishment from the villi, tiny root-like tubes in the womb lining. These will soon gather together to become the placenta, connected to the baby by the umbilical cord. At this time the foundations for the brain, spinal cord, and entire nervous system are established.

The four-week-old embryo has come a long way from its minuscule beginning. It has a huge bulbous head, a temporary tail, arm and leg buds, and a mouth which it can open and close.

By six weeks the embryo is developing at a tremendous pace, more than doubling its size in two weeks. It has rudimentary eyes, ears, teeth (in the gums), and facial muscles. The limb buds are lengthening; the liver begins to make blood, and there are now intestines, a stomach, and a primitive brain.

Between twelve and sixteen weeks all the organs, muscles, and the nervous system become interconnected so that the fetus kicks, curls its toes, and moves its head, although these movements are too small to be felt by the mother. The kidneys form urine, and the bladder urinates into the amniotic fluid. This is recycled every three hours through the mother's system at the rate of about 6 gallons/22 liters a day.

The five-month-old fetus is a recognizable human being with its own habits of sleeping and waking, which the mother may notice.

At six months the heartbeats of the baby can be heard with a stethoscope.

At seven months the baby is "viable," that is, if he were born now he would stand a chance of surviving. He measures about 12 in/30 cm from buttock to crown and weighs an average of 2.2 lb/1 kg. The bowel begins to accumulate meconium, a dark, greenish mass that will be discharged shortly after birth. As the mother can testify, the baby's movements are quite energetic and vigorous. In the last three months the brain develops rapidly, and the number and complexity of the neurons multiply a millionfold.

During the final ten to twelve weeks, the baby's lungs and liver develop toward full functioning. The most apparent change in the baby is in his size. His length increases from about 12 to 20 in/30 to 50 cm and his weight increases from 2 to 7 lb/1 to 3 kg as he gains strength.

Usually, the fuzzy hair, or lanugo, which covered the baby, and the protective creamy vernix caseosa drop away and in the last month he gains important antibodies from the mother. At last the baby's pituitary gland sends hormone messages that pass through the placenta into the mother's bloodstream and set off the mechanism of birth, making imminent the onset of labor.

How your baby develops

Below : The womb at four months has enlarged from about 3 in/8 cm to approximately the size of a small melon. The bump is only slightly visible from the side.

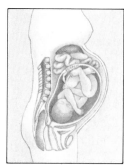

Above : At nine months the womb is about 12½ in/32 cm high and 9½ in/24 cm from front to back. The baby's head has descended into the pelvis ready for the beginning of labor. The pressure on the mother's insides is now at its greatest.

Fears and fantasies, which may sometimes seem quite lurid, need not be a cause for worry or guilt. They are natural and normal and it is sensible to share such thoughts with your husband. He should be involved as much as possible with the pregnancy and prepare for the birth along with the mother. The father-to-be can give great emotional support to his partner during this time through his understanding and involvement, and by doing so will himself benefit greatly.

How fathers can help

The father can and should help in the last three months by taking on more of the household chores, especially the jobs that require most effort, such as the heavy housework and carrying groceries. If there is already a child in the family the father can look after him as often as possible, so that the mother can relax on her own. This too can be a rewarding opportunity for both father and child to establish a closer relationship.

Helping each other

It may seem odd, but pregnancy can be a time of strain for the father. He may even experience more emotional difficulties and worry more about the coming baby than the mother.

He is merely an observer. It is much easier for her to accept the inevitable changes of pregnancy. For him there may well be a sense of unreality in watching the girl he married changing before his very eyes into a mother, a figure with whom he has always had a relationship very different from the physical intimacy of young lovers. As he adjusts to this new situation he may well lose his sexual interest in his partner, both during pregnancy and in the months after birth.

Unfortunately this is just the time when the mother will be worrying about things like stretch marks—and how soon she will get her figure back. She may badly need more than bland reassurance. All pregnant women worry to some degree that pregnancy and motherhood will adversely affect their sex lives. If this happens, and both parents become tense, time, free discussion, and understanding on both sides are generally all that is needed to right the sexual balance. However, this is by no means a universal problem; some men find their wives exceptionally desirable during pregnancy. The sexual energy of pregnant women is usually reduced during the early months, rises again in the second three months, and then declines as the time for birth approaches.

Giving up work

There is normally no need for a woman to give up work the moment she finds herself pregnant. However, chronic fatigue may prevent the baby from receiving adequate nourishment. There are no hard and fast guidelines. The decision to stop working will be largely dependent on how she feels, on the kind of work she is doing, and how far she has to travel each day. Some women choose to work right up to the end; most do not. With a hugely expanded womb and organs now crammed into a much smaller space, the last months of pregnancy can be uncomfortable.

If she has been used to an active, independent working life, a woman who gives up her job in mid-pregnancy may become depressed. The doubts that a mother-to-be naturally feels can easily be exaggerated if she lets herself become isolated. It is important not to give up friendships as well as work and to make the most of this unique opportunity to make new friends and to do all the things you enjoy but have not had time for—leisurely lunches with friends, outings to galleries or a matinee, or choosing new curtains for the living room.

The lightening

If this is the mother's first pregnancy, in about the thirty-sixth week she will normally experience the "lightening," when the baby's head drops into the pelvic girdle. This does not usually mean that birth is imminent. The baby will continue to grow for the next four weeks, pushing back toward the chest.

How a mother's body copes

The changes in the mother's own body during pregnancy are enormous. The womb itself grows from the size of a small orange to the size of a large fat squash to become by far the biggest muscle in the human body, male or female. This is not only done by stretching. New muscle fibers develop, and the old ones grow thicker and longer.

To supply the womb and the growing baby inside, the mother's blood supply increases by as much as a third. This accounts for the pregnant woman's great need for iron, which is required to make the new red blood cells. The blood pressure often drops, especially in the middle third of pregnancy, as blood vessels relax under the influence of placental hormones. The extra blood increases the workload of the heart and, although its rate and rhythm of beating should not change during pregnancy, its size must, by anything up to forty percent. And it has to enlarge while being squeezed higher and higher into the chest by the growing womb as the pregnancy progresses.

This is one reason why a woman will cope with pregnancy better if she is physically fit before it starts. It is also the main reason why she should not put on too much weight during pregnancy; the more weight, the more work for the heart.

The mother's lungs too are pushed up into her chest, which gradually expands, the ribs spreading to make room. The mother may find herself taking shorter and lighter breaths, punctuated at intervals by deep sighs, because placental hormones affect the brain center controlling the depth and speed of breathing.

The demands on the heart and lungs explain why a pregnant mother can feel very lethargic in the last two months. The squeezing of all her other organs can cause some discomfort too, although very rarely actual pain. There is no doubt that whatever the joys of parenthood, the last six weeks of pregnancy can be a wearisome time of waiting. Even simple things like peeling potatoes or getting a toddler off to nursery school are an unexpected effort.

Father's presence at the birth

Traditionally, men have always been excluded from both the hard physical work and the emotional pleasure of childbirth. But in recent years this has changed radically. Although for some fathers it is somewhat harrowing to contemplate, their presence will prevent the mother from feeling lonely and frightened. Whether or not he actively helps, just by being there the father deepens the experience of birth for them both.

Most hospitals will now allow the father to be present during labor and birth, although the parents may have to be firm about this. The practice of removing the baby entirely from the mother, returning him only for strictly regulated feedings, is now almost completely gone, but it is worth checking about this carefully, too. Say what you want and ask for it to be written on your record.

Home or hospital birth?

During the pregnancy the parents should discuss, both between themselves and with the professionals, the choice between a home and a hospital birth. If you prefer to have a home birth, make sure that there are competent professionals in your community who are willing to care for you on that basis—communities differ in their acceptance and encouragement of the practice.

It may also be the judgment of your doctor that he can foresee complications that may make the hospital setting safer. Should you ultimately decide on a home delivery, however, there is no question that the familiar surroundings will make it easier to accept the naturalness of birth and intensify the joy experienced by the total family unit. And away from the distraction of hospital routine the mother is able to get to know her new baby without interruption, from the moment he is born.

Induced birth

Although births can be induced, this is a controversial medical procedure. It can be useful in the case of expected complications but should hardly be planned merely for the convenience of the patient or the doctor. After all, in the normal course of pregnancy, it is the baby who "decides" when he is ready to be born. When his development in the womb is complete his pituitary gland at the base of his brain starts a chain reaction of hormones, which tells the mother's body to start the labor.

There is a risk in induction that the baby may not be quite ready. This may be the reason that more induced babies have to be put into incubators than normally born infants. Respiratory problems, due to under-developed lungs, and jaundice, due to an immature liver, are among the most common difficulties.

Labor may be induced by breaking the mother's amnion artificially. Another common method is to use an intravenous drip containing a drug, oxytocin, which causes contractions in the mother's womb. The two methods are often combined.

Starting labor

Labor is basically a series of increasingly strong contractions of the womb, coming more and more frequently. In fact the womb has contractions throughout pregnancy and throughout its life. In many mothers, however, contractions can get stronger and then die away many times during the last two weeks or so, a tantalizing period for the eager almost-mother. Real labor starts when the cervix begins to open. This may happen when the contractions come regularly every twenty minutes and last for forty seconds or more. However, a woman cannot be certain until they come every five minutes.

Sometimes the mother's waters break quite early in this process, and some of the fluid from the womb escapes. This liquid is usually colorless and it is sterile. So while it may be uncomfortable if the mother is out shopping at the time, no harm is done. It shows that labor is near, but again how near will not be certain. Another sign is a "show," when the plug of jelly which has kept the cervix sealed up is ejected, sometimes with a little blood. This means that the cervix is "ripe," and it is a good sign, although it can happen some days, or even longer, before labor starts, or even after it has started. If your waters break, or you have regular contractions, you should call or go to the hospital or contact your doctor if you are planning a home birth.

Some women find the contractions in labor very painful. Others simply find them hard work. A good training in breathing and relaxation helps a great deal. A fearful attitude increases the feelings of pain. A choice of anesthetics is available, including a gas

The excitement of the baby's developing should be shared with the rest of the family. If an older brother or sister puts his cheek to his mother's stomach he will be able to feel the baby kicking and turning, and will be more ready for him when he arrives.

When to call the hospital

Anesthetics

The birth experience

Although you have been aware that the date for your baby's birth is approaching, when you feel the first contractions it is a thrilling moment. Suddenly, you realise that the waiting is nearly over. In all probability it happens not on the exact day predicted seven or more months ago: it can be at any hour of the day or night and anywhere—at home, out shopping or at a party.

After calling your husband, who will be as excited as you are, and who will want to be with you if he can, you relax and start to time the frequency of your contractions. There is no need to call the doctor or midwife until your contractions are coming regularly, about every twenty minutes. If you have decided to have your baby at home, you settle down to wait. If you are going into hospital, in itself perhaps a new experience, either your husband drives you there or you call for an ambulance to collect you. Once there, the calm and professional atmosphere is reassuring.

During the following three stages of labor, you try to put into practice the breathing exercises you have learned. Understanding what is happening to you and your baby, you soon find yourself relaxing into the creative process of birth, giving yourself fully to this highly emotional, as well as physical, experience. It is a challenge unlike any other. During the birth, there are new sensations and feelings; it takes patience and self-confidence and, yes, effort. But it is all worth while when, bringing joy into the quiet delivery room, you experience one of life's most satisfying moments —that of holding your newborn baby in your arms.

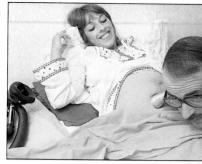

Just before birth, an interested father listens in to his child's heartbeat, using the midwife's eartrumpet.

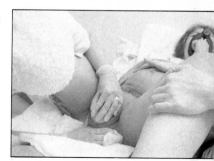

The baby has been crowned and mother and midwife work together to pass his head as gently as possible through the vagina. The mother administers herself gas.

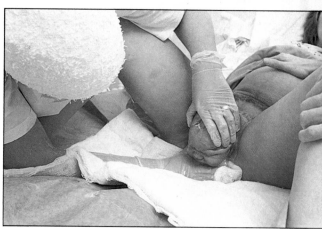

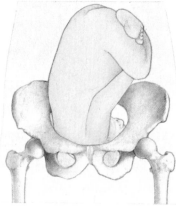

As birth approaches, the baby rotates inside the womb and then, head down, passes through the pelvic girdle.

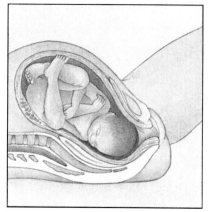

The dilation of the cervix is the longest period of labour, and it must be complete to allow the baby to pass into the vaginal canal.

The head has just emerged fully, but there is still work to be done by the mother. The baby is grimacing from the pressure of the birth canal.

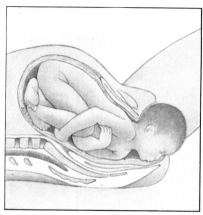

The powerful uterine muscle forces the head of the baby through the birth canal and out into the world.

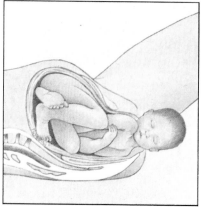

The head turns so that the face looks to one side; and then shoulders, arms, trunk and legs slip out of the birth canal.

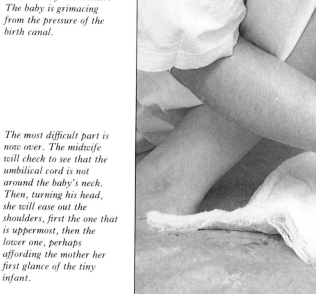

The most difficult part is now over. The midwife will check to see that the umbilical cord is not around the baby's neck. Then, turning his head, she will ease out the shoulders, first the one that is uppermost, then the lower one, perhaps affording the mother her first glance of the tiny infant.

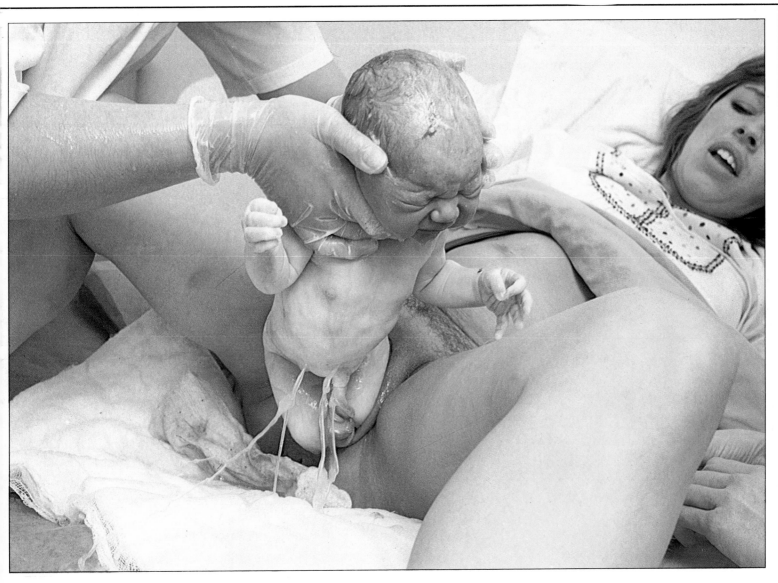

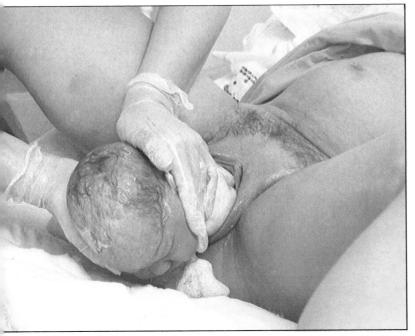

One final contraction and the child slips out. The birth is now almost complete. In fifteen minutes or so the placenta will follow, and the birth will be over.

The last remaining bond between mother and child, the umbilical cord, is cut and tied. The infant is handed to the mother and, although it is time for her to rest, her job has really only just begun.

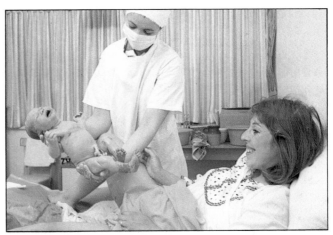

(either trichlorethylene or nitrous oxide) and oxygen mixture inhaled through a mask, or injections of pethidine, which is often combined with a tranquilizer. The most modern method is a local anesthetic that paralyzes and numbs the body below the waist and the legs almost completely. It is given by a tube inserted through the lower part of the back into the spinal canal, and is known as an "epidural."

An injection of pethidine is probably the most common form of anesthetic. The more complete numbing effect of an epidural is often used in an induced birth because the artificial contractions are more painful than natural ones. Unfortunately a forceps delivery is up to five times more likely if a woman chooses to have an epidural. In any case the pain of childbirth can be greatly eased if the mother can relax as much as possible. She will feel rewarded if she has attended classes to prepare her for this moment.

Some mothers nowadays find that they can manage quite well without anesthesia of any kind, or with only a few whiffs of gas. Undoubtedly this is better for the baby. Pethidine can strongly affect the baby. He may not be able to breathe so easily immediately after birth, and the sleepiness of both mother and child will interfere with the first crucial minutes and hours of interaction between the two of them.

The first stage of labor is the time taken for the cervix, the neck of the womb, to become fully dilated. The transition from the first to the second stage of labor, when the baby's head begins to move down the birth canal, is for many mothers the most distressing time. They may feel lost, bewildered, and out of control, sometimes saying things they do not mean. Some women experience severe backache, caused by the pressure of the baby's head on their lower spines. Steady massage

The transition

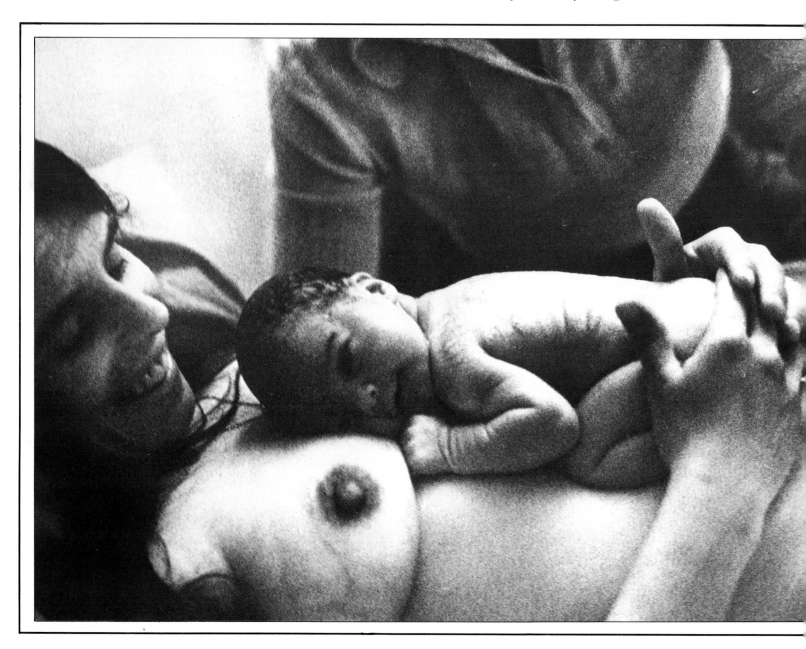

from a caring husband can bring considerable relief to a weary mother-to-be.

Birth

Transition is followed by the second stage of labor, when the baby moves down the birth canal and out into the world. At the end of the first stage more often than not he faces to the mother's side. As his head moves down the birth canal it usually turns to face her back so that he is born facedown.

At last the baby's head can be seen at the peak of each contraction. Soon the baby is "crowned," the top of his head remaining visible between contractions. An exciting moment for father and doctor, although the mother must be patient a little longer. Now the mother must push much more gently so that she does not tear her vagina. If the mother or the baby is having difficulty, the doctor may perform an episiotomy by cutting the tissues between the opening of the vagina and the back passage to ease the baby's passage or speed up delivery. Slowly the little head emerges, its face a bit squashed and puckered with the effort of being born.

The doctor checks to see if the cord is round the baby's neck (it only occasionally is and can usually be easily unlooped). He turns his head to face the side again, and then asks for the last push. Then, so suddenly after all the effort, the little body slithers out, ready to go straight to his mother's waiting arms and breast. And there he is, a new person in the world; so perfect, miraculously grown from the single fertilized cell. Soon his father will tell the world of his safe arrival: for the first moments the three of them are there, together. One senior obstetrician told me that he has never been present at a normal birth without seeing a smile on the face of everyone else there—and smiling himself. The mother herself often looks so radiantly ecstatic that the time immediately after birth has been named the transfiguration.

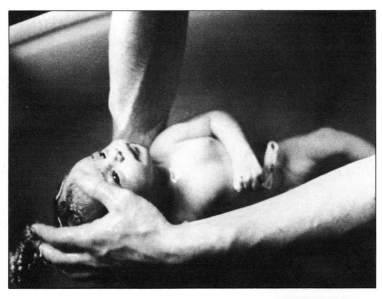

Separated for the first time from his mother, the infant needs comfort and reassurance. Placed in warm water, he opens his eyes wide, already exploring his new world.

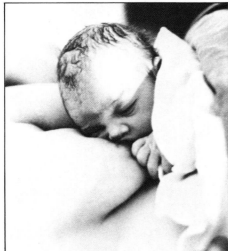

No "back-slapping" is necessary. With the umbilical cord still uncut, the baby is placed on his mother's stomach. Here he can gently stretch his back at his own pace and start to breathe in the new air.

Some babies, brought quietly and gently into this world, may be sufficiently alert to be put to the breast at once.

Easing the shock of birth

For the baby, birth can be a painful and shocking experience. This is the view of the French obstetrician Frederick Leboyer. He maintains that at birth a baby can be affected by the atmosphere into which he is born.

For nine months the baby has lived in darkness and comparative silence. Rather than thrusting the baby into a world of stark lights and sharp voices, Leboyer delivers him into darkened surroundings where only whispers disturb the quiet.

According to Leboyer, a baby needs to be comforted by his mother. So the new baby is placed directly on the mother's belly, where she can caress him and give him the benefit of the warmth and softness of her skin.

Leboyer believes that while a baby is adjusting to his new freedom after birth he requires the continued link with his mother. So the umbilical cord is not cut until it has stopped beating some minutes after birth. Finally, since the baby has spent his life so far surrounded by fluid, Leboyer puts him into a bath at body temperature. Films show the baby calming down dramatically.

Many doctors have responded to Leboyer's belief that newborn babies need to be treated more gently than they used to be, but they have not followed all Leboyer's precepts. They think that in a dim light the blue color which indicates a shortage of oxygen might be missed, and that the bath is dangerous because a newborn is susceptible to loss of heat.

Although research in France suggests that babies born by this method are calmer and mature faster, the "Leboyer method" seems to be catching on slowly. Some hospitals and doctors offer a modified version, but usually the mother will have to ask, and sometimes insist, if she wants the baby to be born this way. Remember it is your attitude and that of those around you at the birth which are more important than the methods used.

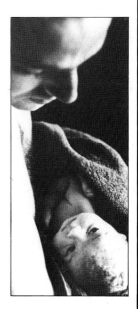

Father and child come face to face. The newborn, watchful and alert, examines the configuration of eyes, nose, and mouth; an image that he recognizes through instinct.

2 *Infancy: The*
TENDER YEAR

From the very beginning
there were unforgettable moments: his life-loving
anticipation of breast or bottle; his eyes
following us closely as we left the room; coming
upon him as he passed his hands before his face with
enchanted concentration. . . . By six months,
he was sitting propped up, gazing quizzically
at his surroundings, expecting our
undivided attention—and getting it.

The newborn baby

The baby has arrived safely, but what do we know about him? At the beginning, while the doctor is busy checking his birth weight and length, the mother notices only the obvious things: boy or girl; arms, legs, flat nose, fingernails, etc. Even if you have had a baby before you will probably have forgotten how tiny and frail he seems. His little limbs may look thin and scrawny. His skin may appear greasy and a little puffy at first; his head perhaps elongated from molding in the birth canal. He may have a great deal of hair or none. The color of his hair, if he has some, will not signify anything because it will gradually be replaced, possibly by hair of a quite different color and texture. If he has had an easy birth his eyes will be open, and he will already be looking around. However, if he has experienced a hard journey, he will probably protest vigorously for a time until he is soothed or held close against his mother. His eyes when you can see them will be a characteristic color — deep, cloudy blue. Only later will the development of the iris give him his own individual eye color.

For himself, he is busy adjusting to his new environment. We know that in the womb a baby responds to touch, taste, and noise. We know that he can see as soon as he is born. His nervous system is busy adapting to life outside the womb. He is learning the new sensations of being held in someone's arms, being picked up, put down, and carried about. For the first time in his life he is not surrounded by fluid and his arms and legs can be waved freely. He is breathing air—as novel a sensation to him as frosty air is to you when you step outdoors on a cold night. Hitherto he has received all his nourishment direct into his bloodstream through the umbilical cord. Now he must learn to use the sucking reflex with which nature has endowed him. His digestive system must prepare itself to take in and use his mother's milk, and his stomach must become accustomed to feeling empty sometimes and full at others.

He needs food, quiet, the closeness and comfort of his mother's arms, and calm handling. As mothers have always known, he will be most peaceful when rocked rhythmically and gently, held with his head against his mother's left side, where he can hear the heartbeat that dominated his life in the womb. But there is more to him, already, than that.

Research during the last few years has shown that newborn babies are much more advanced, and capable of much more, than we ever dreamed of before. For example, you will still find some books which say that a newborn cannot see. We know now that this is simply not so. A newborn baby can see in only a limited way—but he is far from blind.

What a newborn can see

Immediately at birth his pupils will adjust to let in more or less light, depending on the brightness of the room. His eyes focus best at the same distance at which your own eyes focus at rest, about 8 in/200 mm. The convergence of his eyes is very variable at first. He will fix you with a piercing look at one moment; the next he will lose interest, relax, and one eye will be gazing at the ceiling and the other at the window.

A baby's brain develops fastest in the three months before birth and the first year afterward. At birth the upper part of the brain, which controls all of what used to be called the "higher mental functions," lags behind the lower brain, which controls all the "automatic" parts of behavior. The newborn is particularly sensitive to two things: the human face and movement. If you dangle something in front of him and move it back and forth, he will watch intently, within a few hours of being born. But if you stop moving it, he will very soon lose interest. And although he is programed to recognize a face (or as he sees it, a roundish disk with two darker spots side by side), it is interesting that most mothers and fathers bob their heads about when talking to young babies, for this is what the baby needs to help him keep attentive.

Other senses

A newborn can hear quite well, although he will have to learn the meaning of different noises. He will turn his eyes to see where a noise is coming from, and after a month he will move his head, too, although the movements will not be very strong. His senses of taste and smell are well developed.

Your first hours together

In the first hours and days of a baby's life, the relationship he is able to form with his mother, and any others involved in taking care of him, is probably the most vital part of his existence. Some people overexaggerate this importance, believing that there exists a crucial moment, which, if missed, will never return, thus ruining the baby for life. This is foolish, but no more so than the opposite belief that to the baby all other people are exactly the same, and that all he needs is his regular ration of milk. A newborn quickly learns to tell his mother from other people by her smell. And an experiment in a nursery has shown that babies soon get used to one style of being looked after, and know if this is changed, even as early as two weeks after birth, although they do not necessarily find the change upsetting.

The attachment a mother forms for her child is unique. When mothers are left completely free to do as they like with the baby, they normally spend a considerable amount of time caressing and massaging the child. They do this naturally, and do not have to be told. They will usually put the baby beside them where they can look into his eyes, and often talk to him excitedly. It has been found that if mothers who want to breast-feed their baby are not allowed to hold him for 16 hours after birth, they will give up breast-feeding him earlier than if they had held him soon after birth. Research has also shown that mothers of premature babies that are put into incubators, and are therefore separated from them for several days, find it less easy to love the baby when he is finally handed to them. It is almost as though they have to make an effort.

So it seems strange, and sad for both mother and child, that the normal routine of many

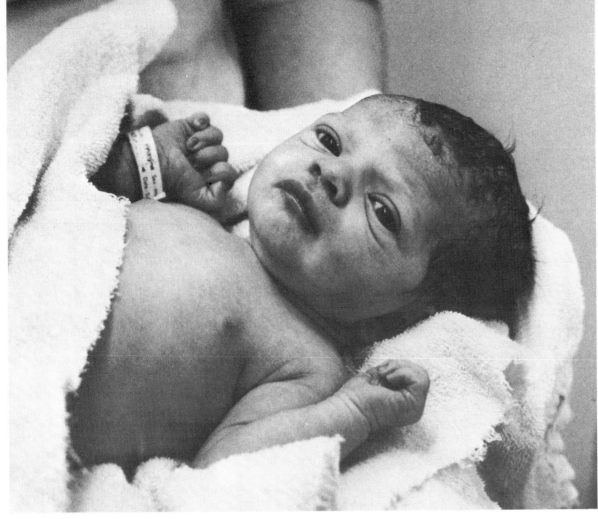

Above : Attracted by the noise and glint of a rattle, a baby follows its movements intently, although perhaps for only a few moments.

Left : A newborn infant is remarkably capable. He is able to see, hear, smell, and is responsive to touch and pain. Calmed and comforted, just minutes after birth, he is alert and observant.

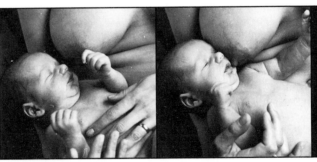

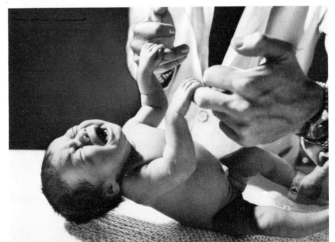

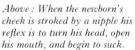

Above : When the newborn's cheek is stroked by a nipple his reflex is to turn his head, open his mouth, and begin to suck.

Left : His tiny hands grasp so tightly that he can easily be raised from the ground—a reflex that probably stems from the infant primate's need to cling to his mother's body.

Below : Just as the infant will grasp with his hands so his feet will respond to touch. If a finger is pressed against the sole of his foot, the toes will curl around it.

Above : The newborn's legs are not strong enough to support his weight, but if he is held with his feet touching a hard surface, he will make vigorous stepping motions as if he were walking.

Right : When startled by a sudden noise or movement the newborn will arch his body and throw out his arms, the fingers stretched. As his actions become more deliberate, this reflex will disappear.

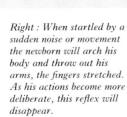

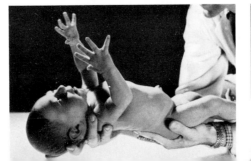

Premature babies

A premature baby is one who is born before the normal period in the womb is completed (technically, before the thirty-seventh week of pregnancy) or who, at birth, weighs less than 5 lb 8 oz/2.5 kg.

A premature baby can normally survive outside the womb, but not in the "ordinary" world. He needs an intermediate environment, so he is taken into special care, and placed in an incubator—a flat crib with a transparent cover in which the air is kept at the correct temperature and humidity, and is oxygen-enriched if necessary.

Many hospitals will now arrange for the parents to visit their baby frequently while he is in special care, helping to avoid the estrangement that can all too easily result. The best have rooms for mothers in the special care unit. A mother who wants to breast-feed can usually do so. If the baby is too immature to suck it may be better for the mother to release her milk manually so that he can be fed either through a tube or with a spoon. The mother should ask to be taught to do this herself. Very tiny babies are often fed with a dropper.

The mother of a premature baby should spend as much time as possible in the same room as the incubator, and she should hold her baby so that she can look into his eyes, and he into hers, for as long as his condition allows, to foster their mutual attachment.

A mother who has had a premature baby may feel that she has let the child down in some way by not completing her full term.

Babies born over 5½ lb
Low-weight babies
Deaths of low-weight babies within twenty-eight days

Premature births represent 6.4 percent of total live births, and only about one baby in every two hundred born will fail to survive beyond twenty-eight days.

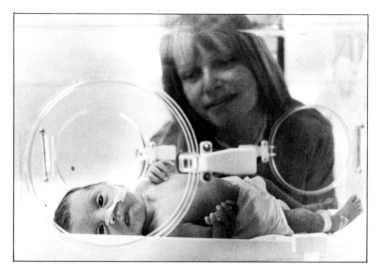

Conversely, she may feel that the child has let *her* down by not being up to expectations. In either case, it is very important that she should strike up a relationship with the child as soon as possible.

Some parents find the sight of their tiny offspring in an incubator extremely upsetting, even though they are reassured that their baby, who is in difficulty, is receiving such advanced and skillful care. However you feel at the time, it is worth emphasizing that frequent visiting is important, and will greatly strengthen the relationship between you and your child in the months and years to come.

Differences that sometimes occur between premature and normal babies are often caused by maternal behavior. Those premature babies who receive attention and stimulation seem to gain more weight and remain healthier than those who are overprotected and isolated.

maternity hospitals tends to thwart the natural formation of bonds. Too often babies are rushed straight from the delivery room to the nursery, or the mother is allowed to hold her baby for only a short time before he is taken away. Today many hospitals provide the opportunity for "rooming in," which allows mother and child to be together during the day, a natural and satisfying arrangement for both. At night the baby is put into a nursery so the mother can sleep undisturbed.

If you want to ensure the best kind of relationship with your child throughout life, with plenty of give and take on both sides, it is best to start him off right, with a secure base, by establishing a bond of love and friendship between you and your baby. If you avoid enforced separation, the mother and child relationship, which started developing during the pregnancy, can be nurtured naturally, without interruption.

Going home with the baby

For many couples it is the journey home in the car with the proudly, perhaps gingerly, held bundle that signals the start of real parenthood. The average stay in a hospital is five to seven days. Nowadays there is an increasing trend toward "forty-eight-hour births," when the mother is sent home as soon as she has had a rest and the baby has been checked and found fit. In home births, of course, practical parenthood begins at the moment of birth.

Some hospitals still follow the old-fashioned practice of doing everything for the mother. The baby sleeps in a separate nursery and is wheeled in at appointed feeding times. The nurses change him and generally look after him, so that the mother's journey home is with a stranger who has already grown accustomed to her absence.

If the mother is fortunate she will not only be allowed to change her baby herself but a nurse will show her how to fold and change diapers and how to dress him. Thus, she will be used to having professional help.

The father's experience so far will be limited to admiring glimpses during visiting hours and to holding him occasionally—an action often frowned upon by the staff. For the father the first involvement in the hourly care of his new child can be both alarming and rewarding. He will suddenly be expected to pick him up and hold him, fetch diapers, and perhaps warm bottles.

Once home a young couple with their first child can feel awfully alone. Some mothers enjoy rising to the challenge by themselves. It is best if the father takes time off work so they can get to know their baby together. If this is not possible, have an experienced friend on call, or the mother's or father's mother to stay for a week. Her experience and ideas on how to treat babies may be very different, but at least she knows some of the problems, and

Friends and neighbors

when not to worry. In the first weeks ideas are not so important. It is the physical skill of handling the tiny baby that counts. Even if your mother cannot remember in detail what she did, she knows it can be done. On her own a new mother can easily feel anxious, even panicky, that she will not be able to cope.

If help from the family is not available to you, or indeed what you want, call on friends or neighbors—anyone who can give practical support doing the housework, shopping, and laundry. A new baby can arouse protective feelings and elicit help from the most unexpected people. A new mother should make a special effort to involve the father in the baby's care as much as possible—the whole family will benefit.

During these early months you will want to be in close touch with your doctor or pediatrician. Many young couples today are isolated from their own families and from grandparents and aunts who in another day would have provided advice and a helpful pair of hands. Some communities are recognizing this gap by establishing discussion groups and centers where young parents can come for mutual support and an exchange of ideas. Parents are less anxious about the stranger in their midst when they can share common concerns.

Having a baby is a stupendous event. The mother will often be tired; the routine of home life may well be chaotic until both parents have become accustomed to their unfamiliar roles. If he is not a first child a bewildered

toddler's need for extra love can be an added strain. Friends and relatives, as well as the father, can give enormous help in those first weeks with household chores and shopping. But this support must never become interference, however well meant. Additional help for the mother should give her an opportunity to concentrate on adapting to her baby, and allow her the peace in which she can begin to understand his needs and ways.

Having a baby completely alters your way of life, and consequently many kinds of emotional adjustments must be made. No matter how thoroughly you have prepared for the event, it is impossible to anticipate all of its ramifications. If there are other children in the family, you will have to give them extra attention so that they do not feel displaced. This is especially true of stepchildren, whose new family may have been created through divorce. Additionally, both parents may have their individual anxieties about this new person and their ability to cope with him. All these emotional readjustments can precipitate a period of postnatal depression for both parents, particularly for the mother.

No relationship, not even that between the parents, can be the same again. So they must accept this as a sensitive time for the whole family, and expect gradual readjustment. For just as their relationship has irrevocably changed, so, with the coming of the baby, has it also been immeasurably enhanced.

But every husband should understand that profound hormonal changes take place in a mother in the days after delivery. The hormones that sustained pregnancy disappear within a couple of days and the body has to adjust to their absence. Because hormones have such a strong influence on emotional states, some mothers experience a short period of tremendous turmoil.

It has also been said that "birth results in a partial lack of self." The familiar bulge has gone suddenly, and with it the pressure inside the abdomen, and the feelings of life within. This may be one element in postnatal depression. The mother may feel as though all hope is lost; the smallest and most insignificant events can precipitate her into floods of tears. Nobody can predict beforehand whether a woman is going to be affected in this way. Some normally calm and confident women are strongly affected, while some normally anxious and excitable women sail through without a tear.

Sometimes a mother feels let down by her baby and wonders desperately how she will ever love this wrinkled, bawling little thing. She may hate herself having such thoughts, but she should realize that they are by no means uncommon. She will find that she will grow toward the baby, and learn to love him as she starts to care for him and know him.

Postnatal depression usually passes quite quickly. In a few women, however, it is believed that the hormone balance does not return completely to normal, which prolongs

Changes after childbirth

Postnatal depression

As you learn more about your baby, he will be discovering about you, too. Watching you, touching you, talking to you. Every little interaction leads to familiarity and closeness between mother and child.

In some mothers postnatal depression can be cured by doses of progesterone, the pregnancy hormone that disappears suddenly after the birth. However, prolonged depression can be caused by the strains a new baby places on a relationship.

the depression considerably. Depression which lasts more than a week can also be a sign that the new mother is not after all ready for parenthood. Or perhaps it is the father who reacts badly, and upsets the mother.

If you are still depressed after two weeks, see your doctor. If you think a marriage counselor would help, then take your problem there. The arrival of a baby can be a good opportunity for resolving difficulties.

Resuming sex   It is unusual though not impossible to resume intercourse before postnatal discharge has ceased, about three weeks after the birth. Some couples start again within days, others wait two or three months. If the mother has had an episiotomy she may be sore from the stitches. This will pass after a couple of weeks.

Some mothers become very child centered and exclude their husband from their emotional life. This can happen whether she is breast- or bottle-feeding. Many breast-feeding mothers find that the physical nature of the process stimulates them to greater intimacy with their husband: others find, on the contrary, that although they love their husband just as much, their need for physical closeness with him is lessened for a time.

Contraception   It is important to resume contraception as soon as you want to start sex again. There is a mite of truth in the old belief that you will not conceive if you breast-feed. The hormone prolactin that promotes milk production inhibits the production of the two hormones involved in ovulation. However, the effect, which diminishes as time goes on, is only to make conception slightly less likely.

The best method is the condom. A new mother often needs lubrication: an additional spermicidal foam or jelly, or baby oil, will serve a double purpose. If she has been using a diaphragm the mother will need refitting and may need a larger one. It is better not to rely on this method for a few weeks. Intra-uterine devices are not fitted for six weeks or more after birth because a mother's womb will eject a coil or a loop. Oral contraceptives are all right if you are bottle-feeding. If you are breast-feeding you should not use them; wait for a month and then use a low-dose variety. Some of the hormones may come through in your milk, and although the quantities will be minute we do not yet know what effect they may have on the baby.

For the first two months of his life a baby needs to be supported when he is not lying down. You will discover that there are two easy ways to hold him. One is similar to the position for breast-feeding, but the baby is cradled at waist rather than breast level. Initially you will need both arms. However, gradually you will become adept at adjusting his blanket or clothing with one hand and holding him with the other. Later he will become too heavy for one arm alone, and if you cradle him you will need both.   *Holding your baby*

The other position is with the baby held against your upper chest, with his head looking over your shoulder. In the first two months you must hold his back and support his neck firmly with your hand, and he will need some support for another two months or so after that. From birth onward some babies attempt to lift their heads so they can see what is going on. Mothers of very young babies soon get to know that tremulous bumping on their shoulder as the baby raises his head momentarily and lets it drop back.

The feeding of babies is an emotional issue about which much has been written. Before the development of modern ways of sterilizing and commercial dried and liquid milk products suitable for infants, there was no real alternative to breast-feeding. Today's mothers have clear options—some are drawn to breast-feeding; other definitely prefer the bottle.   *Feeding the baby*

You will probably have discussed how you want to feed your new baby before he is born. However, whatever decision you made then, you may find, when it actually comes to feeding him, that something makes you change your mind.

Mothers who establish breast-feeding invariably feel that this is the most satisfactory way for both mother and baby. They are probably right. Nature designed mothers' milk for babies, and babies for mothers' milk. Babies like the taste and it agrees with their stomachs. Many mothers find bottle-feeding preferable, and if a bottle-fed baby is fed lovingly and attentively, and not held limply while the adult watches television, for example, he may not miss a great deal. The mother's attitude is of paramount importance. If she feels happy, so will the baby.

Nature provided babies with an instinct for feeding. Many newborns, if they are handled gently and given a chance to relax, will start smacking their lips and making sucking sounds within the first hour of birth. Your baby will find it easier to learn how to feed if you watch for this, take the hint, and give him the breast.

Breast-feeding causes the womb to return more quickly to its normal size. Some women even feel the womb contracting as the baby sucks—so-called "after-pains," especially in the first week after the birth of a second or third baby. The waist of a breast-feeding mother also returns to normal more speedily than that of a bottle-feeder. However, she must take care not to overeat; and she cannot go on a slimming diet while nursing.

Colostrum

Initially there will not be any actual milk in the breast. Mother's milk does not "come in" for two or three days or so after birth. Instead the breasts give out a clear sticky liquid called colostrum, which may vary a great deal in color—white, mustardy-yellow or gray-blue. It contains some protein and is nourishing. More important, however, colostrum is rich in the mother's antibodies, and will give protection from many diseases in the first six months or so. This immunizing effect is lost if the baby is fed on fresh or dried cow's milk during this time.

When the milk comes in

The first feedings will be short, no more than three or four minutes actual sucking on each breast. He is still learning, and the intimacy is good for him, so do not turn him off too early. Gradually, as his hunger increases and he learns how to suck to full effect, he will take longer and steadier feedings. If your baby does not at first take much each feeding and cries for more after only two hours, answer his need and feed him again. You may have to give ten or twelve feedings a day at first, but soon your breasts will be producing enough to keep him happier for longer. Put him to both breasts at each feeding, alternating the one you start with.

The breasts

When your milk first comes in your breasts may feel strange. You may find the sensation of "letting down" the milk disconcerting. It is not something for which modern living prepares women. Once they have got used to it, many women find it surprisingly satisfying.

You may find that your breasts leak between feedings. You can absorb the surplus by lining your maternity bra with freshly laundered cotton hankies. You can buy disposable paper pads or special washable pads that are covered with plastic on the outside to stop the milk from coming through. Be careful that holding the milk in does not make your nipples sore. If there is any tendency to soreness, let the air get to the nipples and go topless for a while.

Leaking may be a problem, especially in the morning when the baby has not been fed for six or more hours. Your breasts may be quite hard and uncomfortable with the milk.

Breast or bottle?

Every mother must decide whether to breast- or bottle-feed her baby. There are advantages, listed below, to both methods. Her feelings and attitudes about her baby will play a large part in her decision.

The benefits of breast-feeding

Colostrum, which precedes milk in the first days after birth, conveys health-preserving antibodies to the newborn baby.

Breast-milk flows fast at first, placating hunger, then slows down, allowing the baby to satisfy his sucking urge without overeating.

The baby is less likely to become fat, develop diaper rash, constipation, or diarrhea.

Milk is always available (once established), sterile, and needs no preparation.

The food is always suitable, agreeable to the baby, and is the correct temperature.

The mother will regain her figure quicker, as breast-feeding contracts the womb and her waist.

Night feeding is less of a chore.

No equipment is needed; this is particularly desirable when traveling.

Skin contact is good for the baby.

The advantages of bottle-feeding

The mother's state of mind has no effect on the milk supply.

The milk will be unaffected by any medications that the mother might be taking.

Baby-sitters or husbands can give the bottle and stand in for the mother.

The mother is better able to keep a watch on the quantity of food that the baby is eating.

Mothers may find it easier to feed the baby in public.

The mother who bottle-feeds will expend less energy and be able to divert it elsewhere. She might, for example, be able to return to work earlier than the breast-feeding mother.

The mother's diet will not affect the baby; she can eat and drink what she likes.

You can easily let off the pressure by releasing the surplus by hand. It is sometimes possible to give this to a hospital to help less fortunate babies, where it is commonly used to feed those premature babies whose mothers cannot yet produce milk.

You may be anxious because your milk looks thin compared with cow's milk. Do not worry: the food value is right for your baby and the different appearance merely reflects the different makeup required to suit a human baby's needs.

Mother's milk

Some women produce copious quantities of milk from the moment it comes in. Others need a week or two to get going properly. Given time, patience, and the will to succeed, only very few mothers are unable to produce sufficient milk for their own baby's needs. Most mothers must wait for their breasts to respond to the demands made on them, which they will do positively. The more you feed your baby, the more your breasts will produce. This is nature's self-regulating arrangement, and it is the reason why breast-feedings should not be supplemented with a bottle. If supplementary bottle-feedings are given, it may be the beginning of the end of breast-feeding, as the milk supply will be reduced. This can be a good thing if you want to switch to the bottle. To do this you should slowly reduce the time on each breast and gradually increase the amount in the bottle.

Supplementary feedings

An infant feeds in bursts. He will suck contentedly at the breast with his eyes closed, pausing now and then to glance up at his mother's face, or around at his surroundings.

After feeding, a baby will often sleep instantly. He will not always be alert, scrutinizing his world ; happy and comforted he may simply fall asleep, not bothering to wait for his crib.

Bottle-feeding

Although many mothers are returning to breast-feeding, some just do not like it. Whatever the reason, whether you are shy, or whether you feel that modern living is not suited to such an elemental practice, if you do not sincerely want to breast-feed there is no need to force yourself. If you have decided to bottle-feed from birth, do try to give your baby the benefit of the colostrum from your breasts for the first two or three days. In addition give him warm (body temperature) boiled water from the bottle, not made-up milk. Start him on milk on the third day. Offer a new baby about 1–2 fl oz/28–56 ml at a time, increasing this gradually until he is taking the full amount for his weight. (See page 36 to calculate his needs.) Some larger babies may take up to 4 fl oz/112 ml each time right from the beginning. Throw away any milk that is left after each feeding.

Storing milk

To avoid having to make such small amounts every two or three hours it is a good idea to make up a larger quantity and store it in the refrigerator, using smaller amounts as needed. These can be poured straight into the bottle, which is then warmed in a saucepan of water. Modern bottles are designed so that the nipple can be placed pointing inward, while a cap, fixed on top keeps it clean.

Preparing the formula and sterilizing the equipment

Before preparing a formula, everything you use, including your hands and tabletop, must be clean and dry. The bottle, nipple, and milk must, of course, be sterile.

In a measuring container, add boiled water to the powdered or evaporated milk a little at a time to make a smooth paste, stirring thoroughly. Then stir in the remaining water. This method will avoid a lumpy mixture that will clog the nipple. Pour the formula into the baby's sterile bottle, which should then be cooled by standing it in cold water. The more rapidly the formula is cooled the more efficiently will germs be prevented from multiplying. To test the temperature splash a few drops of the milk on the inside of the wrist. It should feel barely warm.

Nevertheless, babies will drink cold formulas. When traveling, take the formula made up but cold and, when needed, heat up the bottle in the normal way. If this is not possible, give it cold.

If you bottle-feed your baby, you must sterilize all formulas and bottles. This is to keep them free from bacteria which may be harmless to older children and adults but may make a baby ill until he has developed his own resistance to infection.

First, thoroughly wash the bottle, nipple, and mixing equipment in hot soapy water, using a bottle brush kept solely for this purpose. Milk often congeals inside nipples: rubbing with a little salt will remove any deposit. Rinse everything well before sterilizing them by one of the following methods.

Boil the empty bottles and nipples for at least ten minutes in a covered pan kept for this purpose. All items must be completely submerged during sterilization. Once sterile,

they should be kept sterile until required.

Hospitals make up the daily formulas in bulk batches, and if you prefer to follow this method, boil the filled bottles with their nipples for twenty-five minutes. You will need six bottles and a sterilization pan. The filled, sterile bottles should be kept in the refrigerator until needed.

Many doctors prescribe a premixed formula which is available in cans for individual servings. This can be safely poured into a clean bottle before each feeding and does not require sterilizing. When your doctor feels your baby can handle commercial homo-

A bottle-fed baby should be held close so that his eyes are about 8 in/200 mm from his mother's inclined face, his natural distance for focusing.

genized milk, this, too, can be conveniently poured into a clean nursing bottle.

Many brands of dried milk are available. They differ slightly in their formulas, but their nutritional value is very similar. Some are reputed to be a closer imitation of mother's milk, but it is only by a matter of degree. However, there are differences in the chemistry of the ingredients. Some which have been sold widely are now known not to be suitable for babies (they are known technically as "low solute" milks). You should check with your doctor for up-to-date details. Milks also tend to differ a good deal in their taste. If you are having trouble getting your baby to accept

Dried milk

When using sodium hypochlorite solution to sterilize bottles and equipment, you can buy a special unit (above) which will hold sufficient fluid; alternatively a large bowl with an inner float to hold the items under the water will do.

his bottle, it may be that he does not like the brand you have chosen. Experiment with one or two others until you find one he enjoys. However, if you have to try more than two or three the problem may be a more general feeding difficulty, and you should consult your doctor.

If the milk does not come out of the bottle fast enough for your baby, you can either enlarge the hole in the nipple with a red-hot needle (do not just poke at the edge of the hole with a cold needle or you will leave a ragged edge, which could harbor stale milk and germs) or buy another nipple with a larger hole. The milk should drip from a bottle at the rate of three drops a second.

How much milk?

Most babies, given the opportunity, will regulate the amount of their feedings to their own needs. If you are bottle-feeding you can calculate your own baby's individual needs, which you can do on the following basis: breast milk and properly made formula contain 20 calories per fluid ounce (3 kilojoules per milliliter). Up to five months old, a baby's daily needs are 55 calories for each pound (500 kilojoules for each kilogram) of his weight. So a baby who weighs 7 lb 4 oz/3.29 kg requires 20 fl oz/568 ml a day, and a 10 lb/4.54 kg baby needs 27½ fl oz/780 ml.

If you are anxious about your baby receiving sufficient nourishment, check his weight-gain each week. It is not necessary to weigh him before and after every feeding. By three months he should be getting his requirement with approximately ten minutes on each breast each feeding.

The danger with bottle-feeding is that he may get too much. You must be absolutely certain that you do not make up the milk in too concentrated a form. This will not only give a baby too much food, but it will strain his digestive system and overload him with salt, which can be dangerous. It is also easy to bully the baby with the bottle, jiggling it up and down and encouraging him to go on feeding when he has had enough.

Remember that each individual baby has his own food requirements. It is his general health and vitality which really matter, and which tell you whether he is getting too little, too much, or the right amount.

Thirsty babies

If you think your baby is receiving sufficient nourishment and yet still seems to want something, he may be thirsty, especially in hot weather. After his feeding, offer him a bottle of very diluted orange juice made with cooled boiled water. You will need a nipple with a smaller hole than for milk.

Vitamins

Babies require 400 units of vitamin D every day. Powdered milks are already fortified with vitamin D, but breast-fed babies should be given a supplement. Babies also need a daily dose of 30 mg of vitamin C, which neither breast nor powdered milk contains in any appreciable quantity. By adding fresh

Breast-feeding

Mothers who breast-feed successfully find it a fulfilling experience. It establishes a special kind of intimacy between mother and child and helps to seal the bonding process between them, especially if the first feeding is within a few hours of birth.

A mother who breast-feeds must manage her life to suit—which may mean a more leisurely life style that she will enjoy for its own sake. Her supply of milk can be reduced if she becomes overtired or suffers from anxiety.

The flavor of some foods, such as garlic and strong spices like curry and pepper, can pass into the mother's milk. This will not matter if she eats such food every day, but if she does so only occasionally the change may put the baby off. Alcohol passes into the milk, and a nursing mother should have no more than two small glasses of wine or one pint of beer a day, and no hard liquor.

A breast-fed baby is more likely to stay healthy than one who is bottle-fed. First, there is much less chance of infection of the milk. Second, because the milk was developed by nature to exactly suit the baby's stomach, he digests it much more easily. There is consequently less load on his stomach, liver, and kidneys than there is on the digestive system of a baby fed on a bottled formula.

When the baby learns to suckle, it is important that the mother teaches him to take the whole nipple and areola into his mouth. If he does not, he may not draw down the milk successfully, and his increasingly anxious sucking will make the nipple sore.

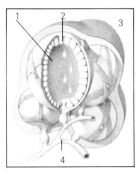

The breasts are composed of fibrous material containing a mass of little cavities, or sinuses (1). Each sinus is lined with many small gland cells (2), which make the milk. The sinuses are grouped together in alveoli (3), which in turn are grouped together into fifteen lobules. Ducts (4) lead from each sinus, linking up as they pass from the alveoli through the lobule.

Behind the areola, the dark ring surrounding the nipple, the ducts enlarge into small reservoirs (5).

Between feedings the sinuses fill until the baby's sucking, or the approach of feeding time, "lets down" the milk into the reservoirs.

While breast-feeding some mothers may find a maternity bra comfortable and convenient. It is adjustable and opens at the front, making the breasts easily accessible to the hungry infant.

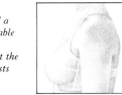 

To release milk, massage the breasts with forward movements. Make a ring with both thumbs and forefingers round the base and squeeze gently toward the nipple. Then hold the breast firmly with one hand and squeeze the areola with the other.

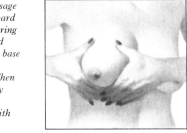 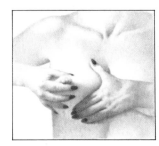 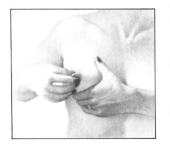

orange juice to your baby's diet every day, he should get an adequate amount of vitamin C. However, your doctor may prescribe a commercial vitamin supplement that contains the proper balance of vitamins A, C, and D.

Vitamins are usually given before a feeding in concentrated drops, which are started when the baby is two to four weeks old.

The provision of supplementary vitamins to babies is subject to controversy, because it has been found that excessive amounts of vitamin D could be harmful to a baby. So it is wise to discuss your baby's nutritional requirements fully with your doctor.

Feeding patterns

A newborn baby has to learn even such an elementary thing as how to satisfy his own feeding instinct. He will probably want to be fed every two or three hours at first. Some babies soon settle down to less frequent feedings; others keep up their two-hourly demand for some weeks. It is best for the mother to accept this. If you are breast-feeding, do not let it panic you into giving up or going on to supplementary bottles until careful weighing shows that he is not putting on enough weight. Some babies are just fussy.

Gradually a baby learns to tolerate near fullness and near emptiness. You should not let him become desperately hungry or anxiously push breast or bottle into his mouth every time he makes the smallest fuss. Let him learn that when he makes reasonable demands they will be met.

A two-month-old baby will usually have settled down to six feedings a day, about four hours apart. You can adjust the schedule to fit in with the life style of your family. Ten, two, six, and two o'clock are common feeding times in the day of the American family, but flexibility is important for all concerned.

A few babies "go through the night" right from the start; others may take three or four months. On the average, at about six weeks the baby will start going without a feeding for six hours or so during the night. How you place that gap depends on the baby and on your own sleeping pattern. Most parents find it convenient to give him a late feeding at eleven o'clock and feed him again at about five in the morning. This is usually better than taking a late evening nap, and feeding him at one in the morning in the hope that he will go through until seven or eight o'clock, because your own sleep pattern makes it easier for you to wake at five than at one. So it is not a good thing to wake a baby on the dot during the day when you think he ought to be fed, but it is right to wake him if he shows signs of sleeping past his nightly feeding.

If he starts whimpering at three or four in the morning, give him a chance to go back to sleep. The house will be still and the quiet may lull him back to sleep if you are lucky.

Going through the night

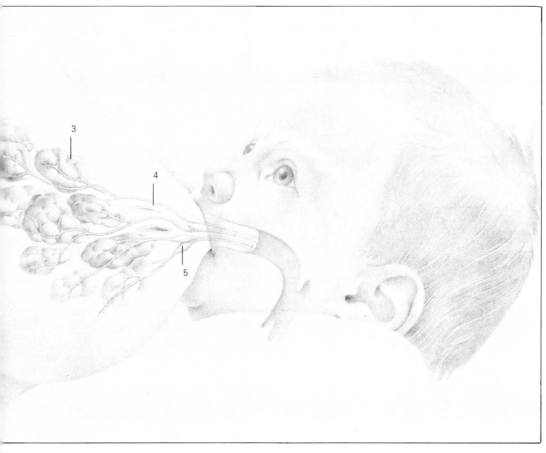

Diet for breast-feeding mothers
A breast-feeding mother should follow the well-balanced diet of her pregnancy. If she does not eat well she will become tired and her milk flow may decline. The extra requirements shown in the table can be met with a diet of at least 1½ pints/0.85 liters of milk, two generous portions of meat, poultry, or fish, and some fresh fruit and vegetables every day; and plenty of cereal, bread (preferably wholewheat), and eggs every week. These foods will also provide all the important vitamins and minerals necessary for a healthy body and for a nutritious supply of milk for her baby. Few mothers will want to calculate their diet as finely as in this chart, which gives a useful comparison between normal levels and those required by pregnant or breast-feeding mothers.

	Before Pregnancy	During Pregnancy	Breast-feeding
Kilojoules	9,200	10,050	11,300
(Calories)	2,200	2,400	2,700
Protein	55 g*	60 g	68 g
Vitamin A	750 µg‡	750 µg	1,200 µg
Vitamin B₁ (Thiamine)	0.9 mg†	1.0 mg	1.1 mg
Vitamin B₂ (Riboflavin)	1.3 mg	1.6 mg	1.8 mg
Nicotinic Acid (Niacin)	15 mg	18 mg	21 mg
Vitamin C (Ascorbic Acid)	30 mg	60 mg	60 mg
Vitamin D	2.5 µg	10 µg	10 µg
Calcium	500 mg	1,200 mg	1,200 mg
Iron	12 mg	15 mg	15 mg

* g = gram

† mg = milligram, or one-thousandth

‡ µg = microgram, or one-millionth of a gram.

Baby clothes & toiletries

When choosing clothes for your new baby, your primary consideration is for the baby's warmth and comfort; second, for the ease of washing the clothes; finally, your budget. For comfort, the baby's clothes must not be tight fitting and are best made from a mixture of man-made fibers, which are easy to wash and dry, and natural fibers, which let the body breathe, thus avoiding overheating or chilling. It is a good idea to buy only a few of the tiny size, as your baby will outgrow them surprisingly fast and he does not need as many changes as the older and more active baby. Better still, buy either stretch suits or outfits in the slightly larger second size. To ensure your baby is winter warm and summer cool, be guided by your own body temperature and that of his hands and feet.

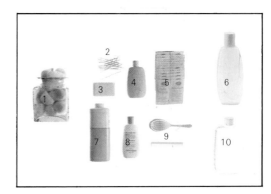

Here is a list of equipment for your new baby. Some things, like diapers, are essential. Others, like toiletries, are less so.

Cotton balls (1) are gentle and hygienic for washing baby's hands and face.

Cotton swabs (2) are handy for cleaning the outside of the baby's ears, nose, and mouth. They should never be pushed into the ears or nose.

Baby soap (3) is better for baby's skin as it is usually free from coloring and perfume.

Baby cream (4) containing a mild antiseptic is sometimes needed if soreness and diaper rash develop.

Baby wipes (5) are squares of fabric moistened with a gentle antiseptic—ideal for wiping baby's face, fingers, and bottom.

Baby shampoo (6) is generally weaker than ordinary shampoos and will not sting the eyes.

Baby powder (7) helps stop moistness and chafing.

Baby lotion (8) used as a cleanser at diaper changes—can prevent dry skin and soreness caused by frequent washing.

Brush and comb (9).

Baby oil (10) can be used instead of baby lotion.

Six receiving blankets (11).

Six diaper pins (12) with safety heads, which lock down over the closed pin.

Two to three dozen disposable diapers (13).

Two dozen diapers (14).

One packet disposable diaper liners (15). These are like extra-strong paper tissues and can be used inside the diaper to cut down cleaning problems.

Six pairs of plastic waterproof pants, can be tie-on (16), pull-on (17), frilly for special occasions (18), or adjustable snap pants (19). It is important to make sure they are not too tight around the baby's waist and legs so that urine can evaporate from the diaper. They should be left off if diaper rash develops and discarded when they become brittle through wear.

Three or four cotton wrap-over shirts with front ties (20) for young babies.

Three or four nightgowns either in the traditional design (21) tied at the back with open-ended hem and cuffs, or, for cold weather, with drawstring and turn-back mittens (22).

OR **Three one-piece stretch garments** (23), which can be worn day or night, are easy to launder, and will expand as the baby grows. Make sure the feet are roomy enough.

A sleeping bag with a detachable hood (24, 25) is warm and easy to carry when traveling.

Three sweaters (26), if you prefer a more traditional outfit for baby, or for emergencies.

One pair scratch mittens (27).

Two pairs outdoor mitts (28).

One bonnet (29).

Two pairs outdoor bootees (30).

One shawl (31). This is a matter of personal preference; a cellular blanket will be just as warm.

Two cellular carriage (32) **and crib** (33) **blankets.** Cellular blankets are warmer in winter and cooler in summer and easier to wash and dry.

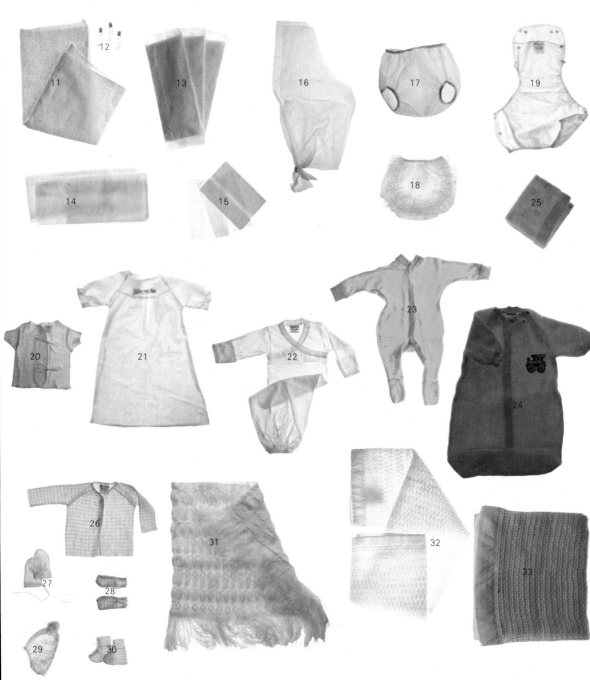

Gradually, as he learns to sleep longer during the night, you can try stretching the intervals between the other feedings, until at five or six months the baby is down to four feedings a day.

Pacifiers

Many babies discover their thumbs early in life as they explore their hands with their mouths and stimulate the sucking reflex. There is no harm in this. It may or may not become a habit. If it does, and soothes your baby when he is tired or fretful, then be thankful for this and do not try to stop him. A thumb is better than the pacifier that some mothers buy—it is cleaner and has its own human warmth. Babies have separate instincts for sucking and for filling the stomach. In most babies these are satisfied at the same time, but in some it seems that hunger can be satisfied before the sucking instinct. A breast-fed baby will often push the nipple forward so that no milk is pressed out, but he continues sucking for the pleasure of it. It may not stop his thumb-sucking, but he will be more contented and secure. Do not let him suck at an empty bottle, which will cause him to swallow air and give him gas.

Gas

It is widely believed that babies suffer chronically from gas. The amount of air a baby normally swallows and its effects have generally been exaggerated. A breast contains none, and a properly held bottle should let none pass. If your baby genuinely suffers and needs to burp a lot, his gas may be produced by the characteristic way his stomach works, as it is in many adults. If he is having to suck too hard at his bottle because of a blocked nipple, or a nipple with a small hole, this will encourage the swallowing of air. The reduced pressure inside his abdomen may also cause gas, which is dissolved in his stomach fluids, to be released from his stomach.

If your baby seems uncomfortable and cries after a feeding, and you know that he has had enough, it may be due to gas. Put the baby up to your shoulder facing over your back and very gently rub his back, putting slightly more pressure on the downward strokes.

Remember that babies differ in their readiness to "bubble," or burp. Some do so very easily; others seem to want to hang on. You will get to know your baby's tendency. When the bubble doesn't come up easily, try putting him down flat for a second and then up on your shoulder again.

Occasionally a baby may stop during a feeding and only resume when he has been burped.

Do not feel that your baby has to burp and that if he brings up no gas after a feeding he has failed in any way. If he is content to be held, but cries when he is put into his crib, then he is suffering not from gas but from isolation and loneliness. Gas has too often been used as an excuse to ignore a baby's distress and real needs.

Spitting up and vomiting

After a feeding, sometimes in the middle, and sometimes when he burps, a baby may regurgitate a small amount of mingled milk and spittle. This is known as spitting up. It is quite harmless. It is advisable to wear a protective garment, or put a towel or napkin over your shoulder, when burping him.

It is very rare for a breast-fed baby to vomit, although bottle-fed babies sometimes do. If the amount is small, there is no need to worry; but if the baby vomits his entire feeding or vomits frequently, or has no appetite, then he may be suffering from some illness, and you should call the doctor. Projectile vomiting, when the baby suddenly shoots out what he has eaten, often a good distance across the room, is rare and usually serious, although not lethal in itself. Consult your doctor at once.

Stools

For the first two or three days after birth a baby will pass the meconium that has accumulated in his intestine during the last six months of pregnancy. These stools are distinctively greenish-black. When these are finished and the baby is feeding properly the normal products of digestion appear.

A breast-fed baby's stools are colored an orangy-yellow and are of a soft, even consistency. They have a sourish but "clean" smell, quite unlike feces passed later in life. A bottle-fed baby's stools are harder and more smelly—more like those of a baby who is eating solid food.

Breast-fed babies very rarely suffer from intestinal infections. The mother will soon notice if the baby is affected by anything she eats, and she should then cut out that food rather than give up breast-feeding.

Babies very often have movements highly irregularly. Sometimes they may have four or five a day, sometimes they may go for a whole day or two between movements. It often seems that babies save it up until just after their diaper has been changed.

If your baby is bottle-fed and seems constipated, you can loosen him by giving him a drink of boiled water and sugar.

Diapers

You will need at least two dozen large cotton diapers. Do not skimp on the quantity. Even with the best home laundry equipment there are breakdowns and emergencies, and you won't want to be caught short. Sometimes for added protection you may also want to use two diapers at a time—at night, for example, or when you take the baby away from home for part of the day.

When the baby is only a few days old and is passing only meconium, which is sticky and hard to get rid of, it is best to use disposable diapers. If prefolded, smaller-sized diapers are available, they are useful for tiny infants. The larger sized ones are necessary for babies more than two or three months old.

Plastic pants are essential, and you will need three or four pairs. It is best to wash these by hand and to hang them on a rod to dry, since they are bound to get ruined in an automatic dryer.

Some mothers find it convenient to use disposable paper diaper liners, which keep the diaper itself less messy.

Changing and washing diapers

There are three basic ways of folding a diaper.

1 The quickest : fold the square into a triangle. Place the longest side under the baby's waist and bring the lower point through his legs. Cross over all points at the front, pinning through with a diaper pin.

2 The crudest : fold the square into an oblong. Bring the lower half of the oblong through the baby's legs. Pin each side.

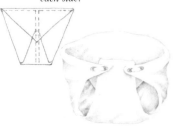

3 The best : fold two corners into the middle and overlap to make a kite shape. Fold the upper point down to make a straight edge, and the lower point up to meet it. Place straight edge under baby's waist and bring narrow part up through his legs. Pin side points over short edge.
    This method is adjustable by varying the amount of overlap, and it provides the greatest thickness at front and back and avoids bunching cloth between the legs, making movement easier.

Washing and bathing

Although it is possible to change a baby on your lap, the most convenient arrangement is a changing table or bathinette, which will be easier on your back. It also has handy places in which to store the equipment you need.

Only during the first two or three months is it safe to leave a baby on his back in the middle of a table or a bed. (Always lay him across a bed, not along the length of it.) When he is able to roll over, you must be vigilant and right there at all times.

Cover the surface of the table with a towel or receiving blanket so the baby is comfortable. If you are using a bed, a waterproof sheet under the towel or receiving blanket will give you additional protection.

Many babies do not seem to mind a wet or dirty diaper. Others are uncomfortable and complain readily. Unless the baby is wearing plastic pants, the evaporation will make him feel cold. But even if your baby is not complaining it is unwise to leave him in a wet or dirty diaper for long. The ammonia in his urine will soon be likely to cause a diaper rash. And the longer a soiled diaper is dirty, the harder it will be to get it clean.

Washing the baby off each time you change him and using powder and/or petroleum jelly are important. If diaper rash does develop and you feel it is getting out of hand, consult your doctor.

Diapers should be rinsed off immediately, put into a waterproof can with a plastic liner, and washed every day or two. Although commercial laundry detergents are usually suitable, some babies may be allergic to them, and if you suspect this, try washing your baby's clothes in a mild soap and give them an extra rinse. Electric or gas dryers are a boon. Our grandmothers and some of our mothers boiled diapers, but with today's automatic equipment that should not be necessary.

Diaper service is available in many communities, but it is expensive and it is unnecessary for a family that has access to a washing machine and dryer. It can sometimes be convenient, however. Since most babies are in diapers for two to three years, many mothers may confront a double mountain for a while, with two children to care for. With twins, diaper service is also a boon. The diapers are usually very thoroughly cleaned, as well.

Although disposable diapers are expensive they are exceedingly popular with American mothers. Disposable goods in general have a great hold on our culture, and our fast-moving, convenience-oriented society has responded enthusiastically to this important labor-saving device. To what extent a mother uses them will depend on her own budget and the pressures on her time.

Most mothers will learn how to bathe the baby safely and efficiently while they are in the hospital. You should be careful not to wet the umbilical cord during the few days when it is still attached. The most important rule

Above : After bathing a baby, lay him on a large soft towel and blot him dry, keep him warm. Gently wipe the creases in his neck and thighs. Right : Once you have dried him thoroughly, apply a mild antiseptic cream if his skin tends to get sore. You may like to apply talcum powder, patting it gently all over. Slip his shirt on as soon as you have done this to keep him warm.

Some mothers like to use a softer muslin diaper to line the thicker diaper. This can be wrapped around the baby first or folded in with the main diaper. Bring the side flaps across the baby's tummy and lift the lower edge through the baby's open legs.

is obvious, but worth repeating: NEVER leave a baby or a young child in a bathtub unattended.

You can bathe the baby at any time of the day, so arrange bath time when it is most convenient for all. A toddler can help by handling the soap and powder, and father might want to join in or just watch. Early evening is a good time. Most mothers find it best to give the bath before a feeding, because a baby often falls asleep immediately afterwards, especially in the early months. Babies may fall asleep after a bath, too. So if the baby has a crying time in the evening, the bath may help him to get off to sleep. Feed, bathe, pick up until contented, and put down.

Babies get cold quickly in the early weeks, so make sure the room is warm and draft-free and that everything is at hand: soap, powder, baby lotion, baby sponge, towel, clean folded diapers, and clothes.

If you become over-anxious you will handle

Initially bathe a newborn infant in only a little water, which should be at body temperature. After testing the water temperature with your elbow, gently lower the baby into the bath, still supporting his back and head with your left arm. Wash his face with plain water for the first few weeks, using cotton balls or a soft washcloth. Clean the rest of his body, running a soaped finger inside the folds. (You may find it easier to soap the baby on your lap.) Rinse him and gently pat him dry, especially in the creases.

Right: If you are using a washable diaper, fold it to the correct size and then slip it under the baby's bottom by lifting both his ankles in the left hand. This is the easiest method of raising the baby and will not upset him. Lay the diaper so that the upper edge is at the waist. Place a liner in the middle of the diaper.

your baby roughly and communicate your anxiety to him. This will make him resist and the whole process will become doubly difficult. Talk to him quietly and soothingly. A baby often loves bath time. When you take off his clothes watch how he lies and kicks and crows with delight. Although some babies hate having their clothes off, after the first few weeks small babies love being naked. They love the water too, and will splash with great abandon.

Some babies develop a form of crust, in which the scalp becomes scaly, either in patches or all over. The condition can look very alarming, with yellow crusty scales adhering tightly to the head, but it is not usually serious, and many babies have mild cradle cap for most of their first year. If it is ignored it can occasionally spread to the skin on the forehead and around the ears, where it can cause a more painful inflammation and cracking. This is normally easily prevented.

If cradle cap appears you may be able to cure it with a medicated baby shampoo. You can deal with more persistent scaling by gently rubbing the baby's head with baby oil to soften the scales, preferably an hour or two before his bath. If the condition becomes severe your doctor may prescribe an emulsi-

Cradle cap

Taking hold of all the layers between two fingers and thumb on the left hand, push the pin in with your right hand, guiding it through with your left fingers to the outside. This will ensure you don't prick the baby. Do not pin the diaper too tightly around his midriff.

fied ointment, which you apply at night and wash off next morning.

Where should your baby sleep?

Many parents will enjoy the experience of having the baby sleep in their room for a while, so that they can get used to his sleep patterns (or lack of them!) and feed him easily when he wakes during the night. Others will prefer to have him in a room of his own from the very beginning; the decision is purely an individual one.

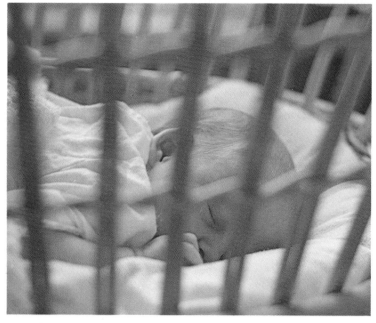

Placed to sleep on his front a baby naturally turns his head to one side. This is the position in which he sleeps best of all.

While he still needs quite frequent feedings it is much more convenient for the mother simply to lean over and lift him out of his cradle beside her than to get out of bed and go to another room.

At this time the baby is still learning night from day, and he will spend a remarkable amount of the night awake, snuffling and smacking his lips and making little grunts and gasps. It is worth putting up with this for the reassurance that he is all right. A tiny baby seems so fragile that most parents nurture a dread that he will somehow just stop living, particularly when he is asleep and you can hardly see whether he is breathing or not. You will find these tiny sounds very reassuring. His presence also helps you to accept that momentous fact—that you actually have a baby and are parents.

A separate room

It will not be long before the baby begins to take notice of his surroundings. Although his sleep pattern will be settling down, he will still rise and fall through the different levels of sleep much more often than an adult, and he will come to the state of borderline sleep quite often. He may make an odd noise or experimental cry in this state. If you are awake or half-awake and make any noise at all he is likely to come to full wakefulness, and then so will you.

So, to help both the baby and you sleep better at night, it is best after the first few weeks to put him in a separate room. You can

leave the door open if you want, although most mothers will wake by the time he is really crying for a feeding. It is surprising how little other children in the family are disturbed by night crying.

Because a baby loses body heat very easily and cannot get warm by moving about or shivering, the temperature of his room should not fall below 65°F/18°C, and for his first month 75°F/24°C is ideal. He will be happy at much higher temperatures than will be comfortable to his parents. However, make sure he is not too hot: listlessness and a stuffy nose can be signs that he is.

Room temperatures

The parents of a baby must be prepared to lose some sleep. Some are lucky and have babies who sleep quietly and drop the night-feeding after a month; others have restless babies who need the night-feeding for three months or longer. It is a time when tempers can become very frayed, and when sharing the burden becomes especially important.

If the baby is a frequent feeder, difficult at night, and is being breast-fed, there is not much the father can do to help directly. He can, however, assist the mother by bringing her breakfast in bed, and do anything else necessary to help her catch up on lost sleep. The father can also give a bottle-fed baby the occasional night-feeding to help a mother after a tiring day. It is usually the father who has to go out and earn the family living the next day, and he may feel entitled to a full night's sleep. But it is not as easy as he might imagine for a mother to sleep during the day.

Disturbed nights can become an even bigger problem if the baby has bad night colic. Then it is essential to share the sleep loss by taking shifts. Either the parents can divide a long night between them or they can alternate nights.

Your own sleep

A glamorous frilly bassinet may please a mother and impress her friends, but it will make no difference to a baby. It is much more economical to let him sleep in the portable crib in which you take him out during the day. If you leave this on its carriage (with the brake on), the movement that the springing allows will help to soothe him.

At about three months, however, he will begin to roll himself over, and soon you will need a regular crib. Those with a side that lets down will keep him safely in place, and will save you having to lift him in and out over a high side.

Cribs

As in everything else babies vary in how much they sleep. Some sleep a great deal of the time with very little disturbance; some sleep a lot but wake frequently; and others sleep much less. One thing is certain, however—most newborn babies sleep much less than we used to think. Over the first three weeks of life a baby is awake for an average of nine hours out of twenty-four. So, apart from the time when he is being fed, washed, changed, or played with, he is spending three to four

How much sleep?

hours lying quietly awake, looking, listening, and getting used to just being there.

As he grows older his sleeping will normally settle down into a pattern, so that at six weeks he is beginning to "know" when he should be asleep and when he should be awake. You can help him to acquire a routine by always putting him to sleep in the same place. In that way he comes to associates a particular environment with sleeping.

Sleeping posture

How should you put your baby down to sleep? The best way is prone on his stomach. In this position he is less likely to roll. His digestion works better, and if he should bring up any milk it is less likely to pass into his bronchial system and choke him. He will not suffocate in this position because he turns his head to the side. Do not give him a pillow until he is at least six months old, and even then make sure it is low and firm.

Some mothers still prefer to put a baby on his side, pulling the blankets tight about him to stop him from rolling over. He should be placed on alternate sides, right for one sleep and left for the next. This is because the bones in his head are still soft, and their shape can be distorted if he always sleeps on the same side. Alternatively, you may like to put him into a baby sling and let him sleep against your own body while you get on with your own activities.

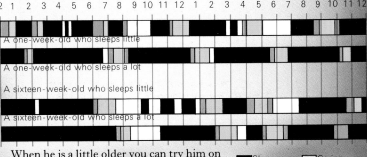

When he is a little older you can try him on his back and front to see which he prefers.

If you have a room hot enough for the baby to sleep without blankets, you will find that, if you put him face down, he will pull up his legs beneath him in the fetal posture. Many children do this until they are two or older.

By 16 weeks your baby will have developed regular eating and sleeping habits.

Lulling to sleep

If you want to get your baby to sleep, the age-old remedy of rocking has been shown to be highly effective. The rate of rocking should be surprisingly high—sixty rocks per minute. Another novel way that has had tremendous success in Japan is to make a tape recording of the mother's heartbeat and play it with the machine or speaker as close to the baby as is convenient.

Always remember, he will sleep as much as he wants. Do not worry if he sleeps less than other children. No baby ever made himself ill through lack of sleep.

Crying

Crying is a form of communication. It is a signal that something is wrong. You may still hear someone say, "It's good for him; it exercises his lungs"; but it is not what he needs.

That is not to say that a baby should never cry. As his satisfactions and comforts come and go there will be many times when he is unhappy and will want to communicate this to his mother.

Most mothers in the hospital very quickly recognize their own baby's cry, once they have been given the chance to get to know him. Within a week or two they will also be able to tell from his crying roughly what is the matter. To those with sensitive ears, a baby's hunger cry is very different from his pain cry, and his cry of boredom and loneliness is different yet again. Some breast-feeding mothers find that their milk begins to flow in response to their baby's hunger cry. If this cry is ignored it will change to a pain cry.

Very young babies appear not to mind wet or soiled diapers. If they stop crying when they are changed it is because they were lonely and bored. Later, however, they certainly do object to full or soggy diapers, and they will cry to be changed.

Although it happens very rarely with properly shaped diaper pins, they occasionally come undone and stick into the baby. It usually occurs later when he is crawling or walking. If the baby seems particularly agonized as though with a sharp pain, it is worth checking, unusual though the event is. If the baby increases his crying when you pick him up instead of calming, this might be the cause.

Babies who are kept to a strict feeding schedule cry more than those who are fed on demand. Some research suggests that babies whose mothers had a general anesthetic during the birth may be more easily upset, harder to soothe, and do not respond so well to cuddling.

How to stop your baby's crying

In the first two or three weeks of life a baby's crying probably means that he is hungry. It can usually be stopped by a feeding, but some mothers fear that this will spoil the child. In fact, babies who are fed on demand are much less likely to be fretful and demanding later on.

In the first two months or so many babies cry when they are put down to sleep. This is probably triggered by feelings of insecurity. Whatever the cause, such babies can be soothed by wrapping them tightly in a shawl or blanket so that their limbs are held firmly.

After two months, if he cries within half an hour of a feeding it is usually not because he is hungry. Picking him up and cuddling him will often be enough to calm him. Only in Western cultures are children left alone in cribs or carriages. In most societies they are kept close to their mothers and are not left in such isolation. Human society is natural for a baby, and consequently soothing for him. You will not be spoiling him if you treat him as the dependent infant he is. He will often go to sleep on your shoulder, and you can then put him gently into his crib.

Talk to him as you hold him, and walk up and down, rocking him. Sometimes he will want to be held over your shoulder; at other times to lie in your arms so that he can see your face.

The parents' feelings

Some babies are fractious and cry a great deal whatever is done. This is very trying for the parents—the mother, in particular, can feel afraid and inadequate. But if you are sure that you are doing everything that is possible—and reasonable—then you should resign yourselves to allowing him to yell for at least some of the day.

Colic

Many babies go through a period when they cry bitterly and frenziedly for no apparent reason. It nearly always happens in the evening, starting at any time from seven to eleven o'clock and lasting for anywhere from half an hour to three or four hours.

Each thing you try—feeding, cuddling, talking, walking, patting his back, rubbing his back, or bouncing him up and down—will probably calm him for a few minutes. Then he will start again, his face twisted, his arms tense, and his legs drawn up to his chest. He will look miserable.

This is evening colic. Its cause is still not certain, but research seems to show that it is due to gas in the baby's intestine. The baby's insides are still soft, and his gut can become looped in knots that trap the gas, causing great pain. The gas is too low in the system to come up in a burp, so ordinary burping will not cure it. Such loops are temporary and

When your baby is just beginning to take solids, he will not know how to cope with a spoon. Until he does, you will have to push the tip of the spoon between his lips and let the food slide into his mouth. He may then push the food out again, but do not despair, you will both adapt to this new method quite quickly.

free themselves after a few minutes. As the baby matures they cease forming. Gentle massage of the stomach and lower abdomen can help to free the bubbles of gas, but it will not provide instant release.

This can be a very difficult time for the parents, who can lose many hours of sleep. When you have been walking up and down with your child for two hours, and it is half past one in the morning, and he apparently makes naught of your best efforts to console him, you can be excused for feeling desperate, and for fleeting fantasies of violence. Do not think, however, that he is testing you, or doing it out of spite. Your baby is suffering, and needs the comfort of your presence and love. Even if you cannot ease the pain of the colic, you should not add to it by withdrawing and leaving him to suffer alone.

Holding a howling, agonized infant in your arms, or even listening to him through the door, drains your emotions. Your body will react with a stress response and you will be tired afterward. The effects will be lessened if you do not let yourselves become angry with your helpless baby.

Colic will pass. A few babies go on as late as nine months, but most get over it long before that. The average duration of colic is about nine weeks.

Weaning

A child cannot live on milk all his life, and sooner or later he will have to move on to solid food. The question is, when? Many mothers seem to feel that it is their duty to get the baby onto solids as early as possible. There is often an element of competition between mothers of babies of the same age to see which child is "more advanced."

This is a great mistake. For the first few months mother's milk or a substitute gives a baby all he needs, with the exception of vitamin D. It is of no benefit to him if he starts on solid food before three months, and it will do

him no harm if he does not begin until he is five or even six months.

Weaning, a phasing out of milk and a tapering in of solids, should be a gradual process. (See the chart on page 46 for details of how to go about it.) Start at about four months with a small amount of baby cereal mixed with boiled milk. Use one rounded teaspoon of cereal and one teaspoon of milk to make a thin gruel, or runny paste. Make sure that it is free from lumps. On no account add sugar.

Many dietitians recommend that you do not start with cereal but with a little puréed vegetable or fruit.

Feed solids to a baby with a spoon, putting a very little on the tip. At first he will not be good at taking it, as he is accustomed to using his mouth and tongue quite differently. He may try to lap the food, and in so doing will push the food back onto the spoon. A lot will spill down his cheeks and his chin. If you are deft and gentle you can collect this in the spoon and try him again with it.

It is best to hold the baby on your lap when beginning to spoon-feed him. This will reassure him during this novel experience. Later on, when he is more used to the spoon, and as he learns to sit better by himself, you may find it easier to put him in a baby seat or high-chair so that you can see his mouth better. Do not start to cut his milk until he is taking food successfully from the spoon.

Before one of his milk feedings, introduce the baby to solid food. Give him solids only once a day at first. Pick the time that suits you best, but it is a good idea to start at the mid-morning (about ten o'clock) feeding. Once he is taking solids well, start tapering off the proportion of his milk to solids at his mixed feedings. Initially, lower the quantity of milk by 1 fl oz/28 ml; continue reducing it by this amount roughly at weekly intervals until the milk has been completely phased out and the baby is entirely on solids.

Once he is well established with a good helping of solids at one feeding daily start a second feeding—the evening feeding perhaps. Follow the same procedure of tapering off the milk and increasing the solid food. When he is used to taking solid food twice a day, you can introduce solids at midday, giving him proper "meals" more like those of the family. Now and then try substituting juice in place of the milk. If he protests, introduce the substitution gradually, and he will very likely accept the change in time.

Many babies, once they are taking cereal well at six o'clock, will cut out their later evening feeding themselves. They are getting all they need and are happy with it. Soon he will not need a morning feeding as early as six o'clock, and you can bring back the ten o'clock feeding to eight or nine o'clock, so that he is having breakfast. At the same time you will need to bring back his two o'clock feeding to about twelve thirty or one o'clock. Now your baby is on the basic three meals a day, breakfast, lunch, and supper.

Introducing the spoon

Eating patterns

After a while your baby will learn how to open his mouth wide enough to accept the spoon, grip it with his lips, and take the entire contents into his mouth at one go.

Weaning your child

Preparing your baby's food

The baby's first solid foods should still be very smooth and rather runny. Baby cereal makes the right consistency, but some dietitians now recommend beginning with puréed fruit or vegetable.

If you are using raw ingredients, do not make the food mushy by boiling it for a long time: cook it until it is just done. Do not add salt. Then either liquidize it in a blender or food processor, use one of those mashers with a handle that turns, or force the food through a sieve with a wooden spoon.

Gradually, your baby will be ready to accept a slightly rougher texture, and by nine months or so you can safely mash some foods merely using a fork.

When you start to give him finger foods, be very careful that you give him nothing that he can bite off in small pieces. Some babies bolt their food and there is always a risk of choking. Zwieback is a safe choice.

Although it is not necessary that everything a weaning baby eats and drinks should be clinically sterile, your cooking utensils must be absolutely clean. All water used to

mix foods, milk, and drinks should first be boiled. After six months, raw fruit and vegetables are all right provided they are washed or peeled. Cow's milk should be pasteurized.

Commercial baby food

Commercial baby foods, in individual or double servings, are a great boon to the mothers of today. They include meats, vegetables, and fruits and make it easy to plan convenient, well-balanced meals. There are a wide variety of brands and items to choose from. Some mothers still prefer to prepare their

A weaning plan

Birth to about three months During the first few months your baby will only be having milk.

* Warning

Do not give a child under three years nuts, unpitted fruit, or shellfish. (See A–Z.) Avoid the following in the first year: Dried fruit (unless soaked and mashed first), dates, sweet corn, berries, uncooked onions, heavily spiced food, coffee, tea, and alcohol. Remember to peel cucumber.

Three to four months When your baby is about three to four months old or more, introduce, before one of his milk feedings, 1–2 tsp/5–10 ml per day of baby cereal (oats, wheat, rice, or barley). This should be mixed to a thin, creamy consistency with a little boiled milk. Or try 1–2 tsp/5–10 ml of fruit purée (not citrus fruit) made semi-liquid with boiled water. Do not add sugar. Increase the amount gradually to 3 tsp/15 ml per feeding twice a day.

Five months When your baby is easily digesting solids, give him plenty of variety of tastes and gradually increase the quantities. The texture should still be smooth, as babies dislike tacky consistencies. Try soups, blended or puréed stewed beef, lamb, or chicken, steamed carrots, cauliflower, peas, cabbage, and white fish. Egg yolk and grated or cottage cheese can be blended into foods as an alternative source of protein to meat. For puddings try an egg custard made with the yolk only, or stewed and blended prunes, apples, apricots, pears, and peaches.

1 Baby cereal
2 Puréed stewed prunes
3 Egg custard
4 Electric blender with pitted prunes
5 Manual blender
6 Grater
7 Grated, cottage, and cream cheeses
8 Puréed chicken and carrots
9 Malt extract
10 Finger foods: fresh fruit and zwieback
11 Orange juice
12 Baby's trainer cup
13 Detachable steamer basket with fish, cauliflower, and peas

own foods and to rely on older, more traditional methods. In any case, the jars are a great help when traveling, or when taking the baby along on a visit or to a restaurant.

Baby cereals are also available, and can be prepared easily by adding milk or water. Some contain preservatives or added sugar, so it is wise to check the ingredients listed on the box, and when in doubt to consult your doctor.

Consumer groups, in fact, are especially conscientious when it comes to monitoring baby food. Keep alert for newspaper and magazine reports, and be conscious of some of the questions being raised about the excessive use of food additives.

Adult food

If you need or prefer to use "convenience" foods, stick to baby foods. Try not to give your child canned or dried foods meant for adults as a great number contain substances which may make children ill. Occasionally, if time is limited, you may use some frozen or canned vegetables as a basis for your older baby's food.

Nutrition

During the baby's first year it is far more important that meal-times are pleasant than that any particular food is eaten in a certain quantity. No foods—even ones that are especially "good" for baby, such as meat, eggs, or vegetables—are indispensable as long as the baby eats some foods that contain iron, vitamins, minerals, and protein. However, to ensure that the baby learns to like and eat all kinds of food, it is best to let him taste everything, but do not worry if he does not take to some foods at once.

His tastes may change, so try him again a few weeks later.

Equipment

We have already referred to the kinds of equipment that will be helpful if you decide to prepare your baby food yourself. Fancy electric blenders, food processors, are not at all essential. Some mothers enjoy the convenience of the microwave oven in warming small amounts of food, but this too is an unnecessary luxury. Small saucepans and plastic containers for leftovers are the essentials.

Six to seven months Your baby's feeding routine is probably well established so continue to increase the range and amount of food. Now he has begun to grasp things include some finger foods such as zwieback, toast (whole-wheat is best), pieces of apple, peeled segments of orange, pear, banana, or carrot. Some foods, such as liver, onions, and tomatoes, are not easily accepted as they are too strongly flavored. If this happens, leave them out for a few weeks. Try lean pork only.

Seven to eight months Your baby can now start eating finely minced food. Its thicker texture will help him learn to chew. You can also try a whole egg, scrambled, poached, or boiled. His meals could contain at least one meat or fish dish and a vegetable with either stewed fruit, an egg custard, half a mashed ripe banana, or grated raw apple. He can eat brown bread fingers, perhaps with jelly or honey on them.

Nine to eleven months As your baby may now be attempting to feed himself and he may have a number of teeth, mash or mince his foods and leave a few small, soft lumps that he can pick up with his fingers. Some new dishes he could eat are omelettes, yogurt, crisp bacon, sausages, lamb chops, and hamburger.

Twelve months Your baby will be able to eat his food roughly chopped and flaked, with small lumps. The choice of foods is almost unlimited and you can give him a small version of the family's meals. Foods fried in fats and heavy oils, especially peanut oil, are best avoided for the first two years. Do not be concerned if your child appears to dislike the foods you consider "good" for him. His eating patterns are not yet established for life and he will astonish you one day by eating with relish the food he hated as a child.

14 Hamburger and mixed vegetables
15 Potatoes, spinach, and hard-boiled egg
16 Finely minced chicken and rice
17 Fresh cow's milk
18 Honey
19 Apricots and natural yogurt dessert
20 Peaches and strawberries
21 A hand-mincer with chicken and carrots
22 New flavors: salmon, mushrooms, celery, tomatoes, and broccoli
23 Broiled kidneys and green beans
24 Steamed potatoes, cabbage, broiled boned lamb chop
25 Sponge pudding and custard
26 Breakfast cereal and milk
27 Cranberry juice

Let the baby choose

While your baby is still learning to eat, allow him to become accustomed to one new food at a time. If, however, he seems positively to dislike one, do not let this hinder his learning, but change after a couple of refusals. You will have to decide sometimes whether he is having difficulty in taking a feeding or whether he does not want the food. If you give him his solids before his milk, he can always make up for any shortage. During his first weeks his appetite for solids may vary a good deal from day to day. Sometimes he will eat enthusiastically, at others he will want to pass on to the milk as soon as possible. If you are worried you can always check whether he is taking enough food by weighing him every week or two weeks.

The human body has its own system of "body clocks," which program the body to do certain things at certain times of day. These vary from one individual to another. By about six months your baby's own internal rhythms will be settling down, and he will to some extent want to control when he eats. So be flexible, and let him have his way. It is better both for him and for you to feed him when he wants rather than to subject both of you to an hour of screaming.

Some infants remain attached to the old, familiar ways and will regard their new cup with suspicion. They will inspect it, play with it, happily let the milk pour down their chins. At first some infants find holding a cup difficult and will need help and encouragement to get them drinking from it.

Drinking from a cup

When you want to wean your baby from breast or bottle (when he is six to ten months old), introduce him to pasteurized cow's milk from a cup. As a transition between the nipple and the cup, you might find a special cup with a feeding nozzle in the lid. Some babies take to these well; others find them only a nuisance and prefer to go straight to the cup itself. You may have to hold the cup quite firmly while your baby is learning to drink. By this stage he will be busy exploring holding things—and he will also love to show his enthusiasm by vigorous waving, which may send cup and milk flying. A good bib should catch the inevitable spillage as he learns to

hold the cup himself while he drinks. A two-handled cup is best for the first few months.

Place a large piece of plastic under and around his high-chair and make a feeding "island." He can experiment with finger foods, too, at this stage.

Ending breast- or bottle-feeding

When weaning is complete depends entirely on mother and child. Some babies practically take themselves off milk as soon as they acquire a taste for solid food and are weaned happily and easily by eight or nine months. A baby ought to have stopped taking breast or bottle by the time he is fifteen months. Most bottle-fed babies are weaned well before this, and some breast-feeding mothers have to stop because their baby chews with his new teeth, making her breasts very tender.

Night bottles

Some mothers give their baby a bottle with which to go off to sleep at night, and even during the day. If you know you will not mind your baby still taking the bottle when he is two or older, there is probably no harm in this. But it is likely that using a bottle as a comforter in this way will condition him to it, and if you would rather this did not happen let him use the more usual soft toy or blanket.

Fat babies

For generations it was thought that a fat baby was a healthy baby. Now we know better. A fat baby is not unhealthy, but there is a chance that he will develop into an unhealthy adult. The diseases caused by obesity in adulthood are many, from varicose veins to coronary thrombosis. A child who is overfed will develop millions more fat cells than he otherwise would have done. For the rest of his life these will demand to be fed, so you will have considerably lessened his chances to be slim.

Do not think that there is one fixed size and shape for babies. People's body type and metabolic style do vary. Today, however, people seem to respond much less enthusiasti-

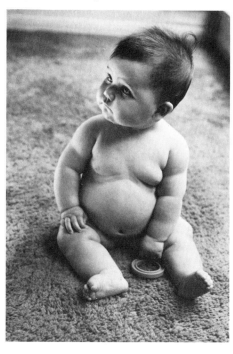

A fat baby will be healthy enough at this tender age, but he may be heading for illness and discomfort later in his life.

Sometime during the first year the infant discovers his mouth and practically everything is then popped into it. Whether he is pensive or distraught, his thumb may be a source of great comfort, and the habit need not be discouraged.

Teething

The two lower front teeth are the first to emerge; a complete set takes another eighteen months.

Teething and health

cally to plump babies, and for sound reasons.

Most overweight babies have either been overfed or given the wrong food. Using a bottle as a comforter, mixing too rich bottle milk, early weaning, too much cereal, cookies between meals, and sweetened drinks and food all help to produce a fat baby. If you start giving him food as a comforter he will go on wanting it. Don't start; give him a cuddle and a romp instead. If he wants something to eat between feedings don't give him a cookie; instead give him something too hard to be eaten quickly such as a piece of carrot, hard apple, or a zwieback.

Although a baby's first set of teeth is already fully developed by about the sixth month of pregnancy, it is unusual for the first tooth to appear through the gum until he is about six months old. As with so many other things there is a great deal of variation about this. A few babies are born with a tooth already through; others do not start teething until they are a year old.

Many parents feel competitive about the age that their baby teethes, and comparisons between children can be a central talking-point for mothers. Remember that there is no particular advantage in teething early or late. The appearance of teeth is unrelated to any other aspect of development.

For generations teething has been used as a catch-all explanation for all sorts of illnesses and childhood ailments. Most of these have been completely mistaken. However, your baby may seem to suffer discomfort. You can get a clue as to whether his distress is due to teething if it appears and goes again as each tooth breaks through. Very often a baby whose new tooth is hurting shows a distinc-

tive reddish inflamed patch on his cheek and has a slightly red gum. There may also be a slight loosening of the bowels.

However, if your baby has a fever or diarrhea, then this will be a genuine illness, and you should take him to the doctor at once. Do not use teething as an excuse to do nothing; if he is teething at the time it is simply a coincidence.

The eagerness with which a teething baby will seize anything hard on which to chew proves that the discomfort is real and that chewing relieves it. But you will probably find that the relief accorded by any one object may be short-lived, and you will have to keep a ready supply of alternatives. You can buy various forms of teething rings and hard rubber objects to chew on, but your baby may prefer to chew on a hard cracker, a piece of raw carrot, or a steak bone. Chicken bones tend to splinter, so beware.

Never attempt to pacify him with sweets. They will not relieve the discomfort in the gum and they may well be the cause of loose stools. If, from his earliest months, he has been used to raw fruit and vegetables and he has not been introduced to sweets until he is old enough to appreciate a treat, a baby is unlikely later on to become a constant sweet-eater. And the detrimental relationship between sweets and poor teeth now appears indisputable.

A very small quantity of fluoride in the diet helps prevent (or more correctly delay) tooth decay. In some areas fluoride occurs naturally in the drinking water, and in others it is added artificially. If you live in an area where the water does not contain fluoride, and you want your child to benefit, you can give him fluoride tablets. Up to the age of two he should have a daily dose of about 1 mg, half a standard tablet. You must not exceed this amount. A dose above the body's requirements is of no advantage to it and will not strengthen the teeth any further. And excess fluoride is believed to cause circulatory problems later in life. Fluoride may also cause yellowish-gray stains to appear in some children's teeth. If you rate your child's appearance higher than his health, you may refrain from giving fluoride tablets for that reason. In the United States, fluoride tablets are available only on prescription from a doctor or dentist.

It is not necessary to clean your baby's teeth in his first year.

If he is well fed and well cared for your baby will be quite naturally healthy.

The antibodies in colostrum and breast milk will help to protect him from any germs that come his way for about the first six months, a period during which he will to a large extent be isolated from most infections. Your doctor will let you know when he plans to inoculate your child against the childhood diseases that are now preventable. He is not likely to be too vulnerable, though, until he

Comforting during teething

It will take anywhere between three months and a year for those first two teeth to appear.

Fluoride

Cleaning teeth

Keeping your baby healthy

is a year and a half or so, when he begins to have more contact with other children. But in families where a child has an elder brother or sister who mixes a lot, try to be aware of any illnesses in the neighborhood or at school with which he might come in contact, so that they are not brought home.

The most common ailments in the first year of life are infections of the respiratory tract, including the ears that branch off it. By far the most frequent is, unsurprisingly, the common cold, usually brought into the house by the parents. There is nothing you can do to cure your baby's colds. Do not give him any adult medicines, even in small doses. If eyes and nose are clogged, clean them very gently with cotton swabs dipped in cool sterile water.

Many babies sniffle because of low nasal bridges which they haven't learned to clear properly; but this does not mean they have a permanent cold. If the nasal mucus is clear and the baby has no temperature or other symptoms, don't worry; if the mucus is thick, perhaps yellowish, and there is either fever, vomiting, or diarrhea, it may signal infection and the doctor should be consulted.

Sniffling is also caused by allowing a baby's room to get too hot and too dry. Once he is past the first two or three months you can drop the temperature a little and rely more on clothes and bedding to keep him warm. Meanwhile, if you need to, use a humidifier, or stand an open basin of water in his room, to keep the air moist.

Fresh air in good weather is good for babies past three months or so. Do not make a fetish of it, however, and remember that in many towns today the air is far from fresh. When the days are pleasant, let your baby sleep outside in his buggy. Try to keep him in the same place, where he can see trees or some other natural feature of interest. Where there are cats or insects about, cover him with a protective net. When he is older he will be able to tolerate colder days. But he must be kept well wrapped up, with mittens, boots and a woolen hat, and always sheltered from the wind. Pushing him in the carriage will give you some relaxation, too.

In hot weather place the buggy in a shady spot or move it around with the sun so that the buggy hood shades him. A cotton sunhat will also protect him, but many babies do not like them and pull them off.

Is your baby ill?

If your child should become ill in his first year he will be unable to tell you. You must be alert to symptoms of illness yourself. You cannot rely on the regular checkups that usually occur monthly in infancy. As you get to know your child better, you will be more and more in tune with his physical ups and downs, and should never hesitate to consult your doctor.

Loss of appetite is the most important symptom of illness in a baby. Normal variations around his average quantity, or a reduced appetite as a result of introducing new food at weaning, are not important, but if his intake goes down for two feedings in a row, you

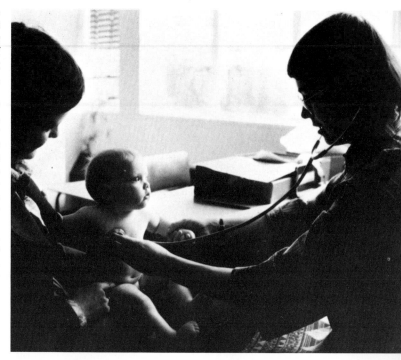

By visiting your doctor regularly you will ensure your baby's progress is being checked. The trip will also provide the ideal opportunity to discuss your worries and to swap experiences with other mothers.

should watch how he takes the third. He may seem reluctant even to start feeding.

Calling the doctor

Should this be coupled with other signs, then you should call your doctor. It is not always easy, however, to describe exactly what the other signs are. They can be subtle changes that only the mother, who is with him most, can sense. Even then she may not be able to say why she is worrying: he may be listless, and his eyes a little dull; or he may be restless and irritable.

If your child has any specific symptom severely or persistently, such as vomiting, or has diarrhea, a rash, fever, red or dull eyes, call your doctor as soon as possible. Keep him warm—but not too warm. If he has a fever he will need to be kept cool; otherwise he may develop convulsions. Until he is examined by the doctor, do not give him any medicine or aspirin. You may mask important symptoms. Do not expect your doctor to make house calls. They have become very rare indeed; if the doctor asks you to bring a sick baby to his office, you should be neither surprised nor indignant. Doctors have found that it is much more efficient to have the children brought in to *them*—not just in time but in the quality of care that can be administered in a professional setting where everything the doctor needs is close at hand.

Do not worry about calling your doctor when you are uncertain whether your child is ill. He knows the difficulties of judging a baby's condition and the doubts of new parents. He would rather be called about a baby who is recovering from some passing ailment than one who has been ill for some time. A doctor can often assess symptoms which you describe over the telephone.

When the doctor has examined the baby, he may decide that there is nothing serious—even nothing at all—wrong. If he diagnoses an illness, such as a throat or a urinary infection, or gastroenteritis, he will prescribe the correct medicine, if one is needed, and advise you on how to care for your baby. He will foretell the course of the illness and say whether and when he will see the baby again.

Looking after a sick baby

While the baby is ill, he will probably not take much milk or food. If he has a fever he will need more liquid than usual. A breast-fed baby has an advantage over one who is bottle-fed because the milk makes less demands on his kidneys and digestion.

A very young baby may sleep more than usual, while an older baby may be more fussy. Remember that your child is not feeling well and he can only tell you by being unhappy. He will require infinite patience and sympathy, and you should give it to him. The father must be alert to any extra demands on the mother and offer additional assistance.

The baby in the hospital

It appears that it is not quite so disturbing for a baby to be separated from his mother as for a toddler, but it is still much better to avoid the separation if you can. So, should your baby have to enter a hospital, arrange to stay with him if at all feasible.

If the hospital does not have facilities for a parent to stay, spend as much of the day as possible with him, and make sure you give him his feedings. Some hospital staff see this as a criticism of their professional skills, but most realize that to a baby no professional can fully replace a parent.

It is best if any older brother or sister can visit too. If they have to be left at home make sure they are given their full share of attention and love when you come home in the evening and before you leave in the morning, lest they be the ones to feel deserted.

Hide any fears you may have about immunization so that you can soothe your baby if it upsets him.

Immunization

You can protect your child against most serious childhood diseases by having him vaccinated and immunized. There is a small risk of side-effects from some injections. The A–Z guide in this book advises you about immunization, but you should also consult your own doctor either before or soon after your baby is born. It is a good idea to keep a written record of all injections, with their dates and notes of any aftereffects.

Temperatures

A baby's temperature is not a very reliable guide to his state of health. It is only one of a number of clues. A child can have a temperature of well over 100°F/38°C and show no other symptoms, and he will be well again before you have noticed anything. Another can be very ill with a "normal" temperature (98.6°F/37°C), although this is not usual.

Many books advise taking a baby's temperature by inserting the thermometer into his anus. I do not think this is realistic advice. It is a method which should be left to the professionals. For a mother it is best to place the thermometer in the baby's armpit. Done carefully, thermometer breakage is scarcely more likely, and the consequences are a great deal less serious.

If you are right-handed, hold the baby on your lap on your left side and place the thermometer on a surface by your right. Tuck his right arm firmly between his side and yours. Take his left arm in your left hand, tuck the thermometer under his armpit with your right hand, and then hold his arm against his side. Be firm and soothing. Clearly you must not fight, and if he is too restless then you will have to leave it to the doctor.

You may be able to take his temperature while he is feeding. If he is breast-feeding, get him started and then put the thermometer into his armpit from behind.

Smiling

Watch any adult in front of a smiling baby. They are at once melted, enchanted, delighted. A baby's smile has a powerful effect on everyone: grandparents, visiting friends, older children, total strangers. The smile is one of the set of inborn expressions that are common to all human beings. Since a baby's survival depends entirely on the goodwill of his fellow humans, the smile is clearly one of his most important assets.

It is strange how the belief survives that babies cannot smile. "He's not smiling," a nurse will say, looking at a baby with the broadest grin, plain for anyone to see, on his face. She will probably say that the expression is caused by gas, which is also supposed to cause so much crying.

Technically, it is perhaps correct to say that the real "social" smile does not appear until the ripe age of about six weeks, but this only means that his first experiments in attracting attention have now been found to work. In those first weeks his smile will often appear fleetingly, and only round the mouth, but your baby will also smile at you, looking you straight in the face.

How much a baby smiles depends partly on his temperament and partly on his social life. Some babies will smile a lot at anyone; others will be more reserved. If you respond by talking to him, cuddling, and playing with him, you are laying the foundations for a more secure adult personality. Babies who are reared in children's homes tend to smile seldom and late. Obviously it is especially pleasant for a mother if she has a baby who smiles a great deal. Her rewards and pleasures from looking after him will be particularly joyful.

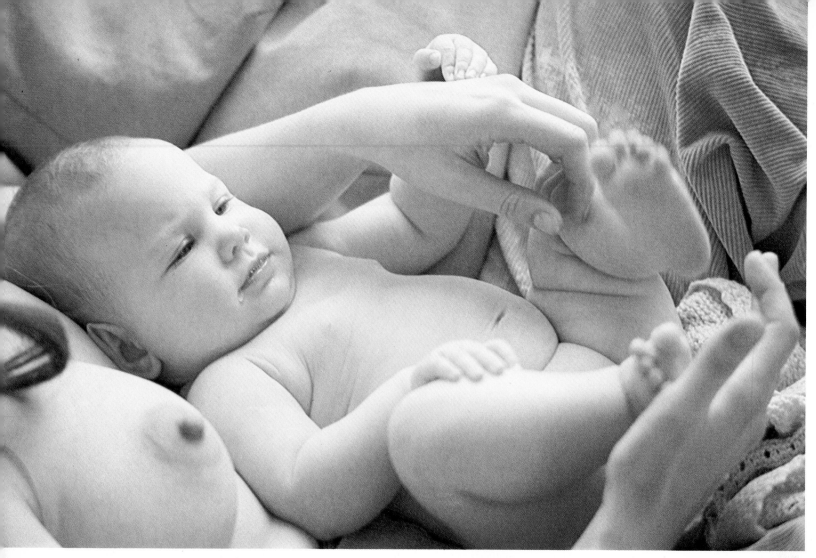

Relationships

A baby is instinctively tuned to respond to other people. He will react positively to a human face long before he can recognize anything else. A young baby does not "know" people as you do—and won't until he is much older—but he starts reacting differently to some people as early as five or six weeks, when he can single out the voices of his parents and respond more happily to them than to any other people.

The face is his most important link with others at first. At two months any face will make him smile, although he will smile longer and more often at his parents.

By three months he will continue to smile and gurgle at anybody who stops to pass the time of day with him, and this can give the mistaken impression that he cannot distinguish between people. However, if you were to time his reactions, you would discover that there is a perceptible lag before he reacts to strangers. In the next months he begins to recognize the rest of his family, and will often be especially excited by the presence of an older brother or sister.

Fear of strangers

Once he is able to comprehend "object permanence," at around seven months, all this changes and he acquires a constant memory of his mother and the rest of his family. Quite suddenly he develops a fear of strangers. You will wonder what has happened to the delightfully sociable center of attention who so charmed anybody who came to visit: now he may react to their interest with terrified yells.

This phase passes about the time he becomes really mobile, at about a year, whether he is an early walker or a rapid crawler, as it presumably arises out of his helpless state. You will soon notice the alteration. He will respond much more actively, and his enthusiastic greetings when you come to him will be more obviously for you personally. If when his mother leaves the room he is awake and restricted to a seat or crib, he will cry. Given the chance, he will crawl after her.

A child at this age may have very definite, but limited, ideas of what and who his mother is, or any other person he knows well. He can cope with some variation, but will be upset by anything beyond this. If his mother appears

A husband will get more out of fatherhood if he can enjoy his wife enjoying being a mother

Direct skin contact is good for your baby. A secure leisurely relationship with his mother is the best foundation for a well-formed personality later in life.

Mixing with the family

Relaxed play with your baby is the best possible thing for him.

The beginnings of personality

in a hat for the first time, or a kind of clothing he has not seen before, or if she changes her hair-style drastically, he may be frightened.

Glasses are another source of confusion. If his father wears glasses, he may treat all bespectacled men similarly, greeting them indiscriminately as "daddy."

It is at this stage that the child starts to piece together his social world, and his own place in it. Relationships are formed, based on identity rather than on the unconscious level of his earlier months. And it is to those people who give him emotional support and care, rather than those who are simply suppliers of food and clothing, to whom he forms his attachments. So it is good for him to lead an active social life within the family. You should not let the mother be the only one who always cuddles and loves him. He will be much more secure in adult life if he can build secure relationships in his first year with a whole family: mother, father, siblings, and grandparents. This is not always possible, but frequently substitutes can be found.

This is important not just for the baby, but for the mother. She cannot remain tied to the baby. Occasionally, a mother does turn her baby into a self-inflicted ball and chain around her legs. There is no need for this. While it is normal for one figure, usually the mother, to loom larger in the baby's world than any other, that person will need to get out and about. At first, a mother's actual coming and going will not be noticed by a young baby, although her absence will be. For the next couple of years, the baby will try to retain her with him. He will protest, perhaps sobbing brokenheartedly, when she leaves him. He has no concept of time and does not know that she will be back. Even though he will usually calm down and appear contented, his joyful response to her return will show how much he has missed her. So it is to her advantage for the baby to be familiar with being cared for by others.

Although it will not be very apparent for the first month or two, your baby has a personality or, perhaps more accurately at this age, a potential personality, very much his own. The way he grows up will depend a good deal on how you treat him, but this will be influenced to a greater or lesser extent by his own preferences.

Some babies are much more easily stimulated than others. They respond to much lower levels of stimulation of every kind: vision, touch, taste, noise, and so on. And since overactivation is distressing to babies, a sensitive child may be upset by levels that one who was less excitable would hardly notice. A game of peek-a-boo with a loud exclamation, which the latter would love, may frighten the more responsive baby, who would prefer it played more restrainedly and quietly.

Some babies have a greater toleration of discomfort. If your child frets when he is hungry or his diaper is wet, do not blame him—he is probably alert to his environment.

But a baby can also be too calm. A placid child may not start to complain of a diaper rash until it is quite bad, and he will need you to look out for such things.

Some babies like being cuddled more than others. They respond positively to physical contact, and later they will snuggle up cosily to mother, father, and any other familiar person. Some will seem to prefer resting in their mother's arms to playing on the floor or with other children.

At the opposite extreme there are those babies who seem almost to resent being picked up. They will put up with sitting on their mother's lap, and will tolerate a supporting arm when they are feeding. But they hate the restriction of a cuddle and will struggle to escape from it.

Inevitably, the majority of babies fall in between these two extremes, but if you have a baby who tends strongly in one direction or the other you will have to behave accordingly. If you have a cuddler who is happy to be put down as well as picked up you have no problem, but, if he cries when you leave him, try to be patient and give him the attention for which he is asking. You can help him toward independence later, and you will do so more successfully if he learns security in his first year or so.

If your child is independent do not feel that he is rejecting you. It is very easy indeed for a mother to react hostilely. "If the little devil doesn't need me, who needs him?" can be an unspoken thought in the mind of a mother who wants to love her baby and who feels he is fending her off.

It can be interesting to compare your baby with any others of the same age that you know (perhaps the child of an acquaintance made at the doctor's office or in the hospital), but do not expect him to behave in the same way or develop at the same rate.

If you are alert to your own baby's preferences and treat him as an individual right from the start, adapting your own behavior to his, you will help to lay the foundation for a happier relationship throughout life.

A child should not be given everything he asks for throughout his childhood. He will have to learn the limits as well as the possibilities of life. If you love your baby and give him a great deal of thoughtful attention in the first year, you will produce a child who is more, not less, likely to be independent later on. You will have provided him with a firm base of self-confidence from which to explore the world and to discover new things to the full.

Once he has settled into the world, a baby is ready and waiting to hear and respond to the human voice. Long before he has any inkling of what speech means, a baby will become excited and wave his arms and legs enthusiastically when he is spoken to, especially by his mother. When chatting to a baby, you should hold him, or else bend over his seat or crib so that he can clearly see your face.

Cuddling

Long conversations of nonsense-talk make good sense for mother and baby.

Spoiling your child

Talking to your baby

A young baby's ears are attuned best to high frequencies, so he will respond more positively to women's voices. The traditional "itchycoo" baby-talk really is the right way to speak to him. Fathers, perhaps, can be excused for feeling self-conscious in such an "unmanly" activity, but they may feel more relaxed and happier if they understand their baby's physiology.

Your baby's first sounds

A baby's first sounds are not much more than little grunts, sniffles, and lip-smacking. Gradually the grunts become different kinds of grunt; and hums and coos creep in. By about six weeks most babies will be making the characteristic cooing gurgling noises that can be so charming to hear; and there may be chuckles to accompany the smiles. By the time your child is about four months old he will have mastered a wide range of sounds, and he will be having "conversations" with you. When you say something, he will make a series of "remarks" and then wait for your reply. He will maintain this for a surprisingly long period, if you will.

A six-month-old baby is starting to develop his consonants, and the sounds he makes are beginning to be organized into phonemes, the basic units of words. The softer sounds appear first, "ma, ma, ma"; "na, na"; harder consonants, as in "da" and "ta," must wait for the upper front teeth. The soft "gher" sound gradually changes into "ger." It is no coincidence that in most cultures a mother is mom, mummy, or mama, and a father is dada or papa. Usually by around eight months a baby has built up a complete range of all the speech sounds it is possible to make. At this stage all babies sound basically alike. There is no difference between babies who are English, American, French, or Chinese. Then comes a stage of two or three months when, to the eager parents anxiously awaiting the magic first word, nothing seems to be progressing. The baby seems stuck with the same kind of complex babbling.

Probably two things are happening. First, he is consolidating what he has already developed and becoming more skillful in the way he uses his mouth and throat to make sounds. Secondly, he is listening to the adults and beginning to get the idea of putting some sounds together in particular combinations (to make words); he is also dropping other sounds because they are not used in whatever language his family speaks.

When a baby actually speaks his first words depends on both his own individual rate of

Sex differences

Although they should not lead you to handle your baby any differently, distinctly male and female characteristics do develop from the moment of conception. On the average girls are shorter and lighter at birth, yet they are several weeks ahead of boys in over-all development. A greater proportion of a boy's body weight at birth is made up of muscle tissue; a girl's has more fat, but her muscle tissue is further developed. The calorie intake of boys is greater from the second month of life, and they develop larger hearts and lungs. A boys grows faster in the womb and until about seven months. After this the girl grows faster until about four years.

Newly born girls tend to have better senses of hearing and smell than do boys, who can see better sooner. Girls react more strongly to pain and touch although there is no evidence that a baby cries more or less because of its sex. Girls are less vulnerable to stress in the womb and during and immediately after

birth. Girls tend to sit up, walk, and crawl earlier than boys, although the movements of boys at birth are more vigorous. Toward the end of the first year boys begin to demonstrate their superior spatial abilities in matching and arranging different shapes and objects. When playing ball they are already better able to aim and judge distances. Girls develop language earlier than boys, and have greater verbal ability at eighteen months.

Girls respond better than boys to speech, and, because they can be reassured verbally, they receive less physical attention from their mothers. Thus, from an early age, girls learn to communicate with language while boys use their bodies.

Boys on the average are longer and heavier than girls throughout infancy, and they have larger lungs and hearts to match. If you plot your child's growth you will find it follows a curve parallel to those on the right, whether or not it lies between the curves for the large and the small baby.

Length gains — 32 in, 28, 24, 20
Age in months: 2 4 6 8 10 12

Nude weight — 29lb, 27, 24, 22, 20, 18, 16, 13, 12, 9, 6½
Boys / Girls
Age in months: 2 4 6 8 10 12

Right: Baby girls choose different toys from baby boys. Their preferences illustrate not stereotyped femininity, but their more rapid early physical and mental development. Girls' greater manual dexterity means that building blocks are already significant playthings for them. Similarly their enjoyment of free play with two toys and with stuffed animals indicates their advanced mental development.

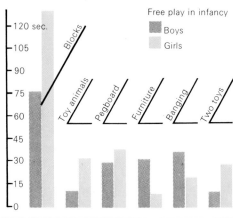

Free play in infancy
Boys / Girls
120 sec., 105, 90, 75, 60, 45, 30, 15, 0
Blocks Toy animals Pegboard Furniture Banging Two toys

Exaggerated head movement and expression make a caricature of the parents during a child's first year—but they are what he needs. From every game, every "conversation," he learns a little more.

The growth of a baby's understanding

The first two months of a baby's life are spent getting his basic systems functioning properly and adapting to life outside the womb. Initially he learns to understand his own body from the inside, and how to use his eyes. For the first month he will move very little. When lying on his stomach he stays almost still for most of the time. If placed on his back he will wave his arms and legs, if they are free, in an uncoordinated way. Then, as his legs straighten and his hands unclench, he begins to discover his own body, and how it moves. His movements will become more coordinated and purposeful, although it may not appear so to a spectator. Each little motion he makes is aimed at getting better at that movement. He is in the same position as a four-year-old learning to kick a ball. He is not interested in scoring goals, and the rules of the game are beyond him; it is enough for him to be acquiring the basic physical skills. So small babies will do the same simple things over and over again, practicing all the time. The first big step occurs at about three months, when the baby discovers that he can make things happen. Earlier than this he might have waved a rattle, but there would have been no intent involved. You would have had to put the rattle into his hand, which he would have waved about with or without the rattle.

One day he will realize that when he does something simple he produces interesting results. He will very likely discover that his body movements cause suspended toys or the mobile hanging over his crib to swing. (Remember that movement is what interests him most.) And he will start wriggling or jerking deliberately, and repeatedly, watching to see the result.

He discovers himself from the outside, so to speak. He realizes that the object that passes back and forth before his eyes when he waves his hand is that hand. He will then spend a good deal of time waving and watching.

If you place a rattle in his hand, he will experiment with it, enjoying the fact that it makes a noise when he waves it and is silent when he is still. His interest will be brief, however. Some parents feel disappointed that the rattle, the toy that everyone seems to think is the central feature of infancy, is cast aside so soon. He may play with it again a little later, around six months, when he is able to pick things up for himself and is more in control. But by then banging may be his chief delight.

By five or six months old he will be attempting to pick up objects. For a young infant this is a difficult task. If you watch very carefully in the early stages you will be able to see how he looks first at his hand, then at the toy that he wants, before steering his hand toward it. Many times he will reach out for something and miss. It will take a lot of practice until he can make his hands do what he wants them to.

At the same time he starts to want things and ask for them, although only his fond parents will recognize the request. He will start stretching out—fleetingly at first—toward objects which attract his attention but which are out of his range. You will probably notice that the way he reaches for something far away is different from the way he stretches out to take hold of something within reach. Later, at about a year or fifteen months, he will clearly point with one finger, exclaiming as he does so. Many babies include "ook, ook," or some other attempt at "look," among their first words.

growth and on the amount of talking he hears and sees around him. If you want your baby to become very fluent with words and ideas, you can help him off to a good start by talking to him a great deal, long before he can actually use words himself. On the other hand, do not worry if, having spent considerable time talking to him, he still does not respond with more than a few syllables when other children are using several words. He will almost certainly catch up later.

A baby understands a good deal before he can actually talk. He will recognize "no" before he can say it. If you hold up his favorite toy in front of him and tell him what it is, like "squeaky duck," and then put it among his other toys and ask him to find it, he will show by picking it out that he understands not only the name but your request.

Don't wait until your child is talking before you introduce him to nursery rhymes. Say or sing them to him, holding him on your knees, and you will find that he loves them. Singing raises the pitch of the voice and he will respond well, particularly if you emphasize the rhythm of the lines. Be gentle, though, and watch his mood. Sometimes he will enjoy being bumped about in time to the rhymes more than at others.

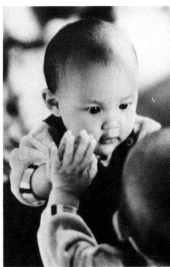

Scrutinizing a mirror, an infant does not recognize himself. He'll watch the expressions, stare at his reflection, but the face he sees is that of a stranger.

Physical development

For the infant the first year is a period of extraordinary physical advances. By their first birthdays many children are tottering, though unsteadily, on their own two feet, but it won't seem so long ago that they were completely helpless and dependent. All children learn to walk eventually and go through the same stages of development, although the rate differs from child to child. Some, though few, can walk at ten months: there are others who will only be starting to teeter at eighteen months. It is important to remember that the age at which your child learns to walk is neither a sign of his intelligence nor of his physical abilities in later life. So don't struggle with him if he seems to be slow, he'll find his feet in his own time.

As with walking so with grasping. Infants learn to handle and manipulate objects through a clearly ordered sequence of stages that cannot be altered or hurried—although it can be delayed. Children learn at their own speed, but they do benefit from simple toys, and from a safe home where they can explore and practice their new-found skills.

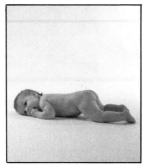

At one month
There will be no dramatic development during the first month, but by this date the baby should be able to lift his chin momentarily, and he will stretch out his legs intermittently.

At two months
As the weeks go by it may seem that the infant is very reluctant to evolve, but he is learning all the time. Little by little he will stretch himself out, and each day he will hold up his head for a moment longer.

At three months
By the end of the third month he should have finally uncurled himself. His pelvis will be flat, and his tiny legs extended. His head, which before seemed so heavy, is at last able to be raised and the position maintained.

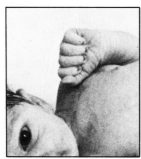

At this young age the infant keeps his tiny hands tightly clenched for much of the time.

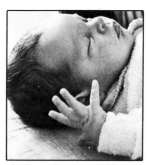

As the weeks advance, his hands will open up and stay open for longer periods with fingers outstretched. Only a slight grasp reflex will remain.

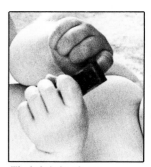

The baby's hands are now loosely open, and, though he will not be able to grasp an object by himself, for a few seconds he will hold a rattle that is handed to him.

Stimulating your child

Some people encourage you to think that if only you give your baby the correct toys and environment from the start, you will produce a genius. Even if this were true, it might not be a good thing, for there is only room for a restricted number of geniuses in the world. There is certainly a limit to what you can put into, and get out of, any one child.

Within this limitation, however, you can assist your baby considerably later in life by giving him a rich and varied environment, which he can explore against a background of secure love and protection.

The most valuable single way to help a child in his first year is to spend as much time with him as you can. Cuddle, bounce him, and carry him with you; play and talk to him. The person who looks after him most—usually his mother—will naturally do most of this, which helps the baby to learn how much variation one constant environment can produce. But it should not all be left to the mother. Father should also take his turn, as should older brothers or sisters.

For the first two or three months delicate and pretty things changed regularly will be lost on your baby. Big, bold patterns are what he likes, kept basically the same, so that he can get to know them properly and be sure of his own reactions. At about two months start hanging some articles at varying distances from him. If you originally fixed up a pop-art mobile about 3 ft/1 m above his crib, move it so that it hangs from the ceiling about 6–9 ft/2–3 m away. In the original position attach a pictorial mobile: one that is very simple and bold, in bright primary colors. Across his buggy or crib string beads or rattles where he can reach them. You can buy a wide variety of objects already strung on elastic. These will do to start with, but it is preferable to make up your own string of articles, which you can change around. Fasten three or four objects at a time, and alter one or two of them every week or ten days.

If he sleeps in a crib or cradle with solid sides, paste shapes or patterns at first, and pictures later, onto the inside where he can see them. When he sleeps outside, settle him where he can see trees or bushes. He will love to watch the leaves and branches moving about in the wind.

In their first six or nine months babies are reduced to a semi-somnolent state if they are

When your baby is two months, and spending some time on his back, put a mobile above his crib. The ever-changing colors and shapes will stimulate him.

At four months
Development during the next few months is rapid. Having mastered control of his head the baby is soon able to gain considerable mobility. Now he will roll from his side to his back, and he will be able to lift himself on his forearms.

At five months
This is the age when the parents must keep a very close watch on their infant. He can roll from his back to his side. Although deliberate crawling will be extremely unlikely, there will be enough movement for him to fall from the edge of a bed.

At six months
The sixth month will see quite an upward advance. He will roll over freely and will be able to sit propped up in a buggy or high-chair. If someone holds him he'll want to put some of his weight on his own two feet.

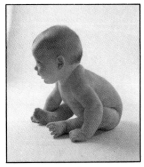

At seven months
The baby's ability to sit up has made real progress. He's reached the halfway stage between lying down and standing, but for the moment he will feel a little wobbly and needs to lean forward on his hand to support himself.

At eight months
He'll now be able to use his hands to play with, and his attention will easily be diverted from the difficult business of sitting up without a support. There will be endless toppling over so make sure there's not far to fall.

This is a time of playing with his hands and of tentative exploration; the infant may pull and tug at his clothes, even pull them over his face.

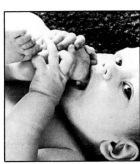

He is still discovering himself: he will grasp his feet and put them into his mouth.

Over the next few months manipulation becomes more deliberate. He will be able to hold an object between fingers and thumb.

The baby can now hold an object in the palm of his hand, and this makes the world more accessible to him; if he wishes he will be able to pick up a zwieback to chew.

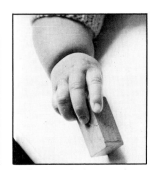

As his dexterity improves he will pick up and hold smaller objects.

on their backs. Even when they are not asleep they are not properly awake either. This is really a wasted period for a baby when he could be looking around him and learning. So when he is not asleep or being fed, put him in a baby seat where he can watch what is going on around him.

How a baby's vision develops

"Can my baby see in color, or in 3-D?" is a question many parents ask. Until recently we could only guess; now experiments have given us a better idea about the vision of a newly born baby.

At birth a baby can probably see in partial color with muted shades, because the color receptors in his eyes are not fully developed. Red and blue are the colors he detects first, followed by green and yellow. Initially, he will only be able to detect bright colors. Baby pink is lost on a new baby.

His world looks flat with some parts in sharp focus and others very much out of focus. Because of this he does not see little details very well.

As early as two weeks a baby will blink and put up his hands to ward off something that approaches him head-on. This is an instinc-

tive reaction, for he will not react to something which approaches as though it were going to pass by a couple of feet from him.

Gradually he builds up a 3-D picture of his surroundings. As he lies in his crib, and feeds on his mother's lap, he will watch her face come and go, now coming to him directly, now going past him as she tucks in a blanket or lifts him up to her shoulder. He will watch her come and go across the room, growing larger and smaller as she does so. He will also see how the world changes in size and shape

Every baby loves movement, particularly if he can make it happen himself. The baby chair or cradle gym will enable him to do this. It will bounce gently when he moves and kicks. It provides support for his head and has straps to prevent his slipping out. The chair's angle will enable him to watch what is happening around him. When he is six months or so and moving quite vigorously, always place the chair on the floor.

At nine months
At last the baby's on the move, but to begin with it may be backward. This won't last long and soon he will be able to crawl across the room to grab a toy or tag along behind his mother.

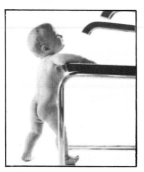

At ten months or later
As soon as he can take his weight on his own two feet, the infant will be trying to walk. He will pull himself up whenever he has the opportunity: in his crib or playpen, or on some nearby furniture.

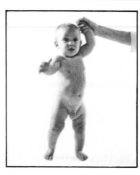

At one year or later
Although he may be putting one foot in front of another, he will need a little outside help in order to keep his balance. Crawling will still be his main method of locomotion, but he's learning fast how to walk.

At fifteen months
Alone and tottering! Most infants will be moving around on their own two feet, somehow or other. Some may be walking whereas others still depend on outside support and will still need a few months before they are freely walking around.

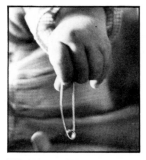

The infant will need a little more practice before he can pick up something as small as a diaper pin.

He will be able to release objects and will enjoy placing them in containers, although his accuracy and coordination are somewhat lacking.

He is learning to give as well as to take, and mother may be the happy recipient of some toy.

The child's coordination has progressed so well that he is now learning how to use his wrist and hand to place an object in a tightly fitting hole.

as he is carried about. At close quarters he will learn the finer points of what is in reach and what is not. So, even before he crawls and starts moving around on his own, he will have built up a good understanding of the third dimension.

During the first six months of his life, although he may not look very active to you, a baby learns an enormous amount. Imagine yourself looking at something you have never seen before. It could be a piece of machinery or a painting by a new artist. If you force yourself to understand it, the chances are that you will end up feeling confused and strained. More likely, you will perceive only a very simplified form of what is in front of you. There will be very many features that you will not notice until they are pointed out to you, such as the details that make up the composition; the individual way the painter has used line and color; and the way a glittering necklace is conjured up from a few blobs of paint.

A young baby is in very much the same position. If you show him something elaborate, he will look only at the outline, not at the detail. He has to learn to build up the world bit by bit as things become familiar to him. At first he will gaze for minutes on end at a single object. By two months he is already beginning to sort out what is more or less interesting, what is new and what is familiar. He recognizes only simple patterns and shapes. Around four months, a baby requires quite an elaborate and varied environment. He soon becomes bored and will look around him to see what is going on, craning to see over the edge of his crib or buggy.

Although the baby will recognize a favorite toy and reach for it more often than his others by the time he is five months or so, he does not remember it when it is not in view. Out of sight out of mind is the rule for things (though not necessarily people) at this age. Should you put your baby in the garden in his buggy with a number of toys to keep him amused, you will probably hear him bawling with frustrated boredom after a time. He will have dropped or thrown the toys one by one over the edge, until there are none left in the buggy —and he will be unable to make out where they have gone.

Later he discovers the joy of dropping things deliberately. This develops about the same time as he learns that when something disappears from view, it does not vanish off the face of the earth. Now the game is a new one, called "Emptying the buggy," But if a willing parent is not there to play the other half of the game, called "Fill the buggy up again," it ends with wails of boredom.

varying effects. Earlier he learned to pull a string to draw a toy toward him; now he invents for himself ways of raking in a toy with something long-handled, or by pulling on the rug on which he is sitting.

Objects that can be placed inside one another fascinate babies at this stage. If you show him how something like a small toy will fit inside a box, a pot, or a can, he will copy you, repeatedly putting the toy in and raking it out again. Interestingly at this age babies seem to prefer the variety provided by unrelated objects: specially made stacking and nesting blocks have much less appeal.

Exploring the world

By a year the child is very active in his exploration, and more systematic in his experimenting. Whereas at six months he banged endlessly with the same block on the same place, he will now use first a block, then a toy car, then a wooden rod, and he will bang with each in turn on different surfaces to enjoy the

When the world comes to stay

A new baby responds emotionally to his needs for food and human contact, but his mental world is restricted to the present. When something moves out of sight, it disappears altogether from his thoughts.

To make the all-important mental steps out

of his cradle he must learn that an object continues to exist even when he can no longer hear it, see it, or feel it; that he can ask for the toy that he dropped to be given back to him; and that his mother is not just a warm body but a person who comes and goes.

 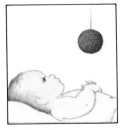 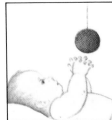 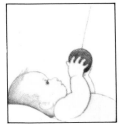 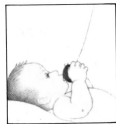

At birth a baby will fail to take notice of an object if it is stationary. He is unaware of its presence and is attracted only by the human face.

By the end of the first month he is taking more interest in his surroundings. He will gaze at a toy hanging above his crib though he will not think of touching it.

A few weeks later he starts his tentative explorations, reaching out toward the toy above. Unable to judge distances and with no experience of holding, he will fail to seize it.

Eye and hand coordination improves so that by four months the infant succeeds in grasping the object.

Soon after this he begins to combine more actions, and by the fifth month he will not only see and hold a toy but will draw it to his mouth and suck.

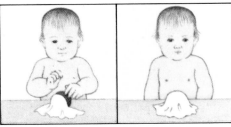 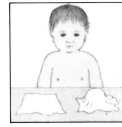 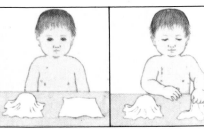

As his coordination develops, the eight-month-old infant shows the first sign of object permanence. If a toy is partially covered he will recognize it by some small clue and reach out for it. However, there will be no attempt to hunt for a well-concealed toy, even if the child sees it being hidden.

By his first birthday he will have grasped object permanence, but will still show a strange inability to locate hidden objects. If a toy is placed under one cover where he finds it and then, in full sight of the child, placed under a

second, he will look for the toy under the first. He is repeating the action that produced the object rather than looking for it where he last saw it placed.

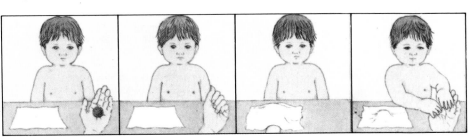

At eighteen months a child will locate concealed objects, but will still be unable to deal with invisible displacements. If you take a coin in your hand,

which you put under a cloth and then withdraw it, leaving the coin behind, the child will look in your hand but not under the cloth for the coin.

During the first two years
he'll be too busy to take any
interest in friends that you
might bring home for him.
Intent on their own
activities, infants will play
independently, oblivious of
the company around them.

Early play

The newborn will look, feel, smell, and listen all the time he is being changed, fed, cuddled, or is lying quietly in his crib. Gradually, he begins to explore this environment that both excites and confuses him—largely through learning to utilize his muscles. He will throw back his head and laugh for the joy of it over and over again. Later he begins to play with things, trying and trying until he succeeds in kicking, reaching, grasping, and throwing.

When the baby learns a new skill well enough to repeat it positively and pleasurably, and perhaps coos and chuckles while he is doing it, he is playing. And it is through this playing that he learns. For the first two years of life, playing mainly consists of practicing, learning, and finally exercising his developing motor skills. He will do this on his own as well as with his mother and other adults and children he is close to.

Much of what a baby does initially will look vague and uncertain. The first recognizable play occurs around four or five months, when he has learned about making things happen. The baby may hit his mother or pull her hair as she bends over him; and if she responds, and he is amused by the reaction, he may attempt it again and again.

Once he can grasp things, at about five to six months, he will spend a great deal of time just waving them up and down. Then comes banging, simply on the first thing he finds around him—the mattress, the floor, his knee, then on any toys that make an interesting noise. Between the ages of six and eighteen months, he will explore things mainly by putting them in his mouth: hands, feet, blocks, rattles, toy cars, and, once he can crawl, dirt, wood, coal, leaves—anything he can pick up.

At first he can handle only one object at a time; if he is given two, he will promptly drop one of them. Toward the end of his first year, he will learn to hold both and bang and shake them, rub them together, and hit them against each other. At about this time, also, he learns to let go—a skill which soon becomes a splendid game as toys and food are hurled from crib, buggy, and high-chair. (He also quickly discovers how efficiently this attracts the attention of his exasperated mother.) Once he has fully understood that although an object or a person disappears from sight they still exist and can return—about nine months—variations of hide-and-seek and peek-a-boo played by himself and with others become endlessly fascinating.

Learning and exercising his skills of mobility—crawling, pulling himself up, sitting down, beginning to walk still holding on—will occupy much of his waking and playing time until he is walking efficiently by himself, probably some time during the first half of the second year. But once he can move around, even if it is only backward, his scope for playing and learning is wide open, and he will require considerable vigilance by his caretaker. As his vocalizing increases, and he tries to imitate more, he will enjoy babbling to the sound and beat of nursery rhymes and tunes. The whole family can be involved in this really delightful activity. Watching a baby develop his play and learning capacities in every aspect, and from day to day, is an endlessly rewarding side of parenthood. Make the most of it, as all too soon it will pass.

Toys

During his first year, a child needs little in the way of specially made toys, as to him everything is a plaything. Blocks are an early favorite, long before he can build anything. They are good for just picking up and putting down; for sucking, admiring the bright colors, and especially for banging.

Model cars will not be cars to him for some time yet; they go straight into the mouth like anything else. Nonetheless they allow him to experience different shapes. Although babies do not dislike soft toys—bears, rabbits, and the like—they seldom form the great attachment for them in their first year that they almost always do at about two.

Children enjoy toys that they can do things with, that give them an opportunity for achievement—and what they can or want to perform at this age is limited. Many children like an engine or an animal on wheels that they can pull toward them with a string, although they need your assistance to return it to the starting point. (You can see who has more patience, you or your child.) Once they can grasp small objects with their fingers and have acquired the ability to let go, some children enjoy playing with a "mailbox" by about a year, although others find it uninteresting until later. Fitting the variously shaped blocks to the appropriately shaped holes makes them more dexterous and teaches them to discriminate between shapes.

For many children the greatest play space is the kitchen floor, and the best toy box is very likely the cupboard. Pots, pans, and wooden spoons will keep your child happier than anything else. He has seen his mother use them, of course, and this is his first opportunity for imitation. They are fun, too, being big and sturdy and easy for him to grasp, push about, and bang. Always make sure that he plays outside the cooking area.

After about eight months a baby will be able to push himself up from the floor into the sitting position. When he is lying, he will be able to roll about and lift the top half of his body off the ground in a kind of push-up. In this position he will soon become frustrated. He can see things across the room which he wants but is still unable to reach himself.

It will probably seem an age to his eager and ambitious parents before his desperate swimming movements produce any real effect. Many babies seem to develop all the techniques of crawling except the knack of getting their midriff and hips off the floor.

At this stage some babies—about a tenth—give up the attempt to crawl and discover bottom shuffling. If your baby does this, do not worry that there is anything wrong. But be prepared for just how fast a bottom shuffler can move about!

These are often sold as devices for helping a baby to learn to walk. In fact they do no such thing, and are usually a hindrance. To walk a baby must first learn to crawl (or bottom shuffle), and to stand on his own two feet.

However, walkers can be extremely useful in giving extra mobility to a child who is not yet walking, and can bring new things into his reach. An infant seat which slants is a handy piece of equipment and will often keep a three-month-old baby occupied for as long as an hour as he watches goings-on around him. It gives him a welcome change of scene.

Crawling

Bottom shuffling

Baby walkers

The traveling child

Mobility for mother and child is essential for both—to prevent the mother from feeling isolated and to expand the child's horizons. It is essential that the baby be safe and comfortable, however. A tiny baby who cannot sit up needs to be protected from the cold and wind. Before buying a buggy, check for stability, good brakes, and fitted harness rings. When the baby can sit up, by all means harness him in. If he is sleeping outdoors unattended, cover him with a netting, and keep a watchful eye from time to time.

Left : Once a child can support his head, a sling gives a parent more freedom for outings. As child and carrier are in close physical contact, which is very reassuring to a young baby, he will sleep in it easily.

Right : This type of carrier is useful for a child who is too large for a sling and likes to see where he is going.

Above : The carriage on the left is handy because it comes off of the frame easily and can be used as a portable crib. It is also light-weight and easy to store. Some mothers prefer heavier carriages which are more substantial and give a smoother ride. The stroller is ideal for older children who are comfortable sitting up but unable to walk very far. No matter which type of conveyance you choose, it is important to make sure your child is carefully strapped in.

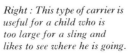

Safety

As adults we take it for granted that we live in a world designed by adults *for* adults. We have to remind ourselves constantly that our small children also live in this large-sized world, and that, although the toddler learns at a remarkable rate, he almost totally lacks judgment of the danger in his surroundings and is extremely vulnerable to serious, sometimes fatal accidents. It is a frightening fact that accidents are the biggest single cause of death in children between the ages of one and fifteen. The commonest cause is traffic accidents, with the proportion of home accidents also significantly large. A recent report showed that of all home accidents, thirty percent involved children under four. These accidents occur most frequently in the living and dining areas of homes, but almost one-fifth of children's accidents take place in the kitchen. Other danger areas are the bedroom and play areas outside the house. Most injuries at home result, first, from household furniture such as chairs, beds, tables, sofas; second, from constructions such as stairs, doors, and windows; and third, from kitchen utensils such as teapots, cups, and kettles.

Baby room
1 Nightwear should be made of nonflammable fabrics.
2 Do not use pillows for babies under one year.
3 Fasten blankets to bed, or use a warm "trundle-bundle."
4 Windows, especially on upper floors, should be locked with safety catches or barred.

Stairways and landings
5 Stairways should be well lit, with switches at top and bottom.
6 Install a safety gate while baby is crawling, ideally at the top and the bottom.
7 Banisters should be firm and should not be wide enough for a small child to get through.

Bathroom
8 Never leave a child alone in the bath or while it is filling. Run the cold water first and test the water before lowering your child into it.
9 Leave no razor blades or medicines within a child's reach.
10 Toilets should have a lid, kept closed.

Living room
15 Fireplaces are delightful, but can be a serious hazard. Fine mesh screens attached to a frame are safer than free-standing ones. Be careful never to leave a young child alone in a room where a fire is burning. Always make sure the fire is out before going to bed.
16 Do not hang clocks or mirrors over fires.
17 Shelving must be securely fixed to walls and preferably above child level to protect both child and possessions. Table lamps, vases, and photographs should

all be placed out of reach.
18 Electric outlets should be of the modern shuttered type or else they should be taped up. For any socket that is switched on permanently, tape the plug into the socket. Dummy or blind plugs can be bought to fill the holes. Disconnect appliances when not in use, especially the TV set.
19 Do not place hot coffee or tea pots, cups, or heavy items on low tables where they can be pulled off by young hands.
20 Never leave anything lying

about where it can be tripped over, especially on stairs or in doorways.
21 Nothing flammable should be stored underneath the stairs.
22 Avoid trailing wires, which could trip your child or yourself carrying your baby.

Kitchen
23 Do not use tablecloths until your child is past the grabbing age.
24 Keep short all cords for electric equipment, especially for coffee pots.
25 Store medicines and first-aid equipment in a childproof cabinet, preferably in the kitchen—the site of most accidents. Avoid cabinets with keys, which can easily be lost.
26 Babies should be secured by a safety harness when in a high-chair.
27 Always turn handles away from front of stove. Turn them to the side.

Never leave a frying pan on the heat unattended.
28 Keep bleach and all other cleaning agents out of reach in a high cupboard.
29 Floor covering should be non-slip, particularly in the kitchen. Vinyl or cork are particularly good. Do not use high-gloss polish; wipe up spilled liquids at once.
30 All doors and large windows should be made of plastic or shatter-proof glass.

Parents' room
11 Do not leave perfumes and cosmetics around.
12 Watch out for trailing wires, which could topple heavy objects down onto curious toddlers.
13 Always close your closet doors and make sure that they can be opened from the inside, as toddlers have been known to get trapped and suffocate inside.
14 Make sure the cord on your electric blanket is not frayed.

Outside areas
31 Doorways must be well lit with convenient switches to avoid dark areas.
32 Keep potentially lethal sheds and garages locked.
33 Ensure your shrubs do not have poisonous berries.
34 Fill in, or drain, or cover garden and swimming pools with nylon nets. Fit lids to rain-water barrels.
35 The gate should be shut and have a childproof catch.

If you have a young child, look at your home carefully, as if through his curious eyes. Are all your windows safe? Is it possible for him to open them and fall out or climb on the sills? Or are they locked or barred? Do you have wide, slatted banisters through which a small body could wriggle? Do you have a balcony that is an invitation to climb or fall through? Prevention is never a waste of time, money, or effort when a child's safety is involved.

In the kitchen, a stove is always the focal point of potential hazard: handles of saucepans of hot liquids should never overhang the edge; kettles and frying pans are particularly dangerous, as are pilot lights or gas flames. Burns and scalds occur frequently when a child grabs a full pot or even reaches for an apparently harmless hot cup of tea. All electric appliances can be lethal to the inquisitive child, especially if their cords trail within reach. Never assume that your child hasn't learned to take out plugs or pull them apart, or to push things or fingers into sockets. A dryer is specifically mentioned in accident reports as a danger spot. Make sure your youngster cannot stand on something so that he can reach into the washing machine. Never leave matches and plastic bags around the house.

The bathroom is also a potential danger area where he should never be left alone with the water running; always run the cold first, then mix it with hot and test the water before he gets in. All containers of water—buckets, wading pools, and rain barrels, even toilets —are dangerous for small children, who may fall in head first and get stuck. A swimming pool obviously calls for the strictest possible safety precautions. It is best to cover it permanently with nylon or wire netting while your child is young.

Adults take for granted so many poisonous products around the house, and tend to be careless about leaving drugs out within reach —all drugs, whether tranquilizers, sleeping pills, cough medicines, or even aspirin, are lethal if taken by a small child. What is more, they often look just like the sweets he enjoys so much. New safety tops on some medicine bottles are harder to open; but never rely on anything except total inaccessibility of drugs. They should be kept out of reach and out of sight so that they are not a temptation to climb for. In the same way, a child exploring kitchen cupboards may come across a bottle of highly poisonous disinfectant, which looks like something appealing to drink. All household cleansers and liquids should be inaccessible. Your garage or garden shed probably contains lethal corrosive fluids, weed killers, and petroleum products, as well as tools; these must all be locked away.

The entire balance of safety for a young child rests on allowing him plenty of opportunity to explore and play while at the same time, because he cannot yet be taught to avoid things he cannot understand, protecting him from elements in his own home environment which are harmful.

From the moment of your baby's birth you have been watching his development, but over the past year the changes have been gradual and it is probably hard to remember just how tiny and helpless he was. It is astonishing to recall that wrinkled being who could be held in one hand.

He has made great strides in developing his abilities. The primitive grasping, sucking, and walking reflexes he was born with have given way to more complex, controlled movements. He can now pick up a small object using just forefinger and thumb; he can sit up unaided, probably even crawl or walk. His sight and comprehension have developed enormously, and he will now distinguish and greet you as his parents with joy. Finally he is beginning to communicate with you; understanding many simple words and phrases and probably reacting to them with a nod or a garbled noise, which means the day that he can talk to you is rapidly approaching.

Your baby's first year

The growth of an infant from birth to fifteen months.

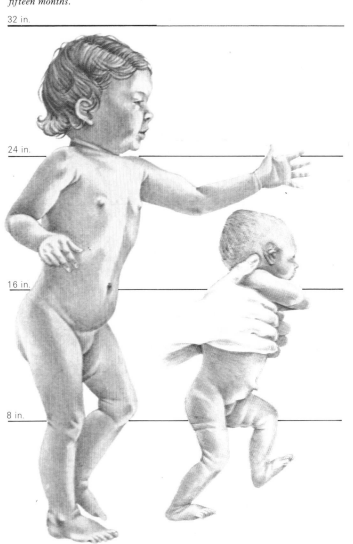

32 in.

24 in.

16 in.

8 in.

3 Toddlerhood:
FIRST STEPS

For weeks, he had
been almost walking—letting go for one step,
two steps, and tumbling, bottom in the
air. Then one afternoon, when we were out for
a walk, he stopped clutching the stroller
and took off—across the path and into the
field, a small, sturdy figure heading
toward the wide sky and the woods. He
spread his arms to steady himself
and his bright scarf blew in the wind.
With every step, his confidence grew; heart in
mouth, I sensed his freedom—and mine.

A parent would have to be a saint always to like her toddler; either that, or the child would not be developing his feelings of autonomy as he should. These years must be stormy ones for both parents and toddler because of the young child's growing demand for independence. This is a period of rapid development on all fronts: it starts with the fifteen-month-old, who has a few words among the babbling as he walks around the living room clinging to chairs; and it ends with the three-year-old, a competent walker and talker, who is emerging triumphantly from the struggles of babyhood.

Physically, he is becoming more independent of his mother all the time: first he is able to crawl, then walk, and finally run away from her. His understanding starts at the point where he knows that objects which are out of sight do not disappear and it develops to the point where he is able to think logically—albeit with a kind of logic that is unlike that of adults. At first he is happy to hide toys and retrieve them; he ends the stage able to build simple structures out of blocks or construction sets. Just as he has to show off his new skills to his mother, so does he increasingly need her warmth and protection. The dependence/independence of a child at an ambivalent age goes on day after day. His moods change rapidly. He will go from smiles to screaming in minutes; in a single afternoon his mother will find him loving, impossible, funny, angry, frustrated, challenging, and charming. Every time he says "No!," which is frequently, he is telling the world that he is a separate person from his parents.

It is rewarding and great fun, but it can be very wearing to be the mother of a toddler. At eighteen months he needs to be watched very carefully indeed. He is always underfoot —and when he isn't, he is probably getting into trouble.

Trying out his new skills he is constantly testing his parents and asking for limits. He has very little inner control, and he looks to his parents to provide it. When his tolerance snaps and he falls to the floor in a tantrum, he is probably frightened by his own feelings. Every time his parents draw the line over refusing another cookie when one has been half chewed and thrown on the floor, they are teaching him acceptable behavior. When he is older, he will be able to impose it on himself.

Toddlerhood is the last stage when parents have their child to themselves completely; soon there will be nursery school and the beginning of a life outside his home. The greater autonomy he achieves in these first three years, the better prepared he is to go on to the next stages of development.

The toddler is receptive and keen to learn about himself and his environment. Whether he's learning about his toes or how to count he will be an appreciative pupil.

First steps

All parents watch eagerly for this milestone in a baby's physical development. Most babies start staggering around a room holding on to the furniture at about a year old, and nearly all will be walking across a room by fifteen or sixteen months. But as in all other areas of development, the age at which a child walks alone varies enormously—from as early as nine months to nearly two years. A rapid crawler or bottom shuffler who gets about very efficiently will have less incentive to start walking. An illness or a bad fall may stop a baby from trying for several days, or make him revert to holding on or crawling after he has started walking alone. So while a parent will naturally encourage a child to walk by himself, he must not be pushed. He will start walking in his own good time, when his body is mature enough and he has gained sufficient confidence. Some babies learn very early to stand, holding on to the furniture or your hand, before they can crawl. You think the unbelievable is about to happen, and that he will walk before he can crawl. Then he discovers crawling, and the joys of mobility, and he may not stand again willingly for another couple of months.

Another baby may seem stuck for months at a stage when he can walk crabwise around a table or around the room, hanging on all the time. You think he will never launch out into the open spaces of the floor. He will move on to the next stage when he is ready. There is rarely any truth in the old idea that walking too soon makes a baby bowlegged. The myth is a survivor of the days when rickets, caused by vitamin D deficiency, led to bone deformities.

At first he walks very clumsily. The effort takes up all his concentration and his muscles and bones are still forming and hardening. As he becomes more expert, he will be able to hold an object in his hand or pull a toy on wheels behind him. Toward two, he will probably be able to run a little, and will attempt to kick a ball in imitation of a parent or older brother or sister. He will also learn to walk up and down stairs, placing both feet on each step to start with. During the third year, he will be able to balance on one leg and hop, which may not seem vital to you, but which can give him a great deal of pleasure.

When he first learns to walk, a baby appears bowlegged and flat-footed with his toes turning in. All this is normal and in most cases will right itself as he matures physically. The bowlegs will be accentuated by diapers. Flat feet are due to undeveloped arches. Most will improve as the toddler's feet mature. It is important that your child's shoes are not too small. The natural thing for a young child is to be shoeless, and many toddlers prefer this, so don't be too quick to put him in shoes all the time. In summer let him play on the lawn without them as much as possible.

Keeping up with a moving person

It seems strange that although a newborn, lying still in his crib, can follow a moving object with his eyes, a toddler has a good deal of trouble following his moving mother. If you take your two-year-old out for a walk, you will find that he will follow for a short distance and then stop. He will do so wherever you are, in the park, in the street, or out shopping. The reason is that children under about three do not know how to keep up. Although they no longer believe that mother, when she moves, is a different person from mother when she stands still, they still cannot relate themselves to a moving target. When they trot happily by your side, it is almost an accident that they are keeping pace with you. If you sit still on the ground a toddler can run

around and come back to your easily enough, but if you move on, even very slowly, he has difficulty in perceiving that you have changed your position. He may even run back to the wrong place.

Most parents understandably think that the apparent reluctance to follow is part of the toddler's growing independence. When they call and the child stands still, they conclude, wrongly, that he is being naughty.

When a child is still learning to walk he needs support—a good opportunity for an older brother or sister to be involved in looking after him.

Getting off the ground is a precarious business, and success a great triumph.

If you have two children quite close to three years old, one older and one younger, you will be able to see how differently they behave when you go out. Holding the younger child's hand is not the answer, for he will lag and want to stop when his attention is caught. So you must be patient when you have the time, and when you are in a hurry you should carry or put the child in a stroller.

Learning to talk

A child's acquisition of language still remains something of a mystery. Psychologists now believe that children have to build up a picture of the language they hear around them, rather like someone in a foreign country starting to learn the language.

When he is about a year old, a child will speak his first word. Usually it is the name of some familiar object, like dog, ball, or bib, but it could be anything. A girl whose parents are very conscious of her femininity might learn "pretty" as her first word. For a few weeks the child builds up a small list of words. Then he starts using them as more than just names. A fifteen-month-old will stand up in his crib and call "Mommy," but what he really means is "Mommy come here" or "Mommy I'm hungry." Similarly, to a toddler in his second year, "Open" may mean "The door is open" or "Open the door, I want to go out in the garden."

Close to eighteen or twenty months he begins to put two words together. These ages are highly variable; children differ widely in their rates of development in speech, more than in any other area. Also, up to the age of three, girls appear slightly ahead of boys in language development. Children learn about fifty words before they put two together. This is a major step in the development of their ability to communicate.

The first sentence

By the time your child is in his second year, he enjoys saying his favorite nursery rhymes with you over and over again, never tiring of the repetition. He probably also loves to hear you sing to him, delighting in the music's rhythms and the simple sounds of the words.

When a toddler starts to speak using more than one word consecutively, he appears to place words in two categories; nouns and a mixture of words that go with nouns. He will use these combinations—as worked out by his own set of rules—to cover many different meanings. He uses the words "Mommy sock" as a kind of shorthand to his mother. When she is dressing him he may use the words to ask her to put on his sock; or he may pick up one of his mother's stockings and hand it to her saying: "Mommy sock." Most children build up a set of words known as "pivot

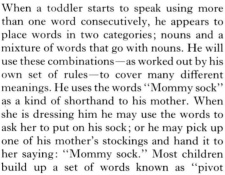

Feeding your child

A child's first attempts at feeding himself are bound to be messy, but a plastic bib with a pocket will collect the spilled food and will be easy to wipe clean after the meal.

Some time during his second year your child should take over feeding himself more or less completely. This will be easier if he has made a start with finger foods toward the end of his first year. Some babies are even dexterous enough to start using a spoon as early as their first birthday.

You will need to buy a special baby spoon, which is a little larger than a teaspoon with well-rounded edges. If you give him a deep dish with vertical sides he can use these to push his food into his spoon.

Some children very quickly acquire considerable skill with eating implements. Others take much longer to master them. All toddlers need some help at first. They can cope with the first half of a meal, but then the effort of their still imperfect skill becomes too great. So you will have to take over when he slows down. That way you will probably find he will eat a lot more, stopping when he has had enough to eat rather than when he is tired of feeding himself.

Some anxious mothers go on feeding their toddlers well into the second half of their second year. This should be avoided, as you are just encouraging your child to be lazy.

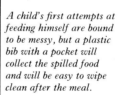

The classical high chair is still the best seat for a baby and toddler. Its broad base increases its stability, and fixing points are provided for a harness to hold the child. The feeding tray is practical, and the child is high enough for the mother to feed him without stooping. Chairs that fit over the back of adult chairs are not sufficiently stable, nor are they safe.

Toddlers (apart from a few paragons of neatness) will go on needing bibs until they are about two. The simple small piece of cloth that is tied around the neck is rarely adequate. It is better if he wears a full apron with sleeves or a plastic bib with a built-in pocket to catch the debris. It is also a good idea to place a plastic sheet on the floor under and around his high chair.

He will inevitably make a mess at first, not only because of his lack of skill but because he enjoys squeezing food with his hands and throwing it about. He thinks this is fun even if you do not. Once he has learned to manage fairly well you can show him that you are not keen on cleaning up more than is necessary and that food, containers, and implements are all to be kept on his tray or the table, not hurled to the floor. As you clean up, encourage him to pick up any larger pieces. This will help him appreciate the consequences of his exuberance.

By now your toddler will be eating the same food as everyone else in the family. Finely chop up his food with your own knife and fork. Toward the end of toddlerhood he may want to start using a knife in imitation of the adults with whom he eats. Let him try. If he is completely unsuccessful he will probably elect to go back to the spoon, with which he can feed himself more efficiently. If he is moderately successful, he will be happy learning to manipulate it. Then you can show him how to cut up the softer foods, such as vegetables and stewed fruit.

It is pointless to expect a toddler, even when he is able to sit up to the table on a high chair, to keep grown-up protocol. The finer points of table manners can come later. Do not insist he stays at the table once he has finished; let him get down, and you will enjoy the rest of your own meal more.

Feeding problems sometimes start because a mother has an unrealistic idea of how much a child should eat, although they may also be caused by a child discovering that what, and how much, he decides to eat has a strong effect on his mother. So if she understands that mealtimes are a potential emotional battleground for toddlers, she will stay cool and cheerful no matter how hard he tries to assert his independence.

If you and your doctor both feel that your toddler is alert and progressing well, even though there are many foods he will not take, try not to be too concerned that your friend's baby, the same age, eats everything he is given—or about how much weight your child is, or is not, putting on. (If he went on gaining as he did in the first year, then you would have something to worry about.)

Give him his meal as though you expected him to eat it and enjoy it quite naturally; and leave him alone. Mealtimes should be pleasant and relaxing. Let him have a reasonable amount of time to eat his food and then, if he is obviously not interested or starts to play, simply remove it. And that's that. Forcing a toddler to eat everything on his plate will lessen his appetite and create ill feeling. But it does not make sense to allow him to fill himself with cookies between meals, even if you are rather anxious that all he ate at lunch were a few bits of potato and some milk. Expect him to be hungry for his next meal, and ensure that he is unaware that his lunchtime antics have upset you unduly—or that there is attention to be gained by his refusal to eat. Experiments with babies from a year old showed that if they were offered a variety of foods and given only what they appeared to want, when calculated over several days they chose an overall balanced diet, although some ate whole meals of fruit or meat or starches. None of the babies became either too fat or too thin.

Now that your toddler is eating solid foods regularly, you will be wondering how to make sure he is getting adequate nourishment.

Foods can be divided up into five major nutrients: protein, carbohydrate, fat, vitamins, and minerals. No single food will provide everything necessary for good health. So, to ensure that your child will get all the nutrients he needs, give him a varied, well-balanced diet. The photograph (above right), which shows a typical day's menu, will give you some indication of how little of the correct foods are necessary to supply all your child's daily needs.

Children from one to two years of age will eat one-third to one-half of a typical adult portion. So don't pile your child's plate high in the hope that he will eat at least some; he will only avoid that food altogether. Let him eat the things he enjoys, but gradually introduce new textures and flavors. Even if he prefers so-called "junk" foods such as cakes, cookies, and hot dogs, as long as they are not eaten to the exclusion of all else he will probably be getting sufficient nourishment.

If he takes a violent dislike to certain foods, why not disguise them: milk can be transformed into custard or a lemon pudding, and liver into pâté.

Breakfast
1oz/28 gm cereal with
5 fl oz/140 ml milk
1 slice bread, butter, and jam
5 fl oz/140 ml milk

Lunch
1 scrambled egg with
1 slice bacon, 1 slice bread
and butter
Stewed apple and custard
5 fl oz/140 ml orange juice

Snack
Whole-wheat cracker
5 fl oz/140 ml
fruit juice

Dinner
1 oz/28 gm liver
1 oz/28 gm green beans
1 small carrot
1 small potato
Rice pudding

Body building and replacement of tissues
from proteins. Animal sources: milk, yogurt, cheese, meat, poultry, eggs, fish. Vegetable sources: peas, beans, lentils, nuts, whole-wheat flour, and bread.

Warmth and energy
from fats and carbohydrates. Good sources of fats: milk, cream, cheese, butter, margarine, cooking oil, milk chocolate, bacon, eggs, oily fish, french fries, potato chips, pastry. Good sources of carbohydrates: sugar, honey, syrup, jams, candy, cookies, cornflakes, oatmeal, pasta, rice, bread, cake, potatoes.

Smooth skin, healthy eyesight, and resistance to infection
from vitamin A. Good sources: liver, fish liver oils, carrots, apricots, tomatoes, spinach, watercress, eggs, butter, cheese, milk, margarine.

Growth, good digestion, clear skin, and health of nervous system
from B vitamins. Good sources: liver, yeast, wheat germ, bread, cereals, eggs, yogurt, peas, beans, lentils, nuts.

Healthy gums and general resistance to infection
from vitamin C. Good sources: oranges, lemons, limes, grapefruit, strawberries, tomatoes, tomato juice, fresh green vegetables, potatoes.

Strong bones and the prevention of rickets
from vitamin D. Good sources: sunshine, fish liver oils, oily fish, eggs, margarine.

Strong teeth and bones
from calcium and phosphorus. Good sources: milk, cheese, eggs, sardines, flour and bread, oatmeal, green vegetables, baked beans.

Healthy blood
from iron. Good sources: meat, especially red meat; liver and kidney; cereal, especially oatmeal; apricots; fresh green vegetables.

words," which they use to make their first attempt at sentences. "Allgone" is familiar as in "Allgone lunch," "Allgone daddy," "Allgone car."

Later, when the child's range of two-word "sentences" is established, he will have to clear the hurdle of making the next step to three words. He knows what he wants to say but cannot fit the words together to say it. And when he can use three words he may get stuck again. For instance, one child who wanted to say "Mommy drink hot coffee" could only say first "Mommy drink coffee" and then "Drink hot coffee."

Understanding early vocabulary

Again, like someone confronted by a foreign language, a child's understanding is often well ahead of his speech. When a toddler is asked as part of a game to point to his eyes, ears, or nose, he will be able to do so long before he has learned the words. Young children start practicing and playing around

with words when they are alone in bed or they cheerfully swap words with another child who is playing near them.

This is part of the charm and fascination of toddlerhood. At first you will have to work out what your child means at any one moment, using one of his limited number of word combinations. Later you will have to wait while he gropes to find the words for what he wants to say—and perhaps fails, unless you are able to prompt. The striving to be articulate is a touching manifestation of the child's natural drive to master the world.

To understand how complex a task it is for a child to learn the structure of language, it helps to remember that while there are dictionaries of words there is no dictionary of sentences. Although a child hears thousands of sentences when listening to his parents and other adults around him, he does not pick up a list of sentences; rather, he has to learn

Learning the rules of language

The toddler's language

Single words will have a much wider application for a child than for an adult. A toddler hears the word "daddy" in connection with his father, but he does not know exactly what it is that makes him "daddy." So he may use the same word for any man—perhaps another male relative, or the postman or milkman. He simply uses the same word to describe them all. He will also guess at word meanings—often accurately—from the general context or tone of voice. It is easy to understand why a child has so many problems with the meanings of words. He is surrounded by a world of complex objects and events. Discovering language is connected with the child's understanding of the world around him; he has to sort out for himself which aspects of his experience and which particular objects are relevant to a specific word.

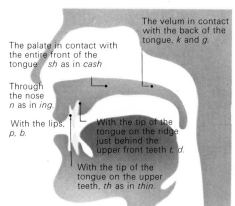

The palate in contact with the entire front of the tongue *sh* as in *cash*

Through the nose *n* as in *ing*.

With the lips, *p, b.*

The velum in contact with the back of the tongue, *k* and *g.*

With the tip of the tongue on the ridge just behind the upper front teeth *t, d.*

With the tip of the tongue on the upper teeth, *th* as in *thin.*

Different sounds are made with different parts of the mouth. Children seem to find it easier to make sounds at the front of their mouth and so may say tot *for* cot *and* darden *for* garden.

BA
BACK
BALACK
BLACK

Very young children tend to drop consonants at the ends of words. Once they have stopped doing this they still find it difficult to pronounce two consonants together; they either drop one or stick a vowel in between. This is deliberate simplification, and it helps them master the complexities of language.

The toddler's perceptual abilities are such that he fails to recognize any real differences between objects that an adult sees as quite dissimilar. Consequently he will label a whole range of objects with one word. But even if he does recognize differences he may simply not have sufficient words, and so he will use one word to describe different objects in which he detects some similarity. The diagram (left) shows how a child, on learning the word car, first applies it to all moving objects. Slowly, as he learns to discriminate and acquires more words, he is able to identify and correctly label the various moving objects.

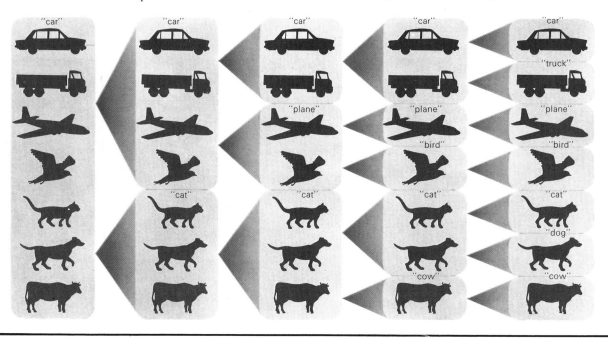

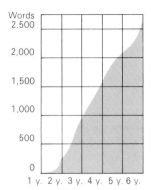

Words
2,500
2,000
1,500
1,000
500
0
1 y. 2 y. 3 y. 4 y. 5 y. 6 y.

For some weeks children will pick up very few words, but soon after their first birthday most start to learn words with remarkable rapidity.

rules that will enable him to make up his own sentences. However, because of irregularities, even these rules cannot be applied universally. Thus, linguistic structures cannot be taught from the outside; the child must learn to construct them in his own head.

Even with only a limited knowledge of the rules a child can produce an enormous number of sentences. The full range of English sentence types—simple statements, negatives, orders, and questions—is produced quite early in language development; but their forms are different from those adults use. When the average length of a child's sentence reaches three words and over, he learns step-by-step the transformations necessary for adult forms.

During his second year, a toddler will try out various utterances that sound funny to a grown-up's ear. This is his way of formulating the rules that govern the making of a sentence. He realizes gradually that they are not always right and will need modifying. Far from being purely imitative, language development appears to be an innate skill, which is developed by practice and some imitation. For instance, a toddler cannot repeat a sentence after an adult unless he is mature enough to have produced the words himself. He will only repeat, when asked, the two or three words that he knows.

Toilet training

For the first year of his life your baby cannot control his bowels—in fact he is quite oblivious that they function at all. He will be at least a year old, and sometimes nearer eighteen months, before he becomes aware of evacuation. He notices the inner sensations first, and only later recognizes the process.

Many babies as early as six months become unhappy with the discomfort of filled or wet diapers; others do not notice them until about eighteen months. But they do not know how they got dirty; only that it has happened.

At about eighteen months, but sometimes as early as fifteen months or as late as two years, you will be able to tell when your baby is passing his stools. He may go red and strain; he will probably take on an absorbed, distracted expression and stop whatever he is doing. (Some babies strain when they are very young: if your child is one you will have to look for other signs that he is becoming aware of evacuating.) He may develop some particular piece of behavior like going to one corner of the room. He may point out a soiled diaper afterward. This is the time to start the toilet-training campaign. But remember, you are only in the first stages.

The opening move is to make him more aware of what is going on. Point out to him, either by a direct statement or with a question, that he is "doing something." It is essential that you make your remarks as matter of fact as possible. Do not indicate that he is doing something "dirty," or you will inhibit the very process you are trying to encourage. Nor is there any need to praise him. This too could be counterproductive when you want to reward the use of the potty.

After a few weeks, depending on the responsiveness of your child, introduce him to the idea of passing his stools in the potty. Keep it ready and when he shows signs that he is about to have a bowel movement, quickly remove his diaper and put him on the potty. It does not matter if you are not able to get him to the potty every time. It is the introduction that counts. You should praise him and make a fuss about him when he does evacuate into the potty.

So that the diaper can be quickly removed, it helps at this stage if you leave off the plastic pants. They are not so essential now that you are watching your child more closely.

Many babies are fairly regular in their bowel movements after their first year. If your baby is one of them you can back up the procedure described by putting him on the potty shortly before he is due in the hope that he will go on schedule. If he does, praise him; if he does not, you may have started toilet training him too early.

Introducing the potty

It takes patience to toilet train your child. You may be tempted to rush the process because it seems to be taking longer than you imagined or perhaps because your older child achieved bowel control much earlier. Don't. Try to remember every child learns at a different rate and that at the very latest he will become trained by the time he goes to school.

The next step is to leave his diapers off during the day. If you use thick terry pants with elasticized legs, these will contain any accidents. A paper diaper liner inside the pants will catch the stools, which will now be quite firm, and make the subsequent washing of the pants much easier.

However, it may be better not to hurry him into pants as soon as he is on the way to achieving bowel control, because most babies

From diapers to pants

do not achieve bladder control until two or three months later, or even more. Small children need to urinate often—every couple of hours—and the need can come on almost instantly. For some time your toddler may need your vigilance to help him stay dry.

As soon as he is able, let him dump the contents of the potty into the toilet and flush it. Toddlers regard stools as their property, and they feel better about their disappearance if they are in charge.

Avoiding battles

There are probably as many variations around this basic method of toilet training as there are babies. The most important rule is: do not turn toilet training into a battleground.

If you turn toilet training into a power struggle between you and your child you may find that he will win either by soiling his diapers or pants deliberately, or by becoming badly constipated. Either way it will be your fault, not his.

This, surprisingly, can happen to a mother who achieves apparent success too early. If your child is as regular as clockwork, and you have been catching every bowel movement, you may mistakenly think that he is potty trained. The success is—temporarily—yours, not his. For as soon as he discovers the pleasant feeling of evacuation, his control over it and the interesting results it produces, his apparent mastery may vanish. When other mothers are starting tentatively to teach the idea of self-control, you will be expecting him to keep to a standard of perfection he gave only the illusion of attaining.

Remember that childhood is a double process of self-discovery and of learning to

Teething

Most babies arrive at the toddlerhood stage with characteristic gaps between their front teeth and their side teeth, or first molars. By the time a toddler is eighteen months old this gap will have been filled by the canine teeth. The childhood set is completed when the second molars appear.

A toddler is better able to cope with any discomfort caused by the emerging teeth than he was in his first year, and you may not even notice without looking inside his mouth that they are coming.

There is a great deal of variation not only in when teeth appear but in the order in which they come through. Most children have the complete set by the time they are three. Only

if your child still has gaps or lacks the second molars after this date, or if any teeth are growing crookedly, need you consult your doctor or dentist.

You should start cleaning your child's teeth after his first birthday before he goes to bed at night. A special small toothbrush is necessary but not a special toothpaste, although the pleasant taste of children's brands may encourage him to let you clean his teeth. How long you will have to do this depends on his dexterity, but it could be until after his third birthday, or later. As soon as he wants to do it for himself encourage him to do so, but you will probably need to finish the job at first.

Right from the start, help your child to clean his teeth, showing him the correct way. Always brush away from the gums, brushing downward over the top teeth, and upward over the bottom teeth, to remove food particles. After this the teeth should be vigorously brushed sideways in order to remove the plaque.

The detailed order in which the teeth appear varies from child to child. This is the most common pattern. The gray teeth are those already through. The white teeth are those emerging. By the age of three, most children have all their first teeth.

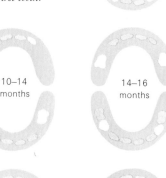

8–10 months

10–14 months

14–16 months

16–20 months

24–36 months

control both the self and the world. When bowel movements at last come to the baby's attention, it is not surprising that they have a special significance. They are not given to him; he makes them, and he makes them out of nothing other than himself. They are unique. Some babies are fascinated by their own feces and will play with them. They have no notion, of course, of the disgust they will learn to feel later, still less of the health dangers that lie behind the taboo. Once a child has grown accustomed to them, he will place no more importance on them then you do—and no less.

Most mothers will come into the bedroom or bathroom at least once to find feces smeared around the crib or walls. If your child does this, rebuke him gently. You must let him know that it is not a thing that should happen again. But do not become angry. He does not know right from wrong, but he does have a very basic awareness of the beginnings of life's game. If you make too much of a song and dance you will arouse his interest and he will do it again for the effect.

The same rule applies to accidents. Most children sometime between the ages of three and five will naturally acquire a sense of shame when they soil themselves. Rather than scolding, you may well find that you have to console a child who has had an accident.

Diapers at night

It will almost certainly be some months after your child is both clean and dry during the day that he is reliably dry at night. Until then, put him in diapers when he goes to bed. Once he is dry more than half the time, you may try leaving off his diapers at night. Putting him on the potty in the late evening before you go to bed will empty his bladder and help him to stay dry throughout the night. You will probably find that you know to within half an hour when you need to catch him before he wets the bed.

During this stage, and for some time after, keep a rubber sheet over the mattress if he sleeps in a bed. Obviously, however, if you have a plastic-covered mattress this will be unnecessary.

When a baby is too young to control himself, he needs you to keep him clean. Once he is old enough, his natural instinct is to be clean. No animal fouls its own home, and, handled correctly, nor does any human. Your child does not need you to force him to be clean, but only to teach him how. And if things should go wrong for you, for whatever reason, and he still seems to be unreliable very late, ask yourself how many children are still in diapers when they start school. The answer will reassure you.

Sleeping

Most babies will stick to approximately the same sleep patterns established during the first year: so a baby who needs a great deal of sleep will continue to do so; a more wakeful baby will again be bursting with energy after much less sleep.

Although many toddlers will settle easily into a straightforward routine of sleeping, others will naturally follow a more fragmented sleep pattern. Their parents, however, will almost certainly be following the usual pattern, and will be greatly inconvenienced if their child sleeps during the day and wakes at night. So they will have to shape his sleeping habits to fit more or less with the rest of the household.

If he has not already done so, he will soon give up the second nap of the day—usually in favor of a long sleep right after lunch, complete with the ritual comforter of blanket or favorite soft toy. Like adults, babies after a year or so will probably resent being waked up for the mother's convenience, perhaps to go shopping or to visit a friend. Also, many toddlers between one and three, waking from daytime naps, need either a little time to "come to" alone or a peaceful cuddle with their mothers. This is the age of tremendous physical activity when a baby is constantly trying out his developing skills of walking and climbing, and taking plenty of spills and tumbles along the way. So he will need odd times in the day when he can rest, apart from his regular nap. He may curl up quite happily on the couch or in his playpen for ten minutes late in the morning while his mother starts to get lunch ready; a long outing in a stroller is a time for him to relax, off his energetic legs, and still have plenty to look at.

Afternoon naps

An active toddler still needs some sleep during the day. You may find it is worthwhile to put your child down for a long afternoon nap so that he will stay awake later in the evening. This gives your husband a chance to be with him before he goes to bed. The later bedtime also means that he may sleep longer in the mornings.

Babies and all young children find comfort and reassurance in rituals—even adults are soothed by them in the late evening. So try to establish a pleasant bedtime routine from the earliest months—the same cuddly toy or blanket, hugs or pats from both parents and brother or sister, a brief look at a picture book before he is old enough for a story. And so to bed. . . .

To prevent, or lessen, a young child's dislike of going to bed, ensure that the change from playing with the family to being put into his crib for the night is not too abrupt. When he first starts balking at bedtime, try lengthening the going-to-bed routine by

Establishing a bedtime routine

starting it a bit earlier. Let him have a pleasant but not too stimulating romp with his father, or a leisurely story. When he is in his crib, sit with him for a few minutes as he settles down. If he still demands attention give him what he asks for in a friendly fashion, *but don't start taking him out of his crib*. This way he is more likely to understand that you mean business.

But if this doesn't always work, be prepared to humor him a little. In the summer, when it's still very light, let him stay up a bit until he is really sleepy. If a night light or the door left open reassures him, let him have them. Don't be too adamant about not picking up a toy flung purposely from his crib, or about ignoring one or two cries indicating another sip of water. . . . He's asking for your attention, which is reasonable enough; and if he's given it when he first asks, he should be encouraged to go off to sleep without demanding too much. A truly tired toddler will sleep wherever he is; and if he exhausts himself by trying to stay awake, he will make up for it by sleeping longer. At the worst, he will simply be a bit irritable the next day. It is important to remember that bedtime problems are resolved much more quickly if the parents don't get too anxious about them.

Bedtime problems

Resistance to going to bed at night is not uncommon once a child is mobile. The one-year-old who goes to bed every night without a murmur is a rarity. Much more common is the toddler who demands yet another drink of water, or endless goodnight kisses. By now, he is old enough to enjoy being part of the family, and may resent being carried away to his room on his own. He may feel a bit frightened in his crib and miss the comfort of his mother's voice. If these difficulties start appearing, try to deal with them when they begin and avoid the situation developing into a tiring and exasperating nightly battle. If the baby stays awake very late and is tired the next day, he can take a long nap to catch up. His parents cannot. (Fathers sometimes imagine that their wives lie around all day. Child care is more tiring than they might think.) Establishing a regular, early bedtime will allow for a peaceful evening.

The toddler who persistently resists going to bed needs to be taken seriously. What is going on in his life to make him so anxious? It may be something as simple as the way you put him to bed. It is pointless to romp with him for a time and then expect him to stop suddenly and go to sleep. However, if sleeping problems are part of a more general anxiety, if he seems high-strung all the time, then you should consult your doctor.

Unfortunately many family doctors take the easy way out and prescribe tranquilizers. This occasionally works if resistance to bed is an isolated habit that can be broken in this way. But if there is some larger problem, then drugs will often mask it, not cure it. A full discussion should lead to a few sessions with a child psychiatrist or psychologist, who can often clear things up quite quickly.

Climbing out of bed

Around the middle of the second year bedtime is further complicated: the toddler learns how to get out of his crib, and may appear, unasked, just as his parents are settling down for the evening. If this happens regularly, then it is almost certainly because you are simply putting him to bed too early, when he is not tired enough to go straight to sleep. You cannot expect a lively child to drop off just to suit your convenience. And it is foolish to decide arbitrarily that a child of his age should be asleep by six-thirty when his father regularly comes home at six-forty-five or seven o'clock. Nor is it reasonable to expect a lively child to remain indifferent when his favorite uncle arrives, or an interesting stranger calls just after he has gone to bed. Let him come down to meet them for a few minutes, and then send, or better take, him back upstairs again.

If you are sure that his coming down is just a ploy, then flexible firmness is what is needed. Let him come down when there is good reason to do so, otherwise send him back. A bright toddler can maneuver the situation, so be firm, but let him have his say.

When your toddler is ready to climb out of his crib, do not use it as a prison beyond its effectiveness. Leave the side down, or at least put a soft rug beside the crib. Falling from the top of a crib onto the floor can cause serious injury.

Disturbed sleep

Like adults, most toddlers half wake in the night many times. Nearly asleep, he may call out for his mother. Give him a chance to go off to sleep again; but if he is awake and crying, he needs you. So see to him, but leave him in his crib. Most parents won't want a toddler sleeping in their bed; so don't start the habit. Losing a favorite toy or blanket in the night can frighten a baby who is only half-awake. Attaching it with string or elastic to the side of the crib will prevent it from falling out. (Do not make it too long or he may wrap it around his neck and strangle himself as he turns over in the night.)

Early waking

Early waking is also very common among toddlers. Exhausted by walking and playing, he may fall asleep at six o'clock at night, or even earlier. Often toddlers are up and ready to start the day around five o'clock. This is rather less of a problem than with a very young baby because if there are toys around he is better able to amuse himself until a more civilized hour. When it is dark, during the winter months, a low-wattage night light will enable him to see what he is doing—and he will fell less alone. Leave some food, such as whole-wheat crackers, in his room where he can find it in the morning—and, of course, all his favorite toys to keep him occupied and content.

Personality

By the time they reach toddlerhood, children have many ways in which to express their individuality. A toddler is becoming more independent of his mother and more demanding; he is learning to speak and becoming more aware of the choices he can make. A strong-willed two-year-old will constantly strive to achieve a bit more than he is capable of, and the resulting frustration may lead to tantrums. A toddler's environment is broadening all the time. He is noticing more than just his single caretaker and his immediate family; he is now remembering a few children he meets on the playground, people he sees in the local shops, aunts and uncles and his parents' friends. All these new people—plus the attitudes of the family he is born into and the experiences he has from day to day—will begin to shape his emerging personality.

Sex-role identification

He is still more influenced by his parents than by anyone else. He starts to copy their behavior—the way they talk and eat, the habits they have, and even the way they walk. Sex-role identification starts early. New research shows that children include their gender in the way they think about themselves as soon as they start to talk; a two-year-old boy or girl taken for the wrong sex probably won't like it.

Parents unconsciously communicate right from the beginning what is expected of being a boy or girl—in dress, in decorating a child's room, in the toys they buy them. From earliest childhood, we tend to reward self-reliance and independence more in boys, obedience and responsibility more in girls. Toddlers perceive this, and are affected by it in the way they behave and in how they see themselves.

Most parents have some preconceived notions—based on their own personalities and experience—of how they feel their child ought to be. If a toddler is rather withdrawn and shows no sign of starting to play with other children, a parent who expects a child to enjoy socializing may become alarmed. This is particularly true because an outgoing personality is highly prized in our society. Similarly, rather quiet parents may be at a loss to cope with a vigorously extroverted child.

In both cases, the attitudes of the parents may modify the child's behavior slightly—but will not change the pattern. And neither should they. The diffident toddler who does not seek out other children is simply expressing his personality and his need to be by himself, as is the rambunctious toddler who can't wait to get into the rough and tumble of the sandbox with the others. Most toddlers will vary between these two extremes; they are at a turbulent age and often feel very differently about things from hour to hour. Sympathetic parents who, whatever their own notions, accept and love a child for himself, are his birthright.

A parent's influence

Thumb-sucking

Virtually all children suck their hands, fingers, and thumbs in their first year, and it is probably a useful part of their development to do so. Strangely, habitual thumb-sucking does not usually appear until later, some time after the first birthday. It might be a sign that your child is not receiving enough love and affection, and is insecure. However, it is much more likely that your child is physically very aware, likes considerable comfort, and has a contemplative frame of mind.

Do not worry, and do not bully him out of it. If you try to, you may start a crisis and cause anxiety where none existed before. He will probably grow out of it later. If he does not, you will have a better chance of convincing him that it is a childish practice that he should leave behind if you have allowed him to indulge in it when he was still a toddler.

Little children love running around without clothes, especially in hot weather. And why not? It feels good, and they are certainly not ashamed of their bodies. They will only come to feel embarrassed if they sense you are.

Many children suck their thumbs for a while mainly because it is comforting, rather in the way an adult enjoys a pipe or cigarette. When a child who does not normally suck his thumb suddenly does so, it is usually because he is very tired or needs a reassuring cuddle.

Security blankets

Most toddlers develop a firm attachment for a favorite soft toy or a particular blanket. The child may carry it with him everywhere, as Linus does in the "Peanuts" cartoon strip, or he may run for it only at moments of crisis, for example after an argument or a fall. By the time he has grown out of it, all that may be left will be a small fragment of the blanket, or an animal that is scarcely recognizable, having had a couple of new faces and all its seams resewn half a dozen times. If you try to replace it with something newer, he will probably resist. His memory is not as good as yours and he will not make the same comparison with its original state.

If your child has such an object, do not deprive him of it. There is nothing wrong, either with him or with you, and he will gradually abandon it as he grows up and becomes more sure of himself.

One day you may notice that your child is sucking his thumb less and less, and you think he has really begun to grow up. Then you realize he has taken to sucking or hugging something else, which he refuses to relinquish. This too should be welcomed as it is an important stage in his development.

A child's increasing perception

After the first year, the child will be able to start representing the world to himself and other people. This is a remarkable advance from infancy as the child now realizes that things can exist beyond his sensory perception. Society encourages him to represent his ideas, thoughts, and needs. His chief way will be through language; he will also draw what he sees around him. He is no longer bound by present time and space and objects that he can actually see as he is thinking; he is also able to reconstruct the past and plan for the very near future. During the second year, a child will imitate the behavior of another child— perhaps some time later. This is when imitative play begins.

A child thinks in a uniquely childlike way. He appears to view the world with a set of patterns that he himself evolves. As he gets older, these patterns become more complex— and he is constantly having to adjust them to what he sees around him. If a child during his first year is used to seeing his father

always working in his study, he comes to associate his father with that room. Even when he is a little older and he is out on the lawn with his father beside him, if asked where his father is he may still point toward the study. So a child's interaction with his immediate environment—and the consequent modification of his basic set of ideas— is still the essence of his intellectual growth.

In the first year, a child knew objects in terms of his activity with them. Although he now realizes that objects exist outside that

The world of a child is full of endlessly fascinating things to touch, explore, and hide in. It can also sometimes be a frightening world as he sees everyday places from a viewpoint no higher than an adult's knees. To an adventurous toddler, the tiny space underneath a parked car or bus can seem a huge inviting den which he can crawl into, putting himself in danger if it moves.

activity, he still sees himself as the center of the world. He will interpret the objective world entirely from the subjective point of view. The child is naturally self-centered at this stage; it is not selfishness as an adult understands it, but part of his normal development. In managing toddlers, it is vital for mothers to understand this: he cannot be reasoned with, or made to do what he does not want to, except by being cajoled.

Independence

Although a toddler is becoming physically more capable, he is still highly aware of how dependent he is on his mother, especially emotionally. He needs her love and comfort all the time, and especially when he is tired or frustrated by his environment, as he so often is. It is this conflict between dependence and independence that can make the years of toddlerhood very stormy. One minute he is clinging; the next minute shouting "leave me alone." Now he likes potatoes, or his toy engine; then he hates them, or it. At times he is so full of confidence that he launches himself headlong at the most impossible tasks; at others so full of self-doubt that he will not attempt anything without his mother's constant support and encouragement. His whole personality never seems quite in kilter for more than a few minutes at a time. His parents admire his growing skills and his guts in trying to accomplish a little more than before, but, at the same time, his relentless exploration and the constant vigilance necessary drive them almost to distraction. But all this energy is a healthy sign that he is developing into the kind of individual who will be able to stand on his own feet.

The magic of books

The importance of sharing with your child the pleasures that a book can give—with rhymes, pictures, and stories—cannot be stressed enough. A child who can associate books with many happy hours spent together with his parents will be more likely to want to read for himself later on.

While you read from a picture book, your toddler will enjoy the illustrations if they are right for his age. If they are to have any lasting meaning for him they must be easily identifiable. Black-and-white illustrations can be difficult for him because they are not a true representation of his world, which comes in full color. He will find easiest those pictures in which the different characters do not overlap and are shown as he knows them —he does not understand perspective.

The story line that accompanies the illustrations should be short and simple. Tangents and diversions would just confuse one- to three-year-olds.

The skill of reading a picture has to be learned. Pictures for a toddler at first need to be simple, with only the essential details picked out to enable quick recognition of the object being portrayed.

Above : A child will get pleasure from pictures that relate to his own personal experience and activities. But, as he cannot appreciate depth in a picture, he may imagine that the dog overlapping the boy in this illustration is in fact eating him. Incomplete figures may also confuse a young child.

A child will identify readily with sympathetic characters in a storybook; those about animals are especially popular as they are an amusing way in which to tell him more about the life that he may eventually experience.

He will see nothing unusual about a picture showing animals sitting down at a table to eat, as he imagines all animals as humans. He will also relish seeing animals enjoying delicious food, especially the sort he loves himself.

The importance of security

Independence comes from security. So if a toddler is rather hesitant and clingy, it is better not to push. He will be less timid with strangers and more adventurous in the park when he feels sure of himself. A child in the park ventures away from his mother not because he wants to lose her—quite the contrary. He toddles off because he is confident enough to know that when he has finished investigating the sandbox or another child's toy, she will be there to come back to. (Numerous stops and reassuring backward glances prove this.)

A toddler needs endless different opportunities to assert his growing independence. Once he has reached eighteen months, he should be allowed to play in the yard or on the playground—even if he does get very dirty and has to be watched every second. Encourage him to meet other grown-ups and children. If he is able to show himself, and his mother, what an independent child he is, he is less likely to be awkward—by refusing to go to bed or by not eating a reasonable meal. He is a prickly little person, who is guaranteed to give his parents plenty of headaches—and fun.

Discipline

With independence must come discipline—the setting of limits. Certainly all parents are familiar with the two-year-old who heads for a forbidden area, turning around to his mother, half daring, half pleading for the inevitable "No!" reaction. A toddler between one and three knows instinctively when he is getting away with too much. Too many choices and too many frustrations panic him, and this is when he is liable to end up on the floor kicking and screaming. He knows that he lacks inner control, and he looks to his parents to provide it.

Don't bother to ask him: "Shall we go out shopping now?"; tell him in a friendly way that this is what you and he are doing—and if he announces that he is not going to wear his hat, unless it is extremely cold, try not to make an issue of it. It probably won't matter very much, and he will feel gratifyingly assertive. A bit of preventive tact can save most confrontation battles with a wayward toddler. He will be happier and far less anxious if his parents provide reasonable guidelines for his behavior in as firm and pleasant a way as possible. Above all, be consistent. Limits one day that are relaxed the next only confuse a young child and make him uncertain about whether or not his parents really mean what they say.

Presenting a united front

Parents who grew up in a happy and healthy family will be likely to discipline their children, quite naturally, as they were disciplined themselves. Occasionally a parent who still resents his own upbringing, which he believes was too controlled or too permissive, may bend over backward to act differently toward his own child—and unwittingly fall into a similar trap. So parents would do well to examine their feelings about toddlers and the way they should be allowed to behave in the light of their own experiences. It is important for both parents to agree on discipline. Even a young child is quick to spot parental dissension over an issue such as being allowed to stay up a bit later. The father should take a hand in setting behavioral limits from the beginning, and should not leave it all to the mother, who is likely to be with the toddler most.

Defining limits

The aim for every individual is self-control and self-discipline; but unless a child is taught behavioral boundaries by his parents, it will be hard for him, as he grows up, to establish them for himself.

During the toddler stage, parents will have to rely on "No!"—plus physical removal. If at all feasible link the child's wrongdoing immediately with your own reaction to it. You cannot permit a child of nearly two to explore an electric plug. Take him firmly away from it, disregarding his protests. Explain that playing with it is dangerous. He will not understand the explanation—yet—but it will help him to recognize that you are not being completely arbitrary.

Most toddlers are highly distractable, and another toy or a quick look at a bus out of the window can soon calm him down. But however outraged he may appear at the time, this firmness will have been just what he was expecting.

Setting certain limits and sticking to them does not mean being inflexible. Your own needs and self-respect will act as a good guide here. Sometimes if he pleads and you have the time, let him have an extra bedtime story; at others, when you have had a long day and want a bit of peace to read the evening paper, be firm that the usual quota is all he is getting. He has had his reading period; now you want yours. There will be another story tomorrow night—and now it's time for him to be tucked in bed.

Disciplining a very young child does not always go smoothly, however much tact, common sense, and sensitivity a parent uses. Occasional blowups are inevitable, and natural coldness and withdrawal of love is cruel; it is much better to admit this to your toddler: sometimes he does make you very cross, just as you make him. But as there is nothing to be gained from feeling guilty on either side, you should make it up afterward. It is important for him to sense that you love him through it all. Then it is done with, the air cleared and calm restored—until the next testing time comes around.

Spanking

There should not be any need, most of the time, to spank a toddler. A little patience on your part when he says "No," or continues to do something you have told him not to, will be much more effective in the long run. Occasionally he will push defiance to the limit, and then you may find that a spank produces instant realization that you mean what you say.

Some people believe that any physical force at all in childhood fosters violence later in life. It seems doubtful that a child who is spanked occasionally as a result of obvious transgressions will become unconditionally aggressive. You may indeed be doing your child a disservice if you do not let him learn that some limits are firmer than others, and that the penalties for going beyond them are real. You will do this most effectively if you spank, but only very rarely, when the reasons for doing so are clear to both you and your child.

Most toddlers react, not with sorrow and defeat, but with rage, and your child is quite likely to hit you back. You will have to be grown-up about this and not be outraged. You are the parent. You can take more than he can—he cannot really hurt you—and it is most important at this age for him to be able to express and experience anger. So let him have his little bang. Be good humored, but do not mock his puny efforts to hurt you. Only if he takes these too far need you show him there is a limit here as well.

Always see that any conflict ends with making up and a cuddle.

Temper tantrums

A toddler is becoming increasingly aware of all the things he can do without his mother. He is still a baby—and all around him there are frustrations such as blocks that do not stay in place or being carted off for lunch when he really wants to stay in his sandbox. His parents are so much bigger and stronger than he is; and he can't communicate very fluently. So it is not surprising that every now and then his tolerance becomes overloaded and the circuit blows. The cause may be trivial, such as not being able to pull his sock off, and it may be aggravated by tiredness. Whatever the situation, it is too much for his tenuous control. And the result, as most mothers of toddlers will recognize, is a full-blown temper tantrum.

Tantrums are the single most violent behavior of this very turbulent period in a child's development. Research has shown that at twenty-one months, sixty percent of all boys and forty-five percent of all girls have frequent tantrums. Tantrums are common in nearly seventy percent of three-year-olds. The child may kick and scream and roll about on the floor, or bang his head against the furniture.

Some children hold their breath and literally turn blue, terrifying parents already alarmed by the sudden anger. If this happens, the child will *not* harm himself; he will start to breathe again as soon as his autonomic (or automatic) nervous system takes control. If he twitches slightly when he is breathing again, this is merely part of the return to normal.

Rage, sorrow, and entreaty are all to be seen in this toddler's face. Whatever the cause, when your child is distressed he needs your understanding and compassion.

How to handle a tantrum

The parent's first duty is to see that the child does not hurt himself. So try to prevent him from falling or banging himself more than necessary, particularly if he is on a hard floor or near the top of stairs. Also take him away from any objects which may get broken in the storm. Otherwise, wait until the mood has passed with as much patience and humor as you can muster. Once he has started you will not be able to stop him. Leave him to get on with it alone, but stay close by. He will probably be frightened by his own behavior when it is all over; and although he needs to know that his mother is not going to reward him for it, he also requires reassurance that she still loves him. It is friendly, loving support that he needs—not black looks. When the tantrum is over, resume normal life. Try out gently whatever suggestion precipitated the showdown. He may accept quite gracefully now. If he still refuses, however, it may be best to pass on to the next phase of the daily routine: into his high chair for lunch or out for a walk in the stroller. A tactful mother will sense when and where her toddler is most prone to tantrums, and try to avoid certain situations. But she won't be able to prevent them all; and neither should she try to do so.

Many parents overreact to tantrums by trying to stop them, or they are panicked by them. They are not a form of infant malingering, nor are they epileptic fits, however much the worst ones may resemble them. Perhaps unconsciously the parents imagine an adult carrying on like this kicking and screaming two-year-old; and they are more frightened and embarrassed by the display of angry frustration than is justified. It may be more difficult for the father to accept them, because they remain strange and incomprehensible to him, whereas a mother has acquired some practice in riding out the storm.

Infant sexuality It is healthy for a toddler if he can observe sex differences naturally; obviously, seeing the rest of the family undressing, in the bathroom and on the beach, is the freest way of all. If a child does not have a sibling of the opposite sex and his parents are extremely reticent, there is some danger that he will notice sex differences rather late, and in circumstances that he may associate with guilt and hiding. Children are fascinated by these differences. They are intrigued by everything around them; they want to "know" everything, and

in the same way they show avid curiosity about their own bodies. They play with their hands, hair, toes, and navel; so it is only sensible to expect them to explore their genitalia, which must give them good feelings even when they are very young. But this rather casual manipulation is not associated with sex, meaning intercourse, until puberty. If it is accepted naturally by his parents at the toddler stage, a child is likely to accept certain limitations on his behavior later.

If a new brother or sister arrives in the household, surely the most natural question in the world is: where did he or she come from? This is simple curiosity; it is an adult who gives it a sexual connotation. A toddler will be satisfied with a matter-of-fact answer on his own level of understanding.

Bathing children together is practical and natural, and if your child decides that he wants to climb into the bath with you he will think it most unreasonable if you refuse him. At this age he will simply regard a communal bath as fun. An added advantage is that the freer you are about your nudity the less chance there will be of your child growing up with reservations about his.

Forming new relationships

If he has known loving and rewarding ties with his family from the beginning, a child is likely, as he gets older, to expect—and receive—similar good feelings in his relationships with others. Many experts believe that an early relationship of trust will affect him positively in his dealings with other people all through his life. These relationships, even when he is a toddler, will also depend on his individual temperament—whether he is outgoing and sociable or inclined to be shy and withdrawn. Young children are quick to sense an aloof adult who is not very interested in them; and they are often put off by an over-enthusiastic approach. A toddler will react best to someone who is natural and un-self-conscious with him.

The importance of playmates

It is good for toddlers to mix with other youngsters as much as possible, particularly if they are first children or if there is a large age difference between them and any older brothers or sisters. Initially, they won't appear to take much notice. They will keep to themselves as they play side by side. After eighteen months, when toys become more interesting because a child is better able to play with them, grabbing and hitting between children are normal.

It is not realistic to expect a two- or two-and-a-half-year-old always to give up a toy to another toddler who decides he wants it; or to expect him not to grab for what he wants. He is not so much asserting a healthy independence as unaware of the meaning of sharing. It is best if one or the other can be distracted by yet another toy; if necessary the children will have to be firmly separated by the caretaker. Forcing more grown-up behavior on a toddler will make no sense to him, and it may make him even more possessive of his own toys—or more ambitious a grabber and pusher! Playing with other children at this time is a preparation for when he is a bit older, around three. Then being with another child will be more of a social and enjoyable activity, and he will want to start to share of his own accord.

Until he is past three, he will probably only play with one child at a time, reverting to long periods of parallel play.

The benefit of grandparents

In other relationships the toddler still makes little differentiation between familiar neighbors, the postman, and the people he gets to know in the local shops. He will tend to adopt the attitudes toward them that he senses in his parents. This is also true of his early relationship with his grandparents: it is difficult to separate *his* feelings about his grandmother and grandfather from the mother/daughter and father/daughter relationships his mother and father have with them. The chances are that if these are good, then he will feel warmly toward them too.

Distance will count also; today many families are widely separated, making close ties a lot more difficult. This is unfortunate because the grandparent/grandchild relationship is a uniquely valuable one for all three

generations. For a toddler, his grandparents are loving adults with whom he feels secure, yet who play a more indulgent role in his life than his parents. It is helpful all around if parents gently encourage a young child to feel close to his grandparents. He has so much to gain: additional protection if his parents go away on vacation, or his mother is ill; his first concepts of aging; and another grown-up who loves to read him stories aloud or to help him build castles with his blocks. If his parents are worried about "spoiling," it won't hurt in moderation; and the quality of such a good relationship can enrich his whole childhood.

Many grandfathers missed a close relationship with their own children. The pleasures of grandchildren can compensate a great deal.

Separation

As a measure of his deep attachment, a young child will naturally react with distress when he is left by his mother. Her love and her presence are his main security; when these appear to be withdrawn, he must feel puzzled and upset—and perhaps a little angry. These separation anxieties also seem to be based on a fear of unusual situations. A toddler builds up a picture of his mother as he is used to seeing her—in the kitchen, shopping, putting him to bed, playing with him. If she is not at hand doing all these familiar things, it disturbs him terribly. So when a toddler cries after he is left by his mother, he is expressing complex emotions: temporary loss of love; bewilderment at the change in his surroundings; feelings of helplessness at being able to do nothing about this new situation;

and, by the degree of his reaction, his own temperament, which may be more or less fearful of change.

When he is taken by his mother on a visit to someone else's home, it will take him a little while to get used to the new environment before he feels secure enough to leave his mother's side. Some very young children even appear upset if their mother goes out of the room by an unfamiliar door, perhaps out on the patio in the summer.

Leaving a screaming toddler is an awful experience for a mother. But it is important for her to remember that her child is suffering separation feelings, *not* separation problems.

He is terribly bewildered and disorientated without her, and he cries and may collapse piteously at the door to show it.

Bedtime apprehension

Although most parent/toddler separations are caused by social reasons—the mother goes out shopping or to the hairdresser or to see a friend—a slightly different kind of separation occurs each night as the child is tucked into bed. Occasionally, a rather fearful toddler finds this bedtime separation quite painful. If you are sure that he is genuinely apprehensive, and not demanding more attention than is necessary, be patient with him. A night light may help, or having one of his parents sit with him every night for a few minutes. He needs to be helped over this fear gently and with understanding.

Explaining your absence

It is easier for him to tolerate short periods of separation when he becomes verbal, around two, and his mother can explain that although she has to go out for a while she will soon be back. She can even tell him where she is going and whom she is going to see. To make her return more definite to him, she can promise to bring back his favorite cookies for a special treat.

Separation from his mother for long or short periods is inevitable in a toddler's life. However upset he may be at the time, it is most unlikely to do him any harm. Separation adds up, however. If a toddler is separated from his mother *and* his father the effects will be greater than from only one parent. And if he is taken away from all his family and his home, then he may be very disturbed indeed. Should both parents have to go away for any reason, then it is best for the toddler to be looked after in his own home rather than moved to the home of his temporary guardian; and if the toddler does have to be sent away from home, then it is best if a parent or brother or sister goes with him.

Baby-sitting

You will have to leave your baby from time to time; this is good for you and good for him. If you have left him briefly with familiar people right from the start, it won't be so hard on him, or you, when he is old enough to mind. And his security will be less shaken if he is left in familiar surroundings with someone he already knows. If you go out a great deal, accustom him to two or three sitters he knows and trusts. Most toddlers will be a bit

suspicious at first, but they will learn to accept caretakers with whom they are familiar —and may look forward to their coming.

Occasionally, a child between one and three is very reluctant to be left by his mother at all, even when he knows the sitter and is in his own home. These very dependent toddlers seem to sense what is in the air and start to cling long before their mother goes out; they may see her ironing a special dress or washing her hair. By the time the sitter comes, even though she may have looked after him many times before, he's already screaming and no amount of reassurance can quiet him down. All dressed up, his mother sets off for her evening out feeling guilty and unhappy and wondering if it's worth it. In his rage he may reject any reassurance you offer him. Do not make things worse by becoming huffy. He is not old enough to cope with "if you won't accept my love you need not have it." He needs unconditional love. Explain that you are coming back, cuddle him, even if he resists, and let him know that his fears are needless.

You will probably find when you get home that he settled down quite happily after you left, an indication of his growing awareness of his lack of power over his mother as well as his genuine anxiety when she leaves.

If your toddler is asleep when you go out and very unlikely to wake up, and the baby-sitter is someone he knows and likes, you may not need to tell him that you are going.

Loving grandparents or older siblings make the best baby-sitters of all, followed by familiar and affectionate neighbors. In some families, baby-sitting with a younger brother or sister is considered a paid "job," particularly if it prevents the older child from going out with his own friends at times.

Although baby-sitting agencies are available in most towns, they are often expensive. Newspaper ads or high school or college students are also good sources.

Another possibility is a baby-sitting exchange in which a group of young parents take turns sitting for each other. Ask about such groups at churches, nursery schools, and other centers in your area. Such groups are usually organized on a point system, through which hours owed and donated are recorded. Such a plan is also a good way of meeting other parents and young children in your neighborhood.

Briefing the baby-sitter

Before you go out, make sure the sitter understands the toddler's routine. If it is during the day, tell her exactly what he will want to eat and when he will nap. At night, let her know if he wants his door left ajar or a particular toy in his crib. Tell her where she can find tea or coffee or a snack for herself; if you object to her having friends in with her, and lots of parents do, make this clear at once. If possible, leave her a number where you can be reached or that of a friend or relative who lives nearby. With young children in the house it is always wise to leave a typed list

Time to yourself

Half a day now and then spent with the family of one of your friends will give your child a chance to get used to being with other people and give you a chance to recharge your batteries. He will make a friend, become the center of attention in a new family, and enjoy exploring a new environment.

permanently by the telephone giving emergency numbers: doctor, police, neighbors.

Leaving your toddler with another child and his mother for one morning a week, while you have both children another day, is a simple and practical idea which can work extremely well for all four people involved. It gives the mothers the invaluable gift of a child-free morning; and it enables the toddlers to have the experience of playing with another child of the same age—and gently exploring a bit of the world outside their own home.

Most mothers find this toddler exchange a lifesaver. A small suburban home, however pleasant, can be very isolating for a young woman who has a demanding toddler underfoot all day. If the exchange is done on a regular basis, she knows that she can count on a few hours to herself every week—and not worry about employing a paid baby-sitter. Knowing another mother similarly placed will give her someone to talk things over with —and she, as well as her child, may gain valuable companionship.

Before starting a half-day exchange, the mothers must know each other sufficiently

well to be sure that they have more or less similar ideas about child-raising and routine. It is helpful for both mothers and toddlers to spend some time together before starting the exchange so the toddlers get to know both caretakers and their surroundings—and the mothers are familiar with the likes and dislikes and routines of both children.

If you do not know another mother with a toddler who wants to start exchanging, ask your pediatrician or a local nursery school for suggestions.

Starting work again

Many mothers think about returning to work and leaving a toddler with a caretaker or at a day care center. On the whole it is preferable not to leave a child under three and a half. Whether or not to do so is a decision that each family must weigh carefully. It is, of course, dependent on the financial needs of the family, the degree of commitment the mother feels to a job or profession, the extent to which she feels frustrated about remaining at home, and the father's willingness to pitch in and share home responsibilities. Chapter 7 contains more information of help to working mothers.

Stimulating your child

A toddler will be stimulated most—and best —by you, his parents. When his mother talks to him and responds to his early sentences, she is encouraging him to develop the skills of language and the rewards of communication with another person. He is a naturally sociable little being; he needs to be stimulated by loving interaction with his parents more than anything else. Experiments with children in institutions show that even when they receive adequate care and have plenty of toys available, it is the lack of individual attention from the same person that appears to retard their development.

A toddler's life will be limited to his home and family. As he becomes more mobile and active, everything he sees around—the contents of drawers and cupboards as well as his toys—will be fair game for his active hands and mind to explore. And there is a tremendous amount his parents can do to lay the foundations for later awareness of his environment; most parents of young children do this naturally. In the garden, they point out birds and trees, let him touch the different textures of snow, sand, and the grass on the lawn, and encourage him to smell mint and roses and flowering honeysuckle. Different noises will fascinate him, too: the roar of traffic in the street, dogs barking, a cow mooing, and the honk of a car horn. Because of his growing skills with language, he will love clapping his hands in time with familiar nursery rhymes.

Introducing books

Although his attention span is still very short, this is the age to take him on brief visits to the local children's library. Many have small tables and chairs where he can sit for a few minutes and look at a picture book. Reading aloud to him at home is a marvelous way of stimulating a toddler. He will identify what he sees in his daily life—people and dogs and houses—before he is able to follow a simple story. Many two-year-olds get so fond of a favorite book that, unlike their parents, they never tire of hearing it. Learning early the magic of words and pictures will help a youngster, in time, into his school and reading years.

Playing and learning

For a toddler, play is hard work as well as enjoyable. It has only recently been understood that what adults think of as play is crucial to a child's normal development. Much of a baby's play during the first two years consists of trying out new skills until he can practice them so effortlessly that they become fun. A fifteen-month-old staggering across the lawn is both enjoying himself *and* learning to walk better. Everything he does— gingerly touching the grass with a bare foot; throwing toys from his high chair—helps him to explore the exciting new world around him. After eighteen months, when he has become a competent walker, his activities branch out. He attempts to run and will start to climb; you can expect anxious moments as you find him perched on the edge of the kitchen table. Trying things out is all part of his playing and learning development; soon he will learn to climb up the first steps of the playground slide. Now he can walk and climb; he will enjoy gentle roughhousing with his father and older brother or sister, climbing over their recumbent bodies, being held in the air, and lowered onto their chests.

During the second year, he becomes increasingly aware of what he can do to things around him, anticipating their reactions. His manual dexterity is improving all the time, and initial scribbles with a crayon will become recognizable attempts to represent his world.

Toddlers are fascinated by the power of their newly acquired speech, and rhymes and imitations become part of play—often practiced in bed before falling asleep or first thing in the morning.

"Eeny-meeny-miney-moe, Catch a rabbit by the toe," is a game that provides an irresistible combination for a toddler: close contact with someone he loves and a funny rhyme that builds up to an eagerly awaited climax. It has variations in almost every culture.

Above : This truck will give your child endless pleasure, and will help to steady him as he pushes it forward. Gradually he will learn how to turn it around corners and how to pull it toward him.

Right : At first glance children under two years old may seem to be playing together, but they are in fact enjoying their own separate games at the same time as checking what those around them are doing.

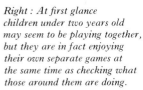

Left : Your child will enjoy expressing his ideas even if at first the result may just resemble a mass of meaningless lines. From out of these scribbles will eventually emerge the beginnings of recognizable shapes and forms.

Right : Teddy is no longer just a comforter for this two-year-old but a friend whom she can confide in and talk to on her own terms. She may also have an imaginary friend who will occupy vacant chairs and otherwise confuse the perplexed adult.

Below : Much of the child's make-believe play involves pretending to be someone else. His parents will stand out as obvious models for him to imitate.

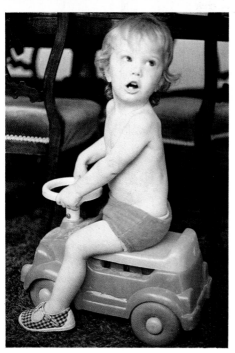

Above : Miniature replicas of real-life objects can be used by the child to explore ideas and to act out scenes based on a mixture of real and fantasy events. This sort of play can help him to understand his own experiences.

Right : With a car his own size the child can feel fully in charge while also learning how to handle a vehicle. By three years of age he will be capable of pedaling himself around the house and yard on a tricycle.

Toys

Simple toys are invariably the best. They last the longest because they cannot go wrong; more importantly, they allow the child to use his imagination to employ them in many different and exciting ways. Before buying toys for very young children be sure that they would be safe if he were to put them in his mouth—and that they have no sharp edges.

Expensive toys that will give him pleasure over several years, such as a tricycle, a pedal car, or sturdy wooden blocks, are more economical than they might appear at first; but inexpensive toys such as crayons and scrap paper are likely to appeal to him just as much.

Kitchen equipment makes marvelous toys: egg beaters, wooden spoons, and pots and pans can be used, indoors and out, for digging and beating and putting things into. If you make pastry, give him a small piece. He will not be ready to cook yet, but will wring endless variations from an increasingly gray lump of dough. There will be many objects around the house that you can pass on to him. Even "scrap" like egg boxes and the cardboard centers of toilet rolls make excellent, though temporary, toys. Most toddlers are fascinated by boxes and tins with lids. These are quite harmless, and allow the child's imagination full play to make them into whatever he wants them to be. Do not give him your old beads. If the string were to break he could swallow or inhale one. (Many toddlers experiment with pushing things up their nose.)

Toddlers must be allowed to play in their own way, at levels appropriate to their development, and without too much interference from parents. Especially with a first child, there is a tendency to give him toys that are too "old" and too complicated for him. There is something to the old joke of a delighted father setting up an elaborate train set while his bewildered two-year-old has more fun playing with the boxes it came in! Also, it was recently shown that girls of eighteen months, given free choice, played with trucks just as much as boys did. So try not to push girls into play patterns that you think they should have.

Most very young children will want to play near their mothers or where the rest of the family is; it is lonely to play by oneself in one's room for too long. With a toddler, having some toys strewn around the house is inevitable, but, if mess is going to worry you, keep at least one room child-free. Make this a rule and stick to it.

A playpen in the kitchen will still be useful for storing toys downstairs as well as for occasional rest periods. Open shelves are invaluable in a baby's room for holding toys, and can be used right on into childhood as books and games are acquired. By the time a baby is two, he can help to pick up at bedtime, with his mother pitching in to finish the job. This is a great age for copying—so make the most of it!

Choosing the right toys

Containing the mess

Fifteen to eighteen months
In addition to playing with only one toy at a time your child will now be combining two toys, such as hollow cups that fit together or blocks that can be stacked into piles. Pull-and-push toys are an obvious choice for this

age group. By seventeen months the child may be able to look over his shoulder as he walks along pulling the toy behind him. He is beginning to say his first words, and simple picture books will help him to associate particular names with familiar objects. During this period you may notice him pretending to drink from an empty cup.

Actions such as this are the very beginnings of make-believe play.

Eighteen months to two years
By twenty months, your child may be able to run, and possibly even jump. Indoor and outdoor swings and wooden toys large enough for sitting on and in now come within his range. A child of this age is beginning to

notice the change in materials that his actions can produce. Sand and water provide endless opportunities for dramatic experiment. A young child is particularly fond of rhyming words and will respond enthusiastically to a well-illustrated book of nursery rhymes. He is now capable of handling slightly

Is your child left-handed?

Although children are often permitted to write with their left hands, schools seldom teach them the correct way to do so. There is one method of writing that reduces the left-hander's problems to a minimum. (1) Always ensure that the right-hand bottom corner of the paper is nearest the body and that the pen is gripped at least 1 in from the point. This reduces the risk of smudging and allows the child to see what he is writing. If not taught this way, a left-hander will invariably pick up one of three incorrect methods (2, 3, 4), all of which are impractical.

For centuries left-handers have suffered unfair disrepute in a world designed for the right-hander; the devil himself was portrayed as a left-hander. But though the prejudices against this small band have diminished, left-handedness is still considered by many to be a form of deviance, and some parents, on becoming conscious of a child's preference for his left hand, begin an immediate campaign to suppress it. But gone are the days when a child at school would be discriminated against for being left-handed and be forced by his teacher to write with his right hand irrespective of his inclinations. Most schools allow a child to use the hand he prefers.

As discouragement has lessened so the numbers of left-handers, not surprisingly, have increased and, though there is no exact figure that covers the entire globe or even the Western world, the rough figure of eight percent gives a general clue to the number of left-handers around.

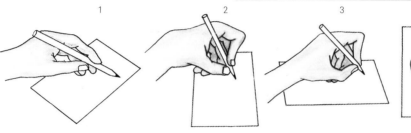

1   2   3   4

Above: There is plenty of evidence to show that hand preferences are established before school age. It may first become apparent early on when the child begins to feed himself.

more complicated fitting toys, such as those where shapes have to be matched together.

Two to two and a half
Instead of pretending to drink from a cup himself the child will now be offering it to his doll or teddy bear. By thirty months the child not only searches for absent objects

that he needs for his make-believe scenes but also improvises with other materials —for example, orange juice may be stirred with a toy rake, used as a spoon. The idea of using one thing to represent another plays an important part in the further development of language and abstract thinking. Encourage your child's

creativity by giving him crayons and paper, and simple musical toys to develop his appreciation of different sounds.

Two and a half to three
Your child's growing language ability means that he can

communicate more effectively with other children of his own age and therefore is able to maintain slightly longer play sequences. Encourage his language development with well-illustrated story-books and poetry records for children. He will also love to talk to his friends on a toy telephone. Simple jigsaws,

of maybe six to eight pieces, should be within the child's capabilities, as are large-piece construction toys such as Lego—which can be turned into a variety of different shapes to be used in play. By now, your child may be ready for his first tricycle.

Health

Toddlerhood can be an anxious time for some mothers. The health of a toddler is highly labile, that is, it can alter suddenly and greatly. This changeability cuts both ways, however. A child may appear to be getting sick rapidly, but within a few hours or a day he will be as right as rain. Usually a mother knows the general health of her own child and realizes that she need not be worried when he is merely "off color." The signs of something more serious are the same as they were in babyhood: listlessness, lackluster eyes, and loss of appetite.

A mother should not take it on herself to decide whether her toddler is suffering from "four-hour fever" or something more serious. Your family doctor will be quite familiar with the problem and will prefer to see a child who recovers soon after than to be called late about one who is really ill.

The most crucial step, then, is to get in touch with your doctor. In the meantime, however, a feverish child can be made more comfortable by gently sponging him with warm water. Cold water will cause the blood vessels to contract and actually prevent the body from cooling.

The ill toddler

Most toddlers who are ill are not old enough to do anything more than follow the dictates of their own bodies. If your child feels well enough to be up and about there is no point in sending him to bed. If he is ill enough to be in bed, he will probably go there voluntarily. If he comes to you sad and listless, give him a hug and suggest that he lie down and rest. Do not force him. He may be better off where you can keep an eye on him and monitor the progress of his illness. More importantly, he will be near you and comforted by your presence. If you put him to bed unnecessarily, he will be more of a nuisance than is worthwhile.

Entertaining a sick child

A child who is in bed will require more of your time than usual. The range of activities that you can use to amuse him is, of course, more limited than when he is up and about, and his attention span at this age is brief. You will have to read to him a lot. Prolong the books by discussing all of the pictures in detail. An extra supply of simple jigsaw puzzles, and of crayons and paper, will be helpful. Pick out the toys that he can play with while sitting up in bed. They will help occupy him for a while at least.

Children's medicines

Modern medicines have transformed childhood illness. They are usually highly effective, and those for children are concocted to taste extra palatable, mostly by the addition of a fruit flavor of strawberry or banana. Some parents are alarmed at how frequently antibiotics are prescribed, because they have heard that they produce resistant strains of germs. This is true in the population as a whole, but it will not affect your child individually. By completing any prescribed course of penicillin, even when your child seems fully recovered, you will ensure that the germs are fully killed off, thus lessening the resistant strains. Too many parents are lax about this.

Routine checkups

Most of the time a toddler should naturally keep in good health. If you are anxious you can take him every six months to your doctor, where he will be routinely weighed and measured, and you will be asked about his eating habits and general condition.

Ask advice about any problem, whether it is a detail such as diet, or a broader query such as how to deal with a generally difficult child.

Going to the hospital

If a young child has to be hospitalized, his chief concern will be separation from his parents. The period from eighteen months to four years old is the time when separation is most likely to have long-term effects. Hospitalization will be a much less frightening experience for him if someone he knows goes with him. So, if you have any choice, make sure he goes to a hospital that allows parents to stay. If it is difficult for his mother to stay with him constantly, she might consider dividing the time with his father: perhaps his mother staying during the day, his father at night. This will be less disruptive if there is another child at home; and it is good for the toddler to know he has equal support from both his parents. But someone else he knows well—his grandmother, an older brother or sister if they are mature enough—can take a turn and give him just as much confidence in his new environment.

He will want his own comforting cuddly toys and night things to make him feel more at home in surroundings that are new to him —and that he may find very alarming. Although it may be hard, it will help him most if those closest to him control their natural anxiety without communicating it to him too urgently. He will know they are worried and be anxious himself; he needs concern, not hysteria.

Visiting the dentist

If your child cleans his teeth regularly and if you control his sugar intake, he is less likely to have bad teeth throughout childhood. Some people, however, simply have vulnerable teeth, so despite the best precautions your child may develop caries (tooth decay). You will be able to monitor this when you—or he—cleans them. If caries start to appear, you should take him to the dentist right away.

Many children are frightened of the dentist, as indeed are many adults. It is sometimes said that young children, in their innocence, are not so frightened, and if you take your child young enough he will learn to like the dentist, an attitude that will persist into adulthood. However, research shows that children who first visit the dentist for treatment before they are three are more likely to be frightened of him later, not less. So, keep your child's teeth clean and safe! It does no harm to take him for a mutual inspection, when the dentist can check his teeth and your

When a toddler decides to dress himself, it is best to stand back until he obviously needs help. It may take a lot longer but it is the only way he will learn to do this difficult but ultimately rewarding task.

child can make the acquaintance of the dentist on a friendly basis. Try to find a dentist who is considered good with children. Perhaps you can let your child watch when you are being treated.

Clothes   A toddler, climbing, falling down, and starting to run, is hard on clothes, so he needs practical long-wearing overalls and T-shirts, with extra sweaters and cardigans for the

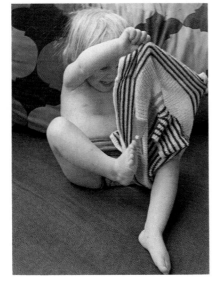

winter. It's best to have at least one "dress-up" outfit for parties and special occasions.

How many clothes he needs depends largely on washing facilities. Dress a young child with about the same amount of clothing as an adult wears on a particular day—overdressing children is quite common. Check that pajamas and nightgowns are made from nonflammable materials. If a toddler is a restless sleeper, a sleeping bag with divided legs will keep him warm. This is also useful if he wakes long before the rest of the family in the mornings, when the house is still cold.

Along with a toddler's growing independence will come his own ideas on dress. Allow him some leeway; he will feel very grown-up, around two, at choosing his red sweater and not his blue. Encourage him to dress himself if he appears interested, even if it means legs stuck in shirt sleeves at first. He will need a lot of help before he can manage very efficiently. Undressing is easier; most babies start to pull down their pants or take off a sock before eighteen months, and some will strip themselves completely by two.

There is no sense in entering needless battles with a toddler over certain preferences he may have. For example, if he strongly objects to wearing the hood of his snowsuit—which may impede his vision when he is out of doors—substitute a woolly hat. Dropping gloves and mittens over the side of his stroller is a favorite winter occupation of many a toddler; so attach them to his sleeves with elastic.

Shoes are necessary only as protection when he goes outside and it is cold or wet; if there is the possibility of splinters in the house, slippers are adequate. Make sure shoes (and socks) are quite roomy; both are liable to be rapidly outgrown throughout childhood.

Getting out

It is extremely important for parents to live as interesting and full a life as possible even when their child is very young; it is healthy for them and for their relationship, and stimulating for the toddler. Naturally, having a toddler entails a restricted social life for the parents; long, leisurely shopping trips and visits to museums are out. So too is the kind of entertaining that requires much cooking and preparation. But getting out of the house on short shopping forays, for a picnic, or to visit friends, will mean that the parents, particularly the mother, will feel less isolated. At the same time the toddler is widening his knowledge of his environment, and learning patterns of social behavior. Because they are kept interested in what is going on around them, most young children behave well away from the home as long as they are not allowed to get too tired or overstimulated.

Outings

Plan outings ahead of time, and with a bit of special thought for the toddler. When you visit friends, take along a familiar toy to reassure him in a different home. Remember that he has a very short attention span. When he is tired of shopping or playing in the park, don't push him to continue. He has had enough; take him home. You want him to think of outings as fun, not ordeals. He will make friends with some of the people he sees in the local shops and start looking out for them and waving bye-bye. Try and shop when he is not tired—in the mornings or after his nap—and take anything vital that you may need like an extra diaper or tissues to wipe his face. Collapsible strollers are invaluable, and can be taken on buses and into most shops. It is better to take a cracker or some pieces of apple with you for a snack; don't get into the habit of always buying him ice cream or candy; he will start to expect them every time, and may create a scene if he doesn't get them.

If you are planning a long shopping trip, it is better to wait for Saturday morning, when he can stay at home with his father, or to get a baby-sitter for a few hours. You cannot expect him to sit in his stroller indefinitely while you try on dresses. If he is not in a stroller don't expect much shopping to be accomplished. So go with a specific purchase in mind, and be satisfied with that. He will need constant watching to keep him from touching things or wandering off—and an escalator, which seems to fascinate most toddlers, can be really dangerous.

Ironically, playgrounds, too, can be treacherous, as every mother who has watched a toddler teeter on the top of a slide well knows. Many playground accidents are caused by toddlers playing on the same equipment as older children, who might push them off jungle gyms and merry-go-rounds.

Eating out

All but the most exclusive restaurants are prepared to cater to toddlers, and plastic seats and high chairs are usually available. Some eating places may even have special children's menus, although you are likely to find that the regular menu will be easily adaptable.

The many chain restaurants which serve "fast foods" are good places for family outings. Since they are relatively inexpensive you are not likely to be too concerned over a half-eaten hamburger or an untouched glass of milk. The informal ambiance makes spills and occasional yells less serious or embarrassing. Picnics are of course ideal. Here relaxation and the joys of an outdoor setting make for a delightful change of pace for both parents and children.

Eating out is not only a way to give mother a break from her constant responsibilities in the kitchen, but it can be an important step in your toddler's socialization.

Vacations

Vacations with a toddler are more enjoyable for everyone if the surroundings can be as much like home as possible. Why not try a trailer, a rented cottage, or a farm that provides vacation accommodation for families. A very young child will have no tolerance for sightseeing, so plan a vacation around outings that he will enjoy—and that you will like too —such as playing on the beach.

Most children are splendid travelers. Unlike weary grown-ups, when they are tired they can go off to sleep without worrying about luggage and tickets. With lots to look at, they will be kept interested. Journeys will go smoothly if they are planned for carefully. Take along your child's special pillow and toy, and crackers and fruit to ward off starvation. On a car journey, frequent stops are the best policy. If a couple of small children start to get restless in the back seat, far better to stop and let them run around for ten minutes than to spend the next hour disentangling legs and arms and listening to a steady whine. In planes or on a long train journey, it will help to bring along a small bag of crayons, paper, and books to keep a child occupied. Don't worry if he doesn't eat very much. If he refuses the food let him nibble on the snacks you bring with you.

You must never permit a child to sit loose on the front passenger seat of a car, nor should you carry him on your lap in the front. It is also important to use a restraint in the back seat that is appropriate to your child's stage of development. Many good devices are on the market. A young baby should be placed

Occupying a child on a journey

Car seats

Most safety seats are designed for children up to about the age of five. You should ensure that the seat is anchored to the main car frame and that it incorporates safety belts. Otherwise, in an accident your child will be catapulted forward, perhaps with fatal consequences.

on the back seat of the car in his portable crib, which should be restrained by special safety straps. Once he can sit up he should be harnessed into a child's safety seat, which should be attached to the floor or to the frame of the car. These seats give a child an excellent view of his surroundings. Make sure you buy a genuine safety restraint and not a flimsy child's seat that offers no protection in the event of a collision.

Car sickness Quite a lot of young children feel sick in cars. This is usually outgrown later in childhood;

but if parents need to travel much with a car-sick child, it can be trying for everyone. It is certainly best for parents to accept, sympathetically, that the toddler does start to feel nauseated by the car's movement; but it is not useful to turn around anxiously every other minute to ask him if he feels sick. Frequent stops and plenty of fresh air in the car may help. It may also assist to take his mind off his discomfort by playing simple "I spy" games. Your doctor may want to prescribe Dramamine or some other drug that is designed to prevent motion sickness.

How your child has progressed

Physical activities such as walking, running, and the exploring of his world form the major part of the toddler's life, and when the little person reaches his third birthday and is already nearly as high as your waist it will hardly seem possible that he was recently so helpless.

His rapid growth will be most noticeable in his height, for though he has another fifteen years of growing he will already be half his final height. But he's not a miniature adult. His head, for example, is still huge in comparison to his body—about one-fifth of his

total size compared to an adult's, which makes up only one-eighth. But though there is still a long way to go, the years of toddlerhood will have witnessed great strides. Every day he will have acquired more skills, learned more words, spoken more fluently, and his legs, though short and bowed, will have carried him with ever greater ease. His co-ordination will have improved; he will have learned to kick a ball, handle a paintbrush, and begin to try to dress himself. Every day he will have aspired to greater things, his life a sequence of striving and achievement.

Though girls tend to be slightly smaller than boys, there are no obvious differences in scale or proportion.

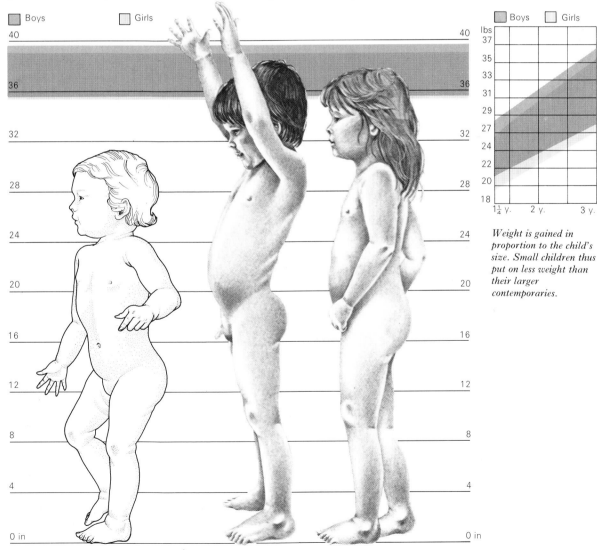

Boys ▢ Girls ▢

Boys ▢ Girls ▢

Weight is gained in proportion to the child's size. Small children thus put on less weight than their larger contemporaries.

4 Early childhood: An
INDIVIDUAL MIND

For a whole month, he insisted
on wearing his red rubber boots wherever he went,
indoors and out. A million questions
formed—and his mind raced on ahead of them.
"What happens to the sea?"
"Where does it end?" "What makes waves?"
Three mornings a week he went off to nursery school, where
he spent hours in the building corner
with his special friend.
In fact, he believed everybody was his friend.
"Will you come to my house for lunch?"
he inquired politely of the pretty stranger as we were
waiting at the traffic lights one day.

Around his third birthday a child can change dramatically. Temper tantrums won't entirely have disappeared—the "terrible twos" can last well into the fourth year—but most of the negativism and balkiness will have gone and suddenly he's a charmer, agreeable, easy to manage, endlessly entertaining.

This is an age of delights for both parents and child. Every week produces a new spate of words, a new trick of climbing, skipping, or jumping. He is alert and vitally interested in everything around him, a joy to be with on an outing. The changes that come with each new achievement go on being dramatic, and make his lucky parents prouder every day.

A three-year-old is beginning to be able to get his body to do what he wants. In the next two years he will (given the right help and encouragement) begin to draw, make simple models, play elementary ball games, dress

sister, or close friends, his talk at three may be full of assertions, "I'm bigger now, aren't I?" "I'm not a little baby anymore, am I?" He's right: his babyhood is gone. However much pleasure you got from it, do not prolong it at the expense of his growing up. Give him the little responsibilities he asks for, and be prepared to stand by while he commits the occasional disaster.

These are the last years he will spend completely within the family before school marks his first step out of the home, so make the most of them.

Once he is out of the toddler stage the child's rate of growth and development slows down. However, in its own way the advances a child makes during the period from three to five or six are just as dramatic, for every change takes him farther away from baby-

Physical development

Left : One child discovers a new prank—an action, joke, or novel phrase—and all the others will want to participate by repeating it themselves. Unlike adult wit, children's appreciation of their own humor increases with the number of repetitions. And so the hilarity escalates, much to the exasperation of any adult audience.

himself, and help with easy household chores. His pleasure in his increasing competence will be matched only by yours.

His mental grasp of the world improves by leaps and bounds. His imagination works overtime; sometimes it is a little difficult to know what is fact and what is fantasy as he tells you about his nursery school.

As his independence and competence grow the child between three and five becomes an individual whose wants and rights his parents must respect.

He resents being treated like the baby he so recently was. If he has a younger brother or

hood and nearer to a state of being more like a miniature adult.

He no longer has to make an effort just to stay upright and to move about. As the whole process becomes more automatic he moves his legs with more assurance and he carries himself more purposefully.

At three he will still be enjoying simple movements, such as hopping, jumping, and running back and forth, just for the sheer delight of it. He will show you with enormous pride how he can run across a room and jump all of six inches. Such a jump will win no world records, but his pleasure in his growing mobility and his own physicality is something you can share with him.

By four he is still enjoying the same activities, but is becoming more adventurous. He will be scrambling over easy jungle gyms and trees. Although he has been able for some time to climb stairs with one foot on each step, he is just now beginning to cope with coming down the same way. He will still often revert to marking time on each step. By five a self-assured child with good physical coordination will be alarming his parents with hair-raising stunts on any suitable climbing object. He will run hard, and enjoy races with other children or his parents. He will be capable of sprinting about 35 yds/ 32 m in ten seconds.

During this period the child begins to separate his control over different parts of his body. Try placing something just out of reach of your child when he is three and again when he is four or more. The first time he will probably lean forward and twist his body. Indeed his whole body plays a part in every movement. By four he is better at keeping still and letting his arm do the work, and at five he will be quite grown up about it.

At three a child is still emerging from the baby stage of placing and handling things. Although he has long had the ability to pick up the tiniest objects between his finger and thumb, the way he uses his hand is relatively clumsy. He may be able to build quite surprisingly high towers of blocks, but each will be placed with great concentration and most will be out of true. When he tries his form board or baby jigsaw he will be very rough and ready about putting things in. Even when he recognizes which hole a piece goes in, and which way, he will not be very exact about positioning it so that it goes straight in. He may then try to force it in, or pat it vigorously.

Increasing dexterity

Above : The seemingly irrational nature of a wheel-barrow takes some mastering but, as with every newfound skill, once accomplished, the sense of achievement makes all the struggle worthwhile.

Right : Bumps and tumbles are inevitable, but if the game is exciting enough they will not stop play for long.

Below and Right : A jungle gym has endless possibilities. It is a means of developing and displaying athletic prowess and daring, but it serves equally well as a house or a spaceship, or for playing king of the hill.

Teaching Swimming

Drowning accidents *are* avoidable. It is never too young to learn to swim and children can be taught as early as eight months. Prepare your child carefully by playing games in the bath in which he gets his face wet and uses his swimming aids. Let him visit the pool before his first session.

For his first lessons, choose a quiet time at the pool and make sure that the water is warm (min. 81°F/27°C). Having reached the water's edge, cuddle your child and enter the water slowly, holding him in your arms. Help him to float on his front or back—whichever seems preferable—with his head "pillowed" in the water. If he wants to splash around on his own, without aids, let him.

Once he is used to the water, make the first move toward swimming. Lift your child so that he lies along your arms, facing toward you. He will hold on to your upper arms, while your hands support his hips. Let him kick his legs, as preparation for the crawl. To help him get used to finding the upright position, move with him through the water. Then hold him in front of you, lying across your outstretched arms, and teach him to do the dog paddle or back paddle with his arms. Once he is confident, make your child go under the water—at least once every session.

Always end the lesson on a happy note. Short daily sessions for three weeks or so will achieve better results than a few, longer ones.

An older child may prefer a suit in which the buoyancy can be reduced as his proficiency increases.

Above : The most important thing is for your child to be relaxed and confident in the water. Aids like water wings will help a toddler while he is becoming used to the water and later while he is learning how to swim.

Left : Holding on to a plastic float keeps him buoyant with his face out of the water while he learns to propel himself with his legs.

At four he will be much more precise. He may even be unable to build such high towers for a time because, in his desire to place the blocks neatly, he may well upset those already stacked. By five he will be in much better control. Hand, arm, and body will all move together under better command of his eye; mere towers will have long since ceased to interest him. He will build a house or a church complete with steeple, though you may still need to be told what each construction is meant to be.

Varying the diet

By three, most children will be eating more or less the same food as the rest of the family. Given the chance, a four-year-old will develop a quite sophisticated palate and will enjoy mildly spicy foods as much as fish sticks and french fries. All of us find some foods more appealing than others—and some downright awful. So it's fair to expect that he will too; as long as his diet is reasonably balanced, it won't matter.

Refusal to eat

It is quite common for a child between the ages of four and seven to sit down for a meal and then suddenly refuse a particular dish, or even to say he does not want a meal at all. This can be a sign that he is over-hungry. The stomach pangs and depression caused by great hunger sometimes make him reject the whole idea of food. This situation takes all a parent's patience and tact, but once you have persuaded the child to take his first mouthful, you will usually find that all

Above : Throwing requires balance, timing, and the coordination of fingers, arms, trunk, and legs. Young toddlers cannot coordinate so many parts and push the ball away using their shoulders and arm. Later they draw the arm back and use their body weight to project the ball, as this five-year-old girl is doing.

his bad temper drops away in an instant and is forgotten, and the meal can proceed as if nothing had happened—calmness is the right way to treat such an episode.

Food fads Extreme faddiness is a perverse eating pattern unique to our affluent society, where food is regarded as more than a means of sustenance. Our indulgent attitude toward what we eat is not surprising with the wide variety and abundance of food available. It is not uncommon to find a five-year-old who appears to eat nothing but a few baked beans and some pieces of sausage; or who insists on cornflakes for breakfast, lunch, and supper. It may be that he is continuing an independence struggle with his mother that began when he was being weaned: he suddenly made the discovery that he could decide what to eat and thereby exert power over his mother. Perhaps he simply finds her personality overpowering—and this is his way of asserting himself.

Regardless of why this faddism has come about, such picky eaters are a nuisance and a worry. It is best not to display the concern you probably feel. It is reassuring to know that if your child is doing well the chances are that he is getting more adequate nourishment than you think. If you feel that, over-all, his diet is badly unbalanced, talk with your doctor. Most children do outgrow such fussy eating habits, especially if little attention is paid to them. Do make

Above: By the age of five the co-ordination of most boys has advanced beyond that of girls of the same age. They are helped by having slightly *longer forearms, which ensure greater velocity and precision. It takes most girls another year or two to reach the same degree of coodination.*

Left: These are the four distinct stages in a child's ability to control a pencil. As fine coordination improves, toddlers employ less arm and shoulder movements, soon learning to use fingers and wrist to manipulate the tip rather than the whole pencil.

because he won't eat any protein except fish sticks. If the rest of the family is having chicken or hamburgers, he can eat a little if he's hungry enough—or make do with vegetables. Fish sticks can reappear—for everyone—the next day.

After three, when a child is feeding himself competently and probably eating most of his meals with the rest of the family, he will begin to copy the table behavior he sees around him. He will also be able to manage a spoon, then a fork—amd finally a knife. Most youngsters will need difficult food, such as meat, cut in pieces for them until they become more adept with a knife.

At three a child is far too young to understand the meaning of etiquette. He is also too young to care. In these still early years teach him the basics of neatness, cleanliness, and consideration for others, but do not expect too much and do not turn mealtimes into a repressive drill of "correct" behavior.

By five he can put his knife and fork straight, if you think that it is important for a child to do so. He can be reminded not to reach across the table, but you cannot always stop him from doing so. He should long ago have learned to put his hand in front of his mouth when he coughs or sneezes, and you will probably have introduced him to the idea of saying "please" and "thank you," but do not allow these words of personal regard to become meaningless ritual obligations that your child will resent.

Inevitably he will lapse occasionally into fidgeting at the table or suddenly leaping down to pick up a toy he has just remembered or to finish a game that he was in the middle of when the meal started. But if you make it clear that he will be more popular if he does the "right" thing without imposing a strait-jacket of rules, you will be preparing him perfectly adequately for when he is old enough to be responsible for his own behavior at the table or elsewhere.

Table manners

If you ever get a chance to watch your own child when he is out visiting, you will probably be astounded at how much better behaved he is than at home, especially as he approaches school age. Many mothers who send their child forth on his first excursion praying that he does not do anything too dreadful are amazed when they collect him later to hear what a little angel he has been.

Unfortunately the opposite also holds true. Some mothers manage by one means or another to produce the little angel at home—and cannot understand why they receive complaints from school and rumors from friends of what a terror he is once he is out of sight of mother.

It seems that a child needs to try things out, to be naughty some of the time to test the limits that you set for him. If the child cannot do this at home, he will do so elsewhere. If he can experiment at home he is more likely to tread the straight and narrow away from it.

Behavior when visiting

sure, though, that your child is not filling up on snacks.

Many children are very conservative about what they eat and drink at this age. They may be reluctant to try anything new. When he is at nursery school or visiting a friend, a child may feel bolder—and be surprised at how good different types of crackers taste.

Don't get yourself into the position of cooking two separate lunches each day

Clothes

The problem with clothes for children of this age is not so much that they don't wear well but that they are so quickly outgrown. So always buy garments that fit generously if you want them to last. Hems of pants, skirts, and dresses can be turned up and then let down again as the child grows. If this is not possible, buy garments with generous hems so that they can be let down later. Skirts and overalls with bib tops are easy to alter, simply by moving the buttons. Elasticized waistbands are an advantage, because they stretch when the child's waist measurement increases and are not outgrown as quickly as fitted waistbands. If pants do not have an elasticized waist make sure they have belt loops.

Fasteners should be easy enough for the child to manage. Zippers without an open bottom end are easiest for a small child, and those made of fine nylon best for his comfort. Buttons and snaps should be large; make sure they are firmly secured to the garment and can stand rough treatment. Avoid small snaps and hooks and eyes. Pajama tops and jumpers with elasticized necklines are easy to pull over his head.

A smock or apron is an essential part of a child's wardrobe. The ideal smock is one that covers the child completely, is elasticized at the wrists and neck so that he can put it on himself, and is either wipeable, such as vinyl, or easy to wash, such as dacron and cotton.

Before you buy any article of clothing for your child check the label for washing instructions. If you want an easy-care garment avoid those that have to be hand-washed or dry-cleaned.

Even special party dresses should be easily washable; polyester/cotton is ideal as it is a

As the drawing shows, your child will grow rapidly, and as he does he will of course outgrow his clothes. "Hand-me-downs" and clothing exchanges will help, since children seldom wear out most items before they become too small.

Children's clothing that is manufactured in the United States is standardized as to size. Imported goods will be sized differently, but you will usually find the American equivalents printed on the label.

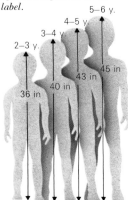

2–3 y. 36 in
3–4 y. 40 in
4–5 y. 43 in
5–6 y. 45 in

What are good shoes?

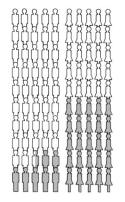

Girls tend to wear ill-fitting fashion shoes earlier than boys and so, as the solid figures in the chart show, by the age of sixteen a higher percentage are developing deformed big toe joints (bunion joints).

Choosing a child's shoes is one of the easiest areas in which to make mistakes—and one where the consequences are most serious. Very few children are born with defective feet. Most abnormalities are caused by unsuitable shoes worn in childhood.

A correctly designed shoe must be broad and long enough to allow plenty of room for movement and growth. It has a straight inside edge and a broad, high toe with no seams. It grips well at the heel and the foot is held firmly over the instep by an adjustable fastener. The sole must be flexible and bend at the broadest part of the foot. A small heel does no harm, but shoes with high heels, if worn regularly, will cause shortening of the calf muscles, pressure on the toes, and hard skin on the ball of the foot.

A child should never wear handed-down shoes as they will have become shaped by the feet that have previously worn them.

The shoes illustrated here show some of the points to bear in mind when buying footwear. It is best to buy leather shoes, which allow a child's feet to breathe; plastic shoes or rubber boots worn for long periods may cause tired or aching feet.

delicate-looking fabric but will wash well and drip dry. A party dress should be practical as well as pretty; long ribbons and bell sleeves are liable to fall into the jelly or get pulled and ripped. Make sure that your child feels comfortable in her dress. A long dress is unsuitable if she is going to want to play rough-and-tumble games or to climb trees. Climbing even a flight of stairs in a long dress may prove a hazard to a four-year-old, especially if it comes down below her ankles.

Many clothing manufacturers include written washing instructions on their labels. Follow them as closely as possible. It is also a good idea to file them away so that you can refer to them from time to time.

Ironing
⊠ Do not iron
▣ Cool iron —up to 120°C
▣ Warm iron —up to 160°C
▣ Hot iron —up to 210°C

Dry-cleaning
⊗ Do not dry-clean
Ⓐ All solvents
Ⓟ Perchloroethylene, white spirit, solvent 113 and solvent 11
Ⓕ White spirit and solvent 113

Drying
▢ Can be tumble dried
▭ Dry flat
▥ Drip dry
▢ Line dry

🖐 Hand wash only
⊠ Do not wash
⊠ Do not bleach

Corduroy and denim are tough and hard-wearing for skirts, pants, and pinafore dresses. Corduroy is warmer than denim, but its pile will soon wear away on the seats and knees of pants. Both fabrics wash easily, but keep to the manufacturer's recommended washing temperature or the color may run. Most denim is preshrunk these days, but inspect the label when you buy.

Cotton needs ironing after every washing, whereas a polyester/ cotton mixture is drip dry and requires little ironing. Nothing, however, is cooler or more comfortable in very hot weather than pure cotton.

If a loose-fitting garment, such as pajamas, is made of polyester or cotton, make sure it is flameproofed, as both these fabrics are highly inflammable.

Wool is the warmest material. Some children are allergic to wool, especially if it is worn next to the skin. If this is so with your child, do not buy him woolen underwear and socks.

Wool mixture sweaters are harder wearing and easier to wash than pure wool, and they are less likely to lose their shape than man-made fibers.

If you do buy an all-wool garment for your child, make sure it is machine washable.

Nylon is not the ideal fabric for a child; it is not warm enough for winter wear, and in summer it will make him hot and uncomfortable.

Nylon underwear is often the cause of minor skin irritations, and nylon stretch socks can constrict the toes as badly as ill-fitting shoes.

Vinyl fabrics are perfect for rainwear and are totally waterproof. However, they tear easily and should be well ventilated; otherwise they tend to be hot and sticky. Sometimes they are available in fluorescent colors which make a child more visible when he is crossing the street.

Below : This shoe incorporates the best design features that enable a young foot to grow normally. Before buying footwear, always measure the length and breadth of both your child's feet. As no two feet are identical, buy for the larger foot.

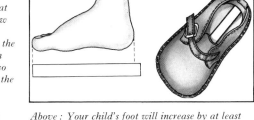

Above : Your child's foot will increase by at least two sizes a year until he is six. To ensure that his shoes fit, place in the shoe a strip of card $\frac{3}{8}$ in/1 cm longer than his foot. This should fit exactly.

Below and Left : A child's shoe should not have a smooth sole, which will slip on wet surfaces ; nor should it have high heels or a high back, which may rub the Achilles tendon.

Left : Sling-backs, ankle straps, and slip-ons do not give adequate support to the foot, which may slip forward and crush the toes. The front inside edge of a shoe must not curve sharply inward, pressure on the big toe joint may lead to bunions later on. Nor should you buy shoes with rigid soles, which are difficult to walk in and bad for your child's posture.

Left : Canvas and leather are ideal materials for play shoes, which should also have rubber soles as they grip well and are hard-wearing. Avoid shoes with seams at the front as they may chafe the child's toes.

Rubber boots should be large enough to allow your child to wear thick socks to keep his feet warm.

Dressing

By three most children can undress themselves, although they may still need help with small or tight buttons. Just how good your child is will depend not only on what you expect of him and encourage him to do but on his dexterity and general physical coordination. His persistence will count for a lot, too; at this age not many children can keep going at anything that is in any way complicated or takes more than a few moments. It's the age above all when nothing succeeds like success. With every little achievement encouragement abounds; any little failure brings near-paralyzing frustration.

As with everything else, children vary enormously in the age at which they accomplish different tasks. Some can barely manage to pull down a zipper at age four; others can dress themselves completely and do up the minutest buttons when they are three.

It really is essential to remain good humored when teaching your child to dress himself. Most children will want to do so as soon as they feel able—which will usually be well before they actually are. Let the child get on with it, however: your role is now to act as advisor and finisher. If you are in a hurry do not make the child feel helpless by rushing him beyond his capabilities; nor should you take over in a way that makes him feel inadequate. Explain that because you have to meet a deadline you must move in and help more actively—for the moment. Let him know that as he grows older he will need your help less and less.

If he is not going anywhere special you can leave his own efforts undisturbed, even if he looks a little disheveled. If you want him to look smarter you can help finish the process off, tucking in the garments in the right order, doing up all the buttons, and making sure that socks, sleeves, and overalls are not crazily twisted.

If as school age draws near, however, your child is still not dressing himself successfully, you will have to show him firmly how it is done. His teacher certainly won't appreciate it if she has to do every last thing for him.

A good way to encourage him is to make him completely responsible for the last garment on, and allow him to work backward as he gains mastery over each item of clothing.

As he gets better at playing constructively, the child is often very willing to help with household tasks. Most of the time the three- and four-year-old will be playing at doing what mommy does—mixing, rolling out pastry, and washing up. This may prove more of a hindrance than a help as he is likely to make a mess and get under your feet in the kitchen. While you naturally have to keep interference with your own work to the minimum, let the child copy and make as much mess as he pleases. He is learning and, most important of all, he is eager.

There are some jobs that a four-year-old can do that will genuinely help his mother. He can pick up his own clothes and put them into the laundry basket. He can put away his own toys, pick up grass cuttings, or help to clear the table—one item at a time! Setting the table will be beyond him for a year or two, but he can carry things to it.

These tasks, where he can see the results, are the kind a youngster performs best. He may also want to help with general cleaning— he should certainly help to clear up any mess he makes himself—but routine housework,

Helping around the house

where there is little visible result, will tire him quickly. Do not force him; he will not understand why it has to be done and you will probably put him off forever.

Putting his own toys away should be a well-established duty by about four—but he will still need you to be present to keep him at it. You don't have to badger him or issue stern orders. He is quite willing to do the donkeywork if you will only mastermind the operation, but with his short span of attention any job that lasts more than a few minutes without the kind of results *he* wants to see will bore him and he will start something else.

The results of a four-year-old's housework may not be immaculate, but do not discourage him by being exacting. He will enjoy helping you and the job can always be discreetly redone once he is out of the room.

How much sleep?

Getting a youngster to bed can be even more of a problem than it is with a toddler. As his active involvement in life grows, so does his determination to get the most out of it. It is during these years that you will first meet the "Can't I just finish this?" ploy, and the endless ruses and new ideas that he suggests to postpone the evil hour.

Nobody can say how much sleep each child should have. As the parent you will have to decide what your child needs and make sure he gets it. As a very rough guide you might take it that a five-year-old needs about twelve hours daily, so that if he gets up at seven-thirty in the morning, then his bedtime is seven-thirty at night. But this is no more than a guide. If your child needs more, then see that he gets it: if less, then do not force him.

Actually, it is doubtful whether you can force a child to sleep too much. If you send him to bed too early then either he will just not go to sleep, or he will get up too early next morning—and be tired too early the next evening. You can, however, let him stay up too late. Timing his bedtime is quite an art. The longer he is allowed to go beyond the time when he ought to be in bed, the less willing he will be to go.

When the child is overtired

Every mother, however good her management, will meet that crotchety feverish activity and irritable insistence that her child is not yet ready to go to bed. This is a sign that he is overtired.

Once a child reaches this stage, he requires the most tactful handling if matters are not to escalate to a really ugly showdown. He is busy asserting his independence. He has gotten beyond the stage of succumbing gracefully to tiredness at the end of the day, yet he is not old enough to be able to assess his feelings and say "enough."

So be firm—you are still the boss—but be kind and gentle. He has a good reason to stay up, for life at this age is almost all fun.

Setting a bedtime

You may find that setting a definite hour for bedtime helps to avoid arguments. "When both hands on the clock point downward it is time to go upstairs and start getting ready for bed," is a rule a child can understand long before he understands time itself, and it will prepare him for using the clock himself when he is older.

On the other hand it is a rare household in which such a rule can be rigidly applied. You may find it better to decide each night just when your child is ready for bed, bearing in mind the time he got up in the morning, what he has done during the day, and what time he has to get up the next day.

Many children, perhaps most, get through the day without a nap by the time they are three or four. There will always be days when your child will be more than usually tired—but too independent to volunteer to go to bed. Always watch for this: a tired youngster will usually respond to a suggestion at the right time.

Dreaming

During a dream the eyes flicker back and forth under the closed lids. Even week-old babies show such eye movements (Rapid Eye Movements, or REM for short) for up to a third of their sleeping time. What can a newborn baby dream about? Nothing very definite or vivid, presumably. It will not be many weeks, however, before you will be able to notice him twitching in his sleep—more evidence of dreaming.

As his understanding of the world grows, so, presumably, do his dreams grow clearer.

It is very unusual for a child under about four to be able to tell you about the dreams he has had in the night. Even then, to an adult they may sound like no more than the usual slightly bizarre imaginings of a child's adventurous mind.

Nightmares

Dreams do not require clear imagery to be frightening: what adult has not woken with some terrible, unformed, and nameless dread upon him? Such dreams are experienced by the child as well, quite early in life.

Toward the end of his second year a child may often stir and cry out in his sleep without wakening. If silence follows you can assume that this was a brief baby nightmare. In his third year a child may start to half-wake, occasionally, but will usually quickly go back to sleep. After another year or so he will sometimes half-wake in a state of considerable distress. He will still not be able to tell you what has frightened him, but it is a pretty safe guess that it was a nightmare.

As he grows toward five, and his mental development continues, he will start to have nightmares—as dreams—about actual events in his life, or about real fears arising out of something he has seen or heard.

When someone wakes in a state of fear for no clear reason he is said to be suffering from night terrors rather than nightmares. He often experiences a feeling of suffocation. Some psychoanalysts believe that this is due to memories of a difficult birth. Another theory is that as the sleeper moves from one stage of sleep to another his breathing becomes shorter and shallower, depriving the body of oxygen.

Many nightmares are directly due to fears aroused by some crisis in the child's life. The death of a close relative, failure at school, or a horrific scene on television can all cause anxiety that the child can suppress, but not resolve, during the day; it then re-emerges at night.

Old-fashioned threats, such as "If you do that the bogeyman will get you," are very likely to cause nightmares, as are any vague threats like "they'll take you away if . . .," or any form of superstitious belief. Children easily convert these into the goblins and witches they hear about in fairy tales. Some nervous children are more prone than others to turn such noises as the whining of cats or the flapping of a curtain at an open window into focuses for fear.

How to deal with nightmares

Often a child will call out once in his sleep and nothing more will be heard. When, at other times, his cries grow louder and come more frequently you must go to him. Often with a younger child you need do little more than cuddle him and murmur reassurance.

Although he may not wake fully, he will still respond to your comfort in his semi-somnolent state and will soon go contentedly back to sleep. This is probably all that is necessary for most night terrors.

If the child seems to be dreaming of something very frightening then you should waken him completely, to "break" the dream. Ask him what he was dreaming about, and encourage him to bring the dream up into the higher levels of consciousness. Show him that whatever was in his dream is not really there. One of my sons once woke complaining that the bones in his legs were bent; another time he thought there was a giant spider on his bed. In the first case I pulled back the bedclothes and showed him his legs and got him to feel them until he knew the bones were not bent; in the second case I made him look again and again at the end of the bed until he was satisfied that the spider was not there.

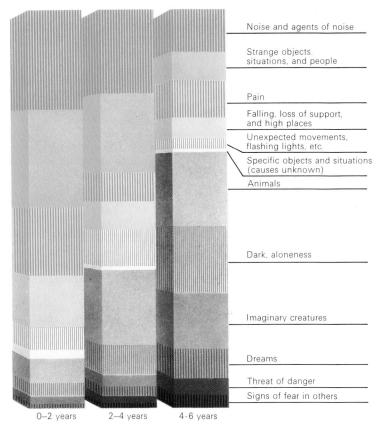

As children gain experience so the nature of their fears changes. A three-year-old who suffers horrors at the sight of a dog may have been quite oblivious to such animals as an infant. As children grow older they come to terms with many physical occurrences, such as loud noises or flashing lights, and the fears that increase are those that stem from their imagination or from their past experiences, such as the loss of a parent.

Noise and agents of noise

Strange objects, situations, and people

Pain

Falling, loss of support, and high places

Unexpected movements, flashing lights, etc.

Specific objects and situations (causes unknown)

Animals

Dark, aloneness

Imaginary creatures

Dreams

Threat of danger

Signs of fear in others

0–2 years   2–4 years   4-6 years

Occasionally a particularly stubborn image will recur, the child going to sleep and re-awakening in a few minutes with the same fear. In this case it is best to bring him out of the bedroom, give him a warm drink, and do whatever is necessary to break the dream. Let him go to sleep on the couch if necessary, and carry him back to bed when he is asleep.

Fear of the dark

Many children at this age are afraid of the dark, even if they were quite happy when they were younger. If this happens to your child give him a night-light, or leave the hall light on and his door ajar.

Bed-wetting

Every child will lapse occasionally from his normal dry state and wet the bed. Often these lapses are inexplicable and, if they are rare, there is no need to seek an explanation.

Boys generally take longer than girls to stay dry at night and are more likely to lapse. Bed-wetting runs in many families, showing that some as yet unexplained physical factor may be at work. This is almost always no more than a cause of delay and the problem will disappear in time.

There is a danger that a father who was savagely treated as a boy for wetting his own bed, or a mother who had a brother who was similarly treated, will, even though they may forget their own history, overreact to their own child's lapses.

Sometimes a child will start to wet his bed as a result of some new stress in his life, such as the arrival of a new brother or sister, a change of house, or an ill parent. If this happens to your child, treat it as a distress signal and give him even more comfort and reassurance than you do already. Buy a rubber or soft plastic sheet (make sure that it is soft, or the crackling may keep him awake) and put it on the mattress. A thick cotton mattress pad goes on the rubber sheet to soak up the urine. It need not be best quality; one made out of an old sheet doubled over will do. Use bed linen that is easily washed and needs little ironing, and always keep a change of sheets and pajamas handy.

Make it clear to him that this is a practical measure; do not let him feel ashamed, or you will make the problem worse. Where there is a clear cause, the episode will pass. If it continues for more than a few weeks or if it starts for no apparent reason you should consult your doctor.

Apart from trying to alleviate any psychological stress that may be causing the wetting very little else needs to be done. Medical treatments are usually kept for older children.

Thumb-sucking

There is nothing wrong with thumb-sucking. Many children do it for sheer pleasure, and why stop them? It is true sometimes that the comfort the child needs is a reflection of an insecure home. A little contemplation on your part should tell you if this is why he persists in this habit.

If your child is still sucking his thumb at five he could possibly displace his front teeth, especially if he tends to pull forward against them. This may mean that when the permanent teeth come through later, they may also be out of place. If you fear that this is happening, consult your dentist.

Washing

Your child may have been washing his hands and face since late in his second year, although this is more usual with girls than with boys. Plenty of children, however, still need a good deal of coaching. They need to be shown how to use a washcloth, to be told to run the taps to get water of the right temperature (cold water in first), to take the soap out of the water, and to rinse out the washbowl afterward. Good teaching now will pay dividends later. Washing is a skill like everything else and the better a child is at it the less of a chore it will be, and the less reluctance there will be to wash, say, before meals.

Bath time will still be fun time, especially if he joins in with a younger or older brother or sister—but don't let the fun detract from the basic purpose of getting clean.

By the time he is three your child's health record should be clear. If his checkups at six weeks, three months, six months, and one year have all shown him to be developing well and healthily, you need only have him checked once a year after this. If you are lucky, your family doctor or pediatrician will advise you when to come, and how often. A more usual practice is for the doctor to give a child a general checkup whenever he sees him for a cold or flu or some other complaint.

Failing this, or if your child never has anything wrong with him and so never goes near a doctor, you still ought to ask for annual checkups, at least around his third and fifth birthdays. Just before starting school is a good time to go to ensure that your child is not suffering from some latent infection or contagion.

A simple check of height and weight and a talk with the mother can tell a doctor a good deal about a child's over-all state of health. He may test eyesight, hearing, reflexes, and

Checkups

The terror a child may feel at the sight of a dentist and his equipment (which may occur because he senses your own fear) can often be dispelled by a social visit.

physical coordination for defects that have escaped notice. If the doctor does not do so routinely you may want to ask for the tests. Not many parents do this, but when they reach school or even later a few children are found to have minor handicaps which could have been detected earlier. Defective vision or a hearing defect can retard a child's intellectual development and make him appear less bright than he really is.

Booster shots
Booster shots for some immunizations (diphtheria, tetanus, and polio) are given when a child is about five years old. Your doctor will advise you on this.

Teeth care
If you help your child clean his teeth punctiliously every evening, and look inside his mouth each time to make sure that the job has been done properly, you may be able to see for yourself if any caries (cavities) develop. If they do, you must take him to the dentist. However, you cannot see between the teeth, and you may feel it advisable to institute regular checkups anyway. It is certainly best if his first visit involves no treatment, but allows him to familiarize himself with the room, the chair, the equipment, and the figure in the white coat bending low over him and peering into his mouth.

Some children are more susceptible to caries than others; the susceptibility is inherited. But even in these children bad teeth can be kept to a minimum if the amount of sugar intake is kept down. Fluoridation of community water is also helpful. This does not mean depriving them altogether: you can insure that the first course of each meal is substantial enough so that they want only a small helping of dessert. Give them lightly sweetened fruit drinks instead of highly sweetened artificial pop drinks, Try to avoid cola drinks altogether because they contain phosphoric acid, which attacks the enamel surface of the teeth and increases the likelihood of caries.

Do not let your child suck candy endlessly, but retain it for treats. (You will be doing his figure a favor, too.) It is not only the amount of sugar that he consumes but also its persistence in his mouth that causes caries.

Teaching road safety
The unconditional rule is that a very young child should never be by himself on a street where there is traffic. This may mean confinement to the apartment or suburban house and yard. Sooner or later, you will have to let him use the sidewalk to get from his house to visit his friends up and down the street. So let him go along once you have judged that he will be sensible about not setting foot off the sidewalk into the road, and not wandering off. If you make your rules clear, and show that you trust him and admire him for keeping them, then he should be safe for short periods of time on the sidewalks of quiet streets.

Even when he notices a car, a young child cannot estimate the speed of traffic. He is all

too likely to rush headlong into the road. So the rule about not stepping into the road by himself must be absolutely cast-iron.

When you are out with him, keep him close to your side all the time, and in busy conditions hold his hand firmly. Never let him cross any road by himself, unless it is a remote country road—and then it should be in full sight of yourself until he is seven or so. When you have to cross the road talk him through it as you go:

"Now we've got to cross the road, but not here because the traffic is coming too fast, and we cannot see properly because of that parked car. Let's go up there to the crossing. Now we are coming to the curb: we stop, we look left, look right, then left again; then listen; anything coming? No? All right, off we go—but walk, don't run. Keep listening and looking all around as we cross."

Give longer explanations about looking all around repeatedly at wide and difficult crossings.

With a good firm grounding like this your child stands a much better chance of surviving the horrible annual carnage on the roads.

As young children are often confused by traffic, they should never be allowed out into the road alone. You should teach them where and how to cross the road safely as well as explaining the meaning of traffic lights and signals and the way in which pedestrians can use them as guides.

Discipline and affection

It used to be said that the best way of disciplining a child was to withdraw your love and approval. If this is done in the right way it is undoubtedly effective. But what is the right way? The advice could be no more than a recipe for emotional blackmail, which could do the child more damage than anything else.

It is important that your own emotions are genuine. If you feel anger, let your child know, and do not bottle it up because it is "not nice." If you disapprove of what your child has done, of course you must make this plain—but be sure he understands that you have not ceased to love him. If you throw your love into the ring as a bargaining point, you may find that you have lost his, and that he feels he has nothing further to lose. More-

over, you are failing in your own role as parent if you behave childishly yourself.

A time-honored way of disciplining a stubborn child is to send him out of the room, to his own room. This restriction can be extremely effective as a last resort and as a short-term measure. Do not leave him banished for long. Make it plain why you are doing it, and what he must do in order to come out. When he has calmed down and undertaken to be good, let him out at once and make friends again. Above all do not make the physical banishment into an emotional one.

This is the age when your child is just beginning to stand up for himself. This method allows him to do so. Spanking does not, and you should have dropped it except

A five-year-old looking at this drawing would probably have no difficulty in understanding that there are more red flowers than there are blue. But if you were then to ask him whether there were more red flowers than flowers he could be confused and say there were. The fact that they are all the same thing despite their different colors is an abstraction that is beyond him.

If you put a set of counters of different shapes and sizes into a bag and ask a three- or four-year-old to take out four that are all the same, you are quite likely to be offered a collection like the one on the right. His mind works like this: the first pair are both yellow, so they are the same; the next pair are both triangles, so they are the same; the third pair are both red, so they are the same; and the last pair are both squares, so they are the same; so they are all the same, aren't they?

Left: If you show a four-year-old a toy car and a trailer, put them into a tube, and then turn the tube over end-to-end a couple of times, he will have no idea whether the car will emerge from the tube forward or backward. He cannot make the picture of the car and trailer in his mind do mental somersaults at the same time as the real ones do. Even when you mark one end of the tube so that he can follow the turns, he cannot visualize the car turning within the tube. When he is six or seven he will be able to do what you do, which is to form an abstract principle: that if you "drive" the car into the unmarked end it will always emerge from the marked end forward.

Below: No young child is safe on the road, however sensible and self-controlled he may be. Not only can he not judge the speed of cars, but he misjudges them in such a way as to put himself into danger. The way in which children judged the relative speeds of these trains shows why. The trains started and stopped at the same time, but one (A) traveled only half the distance traveled by the other (B). Most of the children thought that the faster train (B) was the slower, reasoning that it took longer to make its journey because it went farther. Applied to moving traffic this reasoning would have disastrous consequences.

in extreme cases of deliberate provocation by the time he is four or five.

How understanding develops

A child not yet old enough to go to school cannot separate the world into all its different parts, but he can half-grasp the idea that different things of the same kind are somehow the same thing. His confusion and comprehension are perfectly illustrated by an event recorded by the Swiss psychologist Jean Piaget. He was out walking with his daughter when they saw a snail on the path. A little farther on they saw another snail, and she said, "There's that snail again." Piaget asked her if it was the same snail and she replied "Yes." He took her back and showed her the first snail and she repeated that it was the same one.

However, he then asked her, "Is it another one?" and she again said "Yes," showing that she was struggling between the idea that there were two snails and the idea that all snails were the same snail.

During this period the child is only just beginning to understand cause and effect. He realizes intuitively that hitting a ball with a bat will make it roll, but anywhere above this simple level his grasp is precarious. This is one reason why a small child has such difficulty in playing an organized game. Although he may know that two events go together, he has no idea which is cause and which is effect. For example, suppose your two children have a fight and one comes to you crying. Your conversation might go like this:

"What's the matter?"

"John hit me."

"Why?"

" 'Cause I'm crying."

Between three and five a child is making great strides in understanding things of this sort, and you will probably notice changes almost every day as the sophistication of his thinking grows. Do not expect too much, however. You cannot make a small child grown up when he just does not have the mental equipment. If you try to force him into an adult way of doing and saying things, you will simply restrict his activities and inhibit the joyous interaction between you.

Although he is beginning to develop his own ideas about the world he lives in, these are still simple, and a child is not good at thinking things out. He finds it difficult to comprehend events that he knows are taking place but he cannot see. He is as yet unable to think in the abstract.

But he is developing his power of thought. In fact his own fantasy world uses those elements which he has securely absorbed. But he has little control over reality (to which his fantasies may bear scant resemblance). He cannot yet answer the question "What if?" in any reliable sense. For instance, he has only the vaguest idea of what would happen if a car hit him. And he is unable to master the problem of negotiating traffic because he cannot do the calculations that are needed to estimate whether or not an approaching car will hit him as he crosses the road.

A youngster cannot conceive that other people have thoughts and viewpoints of their own. So when his father comes home in the evening and asks him what he has been doing all day, he may find that the child can say very little. Two things frustrate the child's willingness to please. First the here-and-now nature of his thinking. His recall is not good; he can remember his friend Tom, but not to order. With an effort he will recall charging around the hall on his tricycle, or the ice cream he ate on the way home, but in no great detail.

Second, when he can remember perfectly clearly, he finds it difficult to understand that the memory is his and his alone. He is puzzled that his father does not know the obvious. This difficulty will take him years to get over. (Even some adults are not very good at explaining things because they cannot put themselves in the shoes of someone who does not know what they know.)

However, his alertness to his immediate surroundings makes the young child a delightful companion on a walk or an outing. Instantly responding to every new thing that catches his interest, he will spot much that you miss, and be fascinated and attracted by objects long taken for granted by you, giving you a new pleasure.

And as he grows from three to five, so will his memory improve. He will become better able to describe outings when he gets home and perhaps, if he is good at drawing, he will draw some of the things he has seen. (The resemblance may seem remote to you, but he will know what he sees in his work.)

Up to the age of about six a child cannot properly understand the world except as he sees it at any one time. When he goes along in his parents' car the sun goes along with him; the dog that frightened him in the street a minute ago is the only dog in the world, and he cannot understand why you ask "which dog?"

However, egocentric as they are, most children are not egoistic—they are extremely generous and will naturally share, to the best of their ability, any candy or toys they are given—as long as their own status is not being threatened (boys are more proprietorial and territorial).

Sharing is not easy for a child, even when he wants to be fair. His problems arise quite simply from a lack of understanding. Research has shown that to understand contrasts such as bigger/smaller, longer/shorter, and thicker/thinner, a child first has to learn the idea of quantity—that three, five, or eight apples all mean some apples, and that a rod has thickness, whether it is $\frac{1}{2}$ in or 1 in across. While he is still learning this, the child is unable to understand the concept of "more" and "less."

At the next stage the child gets the idea that "more" and "less" mean a change in quantity, length, or size, but he still confuses the two words, always plumping for the positive end of the scale, so that less equals more. Finally

Trouble with remembering

The world as the child sees it

Grasping the idea of quantity

he comes to understand that "How long is it?" is basically the same question as "How short is it?" and that both mean *What length has it*? Little wonder that sharing candy equally is not always easy for a youngster!

Why? Why? Why?

Many children of about four drive their parents to distraction by continually asking "Why?" Sometimes you can give a simple answer.

"Why are you cutting the meat?"

"I'm getting it ready for cooking."

Some children are not satisfied with this. "Why?" they want to know. "So we can eat it," you explain, with infinite patience. "Why?" comes the inexorable query, until you feel like screaming.

Because he has just grasped the concept of cause and effect, he jumps to the conclusion that everything has a cause. He's not quite sure yet what a cause is, still less that many things do not have real causes. What you dismiss as an accident, or as something with a thousand causes too complicated to analyze, the child believes must have a simple explanation. And so his questions go on and on. You just have to be patient. Try to answer when you can give a reason for what you are doing, or for whatever natural phenomenon (like snow) he is seeking to have explained. Try to make it honestly clear when you cannot explain, or that there is no comprehensible explanation. If he persists he may merely be trying your temper, so do not lose it; just let him know that you are too busy to answer any more questions for the time being.

Learning about right and wrong

A child of three has no idea of "right" and "wrong"—indeed, he is only just beginning to understand this at five. All the three-year-old knows is that there are some things he may not do. For example, a child may learn quite early, as soon as he begins to walk, that he must not touch the stove. He will learn separately not to go near the fire. Not until later, perhaps about four, will he come to realize that fireplaces and stoves are in the same class of things—those that contain fire, are hot, and will burn.

Drawing on the walls is something practically every toddler tries at least once, and may go on doing for a long time. To him one blank surface is as good as another, so if he can draw on paper, why not on walls? Even if you are lucky enough to make him quickly learn that walls are not for drawing on, you may still find scribbles on your books and letters.

Gradually the child begins to put together all that he is not allowed to do, and gets the idea of rules. This first glimmering of "morality" appears at about four or five. He still does not have a sense of right and wrong, for rules at this age are almost entirely prohibitions, things he must not do. Psychologists call this the "premoral" stage, because if you ask a child why he should not do something, he answers that he will be punished if he does. He has no grasp of the principles underlying the rules.

That is no reason, however, why you should not explain why he ought to do this or ought not to do that. While it is wrong to expect standards of behavior and thought of which your child is not yet capable, it is equally wrong to write him off with some dismissive thought, such as, "Oh, he's only a child, he can't understand." You should prepare him for when he can. At the crudest, you can teach him the idea of tit-for-tat. "How would you like it if...?" —though even this level of reasoning requires a grasp of cause and effect which is beyond many five-year-old children.

What is important is that you teach him that what he does matters, that you care about his behavior, and that other people are affected by his deeds. If he learns this now, he is well prepared to absorb all the theory when he is ready for it, and to behave himself well in childhood, adolescence, and adulthood.

As awareness grows, the difference between the two sexes becomes more significant to a child. At around three, a child will want the difference he can see explained. This is the age at which Freud thought that two complexes central to his theories—castration anxiety in boys and penis envy in girls—were laid down. If these do appear later in life, it is probably because the facts were hidden from the child at this age—one at which a child

Sexual curiosity

Some finishing touches, then the masterpiece will be completed to the satisfaction of the child but to the horror of his mother. During those early years most children will experiment with wall painting and will find it hard to understand that wallpaper is not for drawing on. Perhaps the best method of discouragement is simply to give him plenty of alternative materials with which he can satisfy his artistic urges.

may be puzzled by what he or she sees as a lack or an extra. A child may seek reassurance that all is as it should be.

The difference may have to be explained many times. Remember, he is curious, but his understanding is limited. "Boys and daddies have penises, girls and mommies don't" is something you will hear over and over again —unless you stifle the question. This is what happened in the past, often, according to the Freudians, causing problems, and it is still not always easy to be as frank with our children as we know we ought to be.

By about four a child will also be asking, "Where did I come from?" and "Where was I before I was in your tummy?" The best answer is the truth. You do not have to

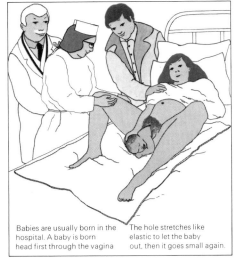

A well-illustrated children's book is a good way of preparing a child for the arrival of a younger brother or sister.

Babies are usually born in the hospital. A baby is born head first through the vagina

The hole stretches like elastic to let the baby out, then it goes small again.

personalize it—an outline of the general principles is all that is needed at the moment. He will add the personal element in his own time. Good books with tactful pictures in the style of children's books are available, and they will help. If you introduce these into your child's ordinary bedtime reading, he will accept the information in a natural way, which will save, rather than cause, embarrassment in the long run.

Coping with sexuality

Although sexuality means nothing to the young child, its emotional side begins to manifest itself. Most children form a special relationship with the parent of the opposite sex. This is particularly true of fathers and daughters. There may be a biological basis to this, but it is mostly a reflection of our culture. Such favoritism is harmful only if it divides the parents or other children and becomes so intense as to distort the child's relations with the opposite sex in adulthood.

The most important thing for a parent to remember is not to suppress his child's sexuality or—on the other hand—respond to it. The line between the two is not an easy one. But if you want a secure and balanced child it is a line you must tread.

Starting real sentences

Once a child has become fluent with his two-word "sentences" he moves on to three words, starting to express two ideas in the

same "sentence." At first this is difficult, and he will hesitate and grope around for the next part of what he wants to say.

Moving on to real sentences, with different parts of speech expressing complex ideas, is an even greater challenge. Again, the child's understanding often runs a long way ahead of his speech. The result can sound strange, but they often have a poetry all of their own. My three-year-old, laughing with delight as a sudden summer breeze stirred his hair and tickled his skin, once remarked: "It did winding me!" An adult would understandably be perplexed when a toddler ventured, "Anything is not to break, only plates and glasses," when he meant, "Nothing is breakable except plates and glasses."

Learning the rules of language

Many of the oddities of children's speech may sound like mistakes to you. In fact, from the child's point of view, if anyone is making a mistake it is you. All language works according to a set of rules, and there is not a language in the world where all the rules stay the same all the time. A child first has to learn that there are rules, and then work out what the rules are. And it will be a long time after that before he can cope with the exceptions to the rules—the irregular parts of correct grammar.

As he grows older and links the idea of the present with that of the past, and at the same time begins to understand about rules of speech, he may change from the correct irregular form, which he has learned by rote, to an incorrect one, which follows the rule. So a child who at two says "It broke" may at three change to "It breaked." Similarly, a child who has learned to use the irregular plural "feet" may later change of his own accord to "foots."

Mistakes such as these may cause alert parents, anxious that their child should make good progress, to think he is regressing. Far from being evidence of this, they are proof that he is advancing.

Problems with questions

If you have a child who is perpetually asking questions it may be hard for you to appreciate that forming a question rightly is one of the hardest things for the young child to sort out.

Many questions in English start with what is called a "wh-" word—the six honest serving men that taught Rudyard Kipling's child all he knew—what and why and when, how and where and who. A three-year-old, perceiving that merely putting one of these words onto the beginning of a sentence makes it into a question, will frame his questions in odd ways. For instance he may say "What you can see?" It takes some time for him to learn that he must also either turn the next two words around or, to put it in the past tense, change a word. In fact, not only are most three-year-old children unable to form questions such as "What did you see?," but they do not understand them when they hear them. This may account in part for their difficulty in answering many of the questions adults put to them. Negative questions may cause

Games with words and pictures

By the time your child reaches the age of three he may have acquired a considerable vocabulary and quite a flair for forming sentences. But children need practice, and through talking and listening to your child you will encourage him to communicate and explore with language. Games with words and pictures will make language seem to be fun as well as useful. As his understanding improves he can be initiated into the world of books, but remember that rather than teaching your child how to read you should teach him to want to read. It is very important that he should arrive at school enchanted by the idea of books and keen to decipher their words by himself. You can, however, help him with the foundations of his later learning.

He may want to be able to recognize and write his own name or the name of some familiar objects; he may enjoy playing with letters, learning that they represent different sounds. Remember, however, that children develop at their own speed and that pushing a reluctant child may simply alienate him from the whole idea of books, hampering his capacity to learn when he reaches school.

Puppets provide a chance for young children to practice language as well as conversation. They can carry on a dialogue with a favorite character from a book or television.

Below : Use a scrapbook to house some of his favorite pictures. Then label each picture to familiarize him with the words, their length and shape.

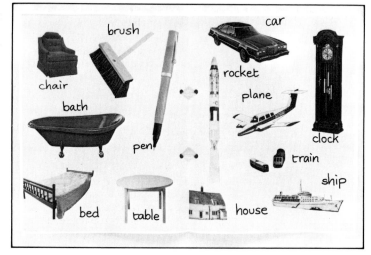

Right : Cut out large letters from different materials so that your child can really come to grips with the alphabet! He will come to know what the letters look like, what sounds some of them represent, and how some can spell his name.

Left : All children like to hear stories over and over again. This is an important part of their learning, so you should give them a balanced diet of familiar stories interspersed with some new material.

In the familiar stories, children will begin to recognize some shorter words if you point them out while you read. Before you start a stringent campaign to teach him to read you should find out what method will be used when he reaches his school.

them even more trouble, and can result in such delightful eccentricities as, "Why not cracker can't talk?"

All these little local language difficulties will disappear in most children by the time they reach five, certainly by six. Many of them are due to an immature brain having difficulties in transforming thoughts into speech, so that if your child starts speaking very late—and some do not really get going until they are four—he will probably skip many of these temporary difficulties and become fluent all in a rush. The progress a child makes between three and six in understanding and communication is truly enormous. Indeed, considering the complexities involved, it is awe-inspiring, and thus a privilege and a considerable pleasure for parents to watch.

The reserved child

Some children are very reserved and speak very little. If your child is one of these, don't leap to the conclusion that he is slow or retarded. He may just be taciturn. Many preschool children, however, delight in their newfound expressiveness, and they will chatter contentedly to themselves for long periods, providing a running commentary on their own play. Some children will happily include you in their "conversation," as long as it is on their own terms. Others will already make more of a distinction between their private world of fantasy and make-believe and the real world, and will become self-conscious and stop their monologuing if they notice anyone listening, especially their father, whose presence is usually (and sadly) more unusual and so more conspicuous.

If you have a child who is a good talker but who is shy, you may catch a glimpse of his enchanted world if you listen from time to time outside the door.

Shyness with strangers

It sometimes happens that a child who talks happily and loquaciously in one situation will be struck almost dumb in another. He may talk well to other children but not to grownups, speak freely to you but not to his teacher or to strangers.

While the strong silent type can achieve a great deal in life, there is no doubt that your child will find success more easily as an adult if he can communicate fluently.

If you find that your child is one who is tongue-tied with strangers, try to draw him into any conversations you have with people he does not know. Perhaps he can be the one to tell an acquaintance where the family went on vacation, or what is happening at the building site around the corner.

Talking with your child

Get your child to tell you about things he has done away from home: an afternoon visit to a grandparent, to nursery school, or to a friend. When he is still three he will have difficulty in remembering and in transforming his memories into words, but if he becomes used to the idea that what he has done is important to you he will be more ready to talk about his experiences when he is old

enough to do so. So when he gropes for the memory of what he did three hours ago and for the way to describe it, gives up, and says he did nothing, do not give up too: ask a new question. In a year or two he will be full of what his teacher or his best friend did.

Whenever you help him or show him how to do something new, talk to him about what you are doing. Tell him in detail your every move, whether you are dressing him, mixing pastry under his watchful eye, or making sure you have enough money in your purse to pay the milkman.

If you want him to do something that he does not want, explain your reasons to him. This is not because you need to negotiate with him—he is still too young for the complexities of bargaining—but because it is a good idea to introduce him to using language to negotiate with. If by the time he is five he is beginning to find that he can use words to persuade his parents to allow him to do something, he is more likely to use language instead of rage or force later in life as a way of expressing his own will.

It cannot be stressed too much that children acquire language at an individual rate, which varies considerably. Only if a child's speech appears unusually delayed and his comprehension uncertain is there legitimate cause for concern. If he is very late in talking, perhaps still using two-word sentences at four years old, you should consult with your doctor. He may refer you to a speech therapist or some other consultant. Occasionally, a child who says very few words between two and three starts to talk later, quite suddenly, coming out with whole sentences. There is some evidence to show that later children in a family are slower to begin speaking but this is not always so.

Late talkers

Eyes, hands, and facial expressions are another form of language that your child will learn. Through watching adults he will grasp many of their subtleties.

Stuttering

Stuttering is quite common between the ages of two and a half and six; a child has so much to say that his thoughts race ahead of his ability to express them. Most children soon grow out of it. Some even pretend to stammer. The years between three and five are a great time for experimenting, and if your own child hears a real stammerer, he may try to imitate him just for effect. In this case you should let him know that you recognize what he is up to, but do so gently. If you bully him you may increase the stammer.

If you are concerned about your child's stammer, take him to your doctor. Speech therapy has improved greatly in the last ten years, and the problem is much more easily corrected in childhood than later.

A lisp is not a speech problem, for it does not affect expression and understanding. If it is bad, however, it may make a child a target for teasing at school. If you fear this ask your doctor to advise you. Many lisps and other difficulties, such as those with the letter "r," disappear in time.

The short attention span

Although at this age children can spend a long time playing intermittently with something that interests them, their attention span is very short. In the days when children were regarded as rather inadequate miniature adults this was thought of as almost a moral fault or a defect of character. Now we know that being able to think about something or tackle a job for a long period of time is an ability that comes with maturity and practice.

You will notice that your child makes huge strides in this during the years from three to five or six. One study found that the length of time a child will stick at one thing doubles from less than five minutes to nearly ten. Jigsaws show well how this span of attention grows. At three he will be able to manage one with only a few pieces which fit together easily and with a picture in bold outline and strong colors so that it is clear where each part belongs. By six he will be able to assemble one with smaller, though not too intricate, pieces and with a rather less strikingly simple illustration.

At the age of three a child needs to pass on from one occupation to another quite quickly, particularly if you give him something to do rather than letting him choose what he does. However, it is easy to underestimate what a child of three can do. He may attend to one

Children are often tired and grumpy at the end of the day after hours of play and excitement. Suddenly every game, every action can be a grueling task. To help your child unwind, encourage him to sit quietly for a short time before putting him to bed. This is a good time for a story; your attention is what he needs.

thing for only a few minutes, or even a few seconds—but he will come back to it again and again, and so keep at it in short bursts for a much longer period.

The agile mind

Most three-year-olds will at some time or another treat you to a commentary on what they are doing. This frequently provides a delightful insight into the workings of their minds, as they hop from one subject to another with bewildering rapidity. This is not a mark of stupidity, but an indication of just how clever they are, for often they will bring three or four different subjects into one brief monologue or conversation. These different subjects will not be mentioned just once and then forgotten; the child will jump backward and forward from one topic to another with little apparent connection.

During the preschool years the child increases his mastery both of language and of any job he has to do. One morning, one of my sons, then about four and a half, was asked by his father to clear the lawn in the afternoon so that it could be cut in the evening. At six-thirty father came home from work to find the lawn all ready, and a very proud son.

"I cleared it all away without asking," said my son.

"Without being asked," gently corrected his father.

"I cleared it all away without being asked," answered this small boy, after a slight pause while he absorbed the correction, thoroughly on top of the world.

It was true that he had not been asked, although he had been prompted when I started the clearing job myself. Whereupon he remembered his father's request and continued the job. This sort of initiative is a great step forward for a child, and my son was right to be proud.

Reading

Some parents are very impatient for their child to learn to read and write. Then, having spent great effort in producing a certain level of achievement in the child, they are shocked to find that they are unpopular with the teacher when the child starts school.

Only in the last twenty years or so have we begun to realize what a complicated skill reading is, and that, if a child is not started right, he may learn bad habits that handicap him later. If your child is exceptionally bright or is good with language and learns with ease,

then you certainly should not hinder him; but neither would it be right to force a child who is not ready. He will learn at school. Teaching him earlier serves no good purpose, and the task may interfere with the freer fantasy and play which are so valuable at this age.

What you can and should do is to help your child toward "reading readiness." When you read to him take the time sometimes to follow the words with your finger. Get him used to the idea of words on paper representing the words he hears in the story. Include some books that are for learning to read. These take certain letters and sounds and

repeat them in different "key words." Without making it hard work, point this out to him. Make a guessing game of which word on a page is the same as the key word on the preceding page.

You can also introduce him to the idea of letters. Modern reading methods use only lower-case (small) letters, which are called not by their names but by the sounds they make (the phonic method): "a" as in apple, "c" as in cow, and so on. Do not teach him the alphabet by rote; this might hinder him from reading whole words later. If your child has a general idea that signs on paper mean certain things, and that certain signs look a certain way and go together, he will have an enormous advantage when he starts school, and will have an early feeling of success.

If, however, you are anxious for your child to learn to read early, or if he has the aptitude, you should visit the school he will be going to and find out how reading is taught, so that you can use the same method, and not handicap him by making him change abruptly at the age of five. The best way to prepare your child for reading is to read to him yourself. Make him familiar with books and with the pleasure they can bring. If you make two or three stories out of books part of the bedtime ritual, you catch the child when he is apt to be ready to sit and listen. You can establish a calm, intimate, and happy atmosphere, which puts reading in the context of an enjoyment, rather than making it a chore—such an activity will also put him in the right frame of mind to turn over and go to sleep quickly when you have finished! If you set this pattern you need not hurry your child into reading; he will learn with a will when he is ready.

What are numbers for?

Some children arrive at school quite capable of reciting the numbers up to ten or more but with little idea of what the numbers mean. When teaching your child to count make him understand that numbers represent actual objects. Let him count the number of buttons on his shirt, or the number of chairs in a room; play number games with him so that he learns to recognize figures and the numbers that they represent. This way he will learn that numbers are not simply sounds to be recited like a nursery rhyme.

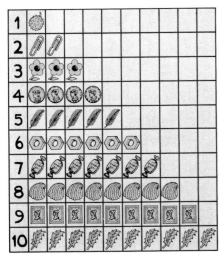

Left : Let your child collect a selection of objects and then help him stick them onto a wall chart. Make sure, though, that the child can see clearly that with each successive number there is one more object. Once the wall chart has been built, it will be an indispensable reference.

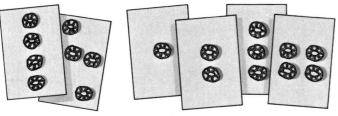

Below : Make two or three sets of cards representing the numbers one to ten. Play games with your child, matching pairs, ordering, and discovering missing numbers.

Left : Cut numbers and animals out of felt and cover a board with flannel. Put a number on the board and ask your child to stick on the appropriate number of animals. Alternatively, ask him to find the number that corresponds with the figures that you have placed on the board.

Writing

Your child will probably spontaneously produce lines of scribble or little symbols that he will call writing. He will be pleased and encouraged by your enthusiastic response. You can introduce him to real writing by getting him to copy his name or the message in his own birthday card to his grandmother or best friend. Write down the titles he gives to his drawings, so that he can copy them underneath. In writing, as in reading, the parent's job is to prepare the child for the learning he will do at school.

Counting

We take counting so much for granted that we forget what a strange process it is. Your child will probably learn to recite the numbers long before he can actually count. Do not be dismayed when the child who can recite one to ten or even further fails to count five chocolate candies in a row. He has to learn that the numbers "stick" onto things in strict order. Even when he seems to grasp this it may be by a careful process of following the sequence of number names. You can test whether he can really count by asking him to bring you three candies or five blocks.

The value of play

An authority once described play as any activity that is not obligatory, or that does not have a useful result. Neither of these descrip-

Which books are best?

One of the most important attitudes you can impart to your child is a love of books. To do this, encourage the idea that within the pages of a book lie exciting worlds and events. He will enjoy sitting on your lap, getting all your attention, and a cuddle too, while you read to him and show him the pictures as you go along. However, try not to make it a chore either for him or for you.

Choose stories that are simple and direct, where the text and pictures complement each other so that the child can pick out the story line for himself. With his egocentric view and limited awareness of life, he will be left behind by stories that stray too far from his experience or are too elaborate. Playing in the park, washing his face, eating his supper, or going shopping with his mother are all situations a child can recognize.

Before a child can read, the illustrations are a vital part of any book. The images must

Above : Pictures showing things from unusual angles may confuse a young child, whose perception is not yet mature enough to understand visual representations of real life.

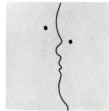

Above : Four- to five-year-olds tend to see only a single face here, where older children would see the two faces.

Below : While younger children would see only the fruit, older children would be able to see a clown's face as well.

Left : As the child's horizons broaden and his imagination develops, he becomes aware of ways of life other than his own. He will enjoy books with illustrations such as this that extend beyond his immediate environment as long as they are linked to his own activities.

be simple and uncluttered, as too much detail will distract the child from the main action and he will not be able to take it all in. It is easier if all the pictures show a child's view of the world—he may be confused by a bird's-eye view.

Understanding perspective is one of the skills we take for granted, but to a young child apparently straightforward pictures can be very confusing. As his grasp of perspective grows, he will be able to appreciate more and more complicated illustrations. Cartoons are particularly enjoyed because they are two-dimensional and exaggerate the important aspects of characters and situations.

Later on, your child can enjoy less mundane stories, such as fantasy and adventure tales. He will love stories that are full of suspense and come to an exciting climax—and preferably have a happy conclusion.

It is not easy to realize when a book is too advanced for your child, especially if he likes the intimacy of reading time. You'll know the books he enjoys most because he will want you to read them again and again.

Above : The child's growing independence will bring him increasingly up against adult wishes, often resulting in feelings of frustration. The world of fantasy is one place where the child can hold his own. He can identify with a child who, in the book, is in charge of monsters like those of his own imagination, and, like him, learn that there is always a road back when it all becomes too frightening.

Above left : A story showing lovable characters with whom the child can identify can also teach him more about the real world.

tions applies to children's play. Children have an inbuilt drive to explore, experiment, and pretend—to play. And the results are decidedly useful because for children playing is learning.

First, there is straightforward physical play. As the child's muscles develop and his strength grows, he needs to be constantly finding out what he can do and practicing his new capabilities. Children are constantly on the go, running, climbing, cycling, rolling on top of each other, usually with what seems like a nonstop shout. It is all wearing for the parents—but essential for the child.

Building and making things also reflect physical development and growth—the increasing ability to manipulate and control

objects using fingers, hands, wrists, arms, and often the whole body. Mastery and achievement in these skills is never a waste. Later in life he will be more confident and self-assured if he is allowed full rein in his play now. So, even if you are not athletic types yourselves, encourage your child to be physically active.

Almost more important than physical play is the fantasy play of the child's mind. In a natural, spontaneous, uncontrived way a child leads a most elaborate life in his imagination. Do not dismiss this as "mere" fantasy. He is trying things out mentally as he does physically. When my son came home from nursery school and announced in a matter-of-

The importance of fantasy

Above : This aerial view of a town at night may well appeal to the eye of an older child, but it contains far too much detail—none of which is very clearly outlined—for a youngster to analyze.

fact way that the place had burned down and that he had been rescued by a fireman, I did not need to guess that the story was rather a long way from the truth. But I entered into the spirit of the play for a few moments, and asked how many firemen there had been, whether anyone had been hurt, and so on. Finally I said "It didn't really burn down, did it?" and he answered "No," in an almost thankful tone of voice. He was glad to have me help him sort out the difference between fact and fantasy.

At other times it is harder to tell whether a story is true or not. Sometimes my sons would own up to things I knew they had not done. It made it easier to keep calm when on other occasions one blamed his brother for something I knew he himself *had* done. It helps a child if you sometimes point out that fairy tales and other such fantastic stories are only stories and not really true.

Make-believe play and toys

It is children's powers of fantasy which make simple toys so much better. My four-year-old son was just as happy with an L-shaped piece of wood for a gun as he was with a replica six-shooter. (Later, of course, he grew to want the more realistic version.)

Make-believe reaches a peak when a child is about four, and lasts for several years. It is an essential way for a child to explore ideas and sides of the world of which he has no direct experience. Lengthy games of mother and father prepare him for his own family later. Playing at doctors or soldiers helps a child to understand roles which he sees performed by other people, and which he may fill himself when he has grown up.

Acting out helps many children to go over experiences they may not have understood fully, especially frightening and unpleasant happenings. A child will give medicine to a "sick" doll, or busily bandage up a teddy that has supposedly been injured in a car crash. A crash might be recreated with toy cars and blocks by a child who has been involved in one, or who has lost a friend.

A child does not need to have direct experience to indulge in this kind of play. Indeed, this is one area where the rehearsal side of fantasy is particularly valuable. A child can make-believe being frightened, and this is good preparation for later life. In today's world anxiety is part of everyday experience.

Two two-year-olds playing in the same room are not really playing together. Each is engaged in an activity which he might just as well be doing on his own. This is known as parallel play. There will be brief interactions, although in many cases one child may merely be grabbing a toy from the other.

By the age of three children are beginning to play together—for very short periods. They will briefly exchange toys, or compare them, and one will join in the other's game, fleetingly. But three-year-olds are still not

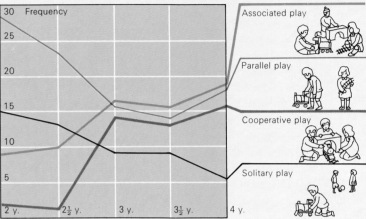

good at coping with more than one playmate at a time. They may copy one another, but doing the same thing is not the same as cooperating in different parts of the same activity. Brothers and sisters will play at closer quarters and more intimately than friends. Rough-and-tumble games begin at about three and gradually become more intense; two siblings or close friends under five will spend a lot of time grappling amidst howls of laughter—and occasional tears when one gets hurt.

Learning to play together

Below: This graph, which records incidents of different types of play, shows that play involving little or no communication between playmates is frequent at first. Gradually children begin to play the same game, but still remain separate; finally they play cooperatively.

For a young girl, a dollhouse is traditionally one of the most wonderful presents she could ever receive. Here, in miniature, is a world where she alone controls the destinies of a family. For hours she dresses and feeds them and creates dilemmas for them.

Sex differences

Although the distinctive character of each sex is often blamed on environmental factors there is plenty of evidence to show that sex differences are actually rooted in prenatal growth. Masculinizing hormones, androgens, are secreted more in the male than in the female during the prenatal period and feminizing hormones, estrogens and progesterone, are secreted more in the female.

As early as the age of three years the presence of androgens in boys is manifested in their greater display of aggression. They are more prone to rough play, to assertiveness, and to competitiveness, while girls show a tendency toward passivity. Boys' inclinations to explore more than girls are directly linked to their greater assertiveness, and all these expressions of aggressiveness form the most significant sex difference. Though no more active than girls, boys do tend to be more vigorous in their activities—a result of their larger muscles and greater speed. In the sphere of more delicate activities girls do better, as they have finer control of their hands and fingers. Boys excel when they aim at targets, and their sense of direction and their understanding of spatial relationships are better throughout their whole development. Perhaps because of this boys play more physical games and their "territory" stretches farther away from home. Girls on the other hand have superior linguistic and oral abilities. They learn to talk earlier than boys, they articulate better, and their vocabulary is always more extensive.

Though research has shown that these differences are real, there has always been a tendency to reinforce and exaggerate them. From birth, children are treated differently according to their sex. Girls are talked to more softly, and discrimination even appears when choosing something as innocuous as a mobile; dangling ships and cars are thought suitable for boys while flowers and dolls are bought exclusively for girls. "Is it a boy or a girl?" is the usual question asked before buying a present. It normally results in a flood of distinctly masculine or feminine toys: guns for boys, miniature tea services for girls. In children's books there is further reinforcement. In most, men and boys are the glittering stars, women appearing only as mothers and wives. One survey of books showed 261 pictures of men to 23 of women. Role stereotypes are changing only gradually in children's literature, and now and then we see women working, or men as caretakers.

By observing what others do, children learn what is expected of themselves. Many parents believe that sex differences can be minimized if they do not subject their child to a display of rigid role-playing based on sex. However, other more traditional influences may well still be brought to bear on the child from his experiences while away from parental influence.

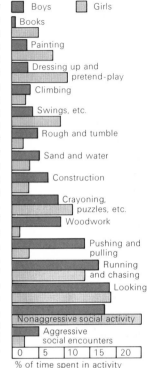

Below : Boys and girls play very differently. Boys prefer physical pursuits such as building and fighting ; girls prefer gentler games.

% of time spent in activity

As the child grows older, so his ability to play with another child improves. As his play becomes more "mental" the opportunities for cooperating increase. Playing doctors and nurses means that two children have to imagine the same thing—or rather, different parts of the same thing. And that is quite a feat for a child under five. Less elaborate games allow more than two children to play together, but it is still almost impossible for five-year-olds to cope with more than three playmates at a time.

If your child has a number of other children close at hand you may notice how one may be singled out as a friend, almost to the exclusion of the others. Gradually his circle of friends grows, and parallel play disappears, as he becomes more of a social being.

How much television?

The amount of television—and the nature of the programs—watched by a preschool child should be supervised by his parents. Television is no substitute for reading aloud, real activities, and personal interaction. The general rule is: children's programs only— and for limited times. Adult programs won't mean much more to him than moving shapes, and, with his limited attention span, he will be unable to follow the long and fragmented plots. Some sports and animal-life programs are admirable, and you will doubtless find your own exceptions to the rule. If you let him stay up late, perhaps to watch a particular program, make sure he realizes that this is a special treat that he can't expect very often.

As a supplement to real life, television can be very valuable for a young child. Many children's programs stimulate his imagination and enlarge his view of the world. Flopped in front of the television, an energetic four-year-old does get some respite from his nonstop activities—and his mother gains a few moments to get on with things undistracted. There will be times when he wants you to sit down and watch with him. If you do, you won't be the first grown-up to succumb to the lure of the excellent television programs for children.

Birthday parties

Most children will be ready for their first real birthday party by the time they are three. They will be old enough to appreciate the significance of the date and to enjoy the occasion and the presence of the other children.

Keep the party simple. Do not ask too many children; half a dozen at the outside. A good practice is to ask as many guests as the age of the child, a plan which helps year by year to mark the host's seniority. Ensure that the party is short, too. Two hours of excitement is as much as most three-year-olds can stand; no more than three hours for a five-year-old.

The centerpiece is, of course, the meal. Do not go to too much trouble; the exquisite trimmings of an adult cocktail party will be

Modeling clay is an ideal toy for a child of this age. With it he will be able to exercise both his physical and mental skills. Often his imagination will run ahead of his modeling abilities, and when he insists that he has just completed a giraffe you may find it hard to decipher the shapeless lump.

Below and Right : While girls often play together in pairs, boys prefer either their own company or large groups. The graph shows that girls have a tendency to be twice as cooperative as boys in their play patterns and assume a caretaking and protective role, helping younger children.

Direction of cooperation

| Boys to younger boys |
| Girls to younger girls |
| Boys to younger girls |
| Girls to younger boys |
| Boys to older boys |
| Girls to older girls |
| Boys to older girls |
| Girls to older boys |

0   10   20   30
% of total cooperative acts by both boys and girls

For boys, acquisitive competition is a major pastime and results are mainly achieved by force. Girls on the other hand prefer to use more subtle methods and will usually submit to aggression from others. The graph divides into percentages all aggressive acts committed by a group of boys and girls, according to their direction. Girls are equally aggressive toward boys and girls, whereas boys display less aggression toward girls than toward boys. Chivalry rules, even in a playgroup.

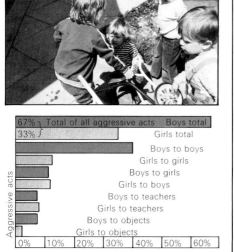

Aggressive acts

67%	Total of all aggressive acts	Boys total
33%		Girls total
		Boys to boys
		Girls to girls
		Boys to girls
		Girls to boys
		Boys to teachers
		Girls to teachers
		Boys to objects
		Girls to objects

0%   10%   20%   30%   40%   50%   60%

Such a portrayal of family activities, clearly depicting different occupations for the two sexes, reinforces traditional sex roles. This sort of picture is typical of many books read at an age when children are impressionable and developing their own social identities.

wasted on small children. Much of the basic food can be the same: hot dogs on buns, small sandwiches, and potato chips. Put out a variety of fillings, so that you cater to any faddishness among the guests. Ice cream is universally popular as a dessert, and a prettily decorated birthday cake with candles—one for each year—marks the climax. Chocolate cake is best at this age; virtually all children love it.

Keep the games simple and give away as many little prizes as you can. Very young children enjoy musical games that are really formalized parallel play, such as Farmer in the Dell or London Bridge.

An entertainer is a good diversion provided that you hire one who specializes in very young children. Magicians, for example, are not suitable for children under six, who will prefer, say, a specialist in characters from Walt Disney.

Nowadays it seems to be accepted that a party ends with a little present for each visitor. This need be no more than a small inexpensive favor like a packet of crayons, or an eraser shaped like an animal. But you may find yourselves involved in a party "circuit," with children critically comparing their loot after each party. You will have to decide then whether you like the idea of competition about something that is supposed to be a symbol of goodwill—whether the party is for your child's sake, or whether its purpose is to impress other parents.

Children's paintings

Children's drawings have such charm and novelty that they are a real source of pleasure for parents. For the child, however, they are rather more serious because they represent an attempt to find some order in a complex world. Although at this age much of his behavior seems quite whimsical, his drawings reveal a great deal of order. Like language, drawing is primarily a form of expression and, just as a child creates his own system for language, so his visual depiction of the world follows a number of rules. Slowly he learns to perceive the world as adults do, but until then he sees and depicts it in his own inimitable way.

A young child does not draw what he sees but what he knows about the world, his mental pictures of his surroundings and the people in his life. Thus the representation of human features and the details of familiar objects increase with mental growth. If a

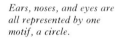

Ears, noses, and eyes are all represented by one motif, a circle.

Special characteristics, such as beards and glasses, are soon picked out.

Legs appear, though a hat seems more important than trunk and arms.

A child gains enormous pleasure from painting, but finds a brush full of paint difficult to control and thus tends to dab rather than paint lines.

child's drawing seems "primitive," it is not just because he lacks coordination and skill; it is also because his perception of the world is limited.

When a child first draws a picture of his mother it will consist mainly of her head; the body will be nonexistent. This is because his image of her is concentrated on her face, especially on her eyes, for it is through her face that she talks to him, laughs, shows her love and approval. Soon a child will begin to draw the body. Initially, he will draw only the legs growing straight out of the head, then he will add the trunk and finally the arms. He may also have gone through a phase of drawing a trunk without legs. It is interesting to note the relationship between comprehension and execution. When young children are shown a head with two lines extending down from it, most will identify them as legs, only later recognizing them as a neck.

In the early stages of drawing, a child's chief pleasure is in making marks on paper.

Early scribbles tend to be circular—but can vary from a dot to a crude curve. As his manual skills develop, lines become more rounded, showing loops and curls. Gradually scribbles become meaningful to him, and you can be certain, once he has completed the masterpiece, that he will name it according to a fancied resemblance. A little later he may draw a circle, and see the possibilities of making it into a face, and so add the necessary features. Even at this stage his plans may change as he notices different images growing out of his marks. It is only later, perhaps as late as five, that he will announce in advance what the drawings will be.

Though there is a systematic development in a child's drawings there is also a great deal of variety. He is always expanding the range of objects that he draws, and he depicts old familiar objects in new ways. He will also experiment with different techniques and within the short space of one day may produce a wide range of symbols.

Right : A picture so full of unrelated incidents may seem like a jumble, but for a child it is his best means of storytelling, of organizing and capturing his imagination.

Before he reaches school and learns to write he will use drawings as his major form of expression, and a child's output at this age can be prodigious.

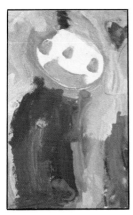

Legs are sacrificed for trunk, mainly for aesthetic reasons.

Though arms are still missing the drawings are becoming more realistic.

By the time he reaches school, a child is depicting the essential parts: trunk, legs, arms, hands, hair, and some simple movement.

A six-year-old will include details of activities and the subtleties of clothing.

Left: Animism is the term applied to a young child's view of the world, where he sees everything that has movement as alive and conscious. For instance, the wind knows that it blows, and many other inanimate objects acquire human characteristics. The sun that he has painted watches and smiles, as alive as the figure in the other corner of the painting.

A young child often employs the same formula for depicting different things. Though modified in small ways, one basic form can cover a whole range of objects. When a child begins to draw animals he depicts them in the same way as he would humans: standing upright with a smiling face, legs, and arms. Only pointed ears may give a clue as to the nature of the particular beast. As the child becomes more aware of the essence of cat so his drawings acquire more feline features, and puss is eventually shown on all fours, tail in the air.

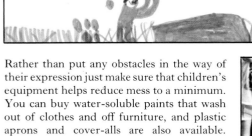

Most children, from toddlerhood onward, are quite concious of over-all composition and draw their figures in relation to the whole page. In this picture the child has depicted the sky at the very top of the page and the ground at the bottom—he knows that the sky and ground can't possibly meet because he stands in between them.

Rather than put any obstacles in the way of their expression just make sure that children's equipment helps reduce mess to a minimum. You can buy water-soluble paints that wash out of clothes and off furniture, and plastic aprons and cover-alls are also available. Young children are as happy painting on the wall as on paper, so make sure crayons are not indelible, since it is not unusual for "mistakes" to occur.

Until about the age of eight a child has little interest in delicacy and detail. Bright vivid colors, large tough brushes, and big sheets of absorbent paper are a young painter's main requirements. Don't waste expensive equipment on him. Powdered paints are very economical and many children may be quite happy to paint on newspaper; sable brushes will be quite lost on him, though an easel with a tray for water and paints may prove an invaluable investment. Clearing up can be hard work, so perhaps a corner given over to his artistic pursuits may be convenient.

Finger paints have a consistency not unlike mud and they are quite as messy, but children enjoy the directness and freedom of expression.

Children's personalities

At nursery school your child learns through play, but in a more carefully planned way than at home. For instance, he may start to learn letters and numbers, and thus be on the road to reading readiness. From playing with sand and water, he acquires an intuitive grasp of quantity, which nowadays is seen as the prelude to learning about number. He will also have access to equipment that is beyond the scope of most homes.

Perhaps the most important thing a child learns is how to get along with others. A group of children constantly changing activities and companions may look like chaos to you, but in fact the children are already forming a regular social order. A French ethologist, Professor Hubert Montagnet, has found five personality types among pre-school children, each of which takes a fairly regular place in the group.

The dominant caring type is very much a group leader. He takes the initiative in games. He shares food and toys voluntarily. He often protects less dominant children and will discipline those who behave badly.

The dominant aggressive type often takes the lead, but holds his position more by the use of power. He may boss the other children, but is less likely to protect or discipline.

The submissive follower is the group member who is not a leader. He is content for the most part to follow the lead of others. He sometimes needs to be rescued from one of the aggressive types, and will beg toys.

There are two outsider types, the aggressive and the passive. The aggressive outsider appears self-reliant but is not good at joining in group activities. He never begs and refuses to share when he has food or a toy. He sometimes picks on submissive followers and bullies them.

The passive outsider is in a sad position. He seems not to know how to join in group activities in any way. He never asks for anything. When he has his own food or toys they are likely to be stolen, but he is rarely rescued by the dominant caring types.

Many children move between these types. A dominant child may use whatever strategy he needs to maintain his position, and be aggressive one minute and caring the next. A follower may be more submissive in some moods than others, although he is unlikely to take the lead. A passive outsider may join in occasionally at the tag end of a group.

One key piece of nonverbal communication seems important in all social activity among small children. This is a soliciting gesture in which a child puts his face close to the face of another child, a little lower, and cocks his head to one side. The gesture is used by all three group member types, but rarely by the two outsiders. It is interesting that this gesture, which indicates appeasement, is also used by dominant caring types when they are offering help to submissive types.

When they collect their children at the end of the day, Montagnet found, some mothers crouch down to greet them, and others bend over them. Bending over someone is a dominant gesture, and children whose mothers do this are more likely to be aggressive types, either leaders or outsiders.

Above : Spontaneous warmth and affection between two playmates are an important part of communication.

Above : Tina is a submissive follower. She gets on well with the other children, even when they treat her like a toy.

Above : Mark and Andrew argue about hoops. Tina, part of the game, looks on, but Simon, a passive outsider, watches from the sidelines.

Left : Simon is left, alone and anxious, while other children play around him.

The importance of nursery schools

With the greater understanding of how children develop and learn, greater emphasis is now placed on the child before compulsory schooling. Some educators believe that the years from three to five are as important to the learning child as any that come after, and that the foundations laid at this time influence for good or ill how a child develops for the rest of his life. Although it is easy to exaggerate this influence, there is no doubt that nursery schools help a child off to a good start.

Traditionally, the chief influence on the child was his family and the village society.

Families today are much smaller than they were, and modern living cuts a child off from close contact with the outside world. Most children benefit from the stimulation and social experiences that a good nursery school offers. No matter how positive his family experience, nursery schools enable a child to begin to learn how to get along with other children, to discover his own abilities in a social setting, and to start on the road to independence from his parents. Nursery school children adapt to school with ease: not for them the tears and terrors of the child left for the first time at the school gate. There

Far left and Left: Jonathan is wheeling Tim in a toy buggy, a very popular toy. Andrew tries to take it over (1). Attracted by the noise, Tina also climbs on (2). Mark now sits on the buggy. Andrew still threatens Jonathan (3). Having failed to win the buggy, Andrew now asserts himself by pushing off Mark (4). Jonathan tries to tip him off, while Mark keeps token possession (5). Mark once again tries to sit on the buggy. Jonathan hangs on grimly (6). Finally he succeeds in up-ending the buggy (7). Andrew is now sole occupant, which is not what Jonathan intended (8). Jonathan now faces a new takeover bid from Mark (9). Andrew and Mark are both dominant types, but Mark is the more aggressive. Jonathan is always a follower, but not particularly submissive. Tim is a contented submissive follower, getting the most out of life no matter what happens.

Above: Harriet is commandeering Julian's tricycle (1). Julian seizes another child's tricycle (2). But he is not dominant enough to hold on to it. His head is lowered and tilted in the appeasing gesture (3). Harriet now changes type and comes to Julian's rescue (4).

will not be such a complete division between the worlds as there will be when he goes to "proper" school later, but a nursery school can expand a child's world enormously.

You will see changes in his behavior when he comes home, and hear all sorts of new expressions, which he learns from his new playmates. More importantly you will discover sides to his character that you would probably otherwise not have seen. His new environment will give him an opportunity to develop parts of his personality that have remained dormant at home. This is not necessarily because you have been deliberately suppressing his personality, but simply because you probably do not recognize those aspects of him that do not fit in with what you expect of your child. And if parents do not recognize something in their child, they do not encourage it—and it languishes. Nursery schools and playgroups do develop the character, perhaps even more than later, more formal schooling. They are much more than just a playground, or time off for mother.

The best way to find the right nursery school for your child is to begin by asking other

How to choose a nursery school

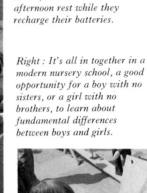

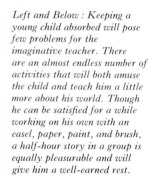

Left : At an all-day nursery school, children need an afternoon rest while they recharge their batteries.

Right : It's all in together in a modern nursery school, a good opportunity for a boy with no sisters, or a girl with no brothers, to learn about fundamental differences between boys and girls.

Left and Below : Keeping a young child absorbed will pose few problems for the imaginative teacher. There are an almost endless number of activities that will both amuse the child and teach him a little more about his world. Though he can be satisfied for a while working on his own with an easel, paper, paint, and brush, a half-hour story in a group is equally pleasurable and will give him a well-earned rest.

Given a good collection of odd objects, children spontaneously create their own play world. Some milk crates, an old steering wheel, and some chairs can easily be transformed into a bus large enough to carry passengers on an exciting imaginary journey.

mothers in your area. Obviously, you do not choose a group just because another mother recommends it; her opinion should be confirmed by a personal visit. Your doctor is likely to be helpful, too, since he will know something about the nursery schools in your community. Another possibility is to check with your local public school or district superintendent.

Nursery schools vary greatly. Some do little more than collect a dozen or more children and put them all in a hall for the morning with some toys and one or two adults who see to it that none gets hurt. Others are stricter than many modern schools and are so formal and tightly organized that they are not really nursery schools at all. The hours they are open also vary widely from only two hours on two mornings a week to three hours on five mornings; some even include lunch, especially if they are arranged for working mothers. Most groups control the ratio of boys to girls, and have a waiting list to help keep the proportions equal.

The character of a nursery school is largely shaped by the person· in charge.

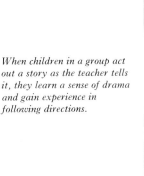

When children in a group act out a story as the teacher tells it, they learn a sense of drama and gain experience in following directions.

Children of this age have boundless energy, but not all nursery schools provide suitable outdoor space where children can let off steam. However, jungle gyms, slides, and ropes can also be accommodated indoors, and they will provide a very satisfactory alternative, on which children can vent their pent-up energies.

In some the children are quiet and well occupied; in others the scene is more like a battlefield, with a large group of children milling noisily around the room.

The kind of group you choose will naturally depend on what you want for your child, and what he will stand. A quiet child will probably not flourish in a noisy group—but you may feel a noisy child would benefit from a quiet group. On the other hand, if you take your child to a nursery school so that he can learn to mix, too tightly organized a group might not give him sufficient freedom.

The person in charge of a nursery school needs to be warm and sensitive, yet firm enough to deal with difficult children, and with several children at once. She must cope with the aggressive and the shy, the bright and the slow. She must genuinely like children, and should view her school as an educational, not a profit-making institution.

You should spend a morning at a group before sending your child, so that you can see how the children behave and how the teacher handles the group. The facilities are controlled by law, but you may still want to inspect them for yourself to see that the minimum standards are well met.

The age at which a child starts nursery school will depend of course on his own stage of development—and what places are found to be available. A few rather advanced children are ready by two and a half; most are mature enough at three, or soon after, to benefit from a good preschool environment. The majority of three- and four-year-olds will take to a nursery school with enthusiasm, though a shy or dependent child may have a hard time at first. If your child clings or cries when you leave, it is well to take your cues from the person in charge; she has seen a lot more children in the same situation than his mother has, after all. She may suggest that his mother stay for the first day or two until he builds up confidence and establishes a relationship with the teacher and another child. Once established in the routine, there should be no staying home except for illness. If at first he's very tired by school, he may return to his nap after lunch. Many three-year-olds need this, as do some older children.

If you are not able to find a suitable preschool group for your child—and feel strongly that he would benefit from attending one—think about starting a nursery school yourself. Lots of mothers have done so successfully. There are three basic options. First, run the group yourself with the aid of helpers you employ; second, set the group up as a co-operative with a number of mothers taking turns at supervising the children morning by morning: third, get together a committee of parents and hire a teacher to run the group.

Of course it will be hard work, but you will be helping actively in your child's first school

Starting at nursery school

Setting up your own nursery school

Don't expect your child to be absorbed by every exhibit in a museum. A fossilized skeleton may catch his attention though the rest of the building may leave him quite unmoved. So let him explore by himself; if he wants to know something he will ask you.

Give your child a screwdriver of his own, a block of wood, and some screws. He may even be able to start them off with a hand drill. When he copies daddy or mommy, he is learning as well as playing.

Even though the purpose of the game may not yet have been learned, a youngster will enjoy kicking a soccer ball around, and will relish his father's participation.

Right : Minute or vast, gentle or ferocious, behind bars or in an open park, all animals are a source of endless fascination to young children.

Above : Puppet shows have fascinated young children for centuries, and this group seems to be no exception.

experience and you will be able to set up just the approach and program that you want. Also, helping to organize a nursery school, working out conditions and costs, can be a way of involving fathers in their child's early education.

With imagination and ingenuity, parents can usually equip a nursery school with second-hand furniture, books, and toys outgrown by older children. Such basic items can be supplemented through a few simple fund-raising activities which can provide for larger items such as children's chairs and tables or a slide or jungle gym, which all the children will enjoy. Always check with your local authority that your plans comply with their regulations concerning the formation and operation of nursery schools and make sure that you are fully insured.

Widening horizons

After three, taking a child on excursions is great fun. He is old enough to enjoy them and his parents will start seeing the familiar with a new perspective. He is toilet trained now, he can eat out at restaurants or on family picnics, and, if outings are carefully planned with time for a rest in the car or on the bus, he won't get too tired. But remember that although he appears so grown-up and asks so many questions, his attention span is very limited. Organize short trips that will interest him. There are lots of places all around you that he will enjoy seeing and learning about. So make use of your local facilities even though you may not have paid much attention to them before.

A trip to the local railroad station is a splendid adventure. If there is an airport nearby, watching planes take off and land is great sport. Why not telephone for an appointment to visit the fire station nearest to you? Small boys are fascinated by construction sites: for a few days let your child watch the progress and see all the bulldozers, earth-movers, and trucks. If you live near a large city, a trip to the museum to see *one* thing—a model of a dinosaur, or a steam engine—will interest him without getting him too tired. Zoos are always fun, especially if you get there at a time when the animals are being fed. Many libraries have story hours and film shows for children; it's worth inquiring. As a special treat, four- and five-year-olds will love a puppet show.

The bakery, the pet shop, the florist, and the post office will all provide something new to see. It is fun to watch the bread baking, to buy a favorite cookie. Horse shows, rummage sales, fairs, and carnivals are also great diversions for a young child for short periods. Bus or subway rides never cease to fascinate young children.

And finally: what does daddy do all day? Take your child on a quick trip to the office to see daddy's desk and some of the people he works with. And, of course, he will enjoy all these trips much more if he can bring along a friend from nursery school or the boy who lives up the road. Young as he is, it's good to encourage these friendships.

After the first three years of very rapid growth children enter a period of slower and steadier progress when the secretions of the growth hormone from the pituitary gland decrease. The proportions of their body develop into a more adult form, and also during this period all their movements become more refined. But if growth seems a little static, general development certainly is not. The child's whole understanding of the world and his ability to become involved with his family and friends have greatly increased. But just as he has become more sociable, so he has become more self-reliant. The dependent days of early childhood will really seem to have come to an end. Brushing his teeth, dressing himself, and wanting to help with household chores are part of everyday life. Out of doors he will have learned to ride his bike, hop, skip, catch, and throw a ball. His greater strength, better coordination, and insatiable appetite for questioning will have transformed him from the toddler of two years ago, and it is now only a very short time before he starts his first day at school.

How your child has progressed

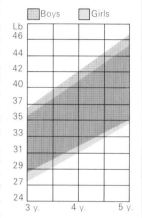

In the second three years of life a child grows steadily taller, but, because his weight-gain slows down, he thins out.

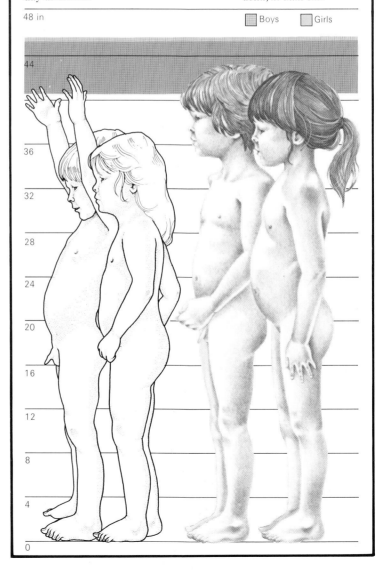

5 *School years:*
THE WIDENING WORLD

On the first morning of school he looked
wide-eyed and apprehensive. By the end
of the first week, the shiny new shoes were already scuffed;
by Christmas, he had grown into his new clothes,
bought too large on purpose. A craze for toy gliders swept the
school—he had to have one. Best friends one day
became enemies the next. Imperceptibly, the transition from
child into schoolboy was made.

Childhood means constant change. But there are periods when the change is more rapid than at others, and none more so than the dramatic transformation at five or six from a little child into a young boy or girl. This is given emphasis by the venturing out of the home and into a wider world.

The young child constantly asserts his independence: his cry of "You can't make me" alternates with "I can if I want to." His fidgeting, balkiness, and propensity for experiments, such as throwing a hard ball around indoors, give his parents moments of great trial. Offer him a choice of ice cream flavors, and he will draw out his indecision to agonizing lengths.

Underlying his independence there is still a large element of babyhood remaining. He still cries frequently, although he is beginning to "be brave" when helped by a parent or older child. Tears of rage can often be diverted to laughter by a persuasive parent.

At seven the child enters another period of quieter, more even growth. His energies may be chiefly directed at the great intellectual strides he is now making toward the achievement of "conservation"—the understanding that some aspects of the world stay the same even when appearances change. Self-absorption characterizes much of his time as he practices his new and growing skills.

In his eighth year, his increasing intellectual powers and physical abilities make him more and more a social being, for he is becoming aware of other points of view besides that of his own.

By nine, boys and girls are growing apart socially. Boys become more strongly group-minded, although they may perhaps have one particular friend. Girls usually do have one special friend, but they may also be part of a more fluid group, which is less important to them than are boys' groups to boys. Traditionally it is now that boys decide girls are silly. No doubt this is a reflection of our male-dominated society, but it surely cannot be a coincidence that it always seems to happen at about this age. Both sexes are learning to take their place in a team, playing softball or volleyball.

The maturity of many nine-year-olds is quite striking when contrasted with that of younger children. But soon they reach another in-between stage. We used to think of adolescence as the period between childhood and adulthood. Now, since we have recognized adolescence as a stage of life in its own right, we are coming to understand that it is the earlier age, between ten and twelve, that is particularly awkward. Then the child is too old to be treated wholly as a child, but still likes to romp with an abandon which his more self-conscious elders are not capable of; he has moments of grace and self-possession, but is not interested in the things that concern teenagers. Girls, especially, are on the verge of the great step into womanhood. Boys, by contrast, may still appear juvenile and unsophisticated.

Catching a ball requires considerable coordination of eye and body. Though a six-year-old child will probably have all the basic skills, it will take some years of practice before he can put them all together smoothly.

Can your child cope at school?

Before your child goes off to school he should be able to accomplish most of the following daily tasks on his own. He will need confidence and independence to cope well with the job of learning. Can he:

○ Say *both* his names and address clearly?
○ Ask to use the toilet when he needs it (without using special words)?
○ Manage coat, hat, scarf, and gloves?
○ Put on outdoor shoes and boots correctly?
○ Deal with buttons, zippers, and laces?
○ Use faucets, towels, flush toilets?
○ Go to the toilet by himself?
○ Eat cleanly with knife, fork, and spoon?
○ Recognize his name when written?

Physical development

By contrast with a four-year old the child between five and six seems mature indeed; when compared with a ten-year-old he seems still very unformed. His body may be slender and his limbs gangling as he finally loses all traces of babyhood physique. He is constantly active, and yet not in full control of his body and limbs. He seems never to walk, always to run. Outside he falls frequently, often for no apparent reason. He runs faster than his legs can safely carry him, changes his mind in full flight, and attempts a turn that would defeat a trained athlete. Indoors he seems to dash about, constantly knocking into things. At meals he fidgets constantly, drops his knife and fork, kicks the table leg, and hops off and on his chair.

Boys like wrestling in an informal way, which often means no more than an unco-ordinated romping. Girls soon learn to skip when they start school—boys can too, if their playground culture allows them.

This is the age of minor tumbles and scrapes, when the first-aid kit becomes an essential household item. You will learn to gauge quickly from your child's cry how badly he is hurt. Often the most anguished crying is for minor scratches, but you will know with dread the awful silence following a loud thud that betokens real hurt. It's almost a rule: if he's howling, let him come to you—it's mostly outrage at the wicked world that trips him up so unfairly; if there is silence, or his crying is in deep sobs, drop whatever you are doing and run to him.

During his seventh and eighth years he stops pushing himself so far beyond his capabilities—largely because his physical abilities catch up. His movements become more measured, more fluid and graceful, and his activity changes from a random letting off of steam to more purposeful pursuits. He is beginning to play regular games, although at first they are still solitary ones, such as roller-skating, hopscotch, or throwing a ball against a wall. Skipping is now done in groups, and most children are good at running into a turning rope.

At nine or ten, a child can become utterly single-minded and pursue an activity to the point of exhaustion. This is the stage when physical types will go on to develop their particular skills; those with a bent toward more leisurely or intellectual activities will quiet down and leave the field.

For the energetic, this is the great age for sports, especially boisterous games with parents, kicking balls, and playing baseball. You can now begin to teach your child the proper techniques of games, as his muscular activity is much better coordinated, and he is acquiring a sense of balance and of timing.

Some children between nine and eleven seem very long-legged and rangy, because their legs are growing faster than their trunks. There is relatively little growth in height in years nine to ten in girls, ten to eleven in boys. Your child's body system is now practically mature in function: respiratory rate is eighteen to twenty a minute (approach-

Right: Fantasy still has a very large part to play in the child's development, and both boys and girls will enjoy dressing up and acting out scenes in which they pretend to be someone else.

Below: Children from seven years onward tend to be less egocentric than younger children. They often have an innate desire to learn and will be eager to find out all they can about something in which they are interested.

ing adult level), blood pressure is increasing, eyes have reached adult size, and sight is completely developed. Brain and spinal cord reach adult size by the age of twelve, though cellular development, on which mental growth depends, is not yet complete.

Growing understanding

Mentally, as research has shown, a child between four and a half and seven is still in transition from the toddler stage, when his thinking was tied closely to action, to that of early schooling, when he is beginning to form concepts. It is rather like the early stage of assembly of a jigsaw puzzle—some of the pieces are coming together to form isolated parts of the over-all picture, but it will be some time before the whole picture emerges. The pieces of experience your child is gaining have to be combined to form the concepts that are the basis of learning.

No amount of teaching of the three R's will mean anything to a child until he understands what symbols such as letters and figures are for, and how they stand in place of the real, concrete objects he handles and sees. Children pushed through the early stages too fast become unhappy "parrot" readers who can

Children's art

As children's experience broadens so their paintings become increasingly differentiated both in style and subject matter. At school they begin to acquire a range of visual tricks through which they can represent the world, and much of the spontaneity of their early painting disappears. Representation is something that children learn to aspire to, and sadly many who fail to capture good likenesses soon lose interest and discard the occupation that once gave them so much pleasure as a means of self-expression.

Above : The peculiar face is simply the outcome of a child's attempt to draw a figure in profile, a result of the conflict that exists between what the child has seen and what he knows to be there.

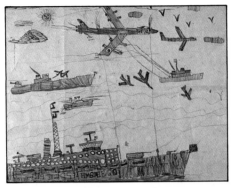

Children's sensuous delight in color tends to disappear during the school years ; it seems sacrificed on the altar of realism.

Far left and Left : Though sex differences have been noted in toddlers' drawings they do not become really apparent until the school years. Then a significant difference can be noticed in their choice of subject matter : boys show a greater interest in objects like airplanes or cars ; girls are more interested in human beings.

Above : As children's cognitive and perceptual abilities improve so they acquire an astonishing eye for detail and might, for example, observe and record the tiny intricacies of playground life.

Right : Just as toddlers have their own visual language so older children create their systems of representation. A detailed pattern, for example, might be used as a structure for a picture.

"read" from the printed page but don't understand its content—doing what one teacher called "barking at print," like a dog doing tricks. Or they will get their arithmetic right but have no idea what it is really all about—being unable to use scales or do simple measurements.

At school the teacher will be giving children opportunities for making experiments in all sorts of ways, building up their experiences by playing with sand, water, and clay, "shopping" at the classroom shop, measuring, and model-making—most of the activities that went on at nursery school. The difference is that she will be guiding their play so that they make the discoveries that lead to understand-

ing the basic concepts of size, shape, order, and succession. She will help them sort out these discoveries by laying the foundation for the three R's, which they will later study with understanding, not merely by rote.

Throughout childhood a child's thinking takes on all sorts of magical forms. For example, children confuse thinking with talking, or with breathing. In one beautiful piece of spontaneous poetry, a six-year-old said, "You think with your mouth. Your thoughts come out like breath, and you can see them on a frosty day."

The sun, the moon, and the clouds are all alive in the mind of the child. The clouds feel

How your child thinks

the wind as it pushes them along. The sun and the moon know their names and they follow you about. You can tell they are following you because when you stop they do too! One child, interviewed by the psychologist Jean Piaget, believed the sun was alive because it gave light. A candle was alive when it was lit, but not when it was out. She thought that a watch was alive because it worked. Another boy thought that a stone was dead, but became alive when he threw it. Life for children means movement, change, and action. As late as eleven or twelve some children still paint the sun with a broadly smiling face.

Even at nine, explaining something is difficult for some children. Piaget asked one boy how Geneva came to be on the edge of a lake. The boy answered, "Because if there had not been a lake, there would not have been any water."

Once he has acquired "conservation," at around eight years old, a child enters the period called "concrete operations." He knows now that when he sees a snail on a garden path, walks on a bit, and sees another one, the snail that he can see must be a different snail from the one he saw before, even though they look identical. He can do math problems (if his kind of school still gives them) such as: "If it takes three men thirty minutes to fill a hole, how long will it take one man to fill the same hole?"

Until now the child has functioned purely on the level of action. Now he can function on the level of representation. He forms a mental picture of a problem and works it out in his mind. (For some children, as for some adults, the picture is so real that they seem almost to have film projectors in their heads; but for most the picture is hazy and unconsciously formed.)

The child can now consider all the "What if . . ." questions that were so far beyond him when he was younger. His mind reaches out beyond him as he begins to understand the world, past, present, and future. It is, however, a very concrete understanding, as is shown by his comprehension of right and wrong. Abstract thought will not come for another eight years or so. In the meantime, there is so much to be learned.

Collecting and classifying

This is the age for classifying and arranging; the "squirrel" age when children's rooms are chock-full of collections—stamps, fossils, coins, pictures—and when they love to spot license plates on out-of-state cars. Parents can enjoy these pleasures too; children make wonderful companions on fossil hunts or on expeditions to collect leaves or berries.

Take your child to the zoo, and he will be able to group the animals into classes. He knows some cars have four cylinders, others six, eight, or even twelve, and they can be sports cars or sedans.

Now, too, he can grasp the relationships within a family—the family tree—and he will like to hear how his grandparents lived, or how his mother dressed as a little girl. History is now developing meaning for him. Quizzes, too, are great fun for all the family: a child now can distinguish more than one kind of classification. Try him with such things as "a yellow flower beginning with *d*."

Recording growth

Throughout these years of growing self-awareness it is good to show a child how he develops. Reserve an inconspicuous part of a wall and mark off his height using a hard-cover book (or tape measure) and a pencil. Measure him every three months or so and date each mark. There is his own increasing stature plain for him to see—better than writing it in a book. If you weigh him each time you can write his weight alongside.

Keep a scrapbook of his drawing, writing, and arithmetic to show him his progress. This is particularly valuable if he becomes discouraged and seems to make no progress for a week or two. Make a tape of your child reading or telling you a story and play it back to him a few months later. He will be able to hear how much his vocabulary and fluency have improved; words and ideas that made him stumble then seem commonplace to him now.

Stages of mental growth

One of the most striking developments in the child's cognitive growth during the school years is his acquisition of "conservation." For a child to grasp this he has to learn that objects retain certain characteristics though they are seen to change their shape. Until they have reached this stage children will always believe that when identical objects change their appearance there is an accompanying change in, for example, quantity or weight. There are different kinds of conservation, which are achieved at different ages. Conservation of volume is not acquired by a child until the very end of the "concrete operational" period.

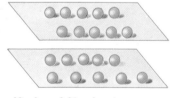

Number : Achieved at six to seven years. Prior to this age the child consider that the line that has been stretched contains more beads.

Substance : Achieved at seven to eight years. Prior to this age a child thinks that the ball that has been elongated contains more substance.

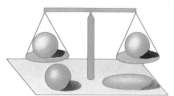

Weight : Achieved at nine to ten years. Prior to this age a child will imagine that the elongated ball will weigh more because it looks longer.

Volume : Achieved at eleven or twelve. Prior to this age a child will think that the elongated ball will displace more water.

Playing and learning

From four to seven the child is developing his personality and building up his sense of individuality. Groups of children at this egocentric age tend to act simply as a number of independent people each concerned with his own particular interests. Rivalry and the desire to do better than others are common at this age, and "showing off" his achievements is natural to the child. He should be encouraged to demonstrate what he can do—it is his way of building up his self-confidence and skill. Through making things where some degree of care is needed, he can also learn useful qualities such as patience and self-control. Older children of eight to twelve years, who have developed these qualities to a greater extent, are thus more likely to enjoy the more complicated type of model-making, where greater dexterity and careful following of instructions is needed.

Many children have a spontaneous interest in flowers and other things that grow. Simple things can be grown indoors all the year round or in a window box during the summer. If you have a garden you could give your child a patch of his own, but make sure it is a decent patch of sunny ground that has been fertilized rather than a useless bit in the shade where you have been unsuccessful in growing anything yourself, otherwise you may only discourage him. Some easy seeds to start off with might include radishes, beans, peas, lettuce, sunflowers, and poppies.

Both boys and girls can get great pleasure out of helping in the kitchen. Or alternatively you might like to help them make their own fudge, or pies and cakes for dessert. However, use of the oven and burners on the stove should be supervised by an adult.

Children from seven years onward very often start collecting things such as stamps, sea shells, buttons, dolls and puppets, flowers and leaves, maps, postcards, rocks, and coins. Through his collection a child can learn a great deal about the world around him. Interest in one subject will very often lead him on to other subjects. He can use his initiative to search out the particular objects

Above: Helping to prepare the meals can be absorbing work. Children will take the greatest care over those little jobs such as cutting out pastry shapes and decorating cakes.

Right and Below: Attractive collages can be made using old bits of material, yarn, and string. Make up your own board games, with a theme such as traffic routes or escaping criminals, that involve throwing dice to move the counters around the board. Boys as well as girls may enjoy sewing and weaving simple things such as hot plates, purses, and belts. Flowers and vegetables that are easy to grow include mustard and cress seeds, alfalfa, carrot tops kept in a saucer of water, and bulbs grown on moist bulb fiber and kept in the dark while the root system is developing.

he wants, and when his collection is large enough he can use his imagination to think up new ways in which to show it off at its best.

For example, shells can be displayed in bottles or strung into necklaces; stamps can be classified into groups and set out in an album, with any spare ones being used to decorate boxes or tins.

A child of this age is very sociable. His desire to excel (developed from four to seven years) has led to greater confidence in his abilities. He now has more to contribute to the social group. Thus children of this age often like to join together in corporate activities for a common purpose. Favorite pastimes often include those we associate with primitive man, such as camping, hiking, fishing, climbing trees, swimming, playing Indians, and trying to handle small boats.

All children up to the age of twelve will indulge in fantasy play, and they can use the most ordinary objects with great effect in their games, so hold on to those bits and pieces for which you may have thought you had no further use.

Above : A tree house provides an unusual den where children can be on their own. Do not allow any form of fire inside. A sandbox makes a good play site for children of all ages and is easily made with sand from a beach or lumber yard. Unfortunately animals, and in particular cats, often foul sandboxes, so keep yours well covered when not in use. Children love to camp in the yard. They will need a tent, a plastic sheet or tarpaulin, plenty of old blankets or a sleeping bag, and a flashlight.

Left and Below : A cardboard box can be turned into a dollhouse, in which matchboxes make marvelous furniture and clay or painted clothespins can be used to model people. Papier mâché is a useful and versatile modeling material with which to make different shapes such as masks and puppets. Soak torn-up pieces of newspaper in glue or a flour-and-water paste and apply wet pieces to a foundation until $\frac{1}{4}$ in/7 mm thick. When dry, it can be painted or decorated with colored paper.

Common childhood diseases

Schoolchildren are particularly susceptible to the common infectious diseases of childhood. Immunization against polio, measles, mumps, rubella (German measles), whooping cough, diphtheria, and tetanus is now easily available, and it is every mother's responsibility to see that her young children are protected. As yet there is no immunization against chicken pox.

When a child enters school booster shots are generally needed. The A-Z section in the back of this book has information on the symptoms of infectious diseases and the course of action to be followed. If your child has any of these symptoms your doctor should be immediately contacted.

Permanent teeth

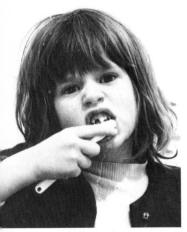

Regular visits to the dentist ensure that the new teeth are growing satisfactorily.

At about six a child begins to lose his "milk" teeth, as his "permanent" teeth grow up underneath them, loosening and pushing them away. The milk teeth drop out in roughly the same order as they first arrived, front teeth, then the molars at the back, and lastly the canine teeth. The process is usually complete by twelve years old, but may take until the child is fourteen. Two extra permanent molars may also appear. The last molars, the so-called "wisdom" teeth which appear at the back of both jaws, do not usually come through until eighteen or much later.

Losing the milk teeth tends to be a painless process. The twinge when an obstinate tooth that has been hanging on by a tiny piece of gum comes away is nothing compared with the psychological twinge felt by the squeamish, which in itself is not to be sneered at. The child, after all, is losing what has been a part of himself. Bleeding for more than a second or two is uncommon.

How much sleep?

The amount of sleep a child needs usually declines steadily during his first five years, but he may then reach a plateau, where it remains constant for some time. This seems to occur partly because of the increasing demands on him, and partly because he reaches the minimum that he can do with for the time being. When he starts school he may actually need more sleep than before, and go on wanting it for several months. As a very rough guide, twelve hours is about right for a six-year-old, lessening to ten and a half hours at twelve. There is great variation around these averages, and by twelve the different patterns of sleep are becoming apparent.

It is very easy, however, for a child to become overtired, and a long-term sleep deficiency may hinder his schoolwork. What we know about the body's own biological rhythms tends to support the old saying that "an hour's sleep before midnight is worth two after," so it is wise to err on the side of an early bedtime.

Dreams and nightmares

Throughout his school years a child's dreams become clearer, more articulate, and better formed. By the time he is twelve they can be quite a useful clue to any untoward stresses he may be experiencing temporarily, as well as a source of amusing self-analysis.

Nightmares reach their peak of frequency in most children at six years old and diminish after this, until at twelve they should be quite rare. If they are not, consult your doctor or an educational psychologist about possible sources of stress in your child's life.

Bed-wetting

About ten percent of all children are still wetting their beds at six, and about four percent as late as twelve. Few people realize just how high the proportion is. Bed-wetting is not normally a sign of abnormality, unless a child starts again having achieved dryness.

However, if a child is still wetting at eight, it is unpleasant both for him and for his family. It makes a lot of extra work and may cause stress. If your child is one of those unlucky ones who reaches full bladder control late, seek the advice of your doctor. Some "soul-searching" as to whether he is under undue pressure at home or at school is in order. Sometimes curtailing liquids before bedtime is helpful. But remember: the less fuss is made about this, the better!

Some doctors may want to prescribe drugs, but you should resist these until your child is at least twelve years old and all other methods have failed.

Getting along with other people

A six-year-old is increasingly aware of group pressures and pleasures. Though not yet ready for teamwork, he is beginning to discover how a group can integrate for a common purpose. He is ready, too, to take on small responsibilities, and to show sympathy for others; though he often still finds it hard to take turns on the swing or wait in line. It helps to remember that at this period there is really no strict social norm of behavior; a child will behave like a much younger one, then suddenly appear quite mature. But at all times he needs us to reinforce his image of himself as a "nice" person, deserving of love. Helping him to keep this image will enable him to survive the doubtful and difficult times when he mistrusts himself.

The age of secret societies

From eight onward is the great age for groups and gangs. Children revel in secret societies, passwords, and codes. It doesn't appear to matter much what a society is for, so long as it has rules. One psychologist, Valentine, reported that one of his boys at nine founded a club for "The Abolition of Ladies" (one wonders how), and another child, a girl, at the same age was president of a "Society for Kindness to Animals." The first notice she sent around to members said, "Anyone who can think of a good rule for the club should send it in to the Secretary."

The reason behind all this clubbing together is largely the search for rules and regulations, which a child wants to obey. It marks a certain amount of progress, in that loyalty to the rules is of paramount importance. A child feels secure in this ordered framework, where the rules are his own.

Children play much more cooperatively now and enjoy group projects and competition among their peers.

Discipline and self-discipline

Amoral
At birth
A baby has needs that must be met, and he develops a primitive inbuilt grievance if they are not. He has no obligations himself.
From about 8 months
He may stop what he is doing and cry when he is scolded. At ten months he will obey simple familiar commands, but he is tied to the immediate situation. He cannot remember prohibitions.
From about 3 years
A child is beginning to learn simple rules of what he must not do. He cannot distinguish between right and wrong as moral concepts, but he can learn that he is a "good" or "bad" child and act accordingly.
From about 5 years
He is beginning to learn more complex rules of what he must and must not do, but his ideas of right and wrong are based on simple hedonism. How wrong an action is depends entirely on the consequences.

Preconventional
From about 7 years
Stage 1
The meaning of right to him is still to defer to a superior power, but he understands that this extends beyond his family.
From about 9 years
Stage 2
He still confuses the value of a human being with the value of his possessions. Human relations are viewed in terms of "you scratch my back and I'll scratch yours," but the concept of fairness emerges as an ideal.

Conventional
From about 12 years
Stage 3
The main motivation is to be thought of as a good boy or girl. What is right is what conforms to stereotyped view of majority behavior and wins social approval.

Above: For the first two or three years a child has no idea of the consequences of what he does. Then he begins to move slowly toward taking responsibility for his actions.

Now that your child is beginning to think for himself, a major question concerning discipline becomes not "how do I make him do it?" but "why should I make him do it?" If you have already been allowing your child a certain degree of self-determination, this will not be so difficult. Nonetheless it is very easy for a parent to ride roughshod over a child's perfectly reasonable preferences.

At six, of course, it may be difficult to find out exactly what a child wants. He is still finding out about himself—you might think that this is a stage we never entirely grow out of—and at the same time he is discovering how much freedom you permit him.

Very often you know much better than the child what is good for him. The danger is that you will always tell him what is good for him. "Don't argue: do it because I say so" are words it is all too easy to fall back on time after time. On the other hand it is equally wrong to pretend that you do not know more than your child. *Avant-garde* "children's libbers" sometimes talk as though there is no difference or ought to be no difference in knowledge and power between parent and child. This is to betray the child's needs.

Your responsibility to your child is both to take care of him and to teach him to look after himself. If, for instance, he decides one cold and wet morning that he does not want to wear his overcoat to school, what do you do? You could just say, "Put it on or else I'll slap you." Or, slightly better, "It is cold and wet, and I do not want you sniveling around the house with a cold, so put your coat on." The best approach of all is, "You will catch cold and be miserable afterward; I know that, even if you can't see it." This is probably about right for a six-year-old, at least when you are in a hurry.

When he is older, or when you have more time, you should try to find out why he is prepared to risk a cold in order to leave off his coat. It may turn out that there is something odd about it, which you have not noticed, but which the other children at school have.

Then there would be several options open to you. Buying him another coat will be beyond most people, but, if you have the money, not unreasonable. You could see if there is a spare one in the family that might fit him. Alternatively you could discuss with him the choice between getting wet, catching cold, and putting up with a little teasing. Even if he insists on going coatless the first day, you have provided him with the basis for changing his own decision later.

The older a child is the more essential, and the more possible, it is to solve differences of this kind by discussion. This will make it more, not less, easy to teach him to recognize that you yourself have needs that it is only fair he meets. If there is a difference over which program to have on television, for example, try to reach agreement on whose needs make their preference more important. If he wants a good children's program and you want a comedy show, it might be the time to let him have his choice. However, if he

wants the kids' cartoons and you select a current events program, then it may be your turn. If you just say "It's my television, so I choose" you are not teaching him how to reach fair decisions—a skill he will need at work and in his own marriage.

It should not be necessary to spank a child by the time he is six, and it will almost certainly be harmful to do so. A few parents keep physical punishment, such as beating with a cane, in reserve for really serious offenses. My opinion is that if they use it they are over-reacting. Nearly all children tell at least one lie in their lives; nearly all steal at least once. Careful research has shown that these tend to be isolated instances, and they do not mean that your angel of goodness has suddenly been corrupted into a life of crime.

Of course lying and stealing are wrong, and you must make your disapproval plain. But try to make the punishment fit the crime. Stop your child's allowance for stealing, and curtail some other suitable privilege if he has been lying. If you make it clear that justice requires some such measure, but that you do not expect to have to do it again, you will be much fairer—and children are very conscious of fairness.

From learning the simple lesson that there are some things he must not do to understanding why he must not do them is a long journey for a child. There are three main stages along the road, and a child is just approaching the first at six or seven. A child's moral behavior usually lags a stage or two behind his thinking.

His grasp of rules in general is still vague. He is still inclined to believe that actions are right or wrong because his mother or father tells him to do, or not do, them. Your child may seem to be following the rules pretty well, but he is doing it for you, as it were. Gradually he acquires a sense that all the prohibitions are for his own good.

At six his ideas about how wrong an action is are strange indeed. Try this little story on your child. "A little boy thought he would

Should spanking stop?

Shades of right and wrong

Lawrence Kohlberg, the world authority on moral development, has established six stages in the growth of moral thinking. The column on the left shows that at ten years the sophisticated stages five and six have not appeared and the two pre-conventional stages dominate. The second column shows that a thirteen-year-old makes most of his judgments in the two conventional stages. Adult thought patterns are only just beginning to emerge.

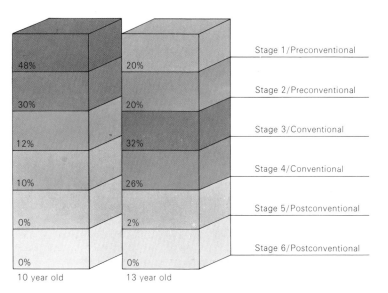

10 year old	13 year old	
48%	20%	Stage 1/Preconventional
30%	20%	Stage 2/Preconventional
12%	32%	Stage 3/Conventional
10%	26%	Stage 4/Conventional
0%	2%	Stage 5/Postconventional
0%	0%	Stage 6/Postconventional

Sex stereotyping

By middle childhood some sex differences are well established, reinforced to a great extent by the social conventions that exist about what is acceptable behavior for boys and girls; about what is considered "feminine" and "masculine."

In the sphere of aggressive behavior there can be found the strongest-held views of how children should behave. As aggressiveness is associated with masculinity, and passiveness considered more feminine, many parents and teachers adopt child-rearing practices that magnify these differences. Girls, for instance, are rebuked quietly and swiftly, whereas mothers and teachers react strongly and loudly to boys, thus reinforcing their aggressive behavior. Research has shown that the repression of aggressive behavior in either sex leads to a decrease in aggressive acts, and this type of repression is reserved almost entirely for girls. Permissiveness in nearly all activities makes children of both sexes more independent and more exploratory—two qualities encouraged in the male and actively discouraged in the female.

Though the women's movement has had an impact on all aspects of American life, sex stereotyping continues to have its influence on the lives of our children. There may be many changes in the wind, but for now many parents seem to remain more ambitious for their sons than for their daughters, a fact which of course reinforces the boys' competitive and ambitious spirits.

There is an increasing awareness, however, that attributes which have traditionally been ascribed to "masculinity" and "femininity" are often quite arbitrary. It is clear that many girls could be quite as aggressive as their male counterparts if they were raised in a less biased fashion. Though it is commonly accepted that boys have difficulty with

As children grow older so many of the activities that they once all played at together become exclusively male or female. Though tree-climbing is a pastime that can be enjoyed by both girls and boys, it is often considered an unfeminine activity and may be distinctly discouraged in girls as they grow older.

their reading and writing, there is little awareness of girls' inferior spatial and mechanical abilities. Teachers will make a great effort to help boys master their deficiencies; girls are often left to flounder with theirs.

There is also a tendency to create a school environment in which children learn that boys are more aggressive. Girls who are timid are usually protected and encouraged to remain where they feel safe. On the other hand, boys who might be quite as timid are

Fights between children are common enough, but girls are seldom the antagonists— stanaing on the sidelines or gently intervening is more common. Boys, on the other hand, become readily involved in open combat, a means through which they attain their ends.

rejected and sent away to fend for themselves. Thus girls' passiveness and dependence are increased and boys are made more independent and outgoing.

It has also been found that teachers tend to prompt and direct boys so that they can solve problems for themselves; girls, however, tend to have things done for them—a process that is hardly conducive to learning and creates the misconception that boys have greater ability than girls. And yet, despite all this, girls do consistently better during the early school years.

help his mommy with the washing up, so he put five cups on a tray and carried them into the kitchen. But on his way he tripped and dropped the tray, and all five cups were broken. The following day, the boy next door tried to steal a tart from his mother's cupboard, and he knocked down a cup and broke it. Which was the naughtier boy?" Virtually all children think the first boy was naughtier, because he broke more cups. The question of accident and what lies behind a bad deed means nothing to a child at this age.

At some point after seven, when he has achieved "conservation," the child is able to make the first step away from this purely egocentric point of view. He is better able to measure the wrongness of different actions such as five cups broken in the course of a good deed against one cup broken in the course of theft.

"Right" for him is still serving his own needs, but he is beginning to understand how his interests are mixed up with other people's. The child grasps the idea of rules, and what is called "reciprocity," which, in moral terms,

becomes fairness. It is the fairness of the marketplace, of "you scratch my back and I'll scratch yours," rather than any high ideals. He will come to those later. Now he is laying the foundations on which he will build his understanding of conduct and society.

During these middle years a child's comprehension gradually broadens, and he starts to move into the second stage of moral development. Rules begin to have their own importance. He feels he must obey a rule just because it is a rule, and not merely because he is likely to suffer if he breaks it. Fairness becomes a question of loyalty and trust, and how other people feel begins to matter, as does his own fear of the consequences of wrongdoing.

A child's first day at "real" school is a momentous experience for him. It marks his first step into the world outside the family. Even if he has had a nursery school experience, the transition is an important one. From being among the oldest of those not

The importance of being fair

Preparing your child for school

Below: The graph shows the reaction time of boys and girls. Though they perform similarly in their seventh year, there is a sharp acceleration among girls soon afterward.

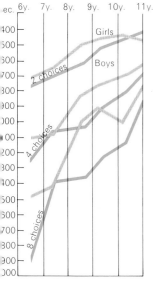

A school playground illustrates perfectly many of the sex differences that are associated with the school-age child. Girls sit in a row quietly chattering while boys indulge in more vigorous activities. Significantly, a teacher has two girls in close attendance; elsewhere a group of boys finalize their plans for some gang warfare.

Right: The diagram shows how masculinity and femininity, defined in terms of aggressiveness and passivity, tend to be affected according to the way in which parents control socialization and aggressiveness in their children and the manner in which they apply punishment. It shows clearly that any form of strictness tends to feminize; a permissive and lax approach masculinizes.

◄ Boys ◄ Girls

Father → Mother	
→	Severity of weaning
→	Level of demands for table manners
→	Severity of toilet training
←	Permissiveness of aggression toward parents
→	Punishment of aggression toward parents
→	Physical punishment
→	Use of ridicule

Right: The diagram shows how involvement with her father in basic areas of development tends to push a daughter toward his sphere of influence, and input from her mother has the opposite effect. These relationships, however, strike different balances through the years.

◄ Mothers ◄ Fathers

Father ← Mother	
←	High proportion infant caretaking
↔	High use of reasoning
←	High use of praise
↔	Low strictness of parent
↔	Satisfaction with socialization
←	High permissiveness for dependency
↔	High reward for dependency
←	High empathy for girls

yet at school, he now finds himself the smallest and newest among a multitude of unknown children, and in addition he is away from home for the greater part of each day.

There is much that parents can do to help the school beginner. Try to adopt a positive, cheerful attitude—not "Wait till you get to school, you won't be allowed to do that!" but "Let's take a walk past the big school today, and watch the children coming out."

Making him personally independent will help him, too, and will give him a head start over those less well prepared.

Choosing a school

Although your child may very well go to the public school in your immediate neighborhood, perhaps you will be considering a private, parochial, magnet, or special school instead. Your decision is one which should be made with great care.

How can you get information about a school? Try to contact families with children already there; watch the local press for notices of events, such as concerts or fairs, held at local schools to which you can go.

Some schools regularly hold open days for next year's parents. Find out if there is an informative magazine or newsletter issued by the school. If the principal is in the habit of making contacts with nursery schools in the area to foster early links with the school, this is the best sign of all; it means that she is concerned and interested.

When you visit, go while the children are there, and notice how they behave. Are they quiet, subdued, conscious of a stranger? Or relaxed, talkative, eager to show you their work? Do they sit at tables or desks, or move about freely? Do they work to the teacher's command, or pursue various occupations in groups or singly? Are lessons stopped at a bell, or do the students move easily from one activity to another? These points will show you whether the atmosphere is formal or free, something you need to consider with reference to your own ideas and your child's temperament.

Be sure to take your child inside his new school well in advance, even if there is no regular "open house" day. Have a teacher point out to you which is his classroom, where to go to the rest room, or where he will be having his lunch. She will have to show him again when he starts, but it is good if his first introduction is made in your company. This helps to bridge the gulf which can all too easily come between home and school.

The first day

The first day at school will be exacting for both of you, so it pays to get everything ready the night before: clothes, shoes, pencil box. Leave time for a leisurely breakfast and journey to school. If you can, it often helps to take an older child with you; it makes the occasion less emotional for both child and parent. A toy or picture postcard brought from home sometimes helps to bridge the gap between family and school, and serves as a useful conversation piece when he first arrives. Make your good-bye as brief and warm as possible—a quick hug and a promise to be there the moment he gets out of school. If there are tears or tantrums, leave the teacher to deal with them; she will probably manage them a good deal more quickly and successfully than you, because there will not be the same emotional tie.

Early anxieties

In a survey in the United States of 250 parents whose children were about to start school, it was found that only thirteen percent of them reported their children were not looking forward to school. Yet at the end of two months as many as thirty-nine percent reported that there had been days when their children were reluctant to go. So you have nothing to worry about if your child occasionally needs persuasion or coaxing—it's natural.

Many early grumbles need taking with a grain of salt: "They wouldn't play the game my way," or "They laughed at me." A light touch and a sense of humor helps more than too much sympathy. Much of a child's initial anxiety about school is due to the length of the school day, which at first seems endless. "Have you just started school?" one teacher asked a glum-looking five-year-old at mid-morning break. "Oh no," said the little girl wearily, "I've been here since nine o'clock!" Fatigue and unfamiliarity may make a child uncertain about school, but these troubles generally disappear.

School is perhaps the most exacting event in a child's life so far, and it's no wonder he is often overtired.

Parent–teacher

Parent-teacher associations exist in most elementary schools, and they are usually helpful in establishing channels of communication between school and home and among parents with common concerns. Today's parents have good opportunities to talk with others and to get firsthand cues from school about teaching methods, discipline, and homework. Many parents also enjoy giving practical help to the school. In some parent-teacher associations, the parents hear their children read in class; they help with the library, make costumes for the school play, and coach at games. If your child's school has no association as such, and you cannot get one formed, there may still be cooperation

with parents; not all principals are willing to have formal associations. Some prefer frequent open days or evenings. The important thing is that school and home should work together; in such an atmosphere your child will be much happier than at a school that virtually says to parents "Keep out."

There may be times when you will wish to go to the school either for reassurance or for information. Try to make these occasions for asking advice rather than for making complaints, for your child needs to feel his parents are on the side of the school and not singling him out for special treatment. If there is something that worries him or you, don't buttonhole the class teacher after school. The first person to talk to is the principal, who usually knows the situation and the teachers in the school. Apart from minor problems, one principal gives these as good reasons for going to see him:

When to see the principal

- If a child takes a sudden dislike to school, or reverts to serious bed-wetting;
- If he shows antisocial habits, such as stealing or lying;
- In times of family crisis: death, divorce, and so on;
- When a child is not getting on as he should in schoolwork;
- If he is being bullied; and
- Where parents feel conditions at the school could be improved.

Matters of policy—punishment, homework, dress—are best brought up by your parent-teacher association, or by a group of parents together.

Tiredness after school

Tiredness at the end of a school day is almost universal among small children, and if your child comes home crotchety or even downright aggressive, you can frequently put it down to fatigue. Don't pester him for a blow-by-blow account of all he has done at school; he may be too tired to tell you, or he may be unable to describe in words all the wonderful new experiences that keep coming his way. Some children jealously guard their privacy over school and need gentle encouragement to share their experiences with you.

After school most children need a period of rest, playing with pets or familiar toys, or perhaps watching television. A comforting evening meal helps them to unwind; the way to a tired child's heart is often through his stomach. A relaxing bath, cool in the summer and warm in the winter, helps too.

Don't be surprised if he brings home new ways and new words from school; one of its benefits is that it brings him into contact with other life-styles and vocabularies. If these are not always to your liking, do not be too shocked, but ignore them and give him time. He will eventually sort out ways and words that are acceptable at home, and drop the others. Except him, too, once he has got over the initial fatigue, to be boisterous when he gets in from school. School can be very confining to an ebullient child, and he may simply need a period of letting off steam without too much criticism from his family.

Different teaching methods

In the schools of today there are many different approaches to teaching, and the past two decades have seen a good deal of experiment and innovation. On the whole the new approaches have been characterized by an emphasis on individualization, on a need to consider the educational needs of each child.

Many methods have been developed which seek to achieve this—what teachers have endeavored to work toward is an understanding of where the child is when he begins a given year's work, and how he can best be helped to move forward from that point.

Individualized teaching, of course, in a classroom consisting of many children, is indeed a challenge for the most conscientious teacher. The luxury of one approach, one lesson, one exercise for all, is not hers. She must be ever ready to work with each child in turn, to "group" and "regroup," as the children progress, to spot weak points and give encouragement. To manage all this and to create a milieu of relaxation and discipline as well is no small task.

Schools differ in their philosophies and in the degree to which they can minister successfully to the needs of children. As economic pressures increase, as costs rise and communities become reluctant to raise taxes in order to keep pace, many schools are finding it necessary to make complex adjustments in the name of economy. And private and parochial schools are also finding it necessary to rearrange and examine their priorities.

Economic pressures and the realization that today's children must be well prepared to take their places in a complicated and competitive society have also led to an apparent swing of the pendulum "back to basics"—a return to more traditional methods of teaching and an emphasis on the "three R's." The factors that are significant in this new/old approach reflect the problems and frustrations that face American society as the seventies draw to a close.

But whatever the threads and complexities, what are important for parents to recognize are the changing perspectives and shifting nature of the educational process and the vital necessity for parent participation in it. Educational theories may come and go and you may be more or less satisfied at any specific time with your child's teacher or his school, but what is most important is your child's feeling that you are positive, on the whole, about the school's efforts in his behalf and supportive of the work he himself is doing.

Middle schools and high schools are usually organized according to specific subjects, and although there is bound to be a range of ability within *any* classroom, children are usually divided according to ability.

Individual teaching styles vary, but most teachers recognize that it is important to get down to the child's level so that he is able to watch the teacher's face and a rapport can be firmly established. Young children appreciate a hug that means "well done, you've got it right!"

Left : In a classroom run along informal lines, where children work together in a fluid "family" group structure, the teacher can circulate and instruct as and when she feels it necessary.

Below : A more formal classroom, in which each pupil has his own desk and stays there until allowed to move. The teacher rarely leaves the blackboard area, and subjects are taught in separate lessons.

There is some feeling that such subtle labeling inhibits the sudden "spurts" which are so characteristic of childhood and adolescence. If you feel a child's placement should be reevaluated, do contact his teacher.

How teachers work

Teachers as well as children can be grouped differently, working either independently or as a team.

Throughout the primary years of schooling the most usual system is for each class to have its own teacher who is responsible for teaching each subject. She is very much "my teacher" to each child. However, specialist teachers may take the class for certain subjects, such as music or physical education. Recently team teaching has become popular: teachers specialize, but pool their skills and resources and work together as a team rather than in isolation. This method demands very good liaison among staff.

How school days are organized

Thirdly, there are different ways of organizing the curriculum. The traditional method is subject centered: what a child has to learn is divided up into separate subjects, such as reading, writing, spelling, arithmetic, geography, history, or social studies. Thus the classroom teacher divides her program by subject areas. For half an hour she teaches the class one thing, and then, after desks and blackboards are cleared, the class turns its attention to a different subject, with no links or relationships sought or explained. Such was the traditional way of organizing curriculum.

The modern way is topic centered (also known as the integrated day). The edges between subjects are blurred, sometimes so much that the divisions no longer exist at all. This is meant to reflect the fact that real life does not fall neatly into the compartments the old curriculum used to reflect.

In some schools topic-centered teaching is done by one teacher, who chooses what the children learn about, perhaps teaching the whole class at once. The result is only one step away from traditional teaching. In other schools it is left entirely to the children to choose. When team teaching is used the children can take a topic or a problem around to each of the specialist teachers in turn.

Open plan or classrooms?

There is also a good deal of variation in how schools are laid out. Many still have separate rooms, especially where children are grouped together in classes. In others—mostly schools built in the last ten years—the space is more open, allowing greater flexibility for teacher and pupils. However, an open-plan school is not necessarily an indication that "open" or progressive teaching approaches are being used. This decision is left to the principal and his staff.

The local school that your child will probably go to may use any combination of these teaching styles and arrangements. There is no rule that a school has to be either "progressive" or "traditional." Very few teach exactly as you were probably taught, a system that changed little for a hundred years. Very few are as unstructured or as undisciplined as you might be led to believe from controversy in the newspapers. Most teachers adopt a middle-of-the-road approach, attempting to use the best that both progressive and traditional styles can offer.

School lunches

School lunches have a bad image in many people's minds, based, perhaps, on a time when they were not as carefully prepared as they are nowadays. All authorities have to prepare their meals in accordance with government recommendations on nutritional content and preparation. It will help your child to adjust if you find out beforehand how lunch is served: on a cafeteria system, perhaps, or on family lines, with pupils sitting at tables in small groups and being served by an older child or teacher.

Many elementary schoolchildren still go home for lunch, although the growing number of working mothers has led to an increasing demand for school lunch programs.

If you are worried about your child eating unfamiliar foods, perhaps served in unfamiliar ways, relax: he will be all right when

Eating for school

During the years of your child's growth, it is essential that he has enough of the right food at the right times. Learning itself requires food, as the working brain uses up large quantities of energy.

Breakfast is vital for mental alertness, health, and weight control. Without it, children are deprived of "fuel" for as long as eighteen hours, a deficit that can lead to apathy, irritability, and restlessness. Current research in nutrition tends to show that adults and children who eat little or no breakfast give poorer over-all performances, are prone to accidents, and are slower and less accurate in ability tests.

Experiments have shown that the type and amount of breakfast we eat is very important. The best start to the day consists of some form of protein, with carbohydrate and fats to provide energy and slow down the absorption of the food. Breakfast should supply roughly one-third of the day's protein and calorie needs: a child from seven to nine needs about 2,100 calories and 53 g protein.

Children particularly need breakfast because their metabolic rate is higher and they are usually more active than adults; it will also stifle their urge to eat fattening snacks and sweets between meals.

If a "hot lunch" is available at your child's school, you can usually assume that it is nutritionally balanced. It should provide about 880 calories and 29 g protein. Children

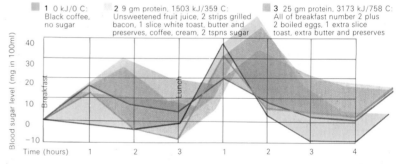

1 0 kJ/0 C: Black coffee, no sugar

2 9 gm protein, 1503 kJ/359 C: Unsweetened fruit juice, 2 strips grilled bacon, 1 slice white toast, butter and preserves, coffee, cream, 2 tspns sugar

3 25 gm protein, 3173 kJ/758 C: All of breakfast number 2 plus 2 boiled eggs, 1 extra slice toast, extra butter and preserves

Blood sugar level (mg in 100ml)

40
30
20
10
0
−10

Time (hours)   1   2   3   1   2   3   4

seem to enjoy the sociability of having lunch at school.

If your child's school does not have a meal service or if you prefer to make the lunches yourself, here are a few points to consider. Soups and drinks may be available, but if not send a hot soup or cold milk or fruit juice in a thermos. In planning, remember to combine different textures and vary the bread and fillings for sandwiches frequently. Moisten dry sandwiches with mayonnaise, ketchup, or pickle. For a balanced packed lunch, give the sandwich a protein filling such as meat, fish eggs, or cheese, and remember that bread itself is a valuable source of protein. Add fresh fruit or raw vegetables for vitamins. Butter or margarine will provide the necessary fats. A slice of cake or a few cookies is a nice dessert for a child, but candy should be avoided since it leads so easily to tooth decay. Tuna or chicken salads spoil on a warm day.

Above: Although this graph shows the results of a study of breakfasts eaten by adults and their differing effects on blood sugar levels throughout the day (despite the fact that they consumed identical lunches), a well-balanced breakfast will give children, too, a high level of performance and a prolonged sense of well-being and satisfaction. The importance of a well-planned breakfast is so widely recognized that many communities provide federally subsidized breakfasts for young children who do not have them at home. Well-fed children are unquestionably more alert and more ready to enter into the day's experiences.

School uniforms are not generally part of the American tradition, although they are still used in some parochial and private schools. Although younger children may enjoy wearing them, older students often resent the intrusion a uniform makes on their own personal taste in dress. They may prefer to wear jeans, the "uniform" of their own peer group.

he is eating along with other hungry, chattering children.

Much care goes into the preparation of school meals to ensure that they are well-balanced, so give your child all the encouragement you can to eat what is on his plate—though few teachers now insist on children finishing every scrap of their lunch.

Private schools

Private and parochial schools provide healthy alternatives to public education in the United States, and it is the right of parents to choose them if they so wish. Their reasons for doing so will vary. In some cases they may believe that the schools in their community are not likely to serve the needs of their particular child or children; family tradition or strong religious conviction may also play a part in their decision. Often children attend the public school at one time and the independent or parochial school at another phase of their academic career.

The issue of subsidies to private education has been hotly debated, and the argument will no doubt continue. In some cases a partial accommodation has been made through various "shared time" arrangements by which a parochial school, for example, may use the science labs of a local high school to supplement its own facilities. In other communities programs are worked out in which children attend public school for their basic subjects and parochial school for supplementary work of religious orientation.

Handicapped children are provided for in most states either within the regular public school system or through subsidies which wholly or partially cover tuition in special schools. Many educators believe that if at all possible a handicapped child will flourish more fully if he attends school with children who are *not* handicapped. This "mainstreaming" approach has proven successful in many school systems. Each handicapped child, however, must be evaluated individually by competent professionals before a determination can be made as to how to best utilize the educational resources available to him.

Boarding schools are generally not recommended for children below high school age, though they may be necessary in special circumstances. In general children do best in family settings, and even at the secondary school level, the decision to send a child away to school must be weighed carefully.

By choosing any one of these sandwiches, and including the food and drink listed below, you will be giving your child a meal that provides all his lunch-time needs. Add 7 fl oz/200 ml milk, pure fruit juice, or vitamin C fortified fruit drink, a piece of fruit or raw vegetable, and some carbohydrate, such as a slice of cake or cookies.

○ *1 soft roll, butter or margarine, baked beans and grated cheese, watercress or chopped lettuce.*

○ *2 slices rye or wholewheat bread, butter or margarine, tuna fish, mayonnaise, and watercress.*

○ *2 slices rye or wholewheat bread, butter or margarine, ham, cottage cheese, and tomato.*

○ *2 slices white bread, butter or margarine, peanut butter and crisp bacon.*

○ *2 slices French bread, butter or margarine, liver sausage, hard-boiled egg, watercress, and mayonnaise.*

Learning to read

Whatever kind of school your child is enrolled in, learning to read will be given top priority, though it may be approached in a number of different ways. Learning to read is a very large task indeed for a child. First he must learn his letters. This is a far more complex assignment than might appear. "A" is easy because it has a distinctive shape. "X" is more or less the same whichever way you look at it. But a child's perception, even at six, is still not as tightly organized as an adult's. So he confuses letters that are the same shape but reversed, as in "b" and "d," "m" and "w." Hence the old saying, "Mind your p's and q's." Next he has to learn the order in which letters go to make up a word, and here he has the same problem: "was" and "saw" can appear the same to him at first glance.

Once he is on the road to reading he can use the context of the word to help him. If he has just read "this is a truck," he can guess the new word in "this is a yellow truck" because he is also learning that words that go before names like truck describe them—and there will almost certainly be a picture of a yellow truck to help him. Knowing what to expect for the next word is an important part of reading: it is what makes some pieces easier to read than others, even for adults. You may find that your child can recognize a new word in one sentence but not in the next.

Perhaps the biggest problem for a child whose first language is English is that a letter may make several different sounds. For example, "a" makes four, alone or in combination, as in "apple," "arm," "angel," and "author"; the letter "o" makes no fewer than six: "toe," "on," "book," "food," "out," and "oil." Even some consonants change, as, for example, "c" in "cat," "chair," and "police."

Because of this many schools have re-introduced the very oldest way of all, teaching the alphabet. The name of the letter, how-ever, is taught together with the phonic method, so that a child is taught that this is an "ay"; and that it makes the sounds "ay," "a," and "ah" ("au" is usually left out, as it occurs only in words a child will not meet for some time). In the United States this method is coupled with teaching both capital and small letters. In Britain, however, it has been found that teaching capitals hinders a child's learning to write, so they are left until later.

How you can help

Parents can give their child great help in learning to read. Every child learns in his own way and needs individual attention, not only when he is being shown new words and sounds, but when he is practicing. Then he needs careful coaching. The amount of time

The basics of reading

The most common methods used to teach reading have been phonics and look-say (or whole word). The first teaches the child the sound that each letter makes and builds up words from single letters, whereas look-say teaches him to recognize whole words at a time. Because they each concentrate on one aspect of reading, both methods show quick results—but of a limited kind. A child taught exclusively by one method has difficulty in learning the other skills needed. Most schools therefore use a mixture of both methods.

The sun is hot.
Mum has a hat, but Dad is in the hut.

Above : A phonic reading book groups together several words containing the same sounds, such as hot, hut, hat. In this way the child becomes accustomed to associating particular sounds with their written symbols, and he comes to realize the alternative ways in which the sounds can be put together to form different words.

However, the reading book can only use words that are made up of the sounds that the child has so far learned, and this tends to lead to awkward phrasing and unusual vocabulary.

The car is at the shop.
Daddy is in the car.
Mummy is going into the shop.

Above : A look-say reading book depends on constant repetition of each word until the child instantly recognizes it in any context. As it may take thirty-five repetitions before a child thoroughly learns a word, building up a working vocabulary is a lengthy business.

The advantage of this method is that reading books can contain interesting and familiar vocabulary, even the long, irregularly pronounced words, such as "television," that a child uses in everyday speech.

Above : There is an enormous range of teaching aids used to help children learn necessary reading skills. These children are using "sentence makers." The child has a large selection of little cards, each of which has a different word printed on it. He chooses from these and slots the cards into the frame in the right order to form a sentence of subject, verb, and object. This exercise improves a child's grammar and enlarges his vocabulary.

the cat iz lꝏkiŋ doun at us

The initial teaching alphabet was invented to solve the problem of all the different sounds that each letter of the alphabet can make. It has forty-four characters, each one corresponding to an exact sound. Once the child has learned to read confidently with ITA, he is transferred to the traditional alphabet. Although most children make this transfer quite easily, some have great problems learning to spell the irregular words in the English language after learning ITA, and its value has been called into serious question.

Learning to write

The first form of writing your child will be taught will be small, unjoined, printed letters; later he will learn capital letters. Most schools teach a rounded form of print, but in the United Kingdom some teach an italic print from the start. All first writing is done in pencil or crayon.

When he learns to join up letters, he may start to use a fountain pen. Many teachers do not encourage the use of ballpoints as they hinder the development of a mature, controlled hand.

There are three major types of "joined-up" writing taught in schools. The children who were taught italic print will learn to link the letters to form an italic script. Those children who have learned the rounded type of print will be taught either a looped form (this is universal in the United States) or "Marion Richardson" (the most popular method in Britain). The latter is simpler for a child to grasp because it uses the same letter-forms as the rounded print the child has already learned.

This is the print script that most children use when they first learn to write. Some are anxious to write even before they are old enough to go to school. If your child seems ready, you can help by giving him an alphabet of simple block letters to copy. The first word a child forms, and the first one he recognizes, is usually his own name.

Above: The process of learning to write is not made into a formal exercise for a five-year-old but is introduced as an integral part of classroom activity. The child will write about the things he is learning at the time.

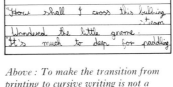

Some European children learn a form of writing that resembles a printed italic, though there seems to be increasing recognition that this style tends to be confusing. Teachers in the United States, however, seem to stress the importance of making the written word resemble the printed word as much as possible so that the letters are more easily recognized by the young beginner.

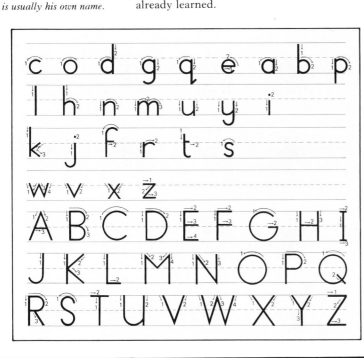

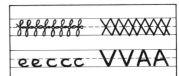

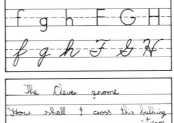

Above: To make the transition from printing to cursive writing is not a simple matter, as many of the letters take unfamiliar forms. Children differ widely in their readiness to make this shift, which requires a much higher level of muscular development than printing. Girls often make the transition more easily than boys. The young child must almost "draw" the words as he learns the complex new shapes. It takes great dexterity for a young child

to write cursive smoothly and legibly, but once achieved an elegant and flowing handwriting will rightfully be a source of great pride. British children often use more rounded forms which can be easily linked into words after they are mastered. This style is called "Marion Richardson." It is often practiced with brightly colored felt-tipped pens or magic markers.

a teacher can give to each child is naturally limited, so supplement the teacher's work with your support. Encourage the child to bring his school reading book home and go over the day's work with him. It should not be work, of course, in the sense of labor. If he is making progress he will enjoy it—and so will you. Do not spend too long or push him too far, especially when he is tired—stop while he is ahead, with a word of praise.

On the whole, primary teachers prefer that parents leave the actual *teaching* of reading to them. But if your child is having difficulty, his teacher may suggest specific ways in which you can help. Remember, too, that all kinds of enriching experiences—a trip to the firehouse or the zoo; the care of a pet—will increase a child's zest for life,

his eagerness to express himself, his vocabulary, and therefore his ability to read.

Reading and writing are two sides of the same coin. There has to be "writing readiness" just as there was "reading readiness," in the sense that a child must have acquired the muscular coordination needed to hold a crayon or pencil and move it from left to right. Perhaps he will acquire this first by "drawing" letters in his sand-tray, or by tracing them with his finger. Later he will be shown how to put letters and words and finally sentences together.

He will have a certain amount of writing practice, but at first he will be encouraged to write labels for various things about the classroom—coat hooks, books—where letters

Encouraging your child to write

can be combined into a single word to give a meaning. When he has managed to produce fairly legible writing in sentences, he may be asked to write these beneath a weather chart, make out a list of instructions for the care and feeding of pets, write out the recipe for cakes made in the classroom oven, or write a letter of thanks after a class visit. You can take all the opportunities that arise at home— ask him to write out your shopping list, write a note for the milkman, or write to grandma. Show him how pleased you are with good work by displaying it around the house.

English language

Later, children will be carrying their writing much further than a few simple sentences. They will be putting ideas together into various forms—what we used to know, perhaps as "composition." Nowadays, however, this activity is not likely to have a special place in the day's schedule but will probably spill over into every facet of school life.

Your child will be writing many different things: it might be the record of the growth of plants or bulbs or, at Christmas time, letters to other children delivered around the school by the school "postman." Sometimes a whole class will get together to write a book, or a series of books, on subjects ranging from astronauts to armor. Poetry will be attempted, too; many children have a natural ear for the music and rhythm of verse. The whole approach to writing and composition is now away from passive copying and toward active experiment with words; trying out different styles for different occasions, expressing feelings as well as facts. "English language" may not figure on the list of subjects studied in many schools; it has just become absorbed into everyday life, by teachers who are conscious of language.

Spelling

You may be surprised to find that your child doesn't appear to have spelling lessons at all. Of course he needs to learn to spell, but teaching in this sphere, at least in the first years, is often done incidentally. This is because attention to accuracy can hold up the flow of words. Spelling is a skill that is quite distinct from the arts of reading and composition.

Your child's spelling skills will be developed not by rote but through reading and through opportunities for written expression. He may make his own personal dictionary of words he needs when writing, and refer to it later. Many teachers encourage the use of dictionaries as storehouses of interesting words on which to draw.

About ten percent of children (mainly boys) have much more than average difficulty in recognizing the "look" of words, and can go on reversing many words and letters for years. Some may continue to be poor spellers for life. Such children will be encouraged to spend more time on their own "dictionaries," adding to them words that they find difficult and having them frequently checked by the teacher.

Punctuation needs to be taught to a child in much the same way as spelling. There is no point in making him too punctuation-conscious to enjoy his writing. He learns best, at first, by ear, hearing where full stops or commas come. Later, he will acquire knowledge by extensive reading and writing, with awareness and care. This applies to grammar, too.

An occasional grammar lesson, when several children meet the same difficulty, can be useful; but wide reading and writing is a better teacher than a grammar book. A child will gradually come to recognize which words are "doing" words (verbs) and which are "naming" words (nouns), but he will not spend a lot of time learning the parts of speech and the exceptions to rules.

Punctuation and grammar

One of the biggest breakthroughs in teaching methods for younger children has been in mathematics. For many parents, math, arithmetic, sums, whatever we call it, was a bugaboo; some people even acquired a permanent block about math, which they saw as some kind of juggling trick with numbers, where answers had to be "right" or "wrong." Too many children simply learned their tables by heart, and tried too hard (or gave up trying) to perform half-understood tricks so as to get the teacher's approval.

No child need fear the "new math" of today; in fact, beginners enjoy exploring not numbers or symbols, which they take time to grasp, but the raw material of math.

Today, learning math is looked on as an exploration, which goes on in all sorts of different settings, at all times of the day, as children handle, experiment, discuss, and record. As one child put it, "math is all around you": in the playground, in the kitchen at home, in the car on a family trip, just everywhere. Children acquire mathematical concepts by examining a ruler or a tape measure, making a plan of their classroom or house, making a graph of the heights of their friends or the family's birthdays, guessing at distances and speeds and checking their guesses.

This does not imply that the basics of arithmetic are not taught or that tables should never be learned. It simply means that the concepts should be understood before the mechanics of math are learned. The courses and the structural equipment that mushroomed during the 1960s were all designed to help children learn and understand through their own activities a process that would give them firm grounding in the concepts underlying the technological, computerized world of today.

Early mathematics

Much of the investigation that goes on in the primary classroom is scientific, though the children may not know the word. Scientific inquiry begins with the child's first questions at the sandbox or in the wading pool—why does this float and that sink? Why is wet sand heavier than dry? Or in the kitchen—why does steam come out of the kettle? Science is

Science

"New" math

Although there are many mathematical courses provided for schools, most teachers combine the better features of these courses with ideas that they may have developed independently. Yet within the apparent diversity, there are certain universal aims: that children should understand mathematical concepts through their own activities, and that the work should be enjoyable so that children gain their own impetus to learn and explore, without having to be forced.

There are a number of mathematical concepts, and children must pass through them in order; solid mathematical understanding can only be built step by step. Furthermore it has been realized that children do not simply learn concepts; assisted by the teacher they acquire them through activity. Most classrooms have a large selection of apparatus with which children can perform experiments and numerical operations that, combined with carefully planned questions, help them discover mathematical relationships for themselves.

A five-year-old's cognitive development is such that he may not understand terms like "longer than" or "shorter than." Therefore the teacher must make sure that he can understand and use mathematical terms with confidence. Learning to sort and to recognize similarities between shapes and colors is another early activity for the schoolchild. After this he will learn about numbers both in the way they relate to objects and to themselves. Only later, with the help of more structural materials, will he begin simple computation: addition, subtraction, division, and multiplication.

It is important that math courses should be flexible and that children should be able to progress at their own rate. They may use individual work cards to help them grasp particular concepts and may carry out structured tasks, one at a time. As each task is completed and understood, the child can move on to some new activity independent of the rest of the class. Math is no longer the chore to be dreaded and feared but an activity that is fun as well as constructive.

Although a wide range of commercial work cards is available, many schools prefer to make up their own. Reading and then carrying out simple instructions is useful practice for young children. The more imaginative cards show how the math he is learning relates to a child's everyday life.

Left: In the early school years children are still strongly visually orientated and find it easier to acquire such concepts as "more" or "less" if they can actually see and handle materials for themselves.

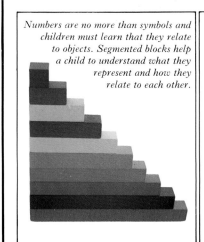

Numbers are no more than symbols and children must learn that they relate to objects. Segmented blocks help a child to understand what they represent and how they relate to each other.

Tables, once taught parrot fashion, can be clearly understood as the child sees the means to the end.

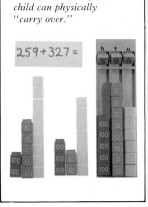

The mechanics of addition are made clearer if the child can physically "carry over."

$259 + 327 =$

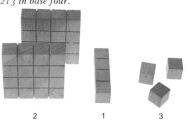

Our everyday mathematics is done to base ten. Other bases are possible and are taught in some schools. In base four a one is carried every time four or a multiple of four is reached. Therefore the number four is shown as 10, and five as 11. These cubes show how thirty-nine in base ten becomes 213 in base four.

2   1   3

not a subject in itself; it involves problem-solving in many fields, so it will be an integral part of various school "subjects," such as math and reading.

Children are encouraged to experiment with magnets, microscopes, and magnifying glasses, to "see what happens" if they play with water, blocks, clay, or scales. In one experiment some six-year-olds dropped water onto various materials. "It's gone," said one, dropped water onto newspaper. "It's spread out," said another, trying it on a piece of glass. "It's a bead," said a third, trying it on waxed paper. Another time, a teacher lit a candle and held a saucer over the flame. "The saucer's gone black," said one child. "Why?" All this leads to discussion and learning.

The world of nature is full of material for scientific inquiry. How does a plant grow? What is a fossil? Here parents can help enormously by letting a child follow up scientific interests out of doors.

Art

Every young child is "artistic" in that he loves to express himself in painting and drawing. Through art he seems to get clear his ideas about himself. It is a matter of technique, rather than of language, expressing feelings and defining experiences. Don't criticize his work because it is not adult; it is his own, and valuable. He wants to practice it at home as well as at school, so let him try, provided he clears up like a workman who is proud of his various tools.

He will also like to model and trace, do paste and paint collages, print, make lino cuts, and try the various crafts—embroidery, basket-making, making things in wood and metal. Give recognition to the gifts he brings home, even if they are not very well made. They are made with love, and you may never again receive such spontaneous presents given with such affection and with so much joy in the making.

Most schools offer children the opportunity to model in clay. Its versatility allows them to create the most varied objects, both realistic and fantastic.

A second language

Unless a second language is spoken at home American schoolchildren often do not have the rich experience of knowing more than their native language. Although some elementary schools do have foreign language programs, inflation and the need to pare expenses have taken their toll. Many schools with a large number of foreign-born children have bilingual programs, despite some questions that have risen about their validity.

Drama

Dramatic expression is very important in these early years. It is not a question of "acting in a play" so much as of improvisation, with everyone taking part freely, there being no distinction between actors and audience. Through "becoming someone else" a child experiences a feeling of release obtainable in no other way; and getting children to act out experiences, hopes, and fears is a very valuable means of helping them to come to terms with living, in addition to fostering good speech and posture.

Dressing up and the disguise thus attained releases many children from their own identities and helps them to act more freely.

Music

It used to be thought that musical ability was a rare talent. Genius is rare, but ability is not. A few unlucky children are tone or rhythm deaf, and others can enjoy music when they hear it but have no aptitude for producing it themselves. Very many children have musical abilities that are never recognized because they are not brought up in musical homes.

If you are musical yourselves, you will probably naturally want your child to join a choir or learn an instrument, Most primary schools have percussion bands or recorder bands. A young child can feel music throughout his body, and will dance spontaneously. The nursery school child often has his first experience in responding to music through movement. If he wants to play a string or wind instrument, it is good to give him a start on the piano when he is eight—at six if he shows he is ready. The Japanese violin master Suzuki has shown that children can achieve high levels of competence on the violin as early as four or five, given concentrated teaching.

Playing in an orchestra teaches a child more than music; he learns that many small parts add up to an exciting whole.

Practice is the great bugbear. A good teacher should be able to grade the lesson in such a way that the child will always be making progress, and will always be interested. But firm encouragement and positive interest on your part will help. Practicing by the clock is not as important as the enjoyment and concentration a child gives to his music.

Social studies

You may be wondering where subjects like history and geography have got to in your child's schooling, for he will not always know them by these names. Often they are combined with "social studies"—a multidisciplinary look at the past and the world around us. Perhaps the children will pursue their natural interest in investigations into local history and past memories of the family and neighbors; what did their town or village look like twenty, thirty, fifty years ago? Geography runs concurrently; children may make a map of their district, visit local docks or railroad stations, or go to the market to see where their food comes from.

Discoveries like these are recorded in various ways: in writing, in graphs, in pictures, and in model-making. Children are in a sense composing their own history or geography books. They will also be visiting museums and galleries, houses of historic

After a day's outing, recapturing some of his impressions in a drawing or painting will help to fix them in a child's memory.

interest, churches, and public buildings—all grist for the learning mill.

The best time to begin sex education is, of course, when a child asks his first questions at home. These should have been answered simply and frankly, so that he has nothing to unlearn when fuller facts are given later.

Today sex education is part of the curriculum in many elementary schools, and it need not arouse any special parental concern or anxiety. If you have done your job as a parent then your child will know much of what the school will tell. If sex is taught as part of a regular unit on biology and human physiology, it will be kept in a healthy perspective. It is likely that your child's school will invite the parents to a discussion beforehand, so that they will understand its factual approach. Sex should always be seen within the pattern of love and family life, but the school will see that as your task. A child needs to view sex as

Sex education

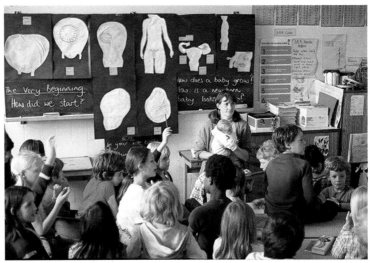

more than a mechanical act; he should see the act as an expression of a deeply felt relationship.

What really matters is sex "education" in the fullest sense of this word; a right attitude toward human bodies and their functions. In a well-run school, teachers will already be prepared for sex questions and sexual awareness as they note their pupils' developing maturity, and they will be able to cope with the problems as they arise within the framework of the school day as well as in those lesson periods set aside for the purpose.

Sex education conducted in an unemotional but informed atmosphere is an excellent way for a child to learn about the facts of life. A mother and baby in attendance add a little reality to the lesson.

These are used in many schools, and include radio, television, films and film strips, tape recorders, slides, and phonograph records, as well as teaching machines. Many children enjoy these extensions of classroom teaching, and are given confidence, especially by using a teaching machine, to learn at their own pace without criticism from the teacher or the class. The teaching machine sets out a learning program to be worked through by an individual child step by step, and it has checks when the wrong answer is given, and

Teaching aids

Intelligence and IQ scores

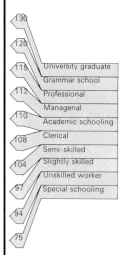

Above : The diagram shows the average IQ scores of children from different backgrounds (combining genetic and environmental influences) and the IQ scores linked with levels of education (shown in brown).

Intelligence can be defined as the ability to absorb new information, remember it, and use it to solve new problems.

It is thought that intelligence has three aspects. To some extent, a person's intelligence is determined before birth and depends on the pattern of genes he receives at conception. But how intelligent he becomes depends also on his early environment: his mother's physical well-being before he is born; in early years how well he is helped to understand the world around him; the attention and stimulation he gets; and to what extent his curiosity is encouraged. Thus, a child who is deprived of stimulation will not develop to his full potential.

Finally there is intelligence as assessed by intelligence tests. These are designed to assess a child's intellectual attainments over a wide field, including many skills that are not directly taught at school. They are most useful in predicting academic achievement. A child's score on an intelligence test is usually expressed in terms of IQ (intelligence quotient). This is merely a way of comparing a child's score on the test with the scores of a large number of children of the same age.

It used to be said that if a child's mental age were higher than the average for his age, then his IQ was above the average (100) by an equivalent proportion, but this does not provide a measure which is the same for all children at all ages.

There are some abilities that intelligence tests do not measure adequately: on the whole they favor the logical scientific mind rather than the creative. IQ test scores are limited in predicting occupational success; a very gifted scientist is no more likely to have a high IQ than his less successful colleagues.

Nonverbal reasoning is one of the three main abilities measured by IQ tests. This test, typical of those used to assess nonverbal reasoning, involves a decision as to which of cards A, B, and C makes the correct fourth card in the sequence formed by the first three.

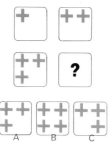

Below : Psychologists have tried various explanations of how intelligence is made up. According to one influential theory, a person has a general intelligence that is made up of more

Spatial ability is the ability to appreciate relationships and manipulate images in space. The test shown requires a child to use his spatial ability to work out from the diagram which way wheel D will rotate when wheel A turns in the direction indicated by the arrow.

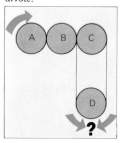

specialized types of intelligence. The two main types are intellectual and functional. Below this level come grouped abilities and then some special abilities. At the bottom on this chart

This is a typical example of the verbal reasoning tests used with young children. The child has to fill the blank in the sentence with the correct word from the list of alternatives. Although three words have to do with "leg," only one has the correct relationship.

Arm is to hand as leg is to—

shoe/sock/foot/walk

come individual skills and abilities. This is one way of explaining why two people with the same IQ can have such different kinds of individual ability.

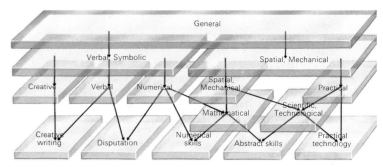

Final exams

The more open approach to what and how a child should learn has naturally meant that there is now less emphasis on tests and examinations than previously. Many primary schools have no examinations or major tests. Instead they continuously assess how well a child is doing. A teacher should know both by training and by experience what an average child is capable of at any age, and she will be able to judge whether a child is above or below average. She should know each child in her charge well enough to decide whether that child is reaching his potential or not. If she has any doubt, then the educational psychologist can give an intelligence and aptitude test.

Later in their educational career examinations become a fixture of life for most children, and, if they do not get practice in taking them, they can find them a rude shock. Thus many primary schools give their pupils some experience with test-taking, through standardized, grade-level tests or

explanations before the next step is attempted. In rural schools the use of these aids enlarges the scope of work considerably.

those designed to measure comprehension of specific curriculum units.

In any case life is competitive. Getting a job, keeping it, and winning promotion all depend on doing well and doing better than the next man. There is a difference here, perhaps, between a child's worth to himself and his family and his worth to an employer. Many parents—perhaps more parents than teachers—believe that exams are the best preparation for this side of life. If exams are a strain on the child, it is probably not the exams themselves but the extent to which he is being pushed by his parents that is making the child anxious. (Some children have anxious personalities, and they need special support.) In the first years a parent's guide to what a child is taking in, or what a school is teaching, will largely be based not on exam results but on the answers to these questions. Is my child generally alert and interested? Can he manage the basic skills of reading, writing, and mathematics at the appropriate age? Is he developing interests and hobbies that enrich him as a person? Does he know where to go for information? Can he talk, discuss, and exchange views within the home?

Learning through their own activities is very stimulating for children, but there are still moments of floundering incomprehension.

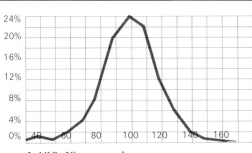

Left : The graph shows the distribution of IQ scores over the population as a whole. Half the population score above 100, half below. Sixty-eight percent of people have IQs between eighty-five and 115. More boys than girls have either very high or very low scores.

A child's IQ score can be strongly influenced by his parent's attitude to his academic performance. Children from demanding homes score highest, but they are also the most tense during tests. Those from less demanding homes are more relaxed, may be apathetic, and score lower.

Demanding homes

Normal homes

Overanxious homes

Unconcerned homes

130
125
120
115
110
105
100
95
90

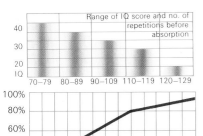

Range of IQ score and no. of repetitions before absorption

70–79 80–89 90–109 110–119 120–129

Left : Some forms of memory are also linked with intelligence. The higher a child's IQ the easier it is for him to learn new words. This is why some people still refer to intelligence as "general intellectual capacity."

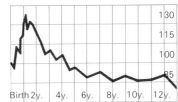

Birth 2y.   4y.   6y.   8y.   10y.   12y.

Above : The growth of intelligence is complete by adolescence. After this, improvements in test scores are due to a mastery of better ways of performing the tasks set in the test.

Birth 2y.   4y.   6y.   8y.   10y.   12y.

130
115
100
85

Above : Since the nature of a child's intelligence changes so much as he develops, his IQ score at an early age tells very little about what he will score when he is older.

Coping with tests

Parents' attitudes toward tests and exams can be crucial. Where conversation at home is dominated by "How did you do in class today?" and "How many marks did you get in last week's test?" a child will sense the pressures and react either with anxiety or by giving up altogether. It is perfectly natural to want your child to do well in exams, but this is best achieved by taking things calmly, seeing that he gets the necessary rest, fresh air, and relaxation—especially the night before—and trying to communicate your own calmness to the child. He will be quick to sense if you are worried about how he is likely to perform. Sometimes you can help by going over the subject the night before. The very fact that he knows you are involved will help to give him confidence.

Homework

Homework is given in some primary schools as a matter of course, whereas in others not at all, or not until the child is nine or ten. It is important to establish what homework is for. For the teacher, it is a means of knowing how far her teaching in class has been assimilated —which makes nonsense of any parental intervention. "Well done, father!" is quite

understandable at the bottom of an essay that the child obviously did not write himself. To do a child's work for him is not to help him at all. On the other hand, for the child, homework is a chance to prepare himself for the independent study he will have to undertake if he carries on his studies beyond school. Any help the parents can give toward establishing this kind of intellectual independence, therefore, will be welcome.

First of all, he will need somewhere to study. It does not have to be a bedroom shut away from the rest of the family. You may find that the kitchen table, where he has only to open the door to ask for help, is the best place. He may even be glad if you are there washing up or preparing supper—some children prefer company. This is not possible for every family, but a child should feel that he is still part of the household and can come to his parents for help when necessary—provided the help is of the right kind.

Often, all a child needs is someone with whom he can discuss a difficulty; he clears his own mind as he talks. Possibly you can suggest ways of tackling a problem, without doing the work for him—reminding him of a rule, perhaps, or taking another example. Parents can enjoy doing this with their children; it can be quite fun to learn alongside your child. You can help him refer to a book or encyclopedia, too, and it will do him good to feel you are also pleased when something comes out right or is at last understood.

Children need a chance for relaxation, fresh air, and time to follow their own pursuits—music, games, or reading—as well as time to do homework. Most schools specify the time to be spent on homework, but have a word with other parents about how long their children are taking. Sometimes a teacher has no idea that a pupil is sitting up the whole evening wrestling with a problem, and is glad to be told. If there is really too much homework being assigned, home/school communication is very definitely in order.

On the other hand, there are schools where homework has purposely been abolished. "I realize this is a big step," one principal told parents, "and that you'll all conclude that your children will from now on do nothing but watch television after school. This is really *why* I am abolishing it. I want your children to spend their time usefully and constructively at home—and you are the people who can best bring this about." The parents were nonplussed, but after a time it became clear that a good deal of interesting "homework" was going on at home, not of the official kind, but of the kind that the principal had hoped would occur: hobbies, collections, reading, and just talk and discussion with fathers and mothers. A bold step, but in that case it worked.

A child can fall behind in schoolwork for many reasons. The most obvious, illness, often has only a minor, short-term effect. Although two or three weeks is a large slice

What to do if your child falls behind

out of a semester, a child who is well-motivated and well-supported at home can usually catch up quite quickly. Find out from the school what he would have covered, and help him through as much of the material as you can when—and not before—he is well enough to cope. A teacher can often assist by giving carefully planned homework. If the school uses teaching machines, these can help him work on his own.

It is not uncommon for a child to have difficulty in one subject or group of subjects. In such a case special tutoring may be useful. Some schools provide this themselves under the chilling technical name of "remedial teaching." Don't be put off by the title. Many teachers tutor in their spare time for a fee. Not all tutoring is good, so make sure that the teacher you go to is qualified, takes a real interest in the children, and meets the needs of your child.

If your child seems to have a succession of minor ailments, colds, coughs, and so on, and appears to be falling behind as a result, it is worthwhile sitting down to consider which is cause and which is effect. Often it is the anxiety caused by learning difficulties that is creating the illness—not the other way around. It is your right to ask for an appointment through the school with the educational psychologist. You might also ask your doctor to recommend a private psychologist or a reputable child guidance clinic. Testing can show whether your child has any special "weak spots," and what a realistic level of attainment is.

Because health problems can often remain undetected for years, it is important to be alert to any indications of illness or disability and to report them to your doctor immediately. It is, after all, the parent who knows the child best, though only the doctor can evaluate the need for treatment or further investigation.

Speech difficulties often lead to backwardness in reading, spelling, written work, and social development. If you notice that your child's speech development is markedly behind that of other children of his age, this is the time to take action.

Poor vision is likely to affect a child's progress in reading, writing, and social development. But more children wear glasses who do not need them than the other way around. This does not cause permanent eye damage, but it will affect a child's concentration at school. Doctors recommend that children be seen by them first for an eye test; if glasses seem necessary, they can then be sent to a specialist. Often a far-sighted child will get headaches if he concentrates on close work for long periods.

Impaired hearing is found in ten percent of children and is often responsible for under-achievement, for the child is unaware of much that happens around him. Deafness is probably present if a child does not respond to visually unprompted sounds such as the telephone ring. Poor hearing leads to social and learning difficulties.

An intelligence test can often reveal a child who is not using his full abilities because of a minor handicap.

Many children's problems are generated by the parents. Many children suffer because their parents are overambitious on their behalf and this tends to make them miserable because they do not come up to quite unrealistic standards. Even bright children can suffer from parents who set their sights too high. One girl was taken to the educational psychologist because her parents thought she was backward. Tests showed that her IQ was 150. She was in fact brilliant, but she compared badly with her elder sister, whose IQ was an astronomic 190! The parents, of course, were highly intelligent, but that did not save them from misunderstanding their children.

The notion that gifted children have special problems has been greatly exaggerated. On the contrary, there is good evidence that gifted people are less likely to have emotional problems than the rest of us, presumably because they are better able to deal with life.

Some gifted children, meaning those with an IQ of 140 and over, do suffer from isolation and persecution at school. Often, it seems, they are the victims of conformity pressures both from the other children and from the teachers. Recent research has shown that only some gifted children suffer from this kind of thing, and they usually are the children of parents who have in some way singled out their child as something out of the ordinary. Being brilliant is unusual, but it is normal. If a child behaves like a freak, then he will be treated like one. It is not his gifts that children and teachers dislike; it is the messages he sends that he is different. Whether he remains aloof or whether he lords it over the other children and demands special attention from the teachers he is inviting trouble. His parents may be contributing to his difficulty.

Color blindness is much more common in boys than in girls: about 7.5 percent in boys and 0.6 percent in girls. Much of modern life depends on color-coded signals: railroad signs, navigation lights for ships and airplanes, traffic lights, fabrics, and cosmetics all involve color. You may recognize color blindness in your child if he colors his paintings in an unusual way. The top picture (1) shows how the scene might be colored by a normal-sighted child; the second (2) by a red/green color-blind child; and the last (3) by a blue/yellow color-blind child. (These pictures are not a test of color-blindness.)

	Vision	Speech	Hearing
90%			
80%			
70%			
60%			
50%			
40%			
30%			
20%			
10%			

This graph shows the incidence of the most common defects affecting learning.

Gifted children

From the age of about seven years onward children are just beginning to follow certain rules of conduct in their games with each other and are becoming aware of "fairness." But children of all ages still enjoy the stimulus of competition and the chance of winning the game.

Team games

Few children can cope with team games before about eight or nine; they are still relatively fluid in their appreciation of rules, and they have not yet grown out of individual or small-group play. However, it is useful to introduce them to teamwork in football or soccer, and to offer the experience of playing on a team. Here fathers especially can be useful with workouts in the backyard.

A child will be into his teens before he can fully grasp the subtleties of the distinctive role of each position on the team—everyone must have watched the swarm of small boys or girls pursuing the ball all over the field. Compulsory games have helped to devalue ball games in the eyes of some, but they really are good experience for a child.

If your child never gets picked for a team, don't nag him because he is "not good enough." Instead, find him something else to excel at, perhaps swimming or judo. Many children greatly enjoy joining sports groups where the play is not always in teams.

School clubs and field trips

Every school has a number of outside activities, and these are as vital to school life as anything learned in the classroom. Don't dissuade your child from joining in. There may be music practice after school; a model club; swimming or skating lessons may be given. It would be a pity if a child could not attend at least one of these.

If your child's school plans a visit to a museum, a factory, or a working farm, let him take part with the others. Such programs are carefully planned to dovetail with classroom teaching, and are not just days out. They also help teachers to get to know their pupils out of school, which can be valuable to both sides. Expenses for school trips can sometimes be subsidized from school funds, so don't allow the money side to deter you if your budget is tight; it is in the interests of your child that he should go. He will benefit enormously from the chance of traveling and living with other children, and become much more self-reliant after even a few days away from his family.

Encouraging his hobbies

School experience needs to be supplemented in a number of ways if a child is to be educated in the widest sense. Parents should give attention to the activities run for young people in their locality, and encourage an artistic child to join an arts workshop or theater group, and a keen young reader to join the public library, which often runs children's reading or literary clubs as well as loaning books. Young naturalists can often join local societies as junior members, and go on nature trails—you can take part with them. Many boys, as well as girls, enjoy dance or ballet classes, or community gymnastic classes—all valuable aids to confidence and poise, even if your child is not likely to turn to professional dancing later on.

Musical children need more encouragement than they can obtain at school. Note whether your child is musical—can he discriminate between different pitches, apprehend rhythms, and grasp melodic patterns? If so, it is worth letting him learn an instrument (if not already taught at school). The piano is a common one to start with, but if you let him learn a string or woodwind instrument he can have the added joy of playing in ensembles. Some children love to learn the guitar, and to sing along—a useful talent at parties later. Try to find a Saturday morning music group for your child, and encourage him to attend some of the children's concerts in your community. He may develop a lasting interest.

Making things can be a very satisfying and rewarding hobby. It is best for everyone if the child can be given some space of his own in which to spread out components and equipment without their being disturbed.

Truancy and school phobia

There is a distinction between truancy, where a child knowingly stays away from school, and school phobia or refusal, where he doesn't understand why he dislikes school but nevertheless feels compelled to stay away. Most of us at one time or another have "played hookey" and philosophically accepted the punishment for it; but this will not help the true school phobic. His fear is irrational and overwhelming. Parents often attribute it to other reasons: "He always has a pain after breakfast"; "He gets sick at school"; "He doesn't like the gym teacher." None of these is the real reason, and no change in routine or physical remedy will help; the child is not experiencing a fear of school, but a fear of leaving home.

School phobics need therapy, of the specialized kind found at a child guidance clinic. Parents must also examine what is happening, and not disguise it by relating it to false physical symptoms. The phobia may arise from classroom problems, bullying, or a family situation. "Families," said one therapist experienced in school phobia, "need to recognize that upset feelings are important in themselves, and quite separate from upset tummies." Where anxieties can be shared with the clinic, by both child and family, there is real hope of the phobia clearing up.

Making friends at school

At school your child will not only be learning from his teachers. Getting along with other people, holding his own in the crowd, making friends and taking responsibilities, and in general getting his bearings are vital ingredients of school life for him.

Making friends is a young child's first job in classroom and playground. It is especially important on the playground, because it is there that he is more or less on his own. Although there is supervision, whether or not he makes friends will be largely up to him; and since quite large periods of the day are spent in this kind of unstructured play out of doors, it is vital to teach him how to approach other children.

One good way for a child who has difficulty making contact is to let him take a toy, like a bouncy ball or a yo-yo, from home and encourage him to share it with the other children. You could also invite some of his classmates home for a snack, or to join him for a special activity. If loneliness still persists, have a word with the teacher; she can see that your child is paired with another in activities such as caring for school pets, and so pave the way for friendship.

Teasing and bullying

Teasing and bullying go on in every school to a minor extent. The bully often has subtle methods, and is not always observed by the teachers; and teasing, which is verbal bullying, often is not noticed at all. Bullying is largely tied up with the bully's own insecurity. An overassertive child may, as the psychologist Adler has shown, seek to compensate for any weakness in himself, finding his inferiority to others quite intolerable; thus he turns to bullying. When frustrated, too, he will take it out on others. The bully is often the child teachers dislikes.

If your child complains of being bullied, you may not need to worry the first time or two. It may be that in the give-and-take of the playground it is his turn to take: next week he will be back on the giving side. But if the bullying seems vicious, or if it goes on for more than a week or two, you may have to give your child some help. Encourage him to give back what he gets. A couple of rude names can sometimes take the wind out of a bully's sails in the most effective way.

On the other side of the coin, some children are very easy victims. They may even invite bullying, possibly to get attention: better to be bullied than ignored. A few children are such passive victims that they are perpetually on the receiving end—and their parents never even know. School phobia and a reluctance to talk about what happens at school can be signs of this.

If all else fails ask the principal to deal with it. A school can often assist a bully by giving him the recognition he unconsciously seeks, perhaps by arranging for him to take on some small responsibility.

Up to about seven, the important factor in a child's life outside his home is his teacher; later, it is the good opinion of the other children that matters. Here the pressures of conformity begin. How can you, his parents, cope with them?

A child needs to feel himself one of the crowd as far as possible, in matters of dress and hairstyle particularly. Though such points may seem trivial, the wearing of jewelry or footwear that is "in," or even the angle at which a hat is worn, may matter a lot to a child. In most areas, blue jeans are the uniform, and it is useless to insist on more formal attire. What you *can* emphasize is the importance of neatness, and you can help assess the right clothing for the day's weather.

Naturally you should not let a child damage his or her feet or risk breaking an ankle by wearing harmful footwear just because it is fashionable; but in other less vital matters it is usually best to give way gracefully. It is a matter of knowing where to draw the line.

Other pressure points may be bedtimes or pocket money. "Nobody else in our class goes to bed till nine"—or ten, or eleven, if you believe your child. "Everybody gets more money than I do." Much of this needs taking with a grain of salt; but one way of dealing with it is to play for time. "When you're nine you can stay up later." Or, "Next birthday your pocket money will be increased." If a child begs for toys that are too expensive on the grounds that "all the others have them," he will need some straight but friendly talking to about things not everybody can afford. "No, we can't afford a new bike like John's this year, but you still get a lot of fun out of the one you have, don't you?" It won't entirely please a child longing for a particularly stylish new bicycle, but it may

The need to conform

Gerbils are almost ideal as pets, cheap and easy to keep, friendly and odor free. Cats and dogs are more expensive, but good with children if acquired young and well trained. Dogs are the most companionable of all pets. Rabbits, mice, and hamsters make poor pets; they are timid yet can bite, and tend to smell. Do not expect a child under six years old to care routinely for a pet, as his attention span is too short. A pet can give a schoolchild good experience in caretaking, and also his first experience with death, preparing him for the inevitable among family friends and relatives.

Playground society

Until he goes to school a child learns his rhymes, games, and rituals from adults. However, schoolchildren until early adolescence have a basic lore and language of their own. It is not shared by adults although it scarcely seems to change from generation to generation. Many of the rhymes and jokes shared today by children of very different backgrounds were being circulated hundreds of years ago. This is the age when children form societies with their own passwords and secret languages, and when everyone is given a nickname. Slang is readily picked up—and by the time adults catch on to new words, they may already be out of fashion.

Like a primitive tribesman, the schoolchild conducts his business with his fellow by means of ritual declaration. The rituals used vary from region to region. For example, any child will be taken seriously by his peers in an area where it is generally accepted that swearing upon your mother's life while making the sign of a cross means that you are telling the truth. Best seats in the classroom are claimed and recognized as being the rightful property of the first claimant. Bargains are made and sealed using whichever gesture or phrase is accepted as binding in the school. One of the schoolchild's most important words is his truce term. This will give him immediate respite from boisterous play until he is ready to continue. It is not the same as giving in.

Children of this age are often very superstitious. They will take careful note of omens and go through their own personalized rituals in order to bring themselves good luck.

Left : In the rough-and-tumble of the schoolchild's world wit and repartee abound, and are kept sharp by a general desire always to have the last word and to be one up on the next person. Puns and jokes are circulated as being original, children little realizing that their grandparents indulged in the same banter.

Left : Nonsense rhymes, popular songs, satirical and improper verse are repeated among boisterous schoolchildren for the sheer fun of it all as well as to accompany their skipping or clapping games. More than being just playthings, these rhymes provide an important means of communication.

Left : Ritual and rhyme are combined here for deciding who is to be "it" in a game of tag or to carry out a dare. Everyone gathers in a circle holding out their fists to be counted in time to the words of a rhyme. By a process of elimination one person is singled out and there is no going back on the decision thus made.

show him that he has got certain things that are very much worthwhile—and (though you should not make the comparison directly) that other children may lack altogether.

Pocket money

A child should have some opportunity to handle money from quite a young age. He will feel more secure about himself if he is able to pay for his own ice cream or comic some of the time, particularly if he sees his friends doing so. The obvious solution is an agreed amount of pocket money each week. It makes no sense to give a set allowance of pocket money to a child under school age; he cannot budget over a number of days, and may not be able to count change effectively. At five or six you could give him a small amount each day, perhaps. Increase it as he gets older and is allowed out more on his own. Change to a weekly allowance as soon as he shows signs of budgeting—at about seven or eight. How much pocket money, and what he is expected to do with it, will vary from family to family. So decide what you think is appropriate for your child, paying no attention to what he *claims* his best friend gets. If this allowance is to have any value whatsoever, a child must know exactly what he is supposed to pay for out of it—just candy and comics, or bus fares too? If he receives larger amounts, perhaps

from grandparents for his birthday, you might encourage him to save at least part of them. This will be more meaningful to him if he has his own savings account and passbook. When he gets older, he can see how the interest accrues.

Once in a while it may be a good idea to tell your child that you will put a small sum toward something he wants to buy, on condition that he also puts his share toward it. This will show you are not a hard-hearted monster, and it will encourage him to save as well. Generally speaking, a child needs to know how much he can expect, and he should be given his pocket money regularly. Only on very rare occasions should it be stopped for bad behavior; this only embitters a child, and may even lead to his taking money to make up for what he loses.

It is quite a good idea to pay a child small sums for any special help around the house in addition to the normal chores of family living. This gives him the chance to save up for something special, and it is an incentive to work. Thoroughly straightening up the garage could be one such occasion: washing and polishing the car, another. This will not encourage him to think that he only works when he is paid, but it will show him he is appreciated.

Helping in the home

Nobody wants to make slaves of children, but nevertheless they should be taught to pull their weight in family living. Jobs have to be done, and children, like adults, need to do their share. One idea is to put up a list of jobs to be done every week, and let your child pick the ones he likes. This lessens grumbling—some children positively enjoy polishing shoes—and ensures that he does not feel like a servant; it also lets him see that his help is needed and appreciated.

Boys sometimes get away with fewer jobs than girls; they have a habit of running out of the back door whenever it is time to wash dishes. They should not be allowed to get away with it, however. Suitable jobs can be found for boys that make them feel proud of having strong muscles and lifting heavy loads. Girls may enjoy putting the finishing touches that they like so much to table settings or to a room for a guest. You may feel, however, that dividing housework on such traditional lines is not for you. "A woman's work is never done" should perhaps be changed to "A family's work is soon done."

Your child's room

When children reach school age, their play needs change, and the space allotted to them has to change accordingly. Most families deal with this by turning what has been a bedroom into a bedroom-den, where a child can not only sleep but work at hobbies, read, display treasures, and entertain friends.

If more than one child has to sleep in a room, try to get privacy for each by using the space wisely. A room divider can be made from an arrangement of chests; bunk beds or stacking beds can be kept to one side and the rest of the room used as play space, where each child can have his own shelves and table. Storage space for clothes will be needed, and also a comfortable chair for each child—guests can sit on floor cushions. Good lighting is essential, and floor coverings should be warm and washable. Some families find carpet tiles, though initially expensive, a good buy as they can be taken up and scrubbed individually, or changed around as they wear.

Storing bits and pieces

A young child needs materials stored where he can easily find them, without always asking for help. Give him a box in which the family puts scrap, such as egg cartons, cardboard, pipe cleaners, fabrics, and ribbons. These, together with scissors and glue, are good raw materials for many creative activities. A trunk is ideal for storing empty eyeglass frames, old clothes, hats, shawls, anything for make-believe. Art materials should be kept separately and checked often. Paints and brushes can get messy unless they are supervised. Scraps of paper, crayons, and charcoal are also useful; clay, kept in a plastic bag or tight container, will occupy many satisfying hours. With a little help, older children will enjoy cutting stencils and making prints from potatoes or linoleum blocks. Scrapbooks offer endless possibilities as well.

Do take an interest in what your child is doing, and display the results for the family to admire. If you can join in, all the better. Projects in which parent and child are involved together bring a good deal of added pleasure.

From eight or nine onward children are great collectors. Give your child a place to keep his treasures. Egg cartons are good, simple containers; shelves are appreciated; best of all is a set of shallow drawers. Sometimes office units can be a good buy.

Children will also need space to play out of doors. If you have no yard, they can enjoy a local park or playground. Climbing trees, building a tree house, erecting a tent are rich experiences of childhood.

You will have to give up the idea of having a neat and tidy yard while your child is still young. He needs at least part of it for active play with balls and bats, somewhere to let off steam, somewhere to ride a bicycle, somewhere to make a hideout from boxes and old curtains. "Dens" are a necessity for children between seven and ten; places where they can hide and conduct their activities free from bossy grown-ups. If your yard has a good den, you will probably find it a center for a gang of friends, constantly coming and going—good company for your own child.

Though trampolines are expensive they have the advantage of requiring very little space, and they will drain energy from the most restless children. They need to be safely placed, however, and carefully supervised.

Outdoor play areas

Right: The seaside is the perfect place for a family vacation. Young children are happy for hours on end with nothing more to play with than sand and water. Parents can relax and enjoy some time to themselves.

Below: The informality and adventurousness of a camping vacation make an exciting change from home for children old enough to appreciate them.

He may like a garden of his own; some children prefer growing vegetables to flowers, because they can eat the results or proudly bring them to the table in the kitchen. Pets are useful companions out of doors; rabbits and guinea pigs can all be kept in covered hutches; they are interesting to care for and can be great sources of comfort.

Family vacations

Family vacations are looked forward to with great excitement, but sometimes a child comes home with a sense of disappointment, and his parents with a sense of frustration. Usually this is because your child has had to adapt to a different routine and to adult standards in a hotel or motel; or sometimes because you have chosen too ambitious a vacation. Children like to be active and informal. They do not get the same interest out of foreign travel as their parents; one beach is much like another when all you can do is wade.

Simple vacations are the best: farmhouse ones particularly, as there is plenty to see and do, even on a rainy day. Choose a working farm where children are welcome; helping to feed the poultry or watching the milking can be enthralling, and there is much more space to run around in, or to dry wet clothes, than in a hotel or motel.

Rented cottages are another good idea, although they can be a poor vacation for a mother. It is more of a change for her if she can share the duties with another family, and this also reduces expenses. Try to find out exactly what is provided, so that you do not arrive without a crib for the baby, or linen for the beds. Resorts for the entire family are also popular, particularly as children are often specially provided for, but in some cases, where there is no all-inclusive price, they can prove very expensive. There are so many attractions that your hand is often in your pocket.

Many families vote camping as the best vacation of all. It is certainly the cheapest. If you have doubts, rent or borrow camping equipment at first; it is much less expensive than buying some and then deciding camping is not for you. Children love the outdoor life, the adventure of the complete change, and the chance to share in camp responsibilities. There is something about a wood fire, however smoky, that invites confidences, and

sleeping (almost) under the stars is an experience children never forget. "I'm in a bag in the desert," the young son of a doctor friend said, in happy amazement.

One of the great joys of family life with children under twelve is taking them on excursions. They are so full of excitement, so full of questions, and ready to go at the drop of a hat! Much of the success of a family outing will depend on good preparation: a telephone call will give you details of admission prices, times of opening, and whether there is a restaurant to save making those eternal sandwiches. Your library will have suggestions for interesting places for children: museums, zoos, historic landmarks, but consider the special interests of your own family. If the boys love soldiers and armor, choose a museum with a good collection of these and stick to that gallery only—much less tiring than dragging around to all of the exhibits. There are various museums with displays of dolls, working models, costumes, toys, and transportation exhibits, and historical sites with special features for children, where they can see what previous inhabitants looked like, how they dressed, etc. Restored villages of an earlier day, often with craft studios and gift shops, are always interesting to school-age children.

Family outings

Fishing requires a patience that is beyond many people. Yet the most active children can find surprising resources of quiet when waiting for a bite.

Road safety

Traffic accidents are today the most serious threat to a child's life, and the need to teach children road safety is obvious. But teaching rules and showing them how *you* cross streets are not enough. Studies have shown that it is not safe to allow children under six out in the street alone, and that even those between six and ten are too immature to be relied upon to cross with safety. If crossing guards are posted on corners between your home and the school, children should be instructed to cross with them.

Young children cannot tell fast from slow traffic or connect the sound of an unseen car with danger. Their vision is restricted by their small size, and road signs are often too high to see. Traffic rules confuse them and lead to some strange beliefs, such as pedestrian crossings ensuring magical protection. Children in the seven- to nine-year age range may not have these difficulties, but they are easily distracted by games and impulsively run across streets. Older children aged nine to twelve usually know the correct way to cross streets, but they may not want to obey the rules or they may copy your potentially dangerous habits, such as crossing diagonally or against a red light.

Safety education should begin at an early age with explanations to very young children of what you mean by "traffic" and "curb" and should be continued throughout childhood and youth.

Improve your young child's awareness of everyday traffic by taking him on walks, pointing out the things to watch and listen for. Remind him constantly of the dangers of running into the street—training a child always to stop at curbs is the hardest task of all. Reflectors on bicycles, and even armbands on clothing, are important precautions. Light-colored clothing is also sensible, especially at dusk.

Show your child how to deal with all types of traffic conditions, emphasizing the basic rules illustrated in the diagrams.

Below : Choose a place to cross that provides a good view of traffic in both directions. Stop, look, and listen at the curb. Wait for traffic to pass, watching particularly for traffic that may be difficult to see, like motorcycles, or cars coming over the top of a hill. If there is no traffic near, keep watching and listening as you cross. Do not forget that traffic may emerge suddenly from side streets.

Below : Whenever possible, cross the street at safe places such as subways and pedestrian crossings. Children must be taught never to run impetuously across streets but to wait for traffic to stop before leaving the curb. Riding two abreast is dangerous and a major cause of cycling accidents.

Left : Never cross between parked vehicles unless there is no alternative ; then it is important to stand at the outer edge of the parked vehicle to see and be seen.
Below : Never run into the street after a ball or a pet, or walk or play along the curb. Always stop, look, and listen for traffic before crossing intersections.

Time off for parents

Summer visits can include forest preserves, nature trails, ball parks, local beaches, art fairs, or craft exhibitions.

Parents need time away from their child, too, and it does the child no harm to get used to this idea. An exchange with friends is one good answer; this can be either for the day, or for a night as well. When parents go out together, tell the baby-sitter when your child is expected to go to bed, and how much television he can watch if he wishes to. When you return, check whether these instructions have been carried out. It is not hard to get the family used to managing while parents are out, and a new face brings a welcome breath of fresh air into the home. Children who are never away from their parents' side can easily become little tyrants and the mother can become overtired and depressed.

When a child is small, parents can protect him from the more obvious risks, but other dangers can arise as the family grows older. It is just as essential to keep medicines out of reach and to be cautious with fires now as it was when he was tiny, but there are other difficulties a child may encounter that have to be thought out in advance.

Bicycling is a great hazard. Make sure that when you buy your child his first real bicycle, it is the correct size; he should be able to touch the ground with his feet while seated. Make sure he can handle the bike well before you allow him out on busy streets. He will need to realize that his bicycle is a vehicle just like his parents' car, and that it should be treated with as much respect and kept with as much care.

Water safety should be taught right from infancy, but once a child has learned to swim,

Preventing accidents

he is not out of danger. Take him swimming yourself and check if he is able to manage; teach him survival techniques as well. When sailing or boating, a child should always have the protection of a life jacket. And on no account should he ever be allowed rubber tubes or inflated toys at the beach—it is all too easy for a child to be swept out to sea.

Safety at play should also be considered. Children need to be warned about machinery, about playing on building sites or near garages or service roads. They also need to be reminded not to accept "dares" such as going on railroad tracks or climbing onto roofs.

There remains another risk—travel, or simply walking alone. Children out by themselves are always liable to meet undesirable people and, without being alarmed, they should be told what the risks are—in public lavatories, on playing fields, in parks, near shrubberies, or in empty lots. Don't pull your punches; tell them that sick people may try to touch them, undress them, or handle their genitals; if this happens, they should get help, even if it means entering a store or calling at a strange house. They also need to be told not to take rides in cars from strangers or to play at another child's house without coming home to tell you first.

Abuse from strangers

How your child has progressed

Physical growth from six to twelve will have been steady with little change of shape compared with what has gone before and what is about to happen. Toward the end of the period some girls will have started their preadolescent growth spurt, and some will have reached puberty. Many boys will still seem much younger in comparison.

The most striking development during these years has been in the child's skills and abilities. His thinking has passed an important stage between six and eight, and his use of his limbs and hands has come increasingly under fine control. He is now capable of the intricacies of model-making or the rigors of hockey or football. He may be learning a second language or a musical instrument, and beginning more complex math.

From six to twelve, children become slimmer. The body grows more than the head, producing more adult proportions. Girls may go through a "puppy fat" stage before starting their growth spurt, which they begin before boys.

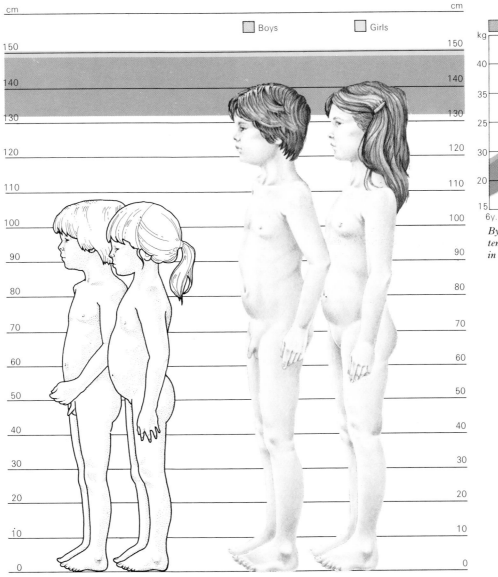

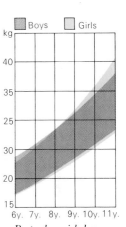

By twelve, girls have temporarily overtaken boys in both height and weight.

6 *Adolescence:* TOWARD SELF-RELIANCE

Just as I was bracing myself to tell the seventeen-year-old reasonably and calmly to straighten his room so that it could be cleaned, he came bursting into the kitchen. "Mom," he said, "I've got an idea. Let's go out to lunch. I'll take you." He grinned. *"And I'll pay!"* Suddenly, it seemed, here I was with an almost grown-up son who could chat on equal terms, share a good laugh—and who wanted to take me out to lunch. Messy bedrooms could wait.

As a proud parent protectively cradling a newborn child it is impossible to imagine such a tiny dependent creature as a strapping teenager. To the parents of a thirteen- or fifteen-year-old it is hard to recall those first nervous and exciting weeks. But the years of dependence are not yet over. The onset of puberty and adolescence only marks the beginning of the developmental sequence that ends in physical maturity. However, even an eighteen-year-old will go on gaining physical and intellectual powers for many more years. He will certainly continue to need your parental guidance and support, although in a very different form from that needed by a younger child.

The hallmarks of childhood are emotional and physical dependency. During adolescence, these dependencies give way to a definite feeling of commitment to meet the expectations of parents, peers, teachers, and, eventually, employers. These challenges, which every adolescent must meet, make this the period in the life cycle when it is crucial that the child defines the nature of his identity. Although the phrase "Sturm und Drang"—storm and stress—is often associated with the turmoil of adolescence, this aspect has been greatly exaggerated. Most adolescents make the transition to adulthood with much less conflict and strain than the mass media, which love reports of trouble and disaster, would have us think. How a child copes with these new demands depends on the quality of his family relationships, his past experiences, and the basic constitution he was born with.

The three stages of adolescence
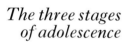

Adolescence is a transitional time in life, starting with the physiological changes at puberty, and extending into early adulthood, when, with no specific rite or timing, a person is socially considered grown up. One definition of adolescence is a "process of adaptation to puberty," but another valid definition might equally be a "process of adaptation to society."

Despite its relatively short time span, adolescence embraces a wide range of development. Bearing in mind the considerable variation of age at which physiological maturity is attained, we can divide the period of adolescence into three stages: at the early stage, from eleven to fifteen, the body changes of puberty dominate the child's awareness; during the middle stage of adolescence, from about fifteen to seventeen, the main concern of the child is to establish his own identity and fulfill his personal needs; in the last stage, from seventeen onward, the adolescent is engaged in training for the roles he will play throughout his adult life.

At twelve a child's self-knowledge is increasing rapidly. His social ability is improving. The ability to do mental calculations and understand the concrete world has carried him a long way forward. Developing this ability further is an important job of schooling. The age is often one of huge enthusiasms, which can be directed in positive ways by the school and the home.

At the onset of puberty, at about twelve and a half or thirteen, most children become uncertain. While parents readily sympathize with these feelings, they are not easily relieved. In fact, they signal normal maturation, and show that the child is starting to know himself in deeper ways. He seizes on events in the outer world and simultaneously tries to organize them and understand them internally. He is beginning to think things through quite deeply, and this may make him uneasy and withdrawn. He chooses fewer friends and may find social contacts difficult. It is no accident that this is the age when many children drop out of organizations such as Scouts, which they had previously entered into with such enthusiasm.

The thirteen-year-old who is shy and withdrawn and who has few friends may become the fourteen-year-old who is more open and optimistic, looking outward to making a life for himself with his own interests. His own circle of friends may widen at this stage: he generally gets on well with other people, peer and adult, but is usually much more involved in peer activities. Verbal comprehension and

Below and Bottom : Over their lifetimes a mother and her child go through a number of changes in their relationship. At first the tiny child is totally dependent on her mother and moves gradually toward the longest and most rewarding stage, of a mutually independent friendship. The cycle is completed in old age when the mother may well be dependent on her daughter.

fluency improve; it is thought that by this age these factors reach about four-fifths of adult peaks.

Then, at fifteen or sixteen, some teenagers again find the going hard. The need for independence makes a child both aggressive and easily hurt—decidedly touchy, as parents discover. The dependence/independence ambivalence causes strain and reserve. At the same time this mid-teenager is extremely loyal—and surprisingly adept at adjusting to different social groups. This is when the new peer group and the old family ties are most likely to compete, causing strains over clothes, parties, and dating.

By seventeen or eighteen, many of these conflicts have disappeared. Independence tentatively resolved, the teenager moves into the later stages of adolescence in a more integrated state of mind. He is better able to cope with the decisions he must now make concerning the future, although to his parents he may still seem to be contemplating a rather short-range future. If he stops to consider it, his own parental role will probably seem light-years away.

Below : As fashions change so do attitudes. Independence is now encouraged at a much earlier age than it was a generation ago and, although most families still go on vacation together, there are also many more opportunities for youngsters to go off on their own or with friends.

How adolescence evolved

Adolescence is the product of modern times. Before the fifteenth century the idea of childhood scarcely existed; let alone the concept of a childhood prolonged beyond puberty. The notion of adolescence as it is commonly understood did not emerge until the last two decades of the nineteenth century. It can genuinely be said to be an American discovery! Major social movements contributed to modern adolescence: compulsory education for children between six and sixteen was widely introduced in America toward the end of the nineteenth century. With the shift from an agrarian to an urban industrialized society, children became decreasingly important to the economic welfare of the family, and their dependent role was inevitably fostered. The increasing child-labor restrictions lengthened childhood until after puberty, and puberty itself came earlier as the standard of living rose. A fourth major factor that has sustained the concept of adolescence in Western societies is the belief in the "promise." This intangible "promise" is the acceptance that if a young

person functions well during adolescence he is then likely to realize status, success, income, power, and so on, when he reaches adulthood. In the middle class, in prosperous economic times, this has remained a reasonably accurate forecast; in underprivileged groups, the disparity between the promise and the grim reality of unemployment—particularly for minority groups in urban areas—is frightening, and a major cause of alienation and rebelliousness.

Today, the word "adolescence" arouses anxiety in perfectly sensible men and women. As our society has become increasingly youth oriented, so the myths surrounding adolescence have proliferated. From the publicity given to extreme cases by the media, one might believe that a high proportion of teenagers frequently runs amok, and that parents have decided to give up parenting. This, of course, is nonsense. It is true that there has been a definite swing toward a more permissive life style since the Second World War, and this applies to adolescents as well as the rest of the population. It is also true that during the height of the youth cult in the 1960s there was a tendency among some parents to relinquish control. But despite the sensational stories of drugs and sex, the most recent research gives a much more traditional picture of the contemporary adolescent. Today's teenagers may regard society as being too competitive and impersonal, and hypocritical in its standards, but the majority are content to remain in the prevailing tradition and strive for conventionally defined "success."

How much have attitudes changed?

Although adolescence has always been considered a time of emotional turmoil, recent studies in Europe and America suggest that the majority of teenagers make the transition through adolescence with less difficulty and tension than had previously been assumed. In fact the incidence of emotional disturbance in adolescence is only slightly greater than it is during the middle years of childhood. This does not mean that adolescents reach adulthood without stress, but it does indicate that most teenagers are well able to cope with the physiological growth, sexual awareness, and social and intellectual development.

Although severe mental distress is found in only a small percentage of adolescents, emotional and behavioral ups and downs, mood swings, are common. To parents of an adolescent, there are days when it seems as though they cannot win, no matter what they do or say, however tactfully. These confrontations, disheartening for parents, are an inevitable side of dealing with an adolescent. It has been suggested that because of the increasing independence that develops during adolescence there is a corresponding regression—the longed-for independence from parents becomes at times rather frightening. It is this independence/dependence ambivalence that is at the root of many a teenager's sullen moods.

Moodiness

Right : During early adolescence having a boy friend or girl friend is a valuable prestige symbol. Open displays of affection between a boy and a girl establish this relationship in the eyes of friends, who respond with studied nonchalance. This is just part of the adolescent's unspoken language, which is an essential feature of his social life.

Above : Adopting the distinctive appearance and specialized jargon of a particular group gives an adolescent a sense of security which is an important source of support when he is breaking his strong dependence on his family.

Coming to terms with sexuality

The need to be alone

The need for love and support

There are many other reasons to account for swings from elation to despair: attempts to establish an individual, coherent identity and doubts about a future job or family are anxieties experienced by all teenagers. Many mood changes have perfectly normal causes, although the reaction may be more extreme, as when acute nervousness and depression before exams give way to elation if the result is satisfactory.

All adolescents must also come to terms with their own sexuality, a new development that is both exciting and worrying. Even today, for boys more than girls, masturbation and sexual fantasies may cause guilt feelings.

The need to be solitary is very usual during the teen years, particularly if a child does not have a very gregarious personality. So an adolescent who stays in his room for long periods listening to music is acting typically for his age, but a prolonged bout of depression, which might be shown by consistent refusal to go to school, dropping friendships, or marked change of behavior, may be serious and need professional intervention.

This transition period from the middle-school years toward early adulthood is a time of insecurity for all children. There is so much newness and uncertainty—a teenager's own body is changing so much that it, too, is unfamiliar. It is because of innumerable half-formed questions—social, sexual, and intellectual—that start germinating in the teenager's mind that he or she needs firm parental support.

At the beginning of the adolescent phase, when puberty starts, he is a schoolchild. His freedom will have specified limits; if he goes off to a football game or shopping with friends on a Saturday, he must know that he is expected home at a prearranged time. As a child progresses through the teen years, a parent must judge how to give him as much freedom as possible—yet still retain the caring control that the adolescent needs and respects. This is not interference on the part of the parents; it is, rather, an ultimate safety net for the teenager to fall back on when he feels he cannot cope with the many new demands that are made upon him.

The more independent an adolescent becomes, the more he will need to retreat, occasionally, to the security of home and family. A teenager is more likely to abide by the rules, without resentment, if he is treated democratically in family matters and allowed his say when decisions are made. Perhaps at no time in his life is a person more vulnerable to parental rejection. Whether he has a case of nerves under exam pressure or a serious emotional crisis, an adolescent needs a strong dose of love and support from his parents.

Above : To an adolescent, a motorcycle is perhaps the ultimate symbol of independence and masculinity.

Below : Even within the strictest teenage fashion movement there is always room for individual taste and personal touches.

Acne

During puberty the surface of the hitherto soft and almost transparent skin becomes coarser, and the pores get bigger. The secretion of fat in the skin becomes more abundant due to the increased activity of the sebaceous glands, and this, sometimes combined with the increasing activity of the hair follicles on the face, causes the skin troubles commonly described as acne. These may sometimes be very troublesome and often, because the consciousness of feeling "different" is greatly increased, lead to quite serious mental distress—which in turn may very well worsen the acne. If your teenager is suffering badly, do arrange for him to see a doctor. The proper treatment will usually bring the situation under good control and thus raise the young person's discouraged spirits.

A high proportion of teenagers suffer bouts of acne, which in a few cases persist beyond the teens. It is very rare indeed for the spots to continue beyond the early twenties, so, however bad the attack is, there is always the assurance that it will end eventually.

The best treatment is cleanliness. Medicated creams can help. In severe cases antibiotics may be prescribed to prevent additional skin infection. The worst thing to do is to apply large amounts of makeup to conceal the spots. Small amounts of makeup may do no harm and can help lower the anxiety of the sufferer. Makeup should be free of perfume and not greasy, and should be applied over a medicated foundation.

Deodorants

During puberty, the sweat glands begin to function more intensively. This often causes body odor, which necessitates greater hygienic attention. An adolescent may be quite unaware of this added perspiration, so a tactful parent should point out the uses of deodorants. Do not stress them too highly; washing thoroughly often has just as good an effect. Excessive use of deodorants can irritate the skin, remove its protective coatings, and encourage infection.

Fatigue

Rapid physical growth during the years of adolescence involves many forms of strain. Restlessness and fatigue that appear so commonly in teenagers are partly due to physical causes. More calories are needed during this time of growth, and meals should not be skipped unless it is unavoidable. Some vigorous adolescent boys at their peak growth rate need a daily caloric intake comparable to that of a large adult doing heavy manual work, about 3,800 calories a day. (This explains why some adolescents always seem to be hungry and enjoy eating vast meals that are high in carbohydrates.) After this peak, however, the extra energy requirement declines to normal adult levels.

All the rapid physical changes cause an adolescent to be highly attuned to his own body. Narcissism—a strong preoccupation with one's own self and body—is often a normal feature at this age. Many adolescents, self-conscious because of their newly acquired shape or added height, feel themselves to be perpetually "on stage"—seeing other people as their constant audience. So the less attractive physical phenomena of adolescence, such as acne and body fat, can assume tremendous importance to a teenager—and to his parents.

Narcissism

Reactions to being overweight vary with sex. Girls are much more disturbed than boys by chubbiness, and are liable to label any excess weight as "fat." Boys are more likely to view

"Puppy fat"

Staying fit and healthy

One in four American children is obese, or seriously overweight. Many parents do not consider obesity a true disability, but research has shown that not only does it lead to social problems but it may well seriously damage the child's health in later life.

Fatness in adolescence is usually a result of earlier bad habits. Indeed, to a large extent the damage may be done in babyhood when a mother overfeeds her baby, whose body does not need the food and, as a result, stores it in increasing numbers of permanent fat cells.

Other danger periods in childhood are between seven and eleven, when the child goes to school and play and energy expenditure are reduced but food intake is not; girls are especially vulnerable at puberty. This is partly because the feminine hormones add a layer of fat on the buttocks, hips, chest, and arms and partly because girls of this age often lose interest in energetic activities like games. Boys do not have this hormonal weight gain as their body patterns tend toward leanness and existing fat is replaced with muscle at puberty. However, after this growth period, at about sixteen for girls and twenty-two for boys, bone growth ceases and adolescents' food intake should slow down as unused nutrients will be stored as fat.

Girls may be less well nourished than boys because, although they need almost as much protein, vitamins, and minerals as boys, they can eat only about two-thirds of the quantity boys eat. Thus, to eat well, girls must choose their foods more carefully, eating less of the bulkier foods and more protein.

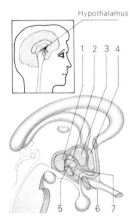

It is difficult for parents to guide their adolescents in the delicate matter of keeping slim as they may not like to be told what they can and cannot eat.

If an adolescent develops the habit of taking regular weekly exercise, he will keep his weight on an even keel and stay healthier. Research has shown that as little as half an hour a week of strenuous activity can reduce the later chances of heart attacks or high blood pressure, can help protect against lung disease, keep us emotionally more stable by providing a good outlet for tension, and help the brain function more efficiently.

Individuals vary, of course, and "string-bean" types will never have to worry about their weight, but an adolescent must be made aware that his future figure and health rest on setting up sound eating and exercise patterns before adulthood.

Above and Left: Adolescents should cut down on snacks and desserts and take up a vigorous activity, which, if it is easy to practice regularly in later life, will help prevent adult obesity.

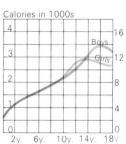

The hypothalamus is a control center for many of the body's basic functions and drives, including sexual drive (1), "pleasure center" (2), thirst (3), internal body temperature (4), aggressive behavior (5), hunger drive, "appestat" (6), thirst drive (7). Research shows that regular exercise helps the "appestat" to control hunger drives efficiently and to maintain an even weight.

The diagram shows the daily caloric requirements from birth to eighteen years. At puberty, there is a sudden growth spurt and increased hormonal action creating high energy needs—the average sixteen-year-old boy consuming more calories than an active adult.

The changes of puberty

Puberty is a distinctive stage in life during which profound and disturbing changes are brought about. Suddenly, or so it seems, although it unfolds over a period of two to five years, the young willowy child becomes a full-figured women or firm-muscled man.

It begins when the hypothalamus (in the brain) signals the pituitary gland to begin hormonal production, in response to which the ovaries and testes increase production of the sex hormones: androgen and testosterone in boys and estrogen and progesterone in girls. These hormones are responsible for the acceleration of physical development and maturation.

The first outward signs of puberty in a boy are the enlargement of the testes and scrotal sac. The beginnings of pubic hair may appear at the same time or within the following year. He will suddenly start getting taller by leaps and bounds: this is called the growth spurt, which in boys generally occurs about two years later than girls and peaks at about the age of fourteen. It is accompanied by penile growth, and the seminal vesicles, where the

sperm is stored prior to ejaculation, now enlarge. During this period a boy may start to have nocturnal emissions, or wet dreams, to cope with the production of sperm. But his penis and scrotum are not fully mature for five years after they begin to enlarge.

Although there is no dramatic change for boys as there is for girls, a boy's first ejaculation can be quite traumatic if he is unprepared for it. Like girls, boys need a factual explanation and unemotional reassurance, preferably from their fathers. Parents should not be coy when discussing the physical changes with a son or daughter; a penis is a penis, a vagina is a vagina. Boys should be reassured that all penises vary, and size is no indication of performance; that circumcision has no adverse effects; and that it is quite normal for a boy to find himself aroused by the slightest provocation at this stage. Fathers should also advise their sons to follow thorough routine genital cleanliness, or else "smegma" may gather under the foreskin and cause odor, irritation, or even infection.

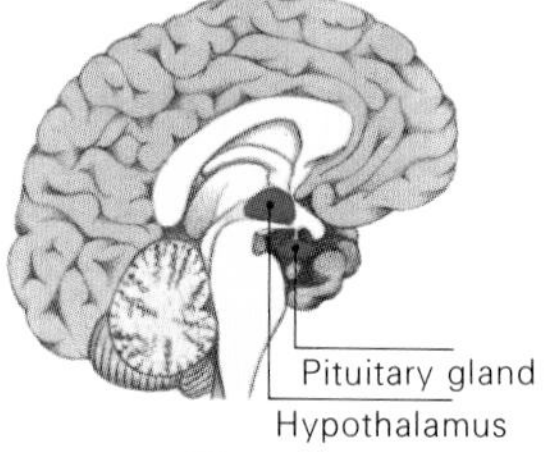

The pituitary is a pea-sized organ situated on the underside of the brain at the level of the eyes. The pituitary produces several hormones which have crucial roles in sexual maturation during puberty. It was originally thought to be the instigator of the pubertal changes, but it is now known that, although the organizer of many other endocrine glands, it is itself triggered by the hypothalamus, which sits just above it.

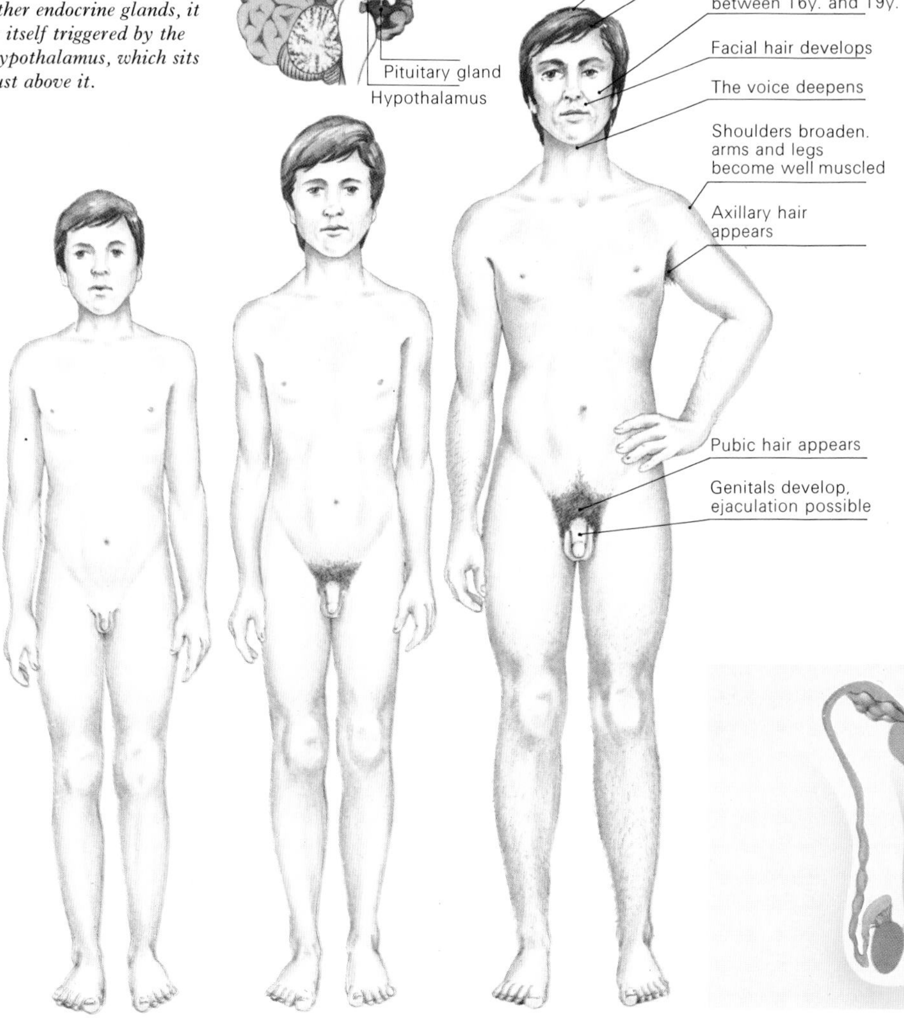

The diagram shows the sequence of events in puberty. The deeper shaded areas represent the period when most rapid growth or change occurs for an average boy and girl. The lighter shading shows the age range between which pubertal changes may begin and end. Although individual growth and change patterns may vary widely from these norms, girls generally accomplish such development earlier than boys.

■ Boys
▨ Girls

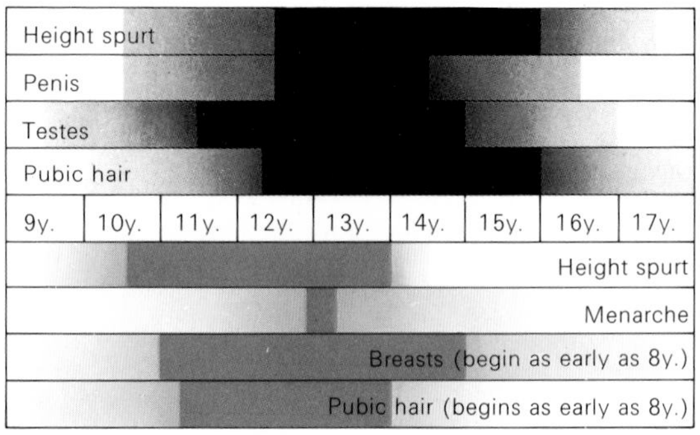

Pituitary gland
Hypothalamus

Increase in height

Hairline begins to recede

Acne usually appears between 16y. and 19y.

Facial hair develops

The voice deepens

Shoulders broaden. arms and legs become well muscled

Axillary hair appears

Pubic hair appears

Genitals develop, ejaculation possible

	9y.	10y.	11y.	12y.	13y.	14y.	15y.	16y.	17y.
Height spurt									
Penis									
Testes									
Pubic hair									
Height spurt									
Menarche									
Breasts (begin as early as 8y.)									
Pubic hair (begins as early as 8y.)									

During puberty the voice deepens as the larynx enlarges and the vocal cords lengthen. Sometimes the voice "breaks" quite suddenly and erratically, at other times gradually and almost imperceptibly.

Between the ages of thirteen and sixteen coarse dark pubic hair replaces the fine, nonpigmented hair at the base of the penis, and usually the testes also begin to enlarge. About a year later the penis begins to lengthen and the scrotal sac skin darkens. Pubic hair does not

cover the abdomen and inner thighs until about the age of twenty-five.

Facial and body hair develop about two years after the start of pubic hair. Facial hair first appears at the corners of the upper lip, spreading across the lip to the upper part of the cheeks, lower lip, and along the sides of the chin. This order is invariable. The amount of body hair your son will have is largely determined by heredity, but chest hair does not develop until late adolescence.

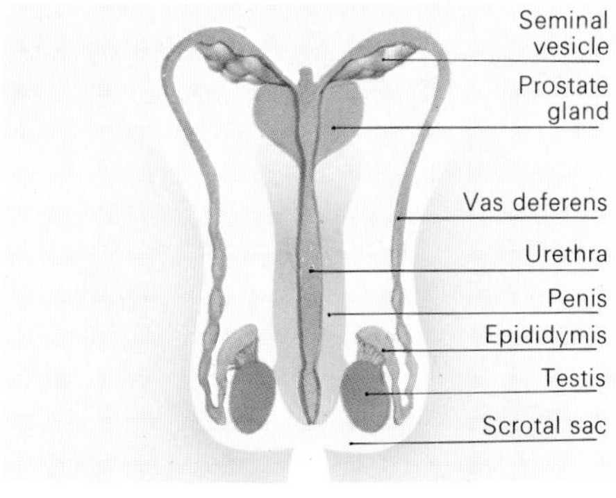

Seminal vesicle

Prostate gland

Vas deferens

Urethra

Penis

Epididymis

Testis

Scrotal sac

The male sex organs are mostly external to the body and consist of two glands, or testes, producing hormones and sperm. The vas deferens conducts the sperm from the testes to the urethra. From puberty, the penis, prostate, and seminal vesicles enlarge. The testes begin to manufacture sperm and the hormone testosterone, which controls development of the sex organs and secondary sex characteristics.

The first outward indication of the inner hormonal changes in girls is the appearance of small breasts and of pigmented pubic hair. The growth spurt occurs at the same time or possibly before this, perhaps as early as nine and a half or as late as fifteen, but generally it peaks around twelve years. Variations in development among adolescents are not a sign of defects or of being less mature, and later developers should be reassured.

The first menstrual period (menarche) is late in the sequence of puberty, most girls beginning their periods when they are about twelve or thirteen, but it is normal to start at any time between nine and seventeen. Although menarche means that the womb and vagina have probably reached a mature stage of development, it does not follow that the full reproductive cycle has been attained. Early periods usually last between three and five days and are often without ovulation.

Apprehensions, such as whether she can safely wear trousers during a period, whether the bleeding may be excessive, whether it

matters if it is irregular, are perfectly natural, but are best talked over by mother and daughter and laid to rest at the beginning. In fact, periods are usually scanty and irregular for the first year or so. You should also draw her attention to the delicate problem of odor during periods, encouraging her to bathe or shower more frequently during periods and discouraging the use of vaginal deodorants, which can cause inflammation.

When a girl's breasts begin to develop, it is quite normal for them to be sensitive, but this will stop as soon as they have grown. Adolescent girls become self-conscious if they believe their breasts are smaller or larger than their friends' and they should be reassured that, whatever their final size, they will function just as efficiently during motherhood. Sometimes girls worry when their breasts grow at different rates, but this does not mean they will always be lopsided. A bra is usually unnecessary until the chest measurement is at least 32 in/81 cm, or the girl is uncomfortable when running.

In boys and girls the skull increases in size at puberty. The jaw lengthens and the chin becomes more pointed; the profile straightens and the nose increases in size. In many there is also a pronounced but gradual change in the facial expression, which is the effect of hormones on the tissues of the face.

Breast development is the first visible sign of puberty in a

girl: the flat chest of childhood gives way to a general enlargement and raising of the breasts and nipple area. As the small breasts grow, the nipples and areolas form a separate contour, which gradually fills out.

The second sign is the appearance of public hair, which precedes the body hair by about two years. Sparse, fine hair grows mainly on the lips of the labia. This hair darkens and becomes coarser and curlier.

Shaded areas on the figure show the major sites of fat deposits, which triggered by hormones develop at puberty and give females their rounded appearance.

Increase in height

Acne usually develops between 14y. and 17y.

Breasts develop

Axillary hair appears

Womb enlarges and menstruation begins

Pubic hair appears

Hips widen

Below: At puberty, the womb enlarges and the production of estrogen and progesterone begins to follow a monthly pattern, causing the menstrual cycle. A girl may be infertile at first but this cannot be relied on.

Once a girl begins to ovulate, however, she may experience "painful periods," which can range from mild cramps and fatigue to severe pain, and usually last a few days. Or she may suffer before the period with a bloated feeling in the lower abdomen; a weight gain due to fluid retention; headache; tension; irritability and depression;

Menstrual control center

Hypothalamus

Progesterone feedback pathway

Estrogen feedback pathway

Pituitary gland

Fallopian tube   Womb

Estrogen

Progesterone

Ovary

Cervix

Vagina

Research shows that there is a significant increase in the number of women admitted to hospitals for emergency and psychiatric treatment; reported absent from work through illness; attempted suicides; and disorderly conduct in prisons during or just before menstruation. As the graph below shows, the frequency of schoolgirls' misbehavior increases just before and during their monthly periods.

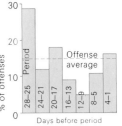

% of offenses
30
20
Period
Offense average
10
0
28-25 24-21 20-17 16-13 12-9 8-5 4-1
Days before period

lack of efficiency. All these symptoms and more are part of premenstrual stress, caused by a hormonal deficiency. Doctors are divided over what causes this deficiency, but one theory is that it is due to a fault in the progesterone feedback pathway.

On the fifth day of the menstrual cycle the menstrual control center in the hypothalamus stimulates the production of hormones, which encourage the ripening of eggs in the ovaries. On the fourteenth day an egg is released; on the ovary, the scar, called the corpus luteum, secretes estrogen and progesterone. These affect the womb and brain. If the menstrual control center is out of balance or inadequate progesterone is produced by the corpus luteum, the premenstrual syndrome results. In some women this can last from ovulation to menstruation, in others it occurs a few days before the period.

Treatment of this problem in the form of progesterone supplements has been carried out effectively on some women, mostly in the thirty-to-forty age group, although symptoms can and do occur earlier. Further recent research has shown that nonhormonal drugs, such as vitamin B_6, have also proved very effective.

it as desirable bone and muscle. Glandular dysfunction (the improper functioning of the hypothalamus or thyroid gland) is rarely the cause of teenage obesity. More often it is because an adolescent has chosen a poor diet, eating too much starch and fat and not enough protein, vitamins, and minerals.

Fat tissue develops oddly in adolescence. Usually a growth spurt in fat tissue occurs before the main body begins to sprout. Thus, especially in some males, before the whole body grows rapidly, "puppy fat" appears and often makes a healthy adolescent look obese. As the body frame enlarges, this "puppy fat" is stretched and used up—presumably by the extra energy required by the growth spurt—and the "string-bean" phenomenon may replace this early fat phase.

In general, the female adolescent does not lose fat; she tends to add it, and the average female has considerably more fat than the male. If a teenager, usually a girl, is genuinely concerned about her weight, it is important for parents to encourage sensible dieting—if possible, in consultation with the family doctor. Teenagers must learn that correct eating habits, not crash diets, are the only long-term method of weight control.

Anorexia nervosa

This is the time to look out for the onset of anorexia nervosa, the starvation syndrome. Most victims of anorexia are adolescent girls; it is a mysterious condition—not a disease but a "maladaptive behavior pattern" which is destructive and out of control. It is serious and needs immediate attention. Though it is a rare condition, it is well for parents to be aware of its manifestations.

Anorexia often, but not always, starts with a girl's idea that she is too fat. But though a normal girl will diet until she decides she is slim enough and then stop, the anorectic girl will go on believing that she is too fat however thin she becomes. Emaciation and severe malnourishment can result. So keep an eye on your daughter's eating, especially if she starts slimming. If you become suspicious, make sure that you really know exactly how much she is eating. Anorexics are very good at pretending to eat.

There is another manifestation of anorexia which is harder to detect and to treat. The victim will eat every meal as normal, possibly even overeating, and then go away and secretly throw it all up. Anorexia can often be treated successfully with behavior therapy or psychotherapy.

Clumsiness

Since different parts of the adolescent's body mature at different rates, boys and girls at this age tend to look awkward and out of proportion. At times their noses, feet, hands, legs, or arms may appear disproportionately large. As growth continues body proportions equalize, and the adolescent will come to look less awkward and gangling. Be assured, the clumsiness of adolescence is genuine and should be treated with sympathy. When an adolescent trips or drops a plate it is best to gloss over it; he

Activism gives the teenager a chance to discover and define his own values.

will be feeling quite self-conscious enough about what he feels to be his huge hands and feet without his brothers or sisters, or even parents, focusing more attention on them.

Intellectual growth

Just as physical maturation occurs during the early part of adolescence, so also will the intellectual growth of most children reach that of an adult. This does not mean that intellectual accomplishments are the same as an adult's; but the adolescent will have acquired the chief mental characteristics that will be the basis for all of his future intellectual development. As he grows and gains experience, he starts to learn more precisely about the world and to gain a better understanding of other people. As this knowledge increases he becomes aware of gaps in his understanding—which he is beginning to be able to fill through supposition.

Learning to think in the abstract

During adolescence a child approaches or enters the stage known as "formal operations" in his thinking. This contrasts with the stage from six to about twelve, which is known as "concrete operations." These two formidable-sounding terms are quite easy to understand. "Operations" means thinking. When you think about something you make a mental picture and operate, that is, work on it.

In the concrete stage a child is still limited to an understanding of the physical world. He can try out experiments, both in reality and in his head, but they are still basically about the physical world. Hence the term "concrete." "Formal" operations are thoughts about abstractions, about matters that only exist as thoughts or rules: they have no physical existence, real or unreal. To make the distinction clear, imagine an extra planet going around the sun. The planet does not exist, so it is unreal: but it is still a physical object. Its orbit, however, is not a physical object, and neither are the real orbits of the planets that do exist.

Just as the age at which a child starts school, at five or six, corresponds roughly to one stage in mental development, so it is no accident that it is at about twelve or thirteen that children start abstract subjects like algebra, geometry, and grammar, and move toward studying literature as something more than descriptions of the world and the people in it. Naturally there is a wide variation in the age at which children become ready for these different skills. It is now that differences among children in intelligence and ability become more obvious, as one son shows skill in, say, the most abstract of all subjects, algebra, another may excel in the language skills of English and French, and a third in woodwork, animal husbandry, or catering.

Some of the stages in schooling are no longer as sharply divided as they used to be: for instance, children are often now given practice in reaching an intuitive understanding of quite advanced mathematics. But the difference is still there, and is marked by the change from intuitive to formal learning.

Concern about the future

Armed with his new ability to think in the abstract, the teenager begins to think about himself, his role in life, his plans for the future—and may well question the validity of the society in which he has grown up. In contrast to earlier preoccupations, he thinks often about the hypothetical, the future, the remote. Because the adolescent sees the world, himself, and the people he knows in such a different way he also speculates about what *might* be instead of what *is*. So it is only to be expected that profound changes occur in his sense of identity and in every aspect of his social relations. The direct results of this higher level of intellectual thought appear in arguments with parents, in academic achievement, and planning tentatively for his future.

This is the period during which a teenager will get away from childish egocentricity and form the patterns in personal relationships that will last a lifetime. He will progress from seeing the world centered on himself and in the here and now to anticipation of the future. This is the age of great ideals and the beginning of theories—many adolescents are attracted by social activism.

The changes that occur in the adolescent's outlook are often regarded as rebellious by parents and teachers. What needs to be understood is that these changes are basically dependent upon the newness of his intellectual advances and will modify with experience. The adolescent is able to deal with hypotheses; he is able to formulate propositions that are not directly connected with what he sees or has experienced. All the changes that are taking place build upon all the previous stages of learning and mark the end of childhood.

An adolescent may be more concerned with moral values and standards than at any other time of his life. This moral questioning will be closely bound up with his new mental capacities and will involve every aspect of his life—social, emotional, and intellectual. Adolescents are subject to the same kinds of social influence as everyone else, and, although they may feel very strongly about certain values and causes, this may not greatly affect how they behave in specific situations.

In the same person, morality tends to be inconsistent throughout life. Actual behavior is highly dependent upon expediency (will I be found out?) and the standards of the surrounding peer group (is cheating in history tests in the classroom considered permissible?). From adolescence onward, standards are often drawn from an ideal. This can be a religious figure, such as Christ or Buddha, a philosopher, or a sports hero. Girls, too, used to pick male figures (God was always male), but now female role models are re-emerging.

From the preschool years, moral development proceeds unevenly. Adolescents can range from the lowest to the highest levels of moral reasoning, which derive in part from the degree of intellectual development and the reasoning ability that results. It appears that the thoughtful, intelligent, and questioning adolescent is more likely to show an early high standard of moral consistency. His attempt to establish his own internal code of moral conduct—and stick to it—may be part of his natural struggle for independence and autonomy in the world.

Immediately before the onset of adolescence a child has reached the level of striving to please people in authority, such as parents and teachers, by abiding by rules and regulations. He has the "good boy" orientation, the first stage of morality, which is known as "conventional" moral reasoning. As his mental capacity develops—sometime during the early part of adolescence—he tends to judge what is right and wrong more subtly: he perceives values as determined by a general consensus in society. He sees that these are based on rules that have been closely examined and agreed upon by society as a whole. He is beginning to understand the social contract view; he appreciates the concept of democracy. Many people never reach this stage, or at least apply this kind of reasoning and awareness to only a small part of their thinking about life and its problems. Many come so far and no further. For those who do, however, the next step can spell trouble.

The preconventional stages of moral thinking are related simply to the individual and the consequences to him of his actions. In the conventional levels, the person judges by social rules; first by his own position in society and then by the need to uphold a stable social order. In the postconventional stages the person becomes aware of the conflicts that can arise between the needs and

Understanding the rules of society

Conventional

From about 12 years Stage 3
The main motivation is to be thought of as a good boy or girl. What is right is what conforms to a stereotyped view of majority behavior and wins social approval.

From about 15 years May be reaching Stage 4
The idea of social order arrives. What is right is what maintains society (or the society the child would like to see). Little flexibility is possible. Authority still reigns supreme. Many adults never progress beyond this stage.

Postconventional

Early adulthood Stage 5
Human life and its quality are what govern everything, with freedom for the individual to decide his own fate. Nevertheless, the standards that guide decisions are still those of society.

Adulthood Stage 6
Conscience and the absolute sanctity of life are supreme. Ethical principles are universal. Society is secondary.

The last few stages in the growth of moral thinking according to leading authority Lawrence Kohlberg. It is important to remember that at any age children and adults vary the stage of their moral thinking from one moment to the next.

Developing a conscience

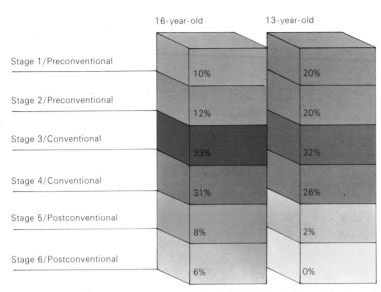

16-year-old   13-year-old

Stage 1/Preconventional — 10% | 20%

Stage 2/Preconventional — 12% | 20%

Stage 3/Conventional — 33% | 32%

Stage 4/Conventional — 31% | 26%

Stage 5/Postconventional — 8% | 2%

Stage 6/Postconventional — 6% | 0%

The right-hand column shows how much of a thirteen-year-old's moral thinking is done in each of the six different stages, according to Kohlberg's theory. The left-hand column indicates that most of a sixteen-year-old's thinking is in the conventional stages. The childlike preconventional stages have dropped sharply, and the adult stages five and six are rising.

rights of the individual and the standards and laws of society. Individual conscience becomes important; for the new arrival at this point it can seem of paramount importance.

As adolescence proceeds the teenager will come to realize that the way in which a person ought to behave will depend on circumstances. He will have the mental capacity to grapple with the problems of weighing the relative consequences of an action for the individual and for society—now and as he thinks it should be. But he will not have the experience on which to base such far-reaching mental arithmetic, and the result can seem childish and even amoral.

At this confused but sophisticated stage many teenagers will reject many of the rules and laws that they have been brought up with. Often this means no more than long arguments and discussions with parents or friends. But in some circumstances the troubled thinking can lead to troubled behavior.

In recent years the refusal of thousands of American adolescents to accept the war in Vietnam was an outstanding example of this moral questioning of society. The extremes to which a small number went to argue and demonstrate their beliefs were evidence of the deep water that lies in wait for those prepared to move beyond conventional patterns of thought. It is rare, however, that young people are pushed to such lengths. Usually they can lead their lives in the safety of conventional patterns until they are ready to test the principles of conscience from a safer, more experienced standpoint.

Sex and the teenager

With the tumultuous hormonal and bodily changes that occur during adolescence arrives an intense sexual drive. This is especially true for boys, who may become easily—and urgently—aroused by the slightest sexual sight or thought. During this period of very early physical manhood a boy has to come to terms with this unaccustomed sexuality, which is both exciting and frightening to him; he may find some release through masturbatory fantasies or, as he gets older, in a genuine relationship with a girl who

attracts him physically and who also shares his interests and outlook. An adolescent who is deeply troubled by his sexuality—or any other puzzling aspect of his age—which he has come to believe is "wrong," may sublimate his mental and bodily turmoil in a particular hobby or enthusiasm.

Although girls also experience increased sexual drive as adolescence progresses, it is usually more diffuse than that of boys. For most adolescent girls, as with females in general, sex is usually linked to tenderness and emotion. Boys and girls should be aware of these innate differences in their attitudes toward sex. During early adolescence, most girls are more likely to be satisfied with the gentleness and reassurance of petting and kissing—whereas boys in late adolescence may find their urgent need for intercourse difficult to control. For boys, intercourse is, first and foremost, an erotic release; for most girls, it is secondary to love and affection. All adolescents must somehow find their own way through this difficult transitional period when they have attained physical, but not yet emotional, maturity.

Because boys and girls become more and more interested in each other as adolescence progresses, it is valuable if they can discuss these differing attitudes with their parents. Parents who have spoken quite naturally about sex to their children ever since those first innocent questions should be able to talk to their adolescent son or daughter in ways relevant to their new mental, physical, and emotional maturity.

It is the attitudes of their parents, whether they are open and understanding and generally at ease with *their* sexuality—as well as what is considered permissible in the society around them—that will have the most influence on their own sexual standards in the long run. So do listen to your children when they talk about sex, however obliquely. In adolescence, they are likely to do this by discussing the actions and relationships of their friends. Remember that no teenager wants to be preached at; he will need his privacy to be respected—but when he is ready to talk or ask, *listen.*

Masturbation

During adolescence, most boys will relieve sexual tension through masturbation. This is rather less common in girls, who tend to be sexually aroused more slowly and to link sex more closely with emotion. (This difference may slowly be lessening now.) It is important for adolescents to understand that masturbation is normal and harmless. Lingering myths that masturbation can cause illness and insanity may even today cause an adolescent to feel guilty and depressed. It will help if parents are able to indicate, rather casually, that masturbation is a private business that continues to some degree throughout life.

Contraception

A child under the age of thirteen or fourteen is unlikely to have a full sexual relationship. Nevertheless, this is the right age to let a boy or girl know that intercourse is an adult act—

Juvenile delinquency

Parents of teenagers who get into trouble should not despair. Over half of all persons cautioned or convicted for indictable offenses are under the age of twenty-one. The peak rate is reached at about fifteen years, after which it declines steadily with increasing age. Figures show that among all delinquents there are a large number of teenagers. Social pressures for good behavior increase markedly during adolescence, and become more effective with adulthood.

Adult criminals are quite different from teenage delinquents. One study of a group of married men (average age forty-two years) who had criminal records found that only fourteen percent had convictions both as juveniles and since reaching the age of twenty-one years. The persistent adult offender is usually solitary, ineffectual, and ill-equipped to cope with the world. He has little in common with the typical young offender,

whose potentialities are often quite sound, but whose energies have just been temporarily misdirected.

Since runaways, however, are highly vulnerable to drugs and prostitution, parents should make every effort to seek guidance.

Chances of reconviction for first offenders	
	90%
	80%
	70%
	60%
	50%
	40%
	30%
	20%
	10%

Under 14y. 14–20y. 21–29y. 30–39 y.

40y. +

Above : The likelihood of reconviction decreases with increasing age. Typical crimes of youth commonly involve larceny.
Left : The awareness of being watched usually acts as a strong deterrent against the temptation to steal.

and that a young person who becomes involved in a sexual relationship must be ready to accept its adult responsibilities. It is essential that every adolescent understands that *any* act of sexual intercourse may result in pregnancy.

A child in his or her early teens may seem rather young, but this is often a good time to talk about contraception. Of course, parents should be careful not to imply that they expect young adolescents to have sexual intercourse, unless they feel otherwise. Nevertheless, the adolescents may later become involved in a serious relationship, or think they may get into a situation where intercourse will result, and they will know that precautions must be taken first. In this case, a parent can explain that contraceptive advice can be obtained from the family doctor, or, if the adolescent feels more comfortable about it, from a local family planning clinic. A sexually active late adolescent boy should always carry a condom in his pocket. Again, contrary to what he, or she, may have heard at school, withdrawal of the penis prior to ejaculation is both unsatisfactory and unsafe. Adolescents who have been sexually educated will then avoid the damaging and potentially tragic decision of having an abortion or bringing into the world a child they will not be able to raise.

Venereal diseases (VD)

As adolescence progresses, particularly if your teenager is having sexual intercourse, or mixing with others who do, he must be told about the dangers of venereal disease. There are four such diseases. Gonorrhea and syphilis are the most serious and the most common. Trichomoniasis and nonspecific urethritis are relatively minor and actually affect the urinary, not the genital apparatus. All four are spread by intercourse, but they can also be caught by engaging in oral genital contact with someone who is infected. Syphilis can be caught by kissing someone who has an open sore on the mouth.

Gonorrhea is the more common of the two diseases that attack the genital apparatus. The signs are usually discharge, which may be yellowish, from the penis or vagina and soreness when urinating. It is less serious than the other, syphilis, and more easily treatable, although sterility can result if the condition is not treated in time.

Syphilis is one of the most dread diseases of all. It is caused by a germ, or spirochete, *Treponema pallidum*. During the first stage a small ulcer, often painless, usually occurs on the penis or vagina, but it may appear anywhere on the body, particularly on the mouth. If the disease is not treated it lies dormant until, years later, it reaches the third stage, in which it may attack the nervous system, heart and blood vessels, causing the victim acute agony, blindness, and madness.

The symptoms do not always appear, however, so prevention really is better than a cure that may come too late. If a teenager is faced with a casual sexual encounter, he is best advised to find out if his partner is free of VD, although putting the question is far from easy. If there is any suspicion whatsoever that he may have been exposed to infection, he should visit a clinic or doctor.

Homosexuality

During adolescence, most boys and girls will experience some kind of emotional attachment to a friend of the same sex. This may take the form of a young adolescent girl having a "crush" on an older girl she admires very much; a boy may experience similar feelings toward a friend he both respects and, perhaps, envies a little.

Although teenagers may feel worried and guilty about this, there is no need; these feelings are quite normal and will be outgrown as interest in the opposite sex increases. Some adolescents may have one or two physical homosexual encounters during these years, particularly in a single-sex boarding school. This does not mean that later, when they mix freely with both sexes, they will be homosexual. However, if toward the end of adolescence a young adult shows exclusive interest in a same-sex partner, it is likely that he or she is indeed homosexual. Although parents naturally find this difficult to accept, the best they can do for their child is not to reject him but to receive his preference with sympathy.

Attitudes toward sex

In a recent survey carried out in America it was shown that sixty-nine percent of all boys and fifty-five percent of all girls agreed with the statement that: "So far as sex is concerned I do what I want to do regardless of what society thinks." It was also found that two out of three adolescent girls from thirteen to nineteen expressed the belief that: "Women enjoy sex as much as men." Only one out of ten adolescent girls believed that: "Women have innately less capacity for sexual pleasure than men." Girls usually display more conservative attitudes toward sexual matters, such as premarital intercourse or pornography. Recent experiments, however, have seemed to show that women and girls are just as easily and fully aroused by erotica as men are. So perhaps the differences in attitudes toward sex are not biological after all, but due to very deep-seated cultural habits, which are now very slowly changing.

It is estimated that more than half of American young people between the ages of fifteen and nineteen have had sexual intercourse. The speed with which such a situation has come about is exemplified by the figures from one Midwestern city, where the proportion of white, middle-class fourteen-year-olds who had experienced intercourse grew from ten percent in 1971 to seventeen percent in 1973. Although most studies suggest a considerable difference between the generations concerning sexual behavior, it is probably much less than it appears—and than many parents fear. It would be wrong to assume that there is widespread promiscuity among young people. It seems that there is a more permissive attitude toward earlier premarital intercourse, particularly among young women, but the frequency has not changed much. Adolescents are, after all, only reflecting the more open attitudes accepted by social generally. In premarital sex and living together before marriage, the emphasis is on mutual feeling—liking each other and having interests in common— rather than on adherence to rigid social and religious rules. For many adolescents sexual activity is simply a lot of fun, some of which is derived from the outrage of older people.

About two in three pregnancies occurring in teenagers are unintended. In 1974 there were over 30,000 abortions performed on girls under twenty in the United States, of which about 17,500 were on girls under fourteen. Teenage marriage is a poor risk. More than one-quarter of first marriages that take place between fourteen and seventeen end in divorce or separation compared to a ten percent break-up rate between twenty- and twenty-four-year olds.

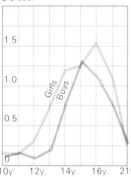

During their teens, young people become highly sensitive to the opposite sex. They recover their composure by the age of twenty-one. The graph shows how much slower a typical group of adolescents subconsciously reacted to emotive words like date, kiss, and dance than they did to neutral words like salt and barley (represented by the horizontal line 0 on the graph). Girls become more sensitive earlier than boys and reach a higher peak of awareness. Boys start to recover their composure sooner than girls, who then catch up rapidly.

A teenager's relationship with his parents will be a key factor in how he makes the transition into mature sexual adulthood. It is obviously valuable for a child of any age to relate well to his parents, but this is particularly important during the stresses and emotional growing pains of adolescence. No relationship between parents and teenagers precludes political arguments at the dinner table or conflicts about what a girl should wear. However trying for parents, the adolescent is asserting a healthy independence.

It is the underlying love and support that matters, because the parent of the same sex provides a model of how the child should behave as a mature man or woman. A loving parent of the opposite sex who gets on well with his partner reinforces the model provided by that partner in the adolescent's eyes and provides the basis for future relationships with the opposite sex.

Throughout childhood, it is the parents who are likely to be close to the child and therefore the prime source of modeling. But any other concerned adult—older sibling, grandparent, or an admired teacher—seen a great deal by a child will also influence sexual identity from childhood, through adolescence and into young adulthood.

Such rewarding relationships help the teenager mature into his or her adult sexual role. But learning and following behavior that is considered appropriately male or female in no way means that stereotyped roles must be adhered to. A teenage girl who admires her mother will naturally seek to emulate her behavior in many ways; but this does not mean that she will be pushed into a culturally conditioned, purely "feminine" role for life—precluding any so-called "masculine" opportunities, such as choice of job or professional achievement. And, of course, a traditionally "masculine" role is no longer necessarily expected of all boys. Extreme stereotyping of the sexes is disappearing and the old rules are fading in favor of wider opportunities for young adults of both sexes.

A vital element in becoming a mature adult is achieving a strong, evolving sense of identity. It is one of the main tasks of adolescence that a teenager comes to see himself as separate from and independent of other people, with his own unique identity, which is generally consistent in different situations and changing relationships.

A sense of self has been emerging gradually since the moment of birth, but the self-image of a child is not just one of a smaller person but one of a different kind. For with adolescence comes the new power of abstract thought, the ability to form concepts outside the solid physical world. A child thinks of him- or herself in a simple fashion: boy or girl, tall or short, strong or not so strong, good or indifferent at studying or games, or not much good at anything; he is the child of his particular parents, who live in a particular house. These are concrete ideas.

Sexual identity

The uncertainties and frustrations of teenage life can cause melancholy and misery. Pressures from peers can lead to recurring anxieties, especially if expectations fail to be fulfilled.

A sense of self

The teenager is aware that there is something else too, the self, which he may start to look for somewhere inside. (In doing so he is falling into a philosophical trap, where, however, he is in very good company.) Suddenly any deviation between his aspirations and his achievements may become glaringly obvious, along with heartfelt searching for the meaning of life.

Paradoxically, it is at this stage in life when the foundations of a young person's personality may be at their shakiest. During the growth spurt the different parts of the body rarely keep pace with each other, so that a well-proportioned twelve-year-old can become quite suddenly plump or gangling. The questions "Who am I? What am I?" are hard to answer when you do not look like the person you were a year ago, when your blood rushes unaccountably around your body and your head at inconvenient times, and you are uncomfortably aware of the smallness of this earth and the remoteness of space.

Life now makes constant new demands—social, sexual, and intellectual. Achievement in all these fields can suddenly matter desperately as a reassurance, while the future takes on a significance it never had before.

The rigors of private study are not to be underestimated, and the need to find the right balance between work and play is essential. Time spent away from books and notes is as important as time spent with them. Resentment or priggishness can build up easily in the teenager who feels himself to be pushed too hard and consequently isolated from his friends.

Self-doubt is very common. Although many teenagers cope very well and manage to live from day to day quite calmly, they may still need support from their parents. Indeed it is probably the ones who ask for the support and receive it who cope the best. But it is surprising how unreasonable some doubts can seem to anyone close. An adolescent may suddenly become an anxious recluse because he thinks he is ugly, when to everybody else he seems a model of what our culture lays down for good looks. One or two bad marks can throw a normally good scholar into an agony of doubt.

Many of a teenager's difficulties in getting his ideas about himself straight are not of his own making but of society's. A child in a simple hunting or agricultural community knows what the adult world holds in store for him because from an early age he lives and works in the adult world, or at least on its fringes. When the time comes for the elders to say "now you are a man," the young person knows what is expected. Indeed he does not experience adolescence as we know it.

For our young people there are so many options. Is the boy to be an accountant, a teacher, or an engineer? Or is he to be none of these things, but an artist or a craftsman, working on his own? A modern girl's position is even worse, for she has to ponder all these options alongside the question of whether she wants a career at all. At any age these questions involve identity, but during the years of adolescence the problem is particularly acute.

Some lucky young people so obviously possess talents in one direction and no other that for them only one path is really practicable. At the same time it may be easy for them to see themselves in the role to which their abilities point, because they clearly fit it. But for many the question "Can you really see yourself as a soldier?" may call forth the answer "Yes—and as a research chemist!" Though professional vocational guidance may be helpful, both parent and child may have to live with uncertainty until the child has evolved more sense of identity.

Self-doubt

Teenage conversions

As part of the search for identity many teenagers become abruptly converted at about seventeen or eighteen to some form of new belief. It may be religion—or atheism—politics, or some form of social philosophy involving voluntary action. These drastic conversions often contain an element of rebellion, either by going against the parents' wishes, or by following the parents' usual beliefs and attitudes, but outdoing them in intensity and activity. Thus the daughter of one Methodist family may join an evangelical church while the son of another (or even the same one) may join the humanists. Such "teenage conversions" are exceptional, although some churches and other groups make a point of encouraging them as a fruitful source of recruits.

No harm usually comes from such enthusiasms, but if a parent is worried it can be difficult to know how to react. Setting up a battle may not help but it may be what is needed—a sign that you really care. This is probably the most important thing. Do not try to convert your teenager to your own views, but show that it matters to you what he believes and does. Ignoring the situation is likely to be a mistake.

The influences of friends

In many ways, the friends of an adolescent play a similar role in his development to those of earlier childhood. "Playing" at this age may seem very different from that of earlier stages, or embarrassingly similar. It has the same function—trying ideas out in order to discover and learn. In relations with friends of the same and the opposite sex, teenagers are coming closer to the kinds of relationships they will have as adults in work, in social situations, and in heterosexual bonds. In early childhood there is a need to explore ways of establishing a pattern of personal relationships; young adults who are unable to form attachments to members of their own or the opposite sex are likely to run into serious difficulties in their personal relationships later on.

As ties with parents become looser and independence increases, the adolescent has a greater need to turn to his peers. Also, as this is often a time of minor family conflicts—arguments, ups and downs in disciplinary matters, the need for love mixed with the need to break away—a teenager often feels more comfortable with friends of his own age than with his parents, however basically sympathetic the relationship. His special friends, and indeed all teenagers, have a common bond that unites them: they have not yet made the transition into adulthood; they are all facing the stresses and the challenges of the future, which seem, at times, rather frightening. With friends, a teenager can fully discuss and try out on an equal footing doubts, hopes, and ideals about jobs, exams, boy or girl friends, war and peace, and a host of other questions involved in the search for identity.

However, although it is true that other young people and teenage culture tend to

become more influential with a teenager, this does not mean that the influence of parents necessarily lessens by an equivalent amount. It is often assumed that after the middle school years the influence of other teenagers far outweighs that of parents; this is not so. Too much peer influence may reflect a lack of genuine interest shown in the teenager at

Above, Below, and Left: Crazes form a large part of the young adolescent's life. They may also provide a mutual point of interest for brothers and sisters. But what might one day be the most important activity in a teenager's life can, the next day, be forgotten and a new activity taken on with the same vigor.

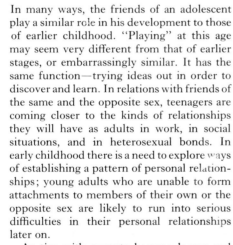

home. But generally teenagers do not choose as their friends young people whose backgrounds are radically different from theirs. Teenage culture has its most important influence on matters such as dress, music, and language. Parental influences persist in deeper questions involving values such as religion, sexual attitudes, education, and the choice of friends.

Although parents are often disturbed by the outward appearances of a teenager's life—the weird clothes and aggressively bad or incomprehensibly mystical language—they must realize that many adolescents need to create a milieu for themselves that is distinctly different from that of their parents. In this transitional stage, neither child nor adult, a teenager needs the opportunity to feel himself separate from his parents; to try out roles on his peers through the way in which he dresses, talks, and expresses opinions. So in the adolescent quest for *who am I?* the peer group plays an important role. Through experimenting with his friends, the teenager gradually clarifies his individual identity to himself. The extent to which a teenager conforms to peer culture usually rises rapidly in preadolescence and the first years after puberty. In later adolescence. there is a steady decline, presumably as the young adult has acquired a better-defined sense of himself and feels secure enough to go his own way if he wishes.

The strong urge to be with friends is balanced in many teenagers by times of needing to be alone. This is all part of the mood swings normally associated with adolescence. Males are more likely to spend their adolescent social lives in groups or gangs; girls tend to pair off with a friend who shares similar interests and talents, although girl groups are not uncommon.

Teenage groups change their membership frequently, and individual members can find themselves suddenly excluded. Sometimes there are reasons for this—their personalities or interests do not suit the new group; at other times the exclusion seems completely arbitrary. If your teenager finds himself in such a position, you may have to offer support, not by running down the group, but by showing that he is just as valuable a person as he always was. Explain to him that groups do change and that the world is not always fair.

Dating The age at which teenagers start dating varies a good deal and depends on their sexual and personal maturity, their family's attitude, and the company they keep. On the whole, the children of parents who accept dating as a natural part of growing up will start early, while those whose parents feel that it is better for such complications to be left until later are unlikely to date until they are sixteen or older. Children from mixed schools, perhaps naturally, start earlier than those from single-sex schools, supporting the findings of one authority that "dating is defined by cultural norms, not by biological development."

Perhaps more in America, the original home of adolescence, than anywhere else, dating is a cornerstone of teenage success. Conformity pressures are high, and the norm is to form "successful" relationships with the other sex. Many youngsters are already dating regularly by the time they reach their early teens.

Relationships with the other sex are one of the great areas of exploration and aggravation throughout adolescence. "Going steady" is a significant commitment. A boy and girl may go out with each other, and with nobody else, two or three times a week yet still not declare that they are "going steady." Or they may "go steady" with a new partner every month. Definitions are important to a young person grappling to understand the elusive phenomena that affect him in new and sometimes disturbingly powerful ways. Is it real love? What is the difference between loving someone and being in love? Can you love someone without liking them? "How far should we go?"

Sooner or later the teenager will experience the stresses and strains of breaking up, the hurt and devastating rejection of being given up, and the mingled relief and guilt on the part of the one who makes the break.

During these times the parents may be called on to steer, caution, welcome, forbid, advise, reminisce about their own youth, and occasionally pick up the pieces of wrecked relationships.

Some ideal matches seem to be made between youngsters who may start to "go steady" in the mid-teens and, having never been out with anyone else, become engaged and marry. But for most people a range of experience with partners of different characters and interests is more likely and in the long run more beneficial. If a boy is deprived of experience, he may think himself in love with the first girl who accepts his advances, and a protected girl may fall too hard for the first person to court her.

Parents often worry about both extremes of behavior. If a son or daughter seems to play the field a little too much, they naturally question whether any long-term relationship is possible for that child. Perhaps greater is the worry of a relationship that seems too serious too soon. The parents will have to face the moral problem about whether the young couple will and ought to sleep together. Then there is the practical worry about whether pregnancy will result. Here parents must advise as they themselves see fit. Most teenagers respect and understand, even if they do not sympathize with, sincerely held and frankly stated views. An angry showdown should be avoided if at all possible. It almost always does irreparable harm. The distance of years makes it all too easy to be cynical about teenage passion, but to those caught in its throes it can be an irresistible force. Its unpredictable consequences must be accepted rather than met head on. Make allowances for rapid swings in mood.

Going steady

Whether it's simply friendship or true love, teenage relationships do help the participants toward self-knowledge and prepare them for deeper relationships in later life.

Try to remember how you felt when you were first "in love." Be as understanding and supportive as you can during an emotional experience that can be almost unbearably tender as well as traumatic.

Lastly, there is the question of education and career. Are studies being neglected? Is homework suffering because the two young people are together every evening?

Each parent must judge how each relationship stands. Sometimes, especially if there is a disturbed home background, a strong teenage relationship can provide an anchor that positively aids educational progress. One study has revealed that married university students have a better record of exam success than their unmarried colleagues.

Overprotective parents

The amount of stress a teenager experiences in adolescence greatly depends on his parents and how they react to the changes in him. Many parents quite simply do not want their child to grow up. They like young children and adore babies; adults do not interest them, and they hate this burgeoning, gangling, most unbaby-like creature that their child is turning into. Such parents may give their child a very happy carefree childhood (although it is likely to have been of a rather restricted kind) and then gradually withdraw from him after the age of eleven or so.

The child is then lost, deprived of the support he has hitherto had in abundance and upon which he has relied. He can do one of three things. He can remain childlike and put off growing up as long as possible—some children of such parents never grow up. He can break away and find his own independence, probably with a good deal of shouting and resentment on both sides, justifying his parents' worst fears as he does so. When this kind of response is particularly strong, teenage delinquency may well be the result. The child may also become an eternal victim of the dilemma, and neither remain a charming child nor mature into a capable adult, instead becoming indecisive, half-alive, sullen, and depressed. For many of this group, their condition shows up only in their own adulthood or middle age, when they seek help from their doctor or a psychotherapist for relief from anxiety or depression.

Parents' stress in the mid-life crisis

Very often the parents' attitudes toward their changing child are not determined by stubbornness on their part but by the stresses and changes that they themselves are undergoing at this time. Unless they had their children when they were very young, parents of teenagers are likely to be at least approaching middle age, if not in the thick of it. They will be facing their own life-change crisis. This has nothing to do with the menopause (though the term "male menopause" dramatizes a stage in the life cycle of both sexes which psychiatrist Elliott Jaques, who

Body types and personality

The three extreme types of the human physique. The endomorph (left) is round, soft, and fat. The mesomorph (center) is broad shouldered, hard, and muscular, and the ectomorph (right) has a fragile and thin physique.

Nearly two thousand years ago there were attempts to link physical characteristics with personality. Black bile, for instance, was thought to make a person "melancholic," pessimistic, and depressed. More recent research by Kretschmer in the 1920s was later refined by Sheldon, who identified three basic body types—endomorphic, mesomorphic, and ectomorphic—and produced corresponding personality traits.

The personality of the endomorph was diagnosed as relaxed, and just as there might be tendencies toward complacency so there could be tolerance and acceptance of others. He was thought to be friendly and companionable and a keen socializer. The mesomorph on the other hand was seen as highly competitive and abounding in drive and enterprise. The ectomorph, slender and thin, inwardly and outwardly aware, was seen as a highly controlled person leading an orderly life and often seeking solitude. Though most people lean more toward one type than another they usually combine some of the characteristics of each type. A thin but muscular person, for example, would be classified as an ecto/meso.

Today, though, it is thought that such emphatic characterization is not possible and that people's personalities are not so rigidly dictated by their bodies. Nevertheless, it is known that different body types do have different requirements. Not until adolescence does a person's body type emerge and once it is established there is nothing that can be done to change it. Despite all the propaganda of the muscle-building advertisers, no ectomorph ever transformed himself into a mesomorph. This does not mean that you should ignore your teenager's figure. Your concerns about nutrition and the benefits of physical activity will undoubtedly be guided by a realization that there is a wide variation between normal ranges in body weight and physique. Whatever stock one puts in this particular way of classifying human beings, what is significant is the need to treat each child (or adult) as an individual.

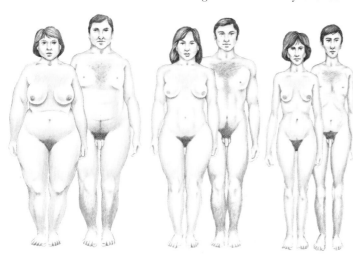

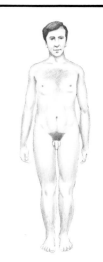

This drawing reminds us that human beings are composites and tend to exhibit the physical and psychological attributes of the basic body types— endomorph, mesomorph, and ectomorph—to varying degrees. The person illustrated here, for example, appears to be mainly mesomorphic. Thus, according to this scheme of generalizing about human beings, he would tend to be competitive and outgoing.

first put his finger on the phenomenon, called "the mid-life crisis.")

Crisis is perhaps too strong a word for what happens to many people. It is a crisis in the technical sense that there is a challenge to be met and overcome, but not in the sense that there is a disaster—at least, not for most people. The mid-life crisis typically hits people at any time between thirty-five and forty-five. It can come very gradually, or it can arrive suddenly. It is the time when a person looks up from his everyday concerns, views the world around him, and himself, takes stock, and realizes that he is not young anymore. His own death appears on the horizon. It may be so remote as to be barely discernible; certainly there is no question of death seeming imminent: but it is now real, in sight, and waiting.

This turning point need not have anything to do with declining mental or physical powers. Indeed, Jaques pointed out that many people start to realize their full poten-

restlessness to affect relationships within the family. It may even be that the more parents repress the desire, the greater the disturbance will be, for they will be depriving themselves of the chance to make changes within their marriage and family.

A father may at this middle point in life be coming to realize, suspect, or fear that he has advanced as far on his career ladder as he can go. Whether this is because he has reached his own limits, or because of limited opportunities, frustration will result, upsetting his self-confidence. If his wife has cherished her husband as a successful go-getter, she, too, may be disillusioned.

For the mother, career changes may work in the opposite direction, for this is the time when many mothers go back to work, having brought their children to this stage of physical, if not psychological, independence.

These turbulent years, it is hoped, will bring growth and maturity, not only to the adolescent but to his parents as well.

One of the pleasures of life with older children is that the whole family can enjoy doing more things together. And when there is a celebration, going to a restaurant or movie is fun for everyone, especially now there is no need to rush home to relieve a baby-sitter.

tial only when they reach this turning point, which can be a spur to achievement. Nonetheless, in the majority of parents, who will be in their forties when their children reach fourteen or fifteen, some small measure of physical decline does set in. The realization comes that they cannot sprint for the bus, run upstairs, or dig the garden with quite such carefree abandon. Hearing and eyesight may also deteriorate, as may a person's looks. In our culture it is difficult to accept this with complete equanimity, even if we are not too concerned about our appearance.

Relationships between the two parents may also be at a delicate stage. Now that they have been married for twenty years or so, even if not to the same spouse for the whole period, a certain restlessness may make itself felt, an unconscious feeling that this is the last chance for a little variety. It is a time when many married people have brief affairs. Many more, however, do no more than dream from time to time. No affair is needed for this

Growing together is easier for parents and children if teenagers can accept change in their parents too. If they have a highly idealized, rigid view of the kind of people their parents are and ought to be, the least slip below these standards may cause bitter disillusion and estrangement. Adolescence is a time when children make huge demands on their parents: it will help them if they already know that their parents are not superhuman and have needs and frailties of their own, as well.

Although some of the difficulties that some families experience during the child's adolescence may be caused or aggravated by the parents' own problems at the time, this is definitely a period when a child imposes very special burdens on his parents. Perhaps your own parents never reproached you for "using the house as though it were a hotel," but you are almost certain to have heard the familiar phrase from some quarter.

Fitting in with the family

Once they have reached young adulthood, teenagers can keep very outlandish hours, coming in at any time of the day or night. Your own sex life may be interrupted, and in this and many lesser ways parents of teenagers can feel that all privacy has gone out of their home and their lives.

It is perhaps an inevitable consequence of the new independence of teenagers that they roam far and wide, returning to the home only for meals and bed. But there is no reason why they should not do a fair share of the housework. It is no good, however, issuing general admonishments to busy and active young people. If you feel that your child is not pulling his weight, convene a family conference in which all the household tasks are evaluated and allocated. Then set up a schedule showing who is to do what and when, and let everybody check off week by week that they have done their allotted duties. Many families set penalties for backsliding, and it is often

are secretly worrying about whether next year's promotion will come through, and whether the attendant increase in earnings will keep pace with the rising family budget, will feel that they have enough to deal with without being drawn into arguments about politics, philosophy, or religion. Their incautious generalized remarks may be seized on by a self-righteous young person, who, the parents wearily think, has no idea of the true priorities and practicalities of life.

It is strange that arguing seems so typical of a family with teenagers, because it is quite clear that few children have ideas that are drastically unlike their parents'. They would be surprised to realize that their own children are likely to grow up with the same political learnings as themselves. Most children follow in their parents' footsteps in career and recreation. So this arguing is not usually a sign of rebellion and deviance but part of a valuable process of creative discovery.

Differences of opinion between people of different ages are a healthy sign rather than something to be avoided. They can make doing things together all the more stimulating, each person learning something new from the other.

the parents who have to protect the child against his own zeal in setting penalties that are out of all proportion to the offense.

Sometimes resistance by a teenager to taking part in housework can be a sign that his parents are already pushing him hard enough. If from the young person's point of view he is already working as hard as he can to reach goals that have been set by his parents rather than by himself, he will see it as unreasonable to be asked to do chores as well. If your teenager seems uncooperative in this way, ask yourself whether he is not already cooperating as much as you have any right to ask but in some other way, possibly by working hard for exams to satisfy your ambitions as much as his.

Family arguments

As a result of their new powers of thought, their new vision of the world and its larger questions, their idealism and need to make clear to themselves what kind of person they are and how they fit into the world, teenagers can be endlessly argumentative and disputatious. Many unfortunate parents, who

Conflict can make life hard for the parents, not because they find themselves apparently under attack but because of the sheer hard work involved.

You can make it worse for yourself, and for your child, however, if you take the challenge too seriously. In fact, your child will come to no harm if now and then *he* has the experience of being right. The realization that parents are not perfect, that now and then they, too, have feet of clay, is an essential part of growing up. Not only life with your adolescent children, but your own growth as parents will be enhanced if you can give way gracefully when you are bested by your own child. In any case, much of the arguing will be about values, in which there can be no winner or loser, for what is at stake is a matter of choice in which your child has as much right to his own preference as do you.

Some of the trials of parenting adolescents are said to be due to an ambiguous quality in the relationship between parents and children. But this ambiguousness is not new, or

Discipline

ought not to be new, when the children reach adolescence. It is part and parcel of the relationship from the moment the child is born. The ambiguity is between providing care and protection on the one hand and allowing the child freedom and responsibility on the other; between guarding against the child's lack of maturity and experience and depriving him of the room he needs to develop and learn about the world.

However you have handled your children up to this age, you cannot now act the authoritarian parent and expect to have every word obeyed without question. Teenagers need to be treated like sensible people, even when you are clearly taking parental responsibility for their behavior. More than ever, discipline becomes a matter for negotiation.

If your son comes home form school with a bad report or is fired from his first job, avoid the familiar line of "I am horrified that a son of mine can behave in such an irresponsible manner. When are you going to pull your socks up and work properly? And after all we have done for you too?" Remember that your child is working to make his own way in the world, not yours, and that there may well be a good reason for his poor performance.

Although a short, sharp shock may have the desired effect once or twice, in the last resort you should always allow your child—who is so nearly no longer a child—to speak for himself. So you should always approach him for his side of the story and with the offer of support: do not punish him pointlessly. One way of opening the discussion would be to say: "It says here that you are not working hard enough, and that you have no time for your teachers. What is wrong? How do you feel about this report; is it right?" Perhaps the teaching is not as good as you thought (and the school's staff still think). Perhaps the school is pushing your child in a direction he does not want to go. Many schools have strong traditions in sports, science, languages, or economics, and are poor at coping with children who do not fit.

On the other hand, since so much of a child's school performance depends on his home background, perhaps it is you who are pressing him into a career or specialization that does not interest him. Or perhaps you have not shown enough real interest in his achievements. Many parents have very high hopes for their offspring without doing anything serious to help him achieve those hopes. "What did you do at school today?" is just as important a question for a sixteen-year-old as for a six-year-old, even if it is not quite appropriate to ask it on a daily basis.

The change to secondary school

In most communities your child will move on to high school at the ninth- or tenth-grade level. High school or secondary school is a major step in his life, and it signifies far more than a move to a new building. It is clearly a rite of passage that is looked upon with excitement (and a measure of apprehension) by most children. Sometimes attending a summer program at the new institution helps to ease the transition.

Secondary schools are inevitably bigger, even when they are not the monsters that have been created in recent years. The atmosphere is usually less intimate and friendly, unless the school is quite exceptional. Bigger classes, and more of them, in a bigger building and campus create quite a different setting.

The teaching methods are almost certainly more formal. Although children are free for a while of the pressures of vocational decisions and college admissions, the warmth of the traditional neighborhood school is often absent. Whatever the community setting, the course of study will be more clearly defined, and teaching much more traditional in style than most children will have experienced before.

Study and exams

Children become quickly intolerant of situations that are undisciplined. When studying at home it is essential to have a routine time and place. Though their working environment should be quiet, isolation is not ideal for all children; some may work better with company or the gentle drone of television. The length of time for which a child can concentrate is also governed by his individual personality. Generally, extraverts require more frequent rests than introverts, but all teenagers should relax for a quarter of an hour every hour when studying.

Exams are potentially the most daunting tasks that will face the teenager and, to avoid panic, you should help your child prepare well in advance. Make sure that he knows what he is responsible for and help him allot time for each subject. Refrain from placing too much emphasis on exams; obviously, the greater the expectations, the greater the stress. Finally, remember that an early night is preferable to last-minute cramming.

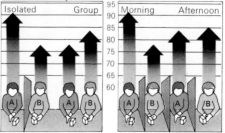

The diagram shows the results on a performance scale of concentration tests among introverts (A) and extraverts (B) working alone or in groups and at various times of day.

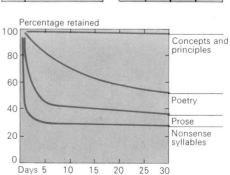

The graph shows our capacity to retain different forms of information. Unrelated facts such as dates can be especially difficult to remember.

Choosing your child's next school

If you are thinking of sending your child to a private school, or if options are available within your local school system, you will need to weigh many factors before you come to a decision. In looking at a prospective school you should be guided by the following considerations:

Are you interested in a public school, a parochial school, a school that provides specialized education with particular talents and interests? Do you think your child would do better in a single-sex school or in a mixed setting?

How far away is the school? A long journey will add expense, tire your child, and may cut him off from his local friends when at school and his school friends when at home. You will have to weigh this against the merits of the school.

Go and look around the school, talk to the teachers, and ask the principal:

o What sort of education is offered to the children: academic, vocational, or general?
o How much interaction is there between the school and the outside world? Does the school arrange field trips, visits to local firms, or talks by people from different walks of life?
o How large is the school?
o Is the school housed in one building, or will your child have to travel between annexes?

o How large are the classes?
o What sort of teaching methods are used: formal, informal, grouped, tracked, or mixed?
o What sort and what choice of courses are offered?
o What sort of discipline is maintained?
o What is the school's relationship with parents: welcoming or excluding?
o What amenities does the school have and will any special abilities or problems that your child may have be provided for?
o Does the school require homework and if so how much?
o How much emphasis is put on sports? Is there a choice of physical activities?
o What extra equipment will the school expect you to provide, e.g., hockey stick, geometry equipment, exercise books?

Left: To overcome the problem of many adolescents' distaste for traditional team games, some schools now provide alternative activities such as judo, fencing, modern dance, and fitness classes (which prove very popular with the figure-conscious).

Above: Large schools can be very impersonal, but they have the advantage of facilities on the premises that smaller schools cannot afford.

At the same time a child may have lost contact with many of his friends because they have gone to other schools. All these changes can add up to a very substantial disruption in the child's life. Some children take this in their stride, but many find it a period of stress. They may need several months to adjust. If their standard of work falls, the principal or school counselor may be able to make special efforts to help them readjust.

If you are considering the possibility of sending your child to an independent or parochial school, many factors will influence your decision and determine your ultimate choice.

Although the American system of public education has traditionally been based on the "neighborhood school" concept, pressures to satisfy federal guidelines for racial integration, particularly in larger cities, have weakened this principle to some extent. Attendance at a school in a neighborhood some distance from home has sometimes been mandatory, in other cases voluntary. Some large cities also offer options within the public school framework that make it possible for students to choose a secondary school that fits his special interests and capabilities, or provide an elementary or "magnet" school that stresses alternate or experimental approaches.

In an effort to make education "relevant" as well as innovative, some schools offer special programs to enrich the curriculum— a unit in outdoor education, perhaps, or a broad study of the city, which may take children to visit and observe some of the

Transferring from his small, local primary school to a large, unfamiliar middle or secondary school is bound to be an unsettling event for your child. Carefully preparing him for these changes will considerably reduce his anxiety about the move.
o Take him to see the school beforehand. If it is a school within the local system, and one to which most of his classmates will be going, a tour will very likely be arranged for the whole group. Usually a child who is going to a new school along with his former classmates will be buoyed by the enthusiasm of the group and will eagerly anticipate the new experience, despite some inner trepidation.
o Sometimes it is helpful for a child to attend a summer program at the school to which he will be moving in the fall.
o Prepare him in whatever ways are necessary to avoid confusion—having the proper supplies, knowledge of homeroom assignments, courses, and schedules, and of transportation arrangements will reduce any anxiety about what is to come.
o Be careful to keep your own anxieties under control. Parents tend to see a child's step forward as a symbol of his gradual movement away from them; it is well to recognize this and transmit a sense of enthusiasm about his growing maturity.

Preparing for middle or secondary school

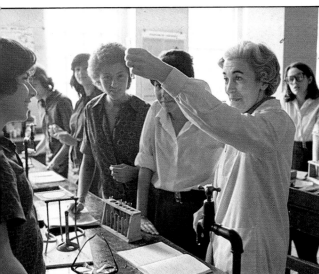

Left : In the past schools tended to teach liberal arts subjects more to girls than boys and the sciences more to boys, but both sexes now have a wide choice of courses from both disciplines.

Below : Private music lessons are expensive, but some public schools include instruction in a musical instrument in their weekly curriculum.

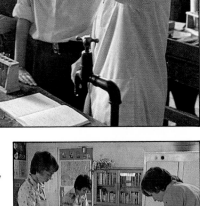

Right : Teaching a child the practical skills of day-to-day living is part of the curriculum in many schools. These days fewer boys and girls leave school versed in the classics ; instead they have learned more practical things : to cook, sew on a button, and maintain a car.

Above : Since young people have been obliged by law to stay on at school well into their teens, many of those who are unsuited to a long course of academic education have become very restless in their last years of schooling. To solve this problem some schools have introduced courses to teach these boys and girls industrial skills, such as metalwork, basic electrical engineering, and cookery, that help them to get a job.

social, political, and cultural institutions of the community in which they live. At the high school level there may be opportunities for independent study and research, or for projects allowing contact with younger children or with senior citizens.

Whether or not your child should participate in such programs will depend on his preferences, but these should be guided by parental judgment. Too often, what may seem like an imaginative, new idea may be merely a novelty, and parents should not be afraid to insist on the solid grounding—at every educational level—that every child needs and deserves. Feel free to discuss your questions and concerns with teachers, principal, or district superintendent—and always with the child himself. He needs the perspective of adults, and yet a healthy balance must be struck with his own goals and desires.

It is also important to forge a close relationship with your child's high school guidance counselor. If your child is likely to go to college, it is important for him to plan his high school program with that objective in mind. If he is unlikely to do so, his program will likewise reflect that outcome. Parents can be helpful, however, in urging a child to "keep his options open." He is at an age when his goals and interests are fluid and often subject to sudden turns, and it is unwise to foreclose possibilities that will interest him as he becomes more mature.

Economic questions are, of course, paramount, and each family must weigh priorities

and resources. However, it is important to remember that scholarship aid is often available, and if you believe that a private school would benefit your child it is wise to explore the possibilities of financial aid before concluding that such a move would be economically impossible.

It is also well to remember that different children in a family will have different needs, and whereas one school may serve an individual child successfully, his brother or sister may need another setting. Which child goes to which school is a matter only parents can decide, but the child who goes to a public school while his sibling is sent to one that requires more expense or even sacrifice is not necessarily "deprived." Conveying this sense of "appropriateness" is an important function of parenthood. Parents must always be vigilant about the pitfalls of projecting the idea that the amount of money spent is a reflection of the amount of love they feel. And whereas the importance of good schooling can hardly be overestimated, educators and parents alike have come to realize that it is the home which has the greatest influence on a child's total development.

One of the hardest things for a modern parent to accept may be a teenager's feeling that high school holds little interest for him and that he would be happier and feel more productive in a daytime job. Many high schools have recognized this possibility by providing work/study programs which allow a student

Allowing for differences

Seeking further education

The first decision a high school graduate must make is whether he wants to go straight into full employment or whether he would like to seek further education in a college, university, or technical school. Although an increasing number of American students are going on to higher education, many are choosing to postpone it for a few years while they gain work experience, accumulate some money, and get more perspective on the career direction they wish to pursue. The high cost of education and the number of vocational options available are making such a plan attractive. Educational institutions, too, are responding to this by adapting their programs increasingly to students of all ages.

The need for women with grown children to seek further education has also been a factor in the growing view of education as a lifetime pursuit.

Thus a young person who is not sure he wants to commit himself at the outset to years of study should be reassured that academic programs will be open to him later on.

Some businesses have organized training programs which combine work experience with academic preparation. Such plans usually include tuition reimbursement.

A young person with energy and determination—and perhaps some guidance—should have little difficulty in choosing a career path that is suitable for him.

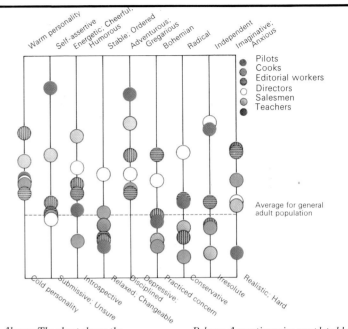

Above : The chart shows the personalities of a number of people in six different careers, each of which is fairly typical of a broad spectrum of occupations, both in the qualities it requires and in the type of work undertaken. Personality more than any other factor determines how successful someone is in his chosen career.

Below : A questionnaire completed by some American students showed that the influences affecting their choice of their major field in college were different from those affecting their choice of career. Surprisingly mothers were more important in influencing future careers, but fathers had more say in the choice of major.

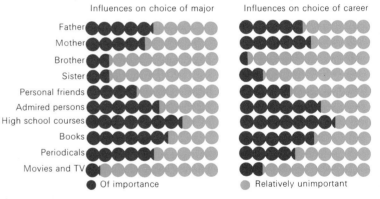

to take his essential subjects during a concentrated period and therefore hold a job for the rest of the day. Another option is to hold a full-time job during the day and attend school at night. Businesses are often willing and eager to participate in training and employing young people in this kind of "earn and learn" program. If such an arrangement seems appropriate for your teenager, consult the principal or guidance counselor in his school and explore the possibility of adjusting your child's schedule to accommodate work as well as study. Most children respond very positively to such an arrangement.

Developing "personhood"

Parents must strive to maintain that thin line between stressing the importance and value of scholastic achievement and allowing their teenager time to "goof off," to relax, to daydream, to pursue interests and activities that may not seem worthwhile, perhaps, but are

part of his struggle to develop his own interests and find his own way. It is often a friendship or an extracurricular activity which has the greatest impact on a young person's direction and development, and it is important that he have the freedom to explore and test activities and relationships.

Developing friendships with people of different ages, participating in political campaigns, helping on community projects, contributing to the life of his family through chores or by taking care of a younger brother or sister, working in a family business—such activities that involve a teenager in the mainstream of life should be encouraged. Too often young people tend to cut themselves off from the wider aspects of the life around them as the interests and standards of their own peer group assume prime importance.

Asserting standards in the midst of protest is a responsibility of parenthood that is not to be ignored. Objections may come loud and clear, but if parents remember that children of all ages want to and need to have limits set for them, the adolescent years will be easier to live through and will be growing years for both generations.

College-bound youngsters will find the academic pressures of high school rigorous, but with careful management of time and a generally relaxed atmosphere at home a teenager should still find time and energy for outside activities. Parents can be helpful here. Finding the right balance between the need to match the competition and the need to remain a whole and integrated person is a goal of young adulthood that is not to be overlooked.

Many parents of teenagers comment on the fact that their children always seem to choose the most inconvenient time to suddenly decide to talk things over with them.

Parents who can be flexible enough to respond to such overtures and keep all channels open will be well rewarded. Heart-to-heart discussions somehow resist programing, but they are perhaps the essence of healthy parenting.

Adolescents who are struggling with their own problems of identity, of career choice, of dealing with sexuality, of forging human

relationships will be comforted and reassured by parents who are responsive to their questioning and who are willing to listen and ready to admit that they, too, are solving similar problems—that such searchings, in fact, are a lifelong process.

Many teenagers are able to decide with some certainty what they want to do when they

The vanity of teenagers is not to be underestimated. Though some may make a virtue of scruffiness, most can be relied upon to keep themselves clean and well groomed.

Going out to work

Reducing the risk of an accident

Youth is the age least affected by illness—it is an age of exploration, when much energy is expended, and to a certain extent accidents are to be expected. The mortality figures given in the graph opposite, however, represent only part of the story—they do not take into account injuries, which, it has been estimated, outnumber deaths by a ratio greater than 200:1.

The twelve-year-old is capable of making reasonably mature decisions. However, pressure from a peer group, say, to perform a dare can often lead to irrational decisions. Typical accidents for this age are as a result of climbing or exploring railroad trestles, building sites, and underground tunnels. Sporting activities also account for large numbers of mishaps. Boys particularly may be aware of their growing manhood, and they may feel the need to prove themselves both to their friends and to themselves.

Motor vehicle accidents show a particularly sharp rise as young people reach the age when they can drive their own motorcycle or car. Many accidents result from an ignorance of how things such as firearms or farm equipment work. Drowning occurs most frequently among males between the ages of twelve and nineteen years.

Genuine accidents cannot be prevented. Many accidents result from unnecessary risks and, in a society where virility and foolhardiness are often linked together, parents have an obligation to point out to their children the dangers involved in their activities as well as the importance of concentration, alertness, and skill.

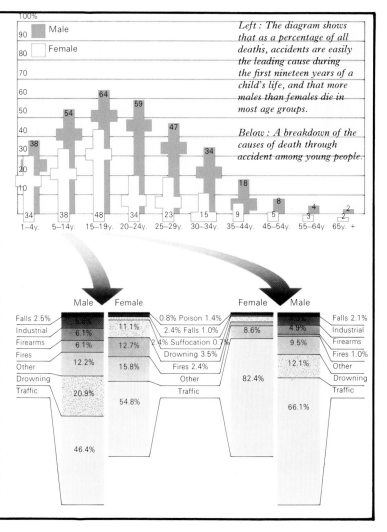

Left: The diagram shows that as a percentage of all deaths, accidents are easily the leading cause during the first nineteen years of a child's life, and that more males than females die in most age groups.

Below: A breakdown of the causes of death through accident among young people.

complete their education. If they make a mistake it is easier for them to change jobs in today's highly mobile society than it was for their parents or grandparents.

As has already been mentioned, it is often wise to encourage a student to work for a year or so between high school and college. He is often likely to have a more mature attitude toward studying when he does return.

One study in America found that higher education is not essential to success. High school dropouts at sixteen seem to do just as well in life (outside certain careers) as those who stay on to study. Clearly there is still room in life for natural ability and experience.

Some children drop out and fail, often unconsciously, as revenge on their parents, who have pushed them too hard or seen their children as objects for their own ambition. Many such rebels, however, eventually find themselves and achieve success on their own terms in their own way.

Allowances

Once a child is able to go out and about with his friends, it is important for him to have more financial independence. If a child has been getting an allowance throughout the growing-up years, a parent may feel that once the mid-teens are reached this is a good time for a more substantial increase. It should be made quite clear at the time exactly what the teenager is supposed to pay for out of this—perhaps movies, concerts, fares, snacks eaten out, and personal items such as curlers and combs. It may work out better for some teenagers if they are given their money once a month, and start learning to budget their resources over four weeks instead of one.

Most teenagers will want to supplement their allowance with money from jobs. Baby-sitting, washing cars, helping neighbors to move are all tasks that quite a young teenager can accomplish. Later in adolescence, part of vacations may be spent working in a shop, factory, or office. Apart from widening an adolescent's experience—and providing money for records and special trips—it will greatly add to an adolescent's self-esteem to know that he is capable of earning. As long as parents are confident that their child is responsible enough to carry out the job he has taken on, they should encourage this healthy step toward independence—however modestly it begins. This is equally so whether the young person is planning to go into business or on to higher education, which will further delay self-sufficiency.

As clothes become more important to both boys and girls parents may feel that a clothing allowance, which the child can manage himself, makes sound sense. Sometimes this can be included in the full allowance: other teenagers still need help in budgeting, and for them it makes sense to keep this element of their income separate (perhaps in a different bank account) and partly under your control.

The financial independence, and thus the spending power, of today's adolescent is greater than it has ever been before. Whole commercial markets, from record companies to motorcycle manufacturers, have opened up, aiming their goods entirely at the young consumer.

Smoking

The health risks associated with smoking are now so well known and well documented that responsible parents must hope to discourage

teenage children from even starting. Once a teenager has reached the age at which he can be spoken to in adult terms, a parent can point out rationally the potential harm a smoker is doing to his body.

If one or both parents are confirmed smokers themselves, they must admit their addiction for the sake of their own credibility. There is no question that such an admission requires courage. How many non-smokers could admit to a bad habit of theirs and could forthrightly say: "I admit I'm hooked. I've tried to give it up and I've failed, and I wish I'd never started. So take my advice and don't start."

Teenagers will spend hours in close confinement, locked away in a bedroom or attic, where they can smoke and talk, far removed from the adult world.

Teenage drinking

Many parents are concerned about teenage drinking because it is becoming much more prevalent. They worry that the effects of even a moderate amount of alcohol on a very inexperienced young person (particularly if there is any driving involved) can be dangerous. While the majority of the population remain controlled social drinkers throughout their lives, the number of alcoholics rises every year. Children start to drink through example. As they see adults—especially their parents—drinking socially, they accept that this is part of the adjustment to adulthood. Every study of alcohol use has found that the drinking patterns of teenagers reflect those of their parents and the community they live in. Boys, it was found, drink more than girls; adolescents in urban areas drink more than their rural counterparts.

If his parents drink, there is bound to come a time when a teenager will want to try it too. In a society in which drinking is so prevalent, this is an understandable and healthy response. Both parents and psychologists feel that there is a lot to be said for allowing first drinks in the home; this must be preferable to experimenting secretly with friends, which

The facts about drugs

Should you tell your child about the dangers of drugs? Will it discourage him from using them or will it prompt him to experiment? The idea of "turning him on" to drugs betrays a fantasy: that the taking of drugs is always extremely pleasurable and at the same time seductive. The fact is, however, that the taking of drugs is not in itself especially pleasurable, and in very few cases does addiction follow experiment. Although taking any drug involves a risk, the effects of drugs are very much a matter of education and learning, and both the pleasures and dangers have been exaggerated.

Research has shown that most teenagers, like most adults, are anti-drugs. So why do children experiment? It is the lack of opportunity that hinders most people, including parents, from indulging. Most children are offered drugs in a relaxed social atmosphere such as a party, and accept an offer simply because of their amiability and desire to conform. The dangers of the drug seem, at the moment, irrelevant; "joining the party" is more important.

Most teenage experiments with illegal drugs are harmless and will have no greater effects than your childhood experiments with alcohol and cigarettes—with one important difference—teenage experimenting with illegal drugs seldom develops into heavy or dependent use of those drugs, while most cigarette experimenters become smokers for life. Illegal drug use harms only a tiny minority of experimenters. themselves only a minority of all teenagers. The main problem is how to reduce the number of experimenters who come to harm.

You can prepare your child for his first offer of a drug. Discuss drugs with him, but do not make wild claims about either their pleasures or their powers of addiction. Describe the types of situation in which drugs might be encountered. Don't divide the world into addicts and nonusers, for it is wrong to make the experimenter feel that he is indistinguishable from the heavily committed user. You might also discuss your own experiences with alcohol, cigarettes, tranquilizers, and sleeping pills and give examples of sensible and controlled use of legal drugs. They will be of more value than the horror stories that so delight the press.

There is no distinct personality type which is drawn to drugs, but a family that uses legal drugs in a slavish fashion may foster that pattern in the children. If you ever feel out of your depth, don't panic. This applies to parents as well as experimenters. Seek out a friend or professional, and listen to his advice.

During their teens most children are offered alcohol; many will experiment with cigarettes, and some will dabble in illegal drugs. Should you discover that your child is experimenting with drugs you should not overreact. First you should try to ascertain whether there is any immediate danger facing the child. Then you can start to evaluate how serious a problem it might be, taking into account medical and legal considerations. Only then will you be able to offer your child some advice.

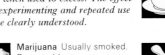

It is important to recognize that all drugs, legal or illegal, are potentially harmful when used to excess. The effect of both experimenting and repeated use should be clearly understood.

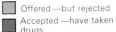
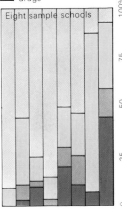

A survey carried out among fifth-formers in some British schools in 1974 measured children's familiarity with drugs. In urban areas children came into greater contact with drugs than in rural areas. Overall the number of teenagers experimenting with drugs was small, and casualties were very few.

☐ No contact—do not know a user
☐ Contact—not offered but know a user
☐ Offered—but rejected
■ Accepted—have taken drugs

Eight sample schools

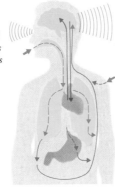

Above: Teenagers do not suddenly decide to smoke twenty cigarettes a day. They may begin by accepting one cigarette from a friend. Later they may accept another. A number of small decisions add up to the intention to smoke regularly. However, someone who, only once in a while, accepts a cigarette is very different from someone who smokes twenty a day. You should draw your child's attention to the way in which the small decisions can add up.

5 Decide to smoke after breakfast
4 Decide not to run out of cigarettes
3 Decide to buy cigarettes
2 Decide to accept more cigarettes
1 Decide to try one cigarette

Children are often offered drugs by someone quite like themselves and in a friendly environment with no pushers or addicts in sight, and the "normality" of the situation may make experimentation seem quite acceptable. Earlier resolutions never to experiment with drugs may then have little influence.

Right: When a drug is injected directly into the bloodstream it will act quicker than when it is swallowed. After a drug has been taken, it finds its way into the bloodstream and from there to the brain, which sends out messages to alter other parts of the body. Return messages from the heart, eyes, ears, and skin about changes in the body are then registered in another part of the brain. LSD disrupts the chemical function of the brain and may cause "flashbacks" long afterward. The total effect of any drug depends on each individual and his situation. If the heart beats faster one person may think he is excited; someone else may feel nervous. If he is happy the drug will exaggerate this. In an unpleasant situation he is unlikely to have a pleasant experience.

Coffee Not recognized as a drug. Repeated use may cause problems in concentration and sleeping. Can be difficult to give up.

Marijuana Usually smoked. Repeated heavy use may cause damage to the lungs, especially if smoked with tobacco. It does not generally cause dependency.

Cocaine Most potent of all the stimulant drugs. It is a white powder from the coca plant, usually sniffed up the nose. Its high cost means teenagers rarely buy dangerous quantities.

Cigarettes Regular smoking damages the lungs and other parts of the body. May cause cancer. Body may grow to depend on them.

Alcohol Socially acceptable. Heavy use causes damage to the heart, liver, brain, and stomach. The body can grow to depend on it.

Pills Mainly in the form of stimulants, which speed you up, and sedatives, which slow you down. Pills are varied and require identification by a doctor or pharmacist. With *any* sedative accidental death. can occur through an overdose. If mixed with alcohol, the effect is intensified.

Opiates Opium, heroin, and other derivatives are sedatives. Heroin, usually injected, is popularly considered to be the most lethal drug, but injection of any drug can cause hepatitis. Repeated use may cause damage to veins and skin, and can all too easily lead to physical dependency.

Solvents Glue, cleaning fluids, gasoline, and similar substances are sniffed by teenagers. The dangers include possible suffocation through loss of consciousness if the head is held within a plastic bag containing glue. Sniffing aerosols can be directly dangerous to the heart.

LSD The "trip," involving unusual thoughts, feelings, and perceptions, lasts several hours. "Bad trips" call for calm reassurance. If a state of prolonged anxiety results, medical care may be needed. LSD can create a highly emotional state. Effects, occasionally, are severe.

Many young people today do not want to plunge immediately into marriage and mortgages. They take the opportunity of their freedom and independence to go to college, travel abroad, or try their hand at a variety of jobs, before shouldering the full responsibilities of adulthood.

the teenager surely will do otherwise. If it is forbidden at home, drinking may automatically become more interesting, and something of a challenge.

A small glass or even a few sips of wine or beer to celebrate a special occasion with the rest of the family is a good way to begin. As the adolescent gets older, and if both parents feel easy about this, it probably makes sense to allow him some beer or wine whenever they are drinking themselves—if he wants it, of course. There is a very good case for *not* permitting an adolescent to drink hard liquor which has a much higher alcoholic content. By taking a reasonable attitude toward beer and wine, a parent can draw this line very firmly. Beer and wine are more frequently used near, or at, mealtimes, and keeping drinking associated mainly with eating is an important safeguard against alcoholism.

Although some older adolescents will take part in the odd drinking binge with friends, the resulting hangover will probably stress the penalties of overindulging. If parents do not take the teenage attitude that this is a praiseworthy achievement, it is unlikely to become a frequent problem. Given standards that are neither too permissive nor unrealistically forbidding, the chances are that a teenager will grow up treating alcohol as something to be enjoyed, not abused.

Stealing

During the adolescent years many teenagers experiment with a little wrongdoing. By far the most common forms are shoplifting and cheating on exams. Often both are surprisingly easy and are usually condoned by friends and other teenagers. The discovery by parents of such breaches of morality often leads to a severe test of the parent/child relationship.

Some people would advise a parent to ignore the odd episode. This may be the best course, if you are *positive* that it is an isolated instance, and if you are absolutely sure that your child does not know that you know. The great danger, of course, is that in avoiding a confrontation, which is bound to be painful and may in the long run be unnecessary, you appear to give silent consent.

If the misdeed is repeated, then you *must* tackle your child. The best course is to follow the soundly humanist advice of St. Ignatius of Loyola: "Hate the sin but not the sinner." Ask him why he did it so that he can understand his own motives. If he has been stealing small items for a dare, point out how out of proportion are the gains and the penalties. If he has been stealing larger items that he desperately wants but cannot afford, then you need to explain financial realities and the facts of the family budget. You may even need to examine your own side of things. Perhaps his behavior is the expression of a grievance. This may be real or imagined, but either way it lies in your power to remedy a real grievance (are you giving him less money than he needs?) or to clarify an imagined one. And it is your responsibility as a parent to do so—not just for your own sake or the good name of the family, but for your child's sake.

It may help to call in professional assistance, as long as this can be done in confidence. If you feel the school psychologist might help, consult the principal in confidence; there is no need for his homeroom teacher to know. Or go to a child guidance clinic. It is vital that if you consult outsiders it is clear, both to yourself and to your child, that you are doing so for professional help, and because wrongdoing does involve the outside world, and not because you are abdicating responsibility.

Above all, try to keep your child out of court. The majority of first offenders are never reconvicted, but the chances of a child's going wrong again are still greater than if he never appeared in court in the first place. Do not help him in the spirit of "getting him off," but on the understanding that you take responsibility for helping him keep within the law in the future.

Growing into adulthood

When the voting age was brought down to eighteen in many countries, the independence and real social power of modern teenagers was recognized. The temptation is to think of the eighteen-year-old as a fully mature adult. The teenager may feel that he is too grown up to ask for support and guidance from his parents, who in their turn may feel that their duty has been done and that their child has no further claim on them.

This is far from the truth. Just as Lawrence Kohlberg has shown how moral thinking develops in sophistication well into adulthood, so our real experience and understanding, both of ourselves and of the world around us, is only just beginning at eighteen.

Studies show that those who develop into the most secure and contented adults are those who had the best relationships with their parents in childhood and who continue them as they move into adulthood. If you as parents can keep in close touch with your grown-up child, you will be able to give him the benefit of your experience, which will always be greater than his, and at the same time continue to learn from him as he grows. A parent's job—and joy—is never done.

How your child has progressed

During the transition from childhood to adulthood dramatic change has taken place. Physically there has been an increase in height and weight. In the space of two to four years your teenager's body has matured from that of a child to that of an adult.

Less visible, and proceeding at a slower pace, have been the changes in his patterns of thought, which have become more far-ranging and more abstract. Self-awareness, and with it self-questioning, have arrived. Society outside himself, at home and school, has been discovered—and perhaps questioned, too. A teenager's whole attitude toward life is deeply thought out, and, whether he conforms or rebels, his reasons for his actions are more strongly felt than his previous unquestioning adherence to the rules which gave him a sense of security.

With his increased sense of individuality he has probably been responding quite aggressively to parental authority. He has lost much of his previous enthusiasm for family activities, and he now forms a social life with friends of his own age. He depends on them to help him establish the basis of his new identity as an adult.

With his growing sexual maturity, he has begun to show a new appreciation of the opposite sex, but it is often not until boys catch up with girls in their development that adolescents of the same age will mix socially.

For some there has been the step out of school into a first job, going once again from being among the most senior to being the most junior and inexperienced member of a community. For others there has been, and possibly still is, the ever-increasing pressure of exams during a long process of education.

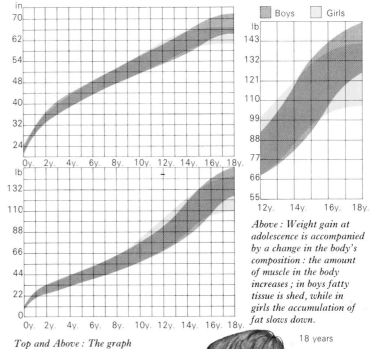

Above : Weight gain at adolescence is accompanied by a change in the body's composition : the amount of muscle in the body increases ; in boys fatty tissue is shed, while in girls the accumulation of fat slows down.

Top and Above : The graph shows a child's height and weight during his first eighteen years. By the time he reaches adulthood he will have grown three and a half times his length at birth and his weight will have multiplied twentyfold.

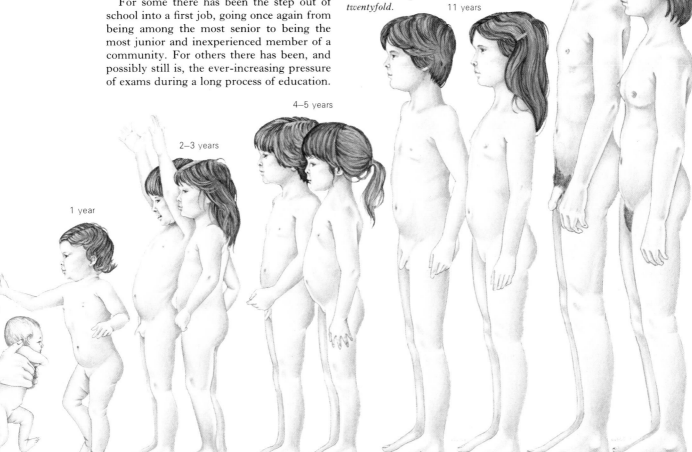

7 The Family
YOUR CHILD'S SUPPORT SYSTEM

We were having an argument,
the nine-year-old and I. With people for
dinner and a meal to be cooked, there were seashells and
muddy boots all over the hall. His father looked
cross and I blew up. He burst into tears and told me I
was mean. Somehow, I felt it. "I'm going to
Grandma's," he announced, "and I'm *never* coming back."
He did, of course, having had a "super"
visit—and just in time to lick the bowl I had made the
meringues in. We all felt happier.

To a child nothing is more important than the family. In his early and most impressionable years his world is virtually enclosed within it. As he grows older and his horizons widen the family is a continuous and, hopefully, steadying influence. And as he ventures farther into the world it can be his refuge in those inevitable times of trouble and self-doubt, a sanctuary within which he can pause to take stock when a confusion of ideas and emotions threatens to overwhelm him. The attitudes and atmosphere within the family and its capacity for love and laughter, its tensions and its problems, together form the most pervasive influence on a child's life.

The changing role of the family

The basic family unit is found in every human society, past and present. It has been, and for most people still is, the key institution of society, guaranteeing its survival. Traditionally there has been in Western society a division of labor within the family, the man taking the role of breadwinner and provider, the woman that of the nurturer and housekeeper. And the major function of this family unit has been to create a secure environment in which to raise children.

In preindustrial times, the family was a working unit: mother, father, and the children all worked, at home or in the fields—many aspects of family life were shared. Industrialization tore the family apart. First the wage-earner left home to work and the family lost its productive functions to the factory. Then it lost its educational function to the school. The mother was left at home with the children, with full responsibility for their upbringing. The mother, without the help and support of her husband, found that she depended greatly on close relatives and friends who lived nearby; and the more she relied on them, the more the father seemed pushed out of the center of the family circle. This situation endured throughout the nineteenth century—and still exists today in many areas.

In the twentieth century a further change has taken place. Social mobility has taken most mothers away from this network of support. Whether she has moved two miles or 200 she is out of immediate personal reach of her own mother or closest friends. This new type of family unit can be very isolating, particularly for the mother who is at home with young children all day. One of her traditional functions, that of doing the housework, has been lessened by the introduction of modern labor-saving devices, and perhaps she has even more free time if she has some babysitting help. In addition she may not have made strong ties with the local community and have no close friends living nearby who could give her advice and support.

The chief reason that a more egalitarian—or symmetrical—family has started to emerge is that, since the push for women's rights, more women now feel that to fulfil themselves as people they must do more as a life's work than take care of home and children. In a consumer society, there is a lot of incentive for the mother to go out and earn to help to pro-

The family is the child's safety net. It should not restrain him from experiencing life but it catches him gently if he should stumble or need support during times of stress.

vide the material benefits that she and her family feel they want. For many young mothers, these advantages outweigh the possible disadvantages of not caring for their own child—of finding a mother substitute, and perhaps regretting it later on. But this is a personal decision in which both parents should be involved; some mothers, having to support their children alone, have no choice.

In theory, if both parents in a family hold down outside jobs this should lead to a considerable change in the division of work and responsibility within the home. However, in many dual-career families this is something of a myth. The mother is likely to find herself with an outside job and with the major share of the housework and child care—in effect, performing two jobs while the father has one. Clearly, this is unsatisfactory for an extended period. There appears to be a trend toward more interchangeable roles within the family, particularly when both parents work—the mother taking on tasks, such as mowing the lawn and redecorating, traditionally considered the male's province; the father being more actively involved in the emotional wellbeing of the child, and in practical domestic chores. Over the centuries, the family has shown itself to be highly adaptable to social change and it will probably continue to adjust to society's demands.

All children have certain basic needs: the need for love and security, for new experiences, for individual recognition, and for responsibility. The love that a child receives allows his personality to develop normally and provides the basis for all of his future relationships. The quality of the care he experiences in his own family setting determines the style and character of the care he will later give his *own* children.

He needs the constant stimulation of new experiences—meeting new people, touching different textures, hearing different sounds such as those of the wind, the country, and the city—to develop his potential for learning. As he develops, he needs the adults who care for him to show him what is expected of him when he grows up—socially, sexually, and morally. He needs to feel that these adults whom he loves and imitates approve of him, and praise is the proof of their approval. As he becomes more competent in dealing with the world, he must have the opportunity to do more and more for himself.

The needs of children

Parents *are* people. Their personal needs do not vanish with parenthood; just like those of children they must be met in order for them to remain whole, balanced people. The way in which an adult reacts to parenthood will largely reflect his or her level of maturity. Ideally, the needs of parents and children should complement each other: the very young child's requirement for a lot of care "matching" the parent's need for this kind of responsibility. The parents should be able to accept the parenting role and be contented with it. If these demands do not suit the parent

The needs of parents

The vital influence of parents

Below : The chart shows how certain conditions and attitudes in the home have links with boys becoming delinquent. A child needs to be brought up in an environment of love, security, and freedom so as to develop his own personality, but he also needs a certain amount of discipline. The family unit has an important part to play in this respect.

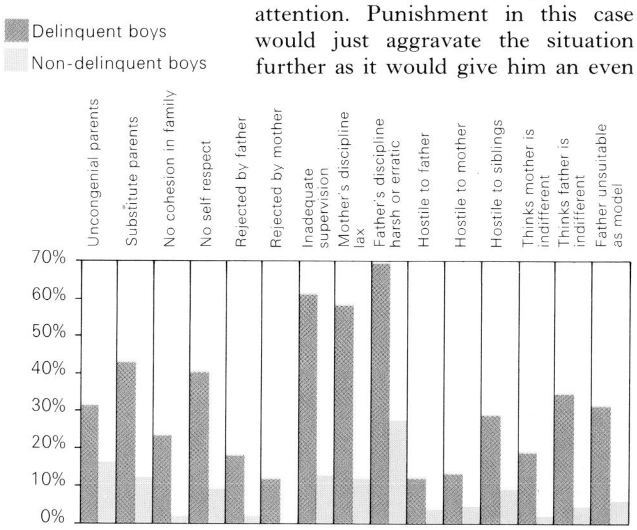

■ Delinquent boys

□ Non-delinquent boys

A child develops feelings of trust and security very early in his relationship with his parents, on whom he is dependent. A child in a children's home, where several mother substitutes (house parents) are provided, may lack that one strong constant emotional bond so necessary to him, as may a child whose parents are inconsistent in showing him their love or who are unsympathetic to the child's need for reassurance.

Through personal love a child can learn self-respect. A child who feels rejected and unloved by his parents may react by becoming truculent, defiant, uncooperative, and antisocial. He pretends he does not care, but in fact he is crying out for attention. Punishment in this case would just aggravate the situation further as it would give him an even greater sense of grievance. Alternatively a child's reaction might be to repress his aggressive feelings, which having no outlet, may then form an unconscious complex. This may emerge later in the form of, say, stealing, by which time it may need psychological treatment to unearth its basic cause.

Social behavior and a respect for other people's property and rights is learned from a child's parents and enforced through their discipline. To be effective, this should be firm yet based on a sympathetic understanding and consideration. A child's delinquent act is often directed against a neglecting parent or a parent who is so overbearing that the child never seems to be able to come up to his standards and get his respect and admiration. It is an attempt on the child's part to penetrate the parent's attention barrier and thus get some response.

Many parents of delinquent children are unable to talk their child into better behavior either because they cannot accept that their child is badly adjusted or because of a general inability to intervene. The parent who has been happy to observe and accept every sign of maturity in his child, and who has accepted his child's failures and emotional idiosyncrasies without agitation, will be in a better position to talk over any problems with the child.

Occasionally, there may be a physical cause for delinquency, such as minor brain damage. Because the cause can sometimes be treated medically, parents could thus avoid feelings of guilt arising from some supposed environmental factor causing disturbance in their child.

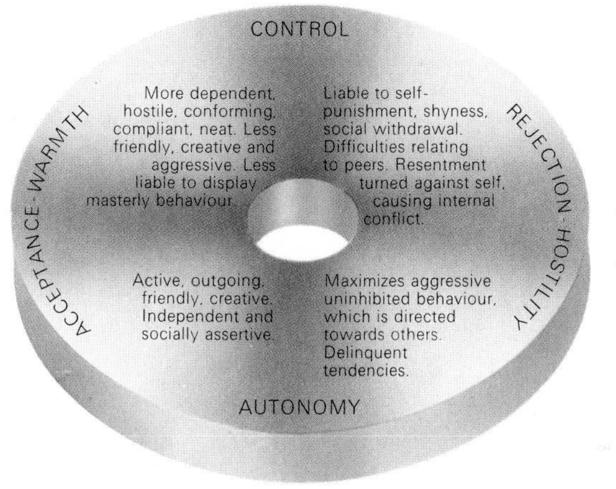

Encouraging independence is not synonymous with permissiveness. Parents should set standards for conduct and activities appropriate to the child's age and thereby create a framework in which a child can lead his life free from unnecessary control. The diagram shows how restrictiveness and inconsistency both have adverse effects on children. Parents who are warm and accepting and who encourage autonomy are the modern ideal.

at his or her particular stage of development, conflict may arise between the two sets of needs. In a healthy, democratic family, this can frequently be resolved.

Parental roles

An important aspect of parenting is serving as a model for the developing child. By observing his father, a boy comes to realize what will be expected of him as a man; similarly, a daughter learns from her mother what it is like to be a woman. It is from their parents that children first learn social roles and behavior; and as their mental ability increases, they develop their moral values and conscience from the standards they absorb from their parents.

Western society has probably never seen such a wide gap between what is expected of men and women as there has been in the last 200 years. With the man away from home each day, often as the sole wage earner, and with the woman shut up in the house as the one who looks after the children, a huge gulf has arisen between traditional concepts of "men's work" and "women's work."

Before the Industrial Revolution the wife was a partner, with some of her own specialities, it is true, but with equal status. To the extent that she was expected to run the household, the woman took on managerial duties. As the husband was present in the home, he was inevitably involved in caring for the children. Naturally, what he could do for a baby was limited, but, as the children grew older, their father assumed increasing significance in their lives, until he became the more important parent—especially for the sons.

Today, however, despite the growing number of working mothers, child-rearing is still considered in many families as "women's work." It is not unusual for fathers, after a hasty breakfast with their children, to arrive home again when they are ready for bed or already *in* bed. Though the myth persists that the father is the head of the family, it is the mother who is making the day-by-day decisions that affect their children's lives. Many fathers function only as a court of last appeal or as an escort to weekly ball games.

It is amazing how potent the myth of male dominance of the family remains. Many women not only do not realize the power that is in their hands, but are also ambivalent about it. Whereas some women campaign actively for equal rights, others complain if they have to call the plumber themselves.

The new patterns that are now emerging are healthy for the entire family unit. A father's involvement in child-rearing is not only a positive force for him and his children but for the mother as well. For she badly needs the help and support of her partner. In matters of discipline, both parents should be involved—each family makes its own decisions on which parent operates in which sphere, perhaps the father having the final say regarding school, and the mother being the chief arbiter in the daily routine and the child's social activities. But despite certain divisions of parental responsibility, the child must never be allowed to play one parent off against the other. If the parental front is united but flexible, a child will grow up respecting the family limits.

The modern father

Perhaps the most important thing to appreciate is that while a child needs mothering, it does not have to be the biological mother who provides it. As long as the child has at least one central figure in his life, with plenty of love and social stimulation, he will do well.

Quietly, without any great parade of complaints, men are gradually waking up to all that they have been missing. One sociologist has pointed out that the sex-role straitjacket restricts men just as much as women. The myth of the male provider locks fathers out of

A father's role is not always to be a serious and restrictive parent. It can be fun.

their own homes, and makes strangers of them to their children. One study found that some businessmen spend less than two minutes a day interacting with their children.

Fathers are changing all this. They come home early to see the children before they go to bed. They read to them. They are ready to show real affection, and are not content to be mere economic providers. More and more a family in which the mother shepherds the children while the father remains aloof is getting to seem like an anachronism.

A recent study by the psychiatrist Ann Dally describes the changes in a mother's role as her children grow up. These changes in mothering fall into three distinct stages. The first phase begins in pregnancy and continues into the first year or two of the baby's life. During this period a mother typically feels as though her child were a part of herself. Not only is the child totally dependent, but the mother's emotions are warm and all-enveloping. When the baby cries, it is as though a part of herself were crying. If the mother is at peace with herself, she can cope with this with ease. But if she is at all unhappy in any part of herself, her baby's crying awakens troubled responses in her. The greater her own unhappiness, the greater her discomfort at her baby's distress. This is the time in the child's life when he needs to be completely surrounded by love and security. It is his needs that shape the kind of mothering he should have—not the maturity of the mother herself.

As the child becomes a little more independent, during the toddlerhood stage, his relationship with his mother changes, and the two of them move into the extension stage. The child remains psychologically a part of his mother, but is now an extension of her. Instead of being enclosed he reaches out beyond her, while retaining powerful links.

During these years, starting with toddlerhood and lasting until adolescence, it is as though the mother, who has been cuddling the child close to her breast, must slowly open her psychological arms and hold him first with one arm around his shoulders, then with one hand on his shoulder, and lastly with one hand in his. He explores the world on his own, but always comes back to "home base."

The third stage is that of separation, during which the mother finally relinquishes all control of her child.

This is a vivid way of portraying the fact that as a child grows so do the parents, as the role required of them changes and expands. Relationships, even those between parent and child, need time to develop. For all of us, parenting involves reliving our own childhood experiences as our own children pass through each successive stage; this empathy can do much to deepen the parents' capacity for all their personal relationships.

All parents are ambivalent toward their children, however much they love them; there is resentment and even hostility mixed in with the genuine desire to protect them and give them loving care. Learning to carry out the job of parenting may be easier if a parent understands that both parent and child are constantly changing—moving along from one stage of their development to another—and that sometimes this spells harmony, sometimes disharmony. There is also the element of "letting go" on the part of the parent as the child grows up and is able to take on more responsibility for himself. It is those parents who accept this gracefully who are most likely to find in their late adolescent son or daughter a new and enduring relationship— that of a friend and companion.

Mothering

From the start, some new fathers are keen to do just about everything with the new baby that a mother can do. This may mean longer changing sessions at first, but it also means the load is shared and somehow made more enjoyable.

Mothers at home

The majority of mothers who have the option feel that, at least while their children are still very young, looking after them themselves is the most worthwhile job they can possibly do. However, no one who has done it for months —or years—at a time will be under any illusion that the routine of looking after small children in the home is easy. It isn't, even if they are your own children, much wanted, and you love them dearly.

A young woman who becomes a mother soon after leaving a job is likely to be ill-prepared for the demands and the isolation of motherhood, which are as inevitable as its pleasures and fulfillment. The hours are long; the pay is usually not very good—a single salary has to be stretched a long way. It is repetitious and frequently humdrum. It is sad that child care, surely the most demanding role any woman will attempt in her lifetime, tends to be underrated in our society. So lots of young women, particularly if they have had higher education or training, when asked "What do you do?" may feel somewhat inadequate if "all" they do is stay at home and look after one or two small children. Perhaps if it were more generally understood how truly important stable and loving care is for children in the early years, more realistic status—not idealization—would be accorded motherhood.

If a woman has her children in her twenties and looks after them herself until they are of school age, she is still young enough to go back to work or learn a skill when they are older—and need her physical presence less. Although a young mother shut in the house all day with a runny-nosed two-year-old will find this hard to believe, children do grow up —in retrospect far too quickly for most parents. And jobs and careers are still there to be trained for and sought. Those early years of childhood—the first words, first steps, tears and all—are swift and precious. And unlike the possibility of a glamorous job, they do not come again.

Being home with a preschool child is exactly what you—as the mother—choose to make it. There is no need to get bogged down with housework and child care unless this is what you want. *And is it?* Of course, every housewife/mother has certain basic chores— shopping, looking after the house, cooking, feeding the baby; with an older child, taking him to and from nursery school and letting him bring a friend home. But many young women have lots of energy and enthusiasm left over when these tasks are done; and there are so many ways, given some thought and imagination, in which a few hours every week can be used constructively.

Above: Raising children could not by any stretch of the imagination be called a glamorous job, but for fortunate mothers it is far more fulfilling than many forms of career success.

Children always love a day out, especially when there's a group of new friends to play with and exciting things to do. Many mothers also find that taking time off from the routine of child care is essential if they are to remain rational human beings.

When to have children

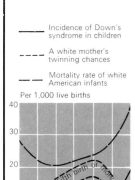

——— Incidence of Down's syndrome in children

- - - - A white mother's twinning chances

— — Mortality rate of white American infants

Per 1,000 live births

The risks to the child at birth are much greater if the mother is under twenty or over thirty-five years old.

Physically, the best years for a woman to have her children are her mid-twenties. The infant mortality rate is extremely high for mothers younger than fifteen. Even at sixteen and seventeen it is still high; thereafter the rate starts dropping until about twenty-five or twenty-six. The likelihood of having a child with Down's syndrome increases slightly throughout the twenties although it remains very low until thirty-five, when it starts to increase at an accelerating rate.

The chances of having twins also increase with age up to thirty-five. Each subsequent pregnancy is also more likely to produce twins.

Some women may need to wait some time until they are mature enough to cope with the stresses and strains of raising a family. There is a danger, however, that a mother who has her children late may be separated from them by too great an age gap, and so have difficulty understanding and joining in with their life-style, both as children and as adolescents.

Many women like to have children early so that they are still young enough to start a career afterward, but it is usually best to acquire professional qualifications before starting a family.

Most urban centers offer a wide variety of adult education classes, during the day and in the evenings. Whatever your particular interest is, follow it. Immaculate houses matter a lot less to most men—and all children—than women believe. So if you are interested in painting or literature or special cookery, make the effort to get a baby-sitter or exchange time with a friend who has a child of the same age so that you can attend classes. A young mother might take a typing course, learn a foreign language with the next summer vacation in mind, or become skillful enough to sew new curtains and slipcovers. She will be doing something of her own which *she* enjoys, working with other adults—and possibly moving in the direction of a part-time job when the children are older. If she can earn some money at the same time, so much the better. For example, I write as well as being a mother. Friends have a variety of jobs that they do for a few hours each week. Finding satisfaction in her own work can only improve the quality of a woman's life.

Working mothers

It helps to keep this rather emotional issue in perspective if one remembers that traditionally most women have made substantial contributions toward the support of their families. It is the women who have tended animals, made agricultural products to use in the home and to sell, spun wool for the clothes, and helped in the family shop or tannery or bakery. Throughout the centuries, the women's economic usefulness to the household has been the rule rather than the exception. After two centuries of being confined

at home, some women are rediscovering ways to develop "cottage industries" that are financially rewarding, thus reverting to a new variation on an old pattern.

But a number of women are taking jobs because they want to work, and not because they need the money. The reasons for this are often complex, and may appear inexplicable to those mothers who think that being a mother is a full-time job and the most important role of their lives. There are lots of mothers who honestly believe that being at home all day with a young child is so tedious for them that neither they nor the child benefit; by getting out to work and coming home with a fresh perspective they are able to be more genuinely caring mothers. These women may have a strong need to achieve independence outside the home; they may have gone through an arduous training which they believe should not be neglected even during the years when their children are very young. They may, quite simply, think they are temperamentally unsuited to the care of babies or small children, and that although they love their children they are more comfortable leaving the daily routine to someone else.

All these are valid, understandable reasons for a mother continuing full-time employment after her child is born; there are also less subtle factors that influence a mother's decision. In many families, particularly in these times of high inflation, two salaries can make the difference in paying the mortgage on the kind of house the family wants, in being able to afford a welcome vacation, or perhaps in paying for private education. In an affluent consumer society, there is relentless pressure on us all for an additional car, travel, fashionable clothes, and good food and drink. Thus, even though her decision is seldom without conflict, a mother may feel that she is doing herself—and her family—more good by helping to earn money to augment the family income than by being a full-time wife and mother.

Financial and emotional considerations aside, the dilemma for mothers today seems to be that working when the children are small—plus shopping and cooking and social commitments—means that she is pushed too far, has altogether too much to cope with; and yet, if she has not established some kind of job or career by the time the children are in school all day, she then finds herself with too much time on her hands. Most women would agree that both employment and nonemployment have their strains and compensations; it is a question of the best balance of personal, financial, and family considerations at each stage of a mother's life.

Several studies have shown that while there is still a child at home, part-time work is the best all-round solution for a working mother. This gives her time to be home after school ready to listen to excited reports on the events of the day. She can also perform the daily tasks of cooking and household management with less pressure. True, there are

Does the child suffer?

drawbacks: part-time work on more than a mechanical level is often difficult to find; it tends to be poorly paid; it is often excluded from employees' benefit packages.

It seems that there is no hard evidence that a working mother harms—or benefits—herself, her child, or the family as a whole. It is the quality of the time she spends with her child that counts, not just the amount of time. Although working mothers inevitably tend to overcompensate by showering too *much* attention on their children, in fact the children of working mothers are likely to become more independent. Each family situation needs to be evaluated separately, as there are so many factors involved. Perhaps the most vital, particularly if the child is small, is the adequacy of the child-care arrangements the mother is able to make while she is at work.

Also important is the attitude of the father: is he glad that his wife is working and is he prepared to be extra helpful, or does he secretly resent her job? It is also important for the mother to enjoy her work and to feel that the additional efforts she must make are worthwhile. If all these factors are positive, there is every chance that the child will not see his mother's work as rejecting him, and as he gets older he may be rather proud of her efforts. So if a mother honestly believes that she is able to set aside time to be with her child after work and on weekends, and if the alternative is sitting around the house all day resentful and depressed, she should keep on working. And if everyone has to help with the housework and shopping, it means that the whole family is learning to pull together.

When to return to work

For many modern mothers the question is not whether to return to work, but when. If you are bottle-feeding, and you are eager to return to work, it will probably be easiest to begin when your baby is between four and six months old. Although your baby needs a consistent caretaker from the beginning, he is usually not aware of strangers until he is about six months old. If you are breast feeding, you will have to wait until the baby is weaned; in few situations is it possible to nurse him at work.

On the whole it is probably best to wait until after the baby's first birthday. It is vital that you prepare the baby. Before you start work again, let him spend as much time as possible with the person who is going to look after him. If he is used to affection from a number of people, he will feel the wrench much less. The father can—and should—play a major part here. If you have not made it in the second year, then the break is best left until your child has started school, or at least attends nursery school or a playgroup.

If a mother decides to work while her children are young, her first task will be to make arrangements for a baby-sitter. Even if her child is of school age, he will still need supervision after school, during vacations, and in case of illness. She must be prepared for the strain of her presence being demanded simultaneously at home and in the office.

But despite the complexities of managing motherhood *and* a job, the fact is that by March 1976 nearly half of all mothers in the United States were in the labor force. The significance of this statistic is emphasized by comparing it with data for the past four decades: in 1965, 35 percent of all American mothers worked; in 1955, 27 percent; in 1940, 9 percent.

Most young children of working mothers are cared for in their own homes by relatives or others. About one-fourth of the preschool children are cared for in someone else's home. Although in many states care for one or more unrelated children must be licensed, only 5 percent of such children are actually in licensed homes. In suburban communities near large urban areas, however, licensing requirements may be met by as many as 50 to 75 percent of the homes performing this service.

Obviously, the need for adequate child-care facilities for the children of working mothers is far from met. Private and community day care centers provide for only one child in ten.

Public schools are attempting, despite budgetary pressures, to meet the needs of school-age children whose mothers work by providing lunch facilities and after-school programs.

If you are thinking of bringing your child to the home of someone else, begin by seeking the advice of one of the child-welfare agencies in your area. Visit the homes they suggest and judge them as well as you can. What kind of attention does the caretaker pay to the children? Does she seem to play with them, give them toys, and keep them amused? Does she have good sleeping arrangements and will she change diapers

Who should care for the child?

Waiting for your child to be let out of school is a good opportunity to meet and make friends with other parents. Many mothers living close to each other form a car pool to take a group of children to and from school. This gives a useful (and entertaining) opportunity to compare different children's impressions of school.

regularly? You should also reassure yourself that the house is safe and that the children will not be left alone.

Many people frown on such arrangements, but if you are sure that the baby-sitter you choose is competent, the arrangement should work out well. The worst thing for a small child is change and uncertainty. A good, reliable sitter is preferable to a succession of friends and relatives.

Brothers and sisters

Modern museum displays fascinate even very young children.

Children are deeply influenced by having brothers and sisters—by their numbers, their sex, and the spacing between them. The child psychoanalyst Erik Erikson speaks of the "irreplaceable experience of a shared childhood" with a brother or sister as a constant

ally against the grown-up world of parents. A child with at least one sibling has many advantages: he learns about loyalty, sharing, and protection; he also gets a taste of conflict, domination, and competition; he has the security of the rough-and-tumble of family life and there is always someone to play with —or quarrel with. All these family experiences will influence the way in which he approaches people in the outside world, both as a child and as an adult.

First children may suffer from overanxious and inexperienced parenting and find that too much is expected of them. Most of us have these attitudes, to some degree, with our first children. However, studies indicate that first children (and this applies to only children as well) generally tend to be responsible and achieving.

It is the first child who must experience the dethroning when the next child arrives. After being the center of his parents' world, he can find this a painful time; an understanding mother and father can do much to help him cope with ambivalent feelings he will have toward the new brother or sister who has suddenly taken his place at the center of family attention. How this stage is handled will largely determine whether serious sibling rivalry develops—or whether a happier, companionable relationship will evolve.

Two children of the same sex, close in age, are bound to be rather competitive. Parents must realize that all children in similar age groups tend to be competitive, whether or not they are brothers or sisters. As the children grow older, it is helpful if the parents concentrate on the strengths of each as an individual; they must not make comparisons between them.

A middle child very often seems to get left out. He misses the wholehearted attention that is more often given to the oldest or the youngest child. His older brother may

Brother and sister make very good company for each other, especially when the age gap is small. Many childhood experiences can be shared together, so forming the beginning of a lifelong friendship.

Coping with three children

appear in a highly privileged light—achieving more and being allowed to go to bed later. Unless the younger child is encouraged to develop his own friends and interests, and allowed a later bedtime himself on special occasions, he may acquire feelings of inadequacy that will last into adulthood. Although few of us achieve it all of the time, parents should strive for scrupulous fairness in the disciplining and daily routine of children. To young children, their parents' word is law—and they must be able to trust it and know that it is fair.

Only children

Today, with the falling birthrate and smaller families, an only child is less of a rarity than thirty years ago. Although the traditional picture of the only child is that of being rather spoiled and lonely, studies do not support this. If anything, it has been found that only children differ very little from those with siblings. Naturally, parents of an only child must be particularly conscientious about getting him together with friends of his own age as often as possible; nursery school is essential. A good deal can be done to help him through contact with other children, and it may be a good idea for parents of only children to get together and share their children for part of the time. The experience of close and continuing relationships with peers is a valuable one as a child grows up, and may be no less important than the close relationship with the mother. He must not be overprotected, whatever the parents' inner feelings may be.

There are also advantages in being an only child: he will benefit from his parents' undivided attention, never experience displacement, and may have a better start, materially, than one of several children in a large family.

With divorce and remarriage increasingly common, there are many children who perhaps have a much older brother or sister who lives away from home and whom they do not see very often. Such children, in fact, have lives like those of only children.

Sibling rivalry

Twentieth-century psychoanalytic writings tend to give the impression—perhaps a bit overstated—that siblings are inevitably great rivals and desperately, if secretly, jealous of each other. Squabbling among children appears either as something that must be stamped out at all costs, or else, to some parents, as an inevitable part of childhood, which it would be wrong to inhibit in any way.

Though it is unrealistic to expect to respond to each child with equal amounts of affection and approval, make every attempt to control your preferences and try to emphasize each child's special qualities.

It is inevitable that children will occasionally want the same toy and fight for it. This is an essential part of learning to cope with life. Whether your own preference is for cooperation or competition, there is no denying that conflict arises and must be dealt with. Many adults have to learn this—a painful, slow, nerve-racking process. The proper time to learn it is in childhood.

Of course, many children test their parents' limits. Two children may fight in collusion to annoy you. A firm hand is needed here. And there must be limits to fighting. This, too, is something that is best learned in childhood. So a parent should always be ready to step in and separate children when arguments become too vigorous or persistent.

Rivalry is sometimes an outgrowth of a sibling's place within the family structure. If the eldest appears to enjoy too many privileges, the younger children in the family may, with reason, be resentful. If the younger appears to receive more love and care than the elder, he may feel excluded and left out. Trying to give each child some time alone with each parent, as often as possible,

may help the family to develop a sensitive balance. The love and attention of grandparents can also be a welcome port in the storm.

The biggest factor in real sibling rivalry is the arrival of the second or third child. If the older child is inadequately prepared for the new baby then trouble will follow.

Tell your child at the same time as everybody else, if not sooner, when you are expecting another baby. You will have plenty of time then to teach him about the changes in your own body as they happen and prepare him for the momentous event. In fact this is the best possible opportunity, provided by nature, to teach your child about sex. His interest is engaged, and you will be able to relate the whole business of intercourse, anatomy, and love and its results. There will be no need to worry about "clinical" lessons at school if you teach your child this way.

If your child is old enough to be involved in the preparation, let him help. Give him a paintbrush of his own if you redecorate a bedroom or nursery. Show him the baby's things as you get them ready.

Though home deliveries are no longer very common, they obviously cause less change in the household routine than when mother is whisked off to the hospital. Your child may well be puzzled by the mood of concern and

On the arrival of a second baby the first child will suddenly find he is no longer the center of attention. Understanding parents will be aware of the child's emotional vulnerability and will make every effort to show that they still care for him just as much as they did before.

Introducing the new baby

The extended family

A child's view of an extended family in which parents, grandparents, aunts, and uncles all live in close proximity. Reaching its zenith in the last century, this type of family has been on the decline ever since, due mainly to greater mobility.

Seldom are the biological parents the only people involved in the rearing of children. The extended family, for instance, once took on many of those duties, and its decline has left mothers with less support in their demanding role. Though doctors, social workers, and teachers have become a modern replacement, their success is questionable and many children are reared exclusively by their mothers. This intense and isolated entanglement is a new and unusual situation and is potentially harmful to both mother and child.

expectation. This puzzlement is an excellent preparation for his meeting with the baby once it has arrived: you should make the introduction as soon after birth as you can, perhaps after an hour or so. If you fear that he may be disturbed by the birth process itself, then you might send him out to a close relative or friend for a few hours—never to strangers.

If you have your second child in a hospital, it is best if someone can move into your house to care for the first child in his own home. Do not send him away unless there is no alternative. Make arrangements for him to visit you in the hospital.

If things do go wrong somehow, and your child resents the new arrival, explain that you understand him. Do not reject his feelings, but make it clear that there is nothing that can be done to change the situation. If he says bluntly that he doesn't like "it" and that he wishes "it" would go away, remember that he is expressing his feelings honestly, and that, although the new baby will not go away, his jealous feelings will if you keep cool. If he goes quiet and sullen, or simply withdrawn, then you must give him extra attention without simply bribing him to "be nice."

If jealousy is in the air, then it will be as well to keep a cautious eye on the baby for a while. It is not unknown for scratches to appear mysteriously on a new baby's face—the expression of the displaced child's grief. If this should happen, do not, whatever you do, treat the older child harshly, for this will only make matters worse, proving to him that his worst fears were justified.

To a young child, a miscarriage may not have the emotional impact that it has on an adult. So if you have already told a child that you are expecting a baby, and then lose it, he may accept the news easily; yet he may think that the baby has not come because he was naughty. A very young child can be told that something has gone wrong, but that you still hope he will have a little brother or sister a bit later on. An older—or school-age—child may be able to understand simple biological explanations. If a mother has been deeply upset by the loss of a hoped-for child, it is her emotional distress that the child will be most conscious of.

It is well known that personality and intelligence are influenced by heredity, environment, education, and child-rearing styles, but they are also affected by the size of the family and a child's position within it.

Evidence for this comes from research into the birth order and intelligence scores of almost all Dutch boys attaining the age of nineteen between 1963 and 1966. It was found that the brightest children came from the smallest families or came along early in a large family.

There is no known biological or genetic reason why this should happen, but one expert suggests each additional child depreciates the family's intellectual environment and that children from large families spend more time in a world of child-sized minds. Another suggestion is that a large family's resources, such as income and parents' time and attention, are spread more thinly, and perhaps diets are understandably less nutritious.

The ideal position in the family is to be first of two children born closely together, as, it is suggested, this gives the older a chance to teach the younger and helps him to develop his verbal and reasoning skills. This is, of course, not so beneficial for the second child who, like only and last-born children, lacks this opportunity. However, last-born children have the advantage of coming into a higher intellectual climate.

A study by the National Children's Bureau in Britain reported that among eleven-year-olds there was a gap of one and a half years in reading score and almost a year in math score in favor of children who, at age seven, had been "only" children, compared with those who had three or more siblings. Where over-all school attainment was concerned, children with one sibling tended to do better than "only" children, but test scores declined for later-born children in families of three or more. Middle children often had behavior difficulties, possibly because the first-born has a certain status and the youngest child is often the family favorite; therefore the middle child may have to struggle for parental attention and to define his place in the family.

As has already been mentioned, it is not unusual for parents to have greater sympathy for and rapport with one child than another.

Miscarriage

Intelligence and family size

The intellectual ability of each child decreases as the size of the family increases. The brightest children are those born first in small families (they are also brighter than only children).

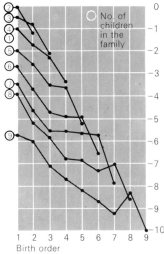

No. of children in the family

Birth order

Each child is different

It is helpful to realize that such feelings are quite natural. We all relate better to some people than we do to others; parents and children are no exception to this. There may also be specific reasons for relating better to one child; perhaps your son shows spontaneous affection to his parents whereas his sister is rather cold; perhaps you or your husband see some of your partner's less appealing traits in one of your offspring.

Although, at a deep level, it is unlikely that a parent loves one child more than another she may like one of her children a lot of the time. And it is healthier if the mother or father admits these feelings to themselves. At the same time, a parent must do everything she can not to let this bias interfere with her handling of her children. Such favoritism is damaging to the whole family. If anything, a parent needs to reach out and try to understand the child who seems to rub her the wrong way. Over the years, this conscious effort can lead to a deepening of the relationship—on both sides.

Twins

Twins account for two and a half percent of all births. Fraternal twins are more alike than any other two children in the same family: they are babies who have shared the same pregnancy but they have no more of their genes in common than any other brother and sister. Identical twins have identical genes. Most mothers are told beforehand by the doctor if they are having twins.

For a mother of twins, the early months can be extremely wearing. At birth, twins tend to be smaller than the average baby. This adds to the frequency of feedings, cutting down on the mother's rest time. But there is no reason why she should not feed the babies herself; the additional sucking stimulates a copious milk supply. If they are breast-fed it is easy to feed both at the same time. Simultaneous bottle-feeding needs only a little extra work and forethought.

A mother of twins needs all the extra help she can get. Cutting corners on housework and child care is something she should not hesitate to do. As they develop, it is essential that the twins are treated by their parents as individuals. Being dressed alike, playing with the same toys, and having friends in common, suit some twins, but others develop better if they are treated quite separately.

Grandparents

Loving grandparents can only add to a child's feeling of security. The relationship between grandparent and grandchild is often an enhancing—and valuable—one on both sides. And it is hard to break the grandparent/parent/child sequence; if a parent/child relationship is close and warm, the chances are that grandparent and grandchild will also have a rewarding relationship.

With grandparents, the problem of authority—and whose—sometimes arises. The moment a child becomes a parent, her parents—now grandparents—must respect her authority as a parent in her own right.

Some parents who are rather authoritarian

Twins usually have a much closer relationship than ordinary brothers and sisters, and may choose to spend a lot of time together. Nevertheless, they should be encouraged to have separate friends as well, so that they learn the social skills involved in mixing with other children.

Most grandparents like to join in with their children's families, especially now they are no longer tied down by the daily needs of their own offspring. A day for the children at their grandparents' gives everybody a welcome change.

do not find this easy; hence the "interfering" aspect of grandparenthood that parents resent, and rightly. Grandparents must remember that they can only advise—often wisely. Children will be confused by conflicts between their parents and grandparents, and this can be damaging to their respect for both.

If conflict arises between the generations, stop to consider why. If the grandparents seem to want discipline that you consider to be too severe, ask yourself if perhaps your own is too lax? If they seem too permissive to you, is it because they resent your growing maturity, and seek to keep everything on a childish level? In either case you can only benefit from learning to cope with the differences, and not depriving your children of their grandparents, and vice versa.

If for any reason a parent must leave a young child, there is no better mother substitute than a familiar and caring grandparent. A grandparent can play a uniquely supportive role: someone in the family who loves the child and yet who is less involved in his daily life than his parents. For youngsters, grandparents mean more grown-ups to read stories aloud, to take them for walks, to play games on wet afternoons, and to run to with their most important news. For an older child a grandparent is someone with whom he can discuss the problems of growing up.

In times of family crises, such as divorce or moving, grandparents can provide much-needed stability—and a refuge from a difficult world. An older grandparent, who has

difficulty walking upstairs or who cannot join in family games, gives a child his first intimate experience with the aging process.

In our society, we try to cover the unpleasantness surrounding death, and open mourning is discouraged. It is never easy to talk about death to a child; our own fears get in the way and unconsciously transmit themselves to the child as he struggles with the idea that nothing can be done to change the reality.

When a child learns to talk, he will mention death, but in a childish way. He will show as he talks that he has no concept of the finality of death; he will think that although he "understands" someone is dead, he can, in fact, return again. Parents may be shocked at a child's speaking in what seems to them an unfeeling way about someone who has recently died. But a child will be eight or more before he starts to comprehend death.

Sooner or later comes the awful question: "Will *I* die?" It is best to take the question seriously, to say "Yes," but probably not for a very long time. It is well to add that young people do die sometimes, but it is unusual. If he knows of a particular child who has perhaps been killed in an accident, you can let him know that you are as unhappy as he is at what seems such tragic injustice. Try not to equate death with sleep; this can initiate going-to-bed and sleeping fears in children. It is never wise to try to shield a child from death; he will surely be touched by it sooner or later. He will observe death in nature in small ways

Death in the family

One-parent families

Child care and household management are often mentioned by single parents as two particular problems. This is especially true of motherless families. When help is not available, children have to take on many of the domestic burdens.

Whereas the one-parent family was once an oddity, it has become more and more a part of American life—especially in larger urban centers. It is increasingly recognized that a parent raising a child without a partner has special problems and needs to develop support systems to fill the inevitable gaps. Single-parent adoptions—once unheard of—are also slowly being accepted, as American society gradually comes to recognize a variety of life styles.

The job of the single parent is lonely and practically endless; seldom do they have someone to turn to for moral or emotional

support, for advice and encouragement. Yet most single parents are conscientious and manage to surmount these difficulties. It is from outside that the worst problems loom. The economics of single parenting are trying; the divorced mother—or the widow—is usually under great financial strain, and the divorced father must often provide now for two households. Housing, employment, and the difficulty of finding adequate facilities for child care present problems hard to solve. On the personal level, the demands of forging new, satisfying adult relationships while fulfilling the unending psychological demands of children are difficult, to say the least.

Problems exist for children, too. Often they feel they are oddities, left out of the main stream. Sometimes they retreat into themselves and parents find it hard to draw them out to participate with their peers. At school it is difficult to determine how academic progress is affected. Many studies have shown that low income and poor housing, two factors that are associated with the one-parent family, affect educational performance, but it is more difficult to ascertain whether the absence of a father or a mother in itself is chiefly responsible. Despite all these problems one-parent families do thrive, and a child who is neither starved of love or stimulation, will do quite as well as a child from a two-parent family.

Family types, USA 1970

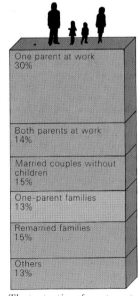

One parent at work
30%

Both parents at work
14%

Married couples without children
15%

One-parent families
13%

Remarried families
15%

Others
13%

The proportion of one-parent families in America is greater than in Britain, where the rate is closer to ten percent. The number of variant families makes traditional assumptions about the basic family unit questionable.

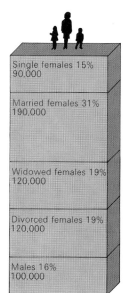

Estimate of one-parent families in Great Britain 1971

Single females 15% 90,000	
Married females 31% 190,000	
Widowed females 19% 120,000	
Divorced females 19% 120,000	
Males 16% 100,000	

Estimates show that one-parent families in Britain have now grown from 620,000 in 1971 to some 700,000 in 1977. The number of dependent children has also increased to over 1,250,000.

all around him—in flowers that bloom then die, in trees that are blown down in storms. Over many years and stages, he must be helped to accept the death of a loved grandmother or an adored pet as an inevitable part of life.

If a close relative is very ill, it is better to prepare a child for the possibility of death. You can tell him honestly that his grandfather is seriously ill, that the doctor is doing all he can to make him better and keep him comfortable, but that he might die quite soon. When a child is actually faced by the death of someone in the family—perhaps even the tragic death of a parent or sibling—let him ask questions, however painful they are to hear. Will he or she ever wake up again? Is the coffin locked? What will happen to all her clothes? The deepest fear that he will have to deal with is that he, and all the people he loves most, will also disappear in this frightening way. And he may also have irrational, guilty fears that he is somehow responsible for this particular death.

As you answer the questions, let him see your own grief—at least part of it. It is dangerous to suppress mourning; grief is best acknowledged and expressed. This is why the rituals of death are so important in all cultures. If a child is mature enough—probably not before he is about six years old—and seems willing to attend the funeral of a close relative, it is better for him to come. A parent can gently prepare him for the ceremony, perhaps arranging for him to leave before a part of the

service that he could find particularly upsetting. If the parents practice religious beliefs, they might feel it helpful for the minister, rabbi, or priest to speak privately with the child. People of all ages tend to find comfort in being included in a ceremony of parting from someone they love. And a child will see that the reality is less terrifying than the fantasies he may have had about it.

A child is well aware when there are tensions between his parents, however hard they try to hide them. Of course, some disagreement is inevitable, and healthy, in every family. Parents may be able to resolve a particularly bitter argument out of earshot of their child, and, if this really clears the air, everyone is better off because the problem has been dealt with. If a child finds you in the middle of a heated argument, let him know that you are having it out—but that you love each other all the same. He will understand because he has battles with his friends, too, and they make up when they are over. Because he understands this, his security will not be threatened. It is constant bickering and quarrels with no resolution that have such a devastating effect on children. Children are always made unhappy by the fact that their parents do not like each other—within a marriage or after it has been dissolved.

With the stigma largely removed from divorce, many couples (or one partner) may be tempted while they are still young enough

Grandchildren bring exquisite pleasure into an elderly person's life. The relationship between children and grandparents is highly idealized and the close bonds that exist between them are very important.

Family strife

Inherited characteristics

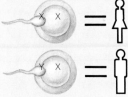

A pair of chromosomes determine a baby's sex. Each ovum contains an X, each sperm brings an X to make a girl or a Y for a boy. The chances should be equal, but 106 boys are born to 100 girls.

At the moment of conception when the sperm fuses with the ovum, the genetic code or blueprint for the future individual is set. Already both parents have done a great deal to shape the appearance and abilities of their child. Each will have contributed to the infant half of their twenty-three pairs of chromosomes to make a new full set of forty-six, as well as the tiny molecules of inheritance called the genes, which are arranged along the chromosomes. This is why no child can ever be an exact replica of one parent or nontwin sibling, although they may share many genes so that they all bear a family resemblance. It has been estimated that there are theoretically 64 billion possible different chromosome combinations in one fertilization.

Genes are responsible for thousands of body functions and aspects of appearance including height, body size, speed of reaction, coordination, physical development, metabolism, temperament, and disease resistance. Even a child's intellectual capacity and creative inclinations can be inherited, although heredity only provides the potential, and a child can subsequently be changed by his environment.

Every part of the code transmitted at conception does not always produce an effect on the individual because, when two genes from different sources meet, one will assert its influence over the other; this is the dominant gene. The weaker, or recessive gene, does not disappear, but remains unused and can still be passed on. The recessive characteristic will come to the fore only if it meets another recessive gene. Prospective parents are wise to seek genetic counseling if members of their families have had congenital defects such as spina bifida or mongolism, or diseases which are thought to be largely hereditary. Many fetuses are tested during pregnancy for such conditions, or careful examinations are carried out at birth for the same reason.

Eyes

Both parents are light-eyed = light-eyed children (98 percent certainty). With mixed light-eyed parents, gray, green, or hazel eyes will dominate blue unless the other parent also carries a blue gene.

One parent is dark-eyed, the other light-eyed = dark-eyed children. (With light-eyed close blood relative = one-in-two chance of light-eyed child.)

Both parents are dark-eyed = dark-eyed children. (With light-eyed close blood relative = one-in-four chance of light-eyed child.)

Hair

Both parents dark-haired = dark-haired children, sometimes red-haired. (With light-haired close blood relative = one-in-four chance of light-haired child.)

Both parents blond-haired = blond children; occasionally brown-haired.

Both parents brown-haired = brown; possibility of blond-haired children.

One light-haired parent, one dark-haired parent = dark-haired children. (With light-haired close blood relative = one-in-two chance of light-haired child.)

Red-haired parents = all red; possibility of light-brown or blond children.

One red-haired, one blond = even chance of red-haired children.

Hair type Dominant = frizzy or curly hair; thick straight Mongolian hair. Recessive = straight hair.

Eyes Dominant = wide or large eyes; drooping eyelids; long lashes. Recessive = deep-set eyes.

Mouth Dominant = thick lips; gap between middle teeth. Recessive = thin lips.

Chin Dominant = narrow or pointed chins; cleft on chin. Recessive = wide chins; receding chins.

Freckles Dominant. **Dimples** Dominant.

Noses are not inherited as an entirety; the shape and size results from a number of separate genes. However, extreme and prominent nose types dominate moderate.

---

to seek another spouse, or way of life, if the present marriage is very unsatisfactory. At the same time, couples with children often feel that they should stay together for the sake of the children. They may be desperately torn by their conflicting emotions and desires.

There is no easy answer to this. Research shows that children of parents whose disharmony culminates in divorce may be less harmed than children who live indefinitely in homes where there is a continuous background of unhappiness. This does not mean that instant divorce is the answer to every deteriorating marriage. Because it appears to be the element of strife that most upsets children, it is valuable for parents who are caught up in such tension and who care about their family, to try to remedy the situation while there is still time—perhaps through seeking marriage counseling. The success of such efforts depends largely on the partners themselves, whether they are both genuine in their aims or whether one is simply going through the motions to satisfy the other. This is also the time for the parents to take a hard look at the practicalities of keeping the two homes that separation entails—and the effects that the resulting lowered standard of living would have on themselves and their children.

All marriages have their ups and downs; it can take a lot more guts to work on a marriage in which there are conflicts than to decide on immediate divorce. Having a child is a good enough reason in itself for making an honest attempt to save, and improve, a marriage.

When parents decide to separate, it is best to tell the children at once. However young, they will probably already have had intimations of the situation between their parents— even if they have not said as much. Depending upon the child's age and level of understanding, stick to the truth as much as possible in your explanations. If a family has been abandoned by the mother or father, it is best to say so—that he or she was terribly unhappy or ill, and chose to leave; that there is a possibility of his or her return, though it is doubtful.

This is a bitter pill for the child, but even so it is better for him to know the truth. In different circumstances you can say that after making every effort to resolve the difficulties between you, you decided that you would both be happier living apart. If you both honestly believe that this is a trial separation, tell the child so. You can explain that you need some time away from each other to try to become friends again so that you will want to live together.

Whatever the reasons, the child must understand that it is not he who has caused the rift between his parents. In their fantasies of omnipotence, children often tend to assume that the separation is due to something they have done; that they have not been "good" enough, have not always behaved in the way

Separation and divorce

their mother or father wanted, and as a result they feel inwardly guilty and unhappy. So assure your child, verbally, that he is in no way the cause; that nothing he could have done would have prevented the separation. He must feel that he is still loved for himself by both parents; that this love is unchangeable; and that their dual responsibility for him will continue.

He will also want to know how the change in family circumstances is going to affect his daily life: Will he be moving? How often will he see the parent who is moving away? Will he have to go to a new school? What will he tell his friends? The questions will be determined largely by the individual situation—and how the parents are able to cope with the added financial burden of running two homes. It is obviously helpful if a child has some time to adjust to the separation without another major change in his life, such as moving away from a familiar community.

The transitional period is never easy for parents or for children. Of course you do not want a child to assume your emotional burdens, but it makes sense to let your child know that you are often unhappy and uncertain. He will know it, anyhow; he will feel more secure if you do not try to keep up a "front."

Some children who are naturally rather adaptable seem to accept the situation fairly smoothly; others remain deeply disturbed and angry for a long time. They may be particularly hostile toward the parent they continue to live with, blaming him or her for the loss of the other parent. Dealing sympathetically with a rebellious child is especially hard for a parent who is experiencing stress and readjustment. Sound professional advice at this time can be invaluable for the future personal relationships of the whole family.

As part of the divorce process a decision will have to be taken about which parent the children will live with. It is clearly best if the parents can agree. Selfish squabbling over who can bring the children up better, or who was the guilty party, can only damage the children themselves. It need not be difficult if both parents keep the children's real interests and rights in mind. And generous visiting rights can help the parent without custody. Nowadays more fathers are being given care and custody of the children if they are able to provide a more stable home.

One thing to beware of is the role sometimes taken by lawyers. They naturally see it as their job to secure the "best" agreement for their client, and to win, or save, the biggest possible portion of the family assets. To do this they usually have to show that the partner they are acting for is the wronged one. The children can easily become pawns in this game, and frequently, if the judge sympathizes enough with one side to give custody, he will allocate alimony or assets accordingly. If you and your partner can reach a friendly agreement in the children's best interests, do not let the expediencies of law change your mind.

Whatever a parent's feelings toward the separated partner, it is best to speak about him or her very carefully to a child. Realistically, it makes no sense to talk about them with affection if there is none; the child will spot the hypocrisy at once. Open criticism only adds to the conflicting loyalties that all children have when parents separate. So be fair—or neutral—or say nothing.

The worst thing that can happen to a child after a divorce is for the parents to keep up their warfare through him. It is enough that a child has to cope with the separation of his parents without being made a channel of communication for their hate and anger.

Once the divorce is over, parents begin to have a new social life. This is healthy both for them and for their children, but it can pose problems. New friends of the opposite sex, particularly if they may possibly represent a replacement for the parent who is no longer living at home, do create anxiety for children. On the one hand, they long for just such a replacement; on the other, it represents a severing of ties with the other parent—and accentuates conflicting loyalties.

Ironically, such conflict may become most acute just as a child is beginning to relate well to, for example, his mother's new boy friend; this will activate the doubts he may have about remaining loyal to the other parent. The adults can help if they understand the difficulties the child is having and are prepared to show a good deal of patience.

The same rule applies to the question of how much a child should know about his divorced parent's sex life—a problem that is likely to crop up. Basically, this will depend upon the ages of the children, how they have been taught about sex, and the attitudes of the adults. While the child must realize that his parent is human, it is also fair to assume that he will tend to expect that his parents' new sexual partners will be permanent ones—an expectation that in today's world of freer sexual attitudes will not always be fulfilled. The best advice is to handle the situation in the way that seems most comfortable for you and the child and to use discretion.

Despite all the trauma of divorce—for parents and for children—if it is handled with care and consideration, it need not be harmful to a child. Like all difficult human experiences, it may make him, in the long run, a stronger and more understanding person. After all, what child really benefits from years and years of seeing an unhappy mother and sensing a tense home atmosphere? It is vital that a child understands that despite the divorce he still has two loving and responsible parents, who are deeply concerned about what happens to him. Marriage can be dissolved; parenthood cannot. Both parents and child must understand this.

Conflicting loyalties

Stepparents

It seems that Hansel and Gretel, whose chilling story has helped to foster the wicked stepmother image throughout the centuries, were just very unlucky. Either that, or, with the increasing rates of divorce and remarriage in recent years—more often than not involving young children—some of the stereotyped attitudes toward step-families have changed. New research suggests that despite the practical and emotional difficulties involved in being a stepparent or a stepchild, the majority of families with stepchildren do very well indeed.

There are many reasons why attitudes should have changed. Most importantly, there are so many more remarriages involving children these days that neither stepfather nor stepmother nor stepchild feels as self-conscious or uneasy about the situation as they might have in the past. This may give the current stepparent more courage to *be* a parent: to discipline when necessary, so that the child feels more secure in his new family environment.

Discipline has always been a major difficulty in the stepparent/stepchild relationship. Children are normally inclined to feel more resentful of being told off by a stepparent than by their own father or mother. A recent study suggested that discipline was more readily accepted by the stepchild when he referred to his stepparent as mommy or daddy. Perhaps this is so traditional that children naturally associate the words with the corresponding authority, or perhaps it shows that the relationship between stepparent and stepchild is a deeper one, with the stepparent being prepared to take, and the stepchild to concede, a large measure of responsibility. Just as in any other family, step-families find the teenage years most demanding, with friction most likely between a stepfather and teenage stepdaughter.

It is always assumed that stepmothers have a more difficult role than stepfathers. Most stepmothers are more actively involved in the lives of their stepchildren than are stepfathers. Also, the innately close relationship between a child and his own mother may make her simply harder to replace. Young women who have not been married before and who suddenly find themselves in charge of stepchildren are more likely to find the situation overwhelming, particularly if they have not fully discussed all the practical ramifications before marriage. Although counselors believe that children should regularly visit the parent they do not live with, many parents report that this causes disturbances within the step-family; fewer, longer visits may be less disruptive.

Many children find the early years of having two mothers or two fathers very confusing; the child may also see the new parent as a threat that may separate him from the parent on whom he now depends so strongly. Perhaps once there has been a remarriage, the idea that "a parent is forever" needs to be modified. Until he works out the facts of life for himself, and can accept that he has loyalties to both his parents, these strains may be shown in hostility and irritability.

Each family must adjust to the influence—emotional, financial, and in matters of discipline and schooling—that stepparents have in the upbringing of a stepchild. And new evidence shows that, nowadays, families appear to deal most capably with these questions. According to this reseach, remarriage is less stressful on a child than was previously thought; indeed, many children are much better off, and lead fuller lives, when the parent they live with marries again. A new baby in the family, far from stimulating jealousy, generally improves relations all around. It can almost be said that "steps" through remarriage constitute a modern version of the extended family.

There is tremendous pressure on a second family to succeed. Parents who remarry have the priceless advantage of maturity in dealing with their stepchildren. They are likely to be more prepared to put themselves out, to be patient and tolerant—and to understand the stepchild's inner conflicts. These attitudes will go far toward getting a step-family off to the right start. And this is important, because the reactions of the children for whom they are responsible affect the new husband/wife relationship; it is naturally helpful for the marriage if these relationships are as harmonious as possible. And in the long run, it must be valuable and rewarding for stepchildren to see an adult relationship "working"—even if it is not between both of their biological parents.

You do not have to become pregnant to have a baby: you can adopt. Nowadays adoption agencies are so well organized that you can usually collect an adopted baby within hours of his birth. It is even possible for an adoptive mother-to-be to take drugs that will help her to produce milk and breast-feed the baby.

A couple's reasons for wanting to adopt a baby are crucial to the eventual success of the adoption. Usually, adoption is only considered when parents have been told that there is no chance of having a child of their own, or if they have been advised through genetic counseling that there is a strong possibility that their child will be seriously ill or defective. A couple who are considering adoption should consult a reputable social agency. Referrals can be made through your physician or through the child welfare department in your state. Today, however, there are few white infants available for adoption, and unless parents are willing to adopt minority, older, or handicapped children, they are likely to experience difficulty and frustration.

Adopting a child *is* different from having one naturally, but not as different as most people believe. It takes time for parent and child—natural or adopted—to establish a loving relationship. Remember that there are no guarantees as to how a child will turn out—adoption adds little to the unpredictability! Adoptive parents sometimes feel excessively guilty. They believe that because they have been entrusted to raise this child they did not bring into the world, they have an extra responsibility. They may worry that any small behavioral difficulties are connected with the child's feeling about his adoption; that

Adoption

Parents who adopt children of a different race or nationality have an added obligation— that of teaching the child something of his own culture and country. As they grow, older children perceive certain differences and parents may have to make an extra effort to reassure them that the differences do not in any way detract from the love and care that they will give. Such adoptions are almost always successful and satisfying to both parent and child.

Organizing your life with children in mind

Traditionally, the most difficult years for children are supposed to be under the age of six and during early adolescence, between about twelve and fifteen years of age. The chart below gives a more clear and detailed breakdown of the truths underlying this belief. It shows the best and worst ages for a parent to choose to take certain actions, which will affect his children, their development, and thus the harmony of the family. However, it must be emphasized that every child is an individual, and his different circumstances and that of his family should be taken into account before following any advice offered here.

Returning to work
For the first two to three years of life in particular a child needs a strong relationship with one or preferably two or three warm, loving people who will be his chief caretakers.

Up to three months The baby recognizes his caretakers by touch, smell, and how they handle him.
Four to six months The baby begins to recognize familiar people by sight. Permanent people in the child's life and baby-sitters should be introduced now.
From about six months The baby may start resisting approaches from strangers and may show "clinging" behavior toward his mother. He should only be left with someone he loves.
Three to five years Working (especially part-time) becomes easier once the child starts going to a playgroup or nursery school.
From five years Once a child starts school full-time, work is more feasible, but remember school vacations, sickness, and the time at which school finishes.

Adoption
The sooner after birth a child can be adopted the easier for both parent and child. Many adoptions are made within hours of birth, and it is possible for an adoptive mother to breast-feed. Tell the child that he is adopted as early as is possible.

Two to three years Storybooks about adoption may help: read them to all the family.
Three to eleven years Telling your child about himself and his past should be a continuous process, not a once-and-for-all lecture. Answer questions as they arise or offer the information yourself. A child will appreciate the truth, but in a form suitable for his age.

Twelve to eighteen years A child whose background is particularly disturbing need not be told *all* the details until he is old enough to understand. During adolescence, when children are particularly interested in their backgrounds, he may want and *need* to know.

Divorce
Whether parents are divorced or not a child must feel that both parents love him, unquestionably, for himself. Divorce must not mean that one parent signs off emotional responsibility for the children.

Up to six years Children between two and three years are particularly vulnerable to the departure of either parent, as this is the time when parents are most needed as models for identification.
There is a significantly higher risk of later delinquency among boys, and illegitimate births among girls, if their homes were broken before they were six years old. At this age a child often interprets anything bad that happens in his life as a punishment for something *he* has done wrong. Thus, it may be better for the child if his parents stay together. However, where the parental relationship is particularly stormy or destructive, the act of separation may actually benefit the child by bringing relief from inconsistent discipline, constant quarreling, and tension.

About twelve to fifteen years
The early years of adolescence may also be a difficult time. The child is undergoing hormonal changes, and just beginning to think of himself as an adult. His parents' example may be very destructive to him.

Spacing of children
A child is most likely to be jealous of the child born directly after him, especially if he himself is under five years old. Some mothers need up to eighteen months to recover from the birth of a child. Older mothers may prefer to have children quickly.

One year Jealousy is least likely at this age. However, the child may suffer from less attention during his second year, when he is learning to speak.
Two to three years Jealousy is most likely now. Parents should explain the situation as fully as possible to their child. The children will be close enough to provide company for each other as they grow up. There is also the practical advantage of looking after children near in age.
About five years It may be better not to let the arrival of a new baby coincide with other major changes in the child's life, such as starting school, or he may "blame" the baby for his new situation and resent him even more.
Six years or older The first child will have the full attention of the parents during his formative years. However, it will make the mother's job of child caring more drawn out.

Vacations and travel
Children in general are not good travelers. Sitting quietly is often physically impossible for them. Plan your journey to start just before the child's normal bedtime so that he can sleep on the way. Have drinks and snacks, amusements, and distractions always at hand.

Up to four months A baby will sleep almost anywhere.
Up to eight months A baby is easy to carry about in a portable crib.
Up to one year Babies are soothed by movement. They travel easily, asleep or awake.
Preschool The place you select for your vacation must suit small children. Beaches and farms are best.
Four to five years A child will be quite happy staying, if necessary, with a well-loved relative in surroundings that are familiar and near to home.
About seven years The child is becoming more independent. He may have developed a particular friend with whom he would like to go and stay—but may still be surprised by homesickness.
Eight years Some children are ready for a "sleep-away" camp experience at this age. Let your child's wishes be the best guide. Scouting and other "club" activities are also popular now.
Twelve to thirteen years An in-between age when children may not identify with adult activities or child's play. A vacation with friends under adult supervision may prove to be the best arrangement.
From fourteen years Teenagers may want more independence, such as that found in going youth hosteling. You should lay down rules—such as to stay in a group, and not to attempt hitchhiking.

they are not suited to raise this particular child; and they may agonize over being fair when they discipline him, and perhaps be less firm at times than they should be. It is important that they realize that *all* parents have these doubts from time to time. If they feel overwhelmed by such feelings, it may be helpful to talk them over with a professional.

The most difficult decision for an adoptive parent is whether, how, and when to tell a child that he is adopted. It is best to tell your child when he is as young as possible—in whatever terms you feel he can understand, as you do when you explain where babies come from. It may be best to tell a very young child the story of how you wanted a baby very much and went to a special place and asked for a brown-haired, brown-eyed baby—and were delighted to be given him (or her). Of course this cannot be the only explanation, but it is a start; as he gets older he will be able to talk about it more fully.

Parents of adopted children fear that they will lose the child's love when he knows that he is adopted, and this may encourage them to be less open with the child about the adoption than they should be. But knowing that he is adopted does not change his need. If the child comes to feel that the adoption is something hidden, not to be spoken about, then he will start to feel insecure about it. Adoptive parents should always speak positively of the natural mother so that the child will not feel that he has been rejected, even when you explain that she was not able to care for him herself. As he gets older, he will want to know more about his natural parents. Curiosity is particularly strong during adolescence, when a young person is vitally concerned with his or her own sense of identity. Even if some of the facts in his early background are unpleasant, and may be painful for the adoptive parents to speak of, it is wiser for a child to learn them from you—his psychological parents.

FIRST AID

From drowning to insect bites: the emergency procedures to be followed when your child has an accident or suffers injury

This First Aid section should only be treated as a guide in case of emergency It is deliberately brief as your doctor should always be consulted as soon as possible after an accident. General emergency treatments are listed first; entries then follow alphabetically, for easy reference.

RECOVERY POSITION

This position is used when the child is unconscious but is breathing and has a pulse. To put the child in the recovery position, turn him gently onto his side.

Draw up the upper arm until it makes a right angle to the body and bend his elbow. Draw up the upper leg until the thigh makes a right angle to the body and bend the knee. Draw out the lower arm gently backward to bend down clear of the body. Bend the lower knee slightly. Make certain the head is kept on one side.

It is also important to see that the mouth is not blocked by blood, vomit, or foreign bodies (clear it with your fingers if necessary); that tight clothing at the neck, chest, and waist is loosened; and that there is good ventilation.

ARTIFICIAL RESPIRATION

When the child is not breathing, mouth-to-mouth resuscitation should be used in almost all circumstances except where there is severe injury to the face and mouth. Get someone to seek medical help urgently.

Meanwhile remove any obstructions and vomit from the child's mouth. Keep his air passages open by placing him on his back, raising his neck, and tilting his head backward. Keep his chin pressed upward. Loosen his clothing around the neck and waist. The child may begin to breathe again when the air passages have been cleared. If he does, place him in the recovery position and watch him carefully until medical help arrives.

If he does not begin to breathe when the air passages are open, take a deep breath, pinch the child's nostrils together, and seal your lips around the child's mouth. (In the case of a young child, seal your lips around his mouth and nose.) Breathe gently but firmly into the lungs until his chest rises. Remove your lips and watch for his chest to fall. Repeat this procedure about twenty times a minute (once every three seconds), until the child begins to breathe himself or medical help arrives.

If his chest does not rise, you may not be covering the child's mouth with a good seal, you may not be closing the nose adequately, or the airway may still be obstructed. If the latter is true, tilt his head farther backward and try again.

External cardiac massage If the child's heart has stopped no pulse can be felt at the wrist, or in his neck. The pupils of his eyes are widely dilated, and his color is ashen gray or blue. Lay him immediately on his back on the floor. Give him a short, sharp thump to the lower part of the breastbone with the edge of your hand. If his heart does not commence beating, start external cardiac massage at once.

Position the heel of your hand on the lower half of his breastbone. Cover this hand with the heel of your other hand and rock forward, pushing firmly and sharply on the lower half of the breastbone. Repeat this pressure rhythmically without removing the hands. The pressure must be applied in a vertical direction. For infants, apply light pressure with two fingers, about one hundred times per minute. For children up to ten years, apply light pressure with one hand, about eighty to ninety times per minute. For children over ten, repeat this pressure at least sixty times per minute.

When the heart stops, breathing will also stop. It is, therefore, always necessary to perform artificial respiration at the same time as external cardiac massage.

It is best if there are two people available to do this. The first person should breathe into the child's mouth, as described in artificial respiration. Then, as the child's chest begins to fall, the second person should give four quick presses to the breastbone, and then pause to allow the first person to repeat a breath. Continue in this way until medical help arrives. If there is only one person available, it is still possible to carry out the alternate breathing and external cardiac massage as described above.

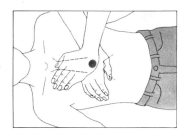

BITES

Animal bites There is always the possibility that an animal bite is infected so, if the skin has been pierced, it should be taken seriously. Being bitten by an animal can be very frightening, so treat the child if he is suffering shock. Then wash the wound thoroughly and apply a clean cloth or dressing. Take the child to a hospital so that the wound can be properly cleaned and a booster tetanus injection given.

Snakebites Some children are shocked by a bite from a poisonous or nonpoisonous snake. The size and swelling of a snakebite indicates the amount of venom, which can be, but rarely is, fatal. Reassure the child and lay him down. Clean the wound very gently with soap and water, carefully washing away any venom around the wound. If possible, support and immobilize the limb. Do not give the child anything to eat or drink. Seek medical help immediately. If breathing falters, start artificial respiration.

Insect bites Apply antihistamine cream or calamine to a bite from a gnat, mosquito, flea, louse, or tick.

BLEEDING

A wound may be incised (by a sharp instrument), lacerated (by an object with jagged edge), contused (by a blow or fall, or by crushing), or punctured (by a sharp, pointed instrument). The wound requires special treatment only if it is large, bleeds profusely or persistently, or threatens an important structure such as an eye or a nerve.

Severe bleeding requires medical attention immediately, so get the child to a hospital emergency room or call a mobile unit. Meanwhile, apply direct pressure to the child's wound with your fingers. Still maintaining the pressure, lay him down in a comfortable position. To help reduce the bleeding, the part should be elevated, unless a broken bone is suspected. Then apply a pad of clean material to the wound and bandage it firmly in position. If blood soaks through apply another dressing on top. Do not remove the original dressing.

If there is a foreign body in the wound, or a broken bone is sticking out, it will not be possible to apply direct pressure. In these cases, pressure can be applied with the fingers to the side of the wound nearest to the heart. If the foreign body is loose it can be carefully lifted out of the wound, but never attempt to remove a deeper foreign body—you may cause more serious damage.

Internal bleeding is caused by an injury or a blood vessel breaking and can only be dealt with by a doctor. The child is apt to be pale, breathless, or restless, with a rapid pulse. Blood may be coughed up, vomited, or passed in the stools or urine.

Have someone call immediately for a doctor or an ambulance while you lay the child in a comfortable position with his legs raised. If he is vomiting, place him in the recovery position. Loosen tight clothing and protect him from the cold. Keep a record of his breathing and pulse rate. Do not give him anything to eat or drink.

Minor external bleeding generally stops of its own accord. If it continues, have the child lie down; if possible, raise the injured part and support it with a pillow, unless a fracture is suspected. Apply firm, continuous pressure on the wound with a sterile gauze square or clean cloth until bleeding stops. Tourniquets are both unnecessary and dangerous.

Cuts It is important that cuts in the skin heal with as little scarring as possible. Use soap and water to clean a minor cut, working outward from the wound. Bring the edges of the cut together. Small cuts will come together without help; larger ones can be held with thin strips of adhesive tape, stretched and applied at right angles to the wound. Cuts that cannot be held together with tape may be stitched by a doctor. To keep a wound clean it should be covered with a porous dressing.

Scratches Superficial abrasions should be cleaned. Remove gravel or splinters with sterilized tweezers and wash with soap and water. Cover with a sterile dressing.

Bruises are a minor form of internal bleeding that often results from a fall or blow to the body surface. Treat the swollen area with an ice bag or cold compress.

BLEEDING FROM SPECIFIC AREAS

Scalp Apply a dressing that is larger than the wound; then bandage it securely in position. Use a large doughnut pad if you suspect an underlying fracture or a foreign body in the wound. Obtain medical help.

Ear canal Cover the ear loosely with a pad or dressing. Lay the child down with his head slightly raised and inclined to side of injury. If unconscious, take him to a hospital immediately.

Nose Have the child sit with his head slightly forward. Tell him to breathe through his mouth. Loosen clothing around his neck and chest. Pinch the soft part of his nose together with your finger and thumb for up to ten minutes. If bleeding continues, pinch nostrils again for a further ten minutes. If this is still not effective, seek medical attention. Once the bleeding has stopped tell the child not to blow his nose for several hours.

Frequent nosebleeds may be caused by the breaking of a small vein on the surface of the nasal lining; this may require medical treatment.

Palm of hand Apply direct pressure and raise the limb if possible as bleeding may be severe.

BROKEN BONES

It is frequently difficult to distinguish between a sprain (injury to soft tissues, either ligaments or muscles around a joint) and a fracture (broken or cracked bone). Children's bones are softer than adults and are therefore more liable to bend. In a young child the break may be incomplete (like a split along one side rather than a complete break) and it is referred to as a greenstick fracture. In general, fractures in children heal well without deformity.

Fractures may be simple (the flesh is not broken) or compound (when there is a wound leading down to the fracture or when the fractured ends protrude through the skin). Either type of fracture may be "complicated." This means the broken ends of the bone have damaged a large blood vessel, nerve, or internal organ. The injured limb is characterized by pain, tenderness, swelling and bruising, loss of control, or deformity.

Treatment In the case of a sprain, support the joint in the most comfortable position for the child and apply a cold compress.

In the case of a fracture do not move the broken limb more than is absolutely necessary. In particular, never move the two parts against one another in an endeavor to confirm the fracture. This will only increase the damage and may pierce the skin, worsening the original fracture. Control any external bleeding. Keep the child still and request medical help. Support the injured part, and, if medical aid is delayed, immobilize the limb, either by using the child's body as a means of support (e.g. for a broken upper arm, bind the arm to the chest with a sling or by using a padded splint (or, in emergencies, a walking stick, umbrella, broom handle, or tightly rolled newspaper). The splint should lie alongside the limb, and should extend well above and below the break. Secure it with a broad bandage along its length, making sure it is firm enough to prevent movement of the fracture, but not so tight that it stops the flow of blood to the limb.

A suspected broken leg may be fastened to the sound leg, after placing a pad of soft material between the ankles and knees.

BURNS AND SCALDS
Dry heat, chemicals, electricity, powder (from fireworks or cap pistols), and moist heat are the most common causes of burns and scalds. Prompt hospital attention should be given to young children who suffer even the smallest burn, particularly if the skin is broken.

To relieve pain and to reduce the spread of heat in the tissues, hold the burned area under gently running cold water for at least ten minutes. See that any constrictive articles—rings, belts, shoes—are loosened or removed before any swelling begins. Pour cold water over clothing that has been soaked in boiling liquid. This will reduce the heat much more quickly than trying to remove the hot clothing. Lay the child down and comfort him. Cover the burned area with a piece of clean material such as a cool, ironed sheet or pillowcase. Immobilize a badly burned arm or leg. Arrange for prompt removal to a hospital if the burn or scald is severe.

Do *not* apply butter, soap, creams, ointments, or oil dressings.

Do *not* burst blisters, or cough over or touch the burned area.

Mouth or throat Arrange transport to a hospital. Lay the child in recovery position. If he is not breathing, give artificial respiration. If he is conscious, give sips of cold water.

Chemical burns Wash the burn thoroughly and continuously with running water until the chemical has been eliminated. Remove contaminated clothing. If an eye is affected, sit or lay the child down, with his head tilted straight back and turned toward the affected side. Flush the injured eye copiously with cool water. Apply a dressing gently over the eye. Arrange for urgent medical help.

Powder burns Remove any foreign particles from the wound and wash with soap and water. Cover with a dry sterile dressing.

Sunburn If reddening, itching, or peeling occurs, this means that the child's skin is starting to burn. Cover with loose, clean clothing. Have the child sit in the shade and give him a cold drink.

If blistering or weeping from the skin occurs, cover with a clean cloth and consult a doctor for further treatment.

Electrical contact burns Switch off the electricity or get the child away from the source of the current by using any dry nonmetallic object or by standing on a rubber mat. If he is not breathing, give artificial respiration. Treat as a burn.

Clothing on fire Douse the flames with water. If not possible, roll the child in a rug, blanket, or coat. Pour cold water over burned area, wrap the child in clean material, and take to a hospital.

CHOKING
Choking occurs when an object, such as a lump of food, gets stuck in a child's windpipe and prevents normal breathing. As a result, his face and neck are congested, and he may cough violently.

Treatment An infant should be held upside down by his legs, and his back slapped vigorously three or four times.

Rather than hitting a child sharply on the back, it is best to use the Heimlich maneuver, which every parent should learn.

FAINTING
A fright, fatigue, a debilitating illness, or injury to some part of the body may cause a child to faint. His face will be pale, his skin cold and clammy, his breathing shallow, and his pulse weak and slow but gradually increasing.

Lay the child down and raise his legs slightly. Loosen his clothing at the neck, chest, and waist. Make sure he has plenty of fresh air; if breathing is labored, place in recovery position. As he regains consciousness, gradually raise him to a sitting position and give him sips of water.

Impending faint If the child feels giddy, his face is pale, and he starts to sweat, reassure him and urge him to breathe deeply and flex his leg and buttock muscles. Loosen his clothing at the neck, chest, and waist. Sit him down and lower his head between his knees. On recovery give him sips of water.

FITS (CONVULSIONS)
These take many forms, from general jerking of the whole body, lasting several minutes, to brief periods of blankness, without any movement, lasting less than a second.

Treatment Place the child in a position in which he cannot hurt himself, by falling or knocking himself. Touch or move him as little as possible while he is actually convulsing. Loosen tight clothing about his neck, chest, and waist as soon as possible. *Never* try to force a peg or spoon or anything else in between his teeth to try to prevent him from biting his tongue. (It is possible to knock out a tooth in the process, which he may inhale into his lungs.) If the child vomits, turn him on his side so that the vomit runs out of his mouth and does not obstruct his breathing. Stay with the child during the fit and, above all, don't panic. Obtain medical help immediately. If the child feels hot, remove his clothing and sponge limbs, face, and body with tepid water. Allow the moisture to evaporate from the skin. This will reduce his temperature while waiting for the doctor to arrive.

POISONING
If your child has swallowed anything poisonous, urgent medical help is needed, so take the child to the hospital.

Treatment If the child is conscious, quickly ask him what he has swallowed as he may soon lose consciousness.

If his lips and mouth show signs of burns (from a corrosive poison such as gasoline, paraffin, strong acids, caustic soda, or strong bleaches), first give him large quantities of milk or water to neutralize the poison. Do not induce vomiting.

If the poison is noncorrosive (tablets, berries), induce vomiting by sticking a finger down his throat. Do not use salt and water, or an emetic.

If the child is unconscious but breathing, place him in the recovery position.

If the child is not breathing, begin artificial respiration immediately.

If possible, take a sample of what you think the child has swallowed to the hospital.

SHOCK
Shock may result from severe bleeding, burns, crush injuries, a ruptured appendix, or loss of body fluid. The child in shock is likely to exhibit the following signs and symptoms: a very pale face, cold, clammy skin, profuse sweating, blurred vision, a feeling of giddiness, rapid, shallow breathing, an anxious appearance, and an increased pulse rate followed by a weak, faint pulse.

Get the child to a hospital promptly. Lay him down with his head low and turned to one side; raise his lower limbs if possible. If there has been an injury to his head, chest, or abdomen, raise his shoulders slightly and support them, with his head turned to one side. If he is vomiting or unconscious, place him in the recovery position. Try to ascertain the cause of shock. Loosen his clothing at the neck, chest, and waist.

Keep a record of his pulse and respiration rates. Reassure and comfort the child.

Do not give the child anything to eat or drink, but moisten his lips if he is thirsty.

Do not warm his skin with blankets or hot water bottles.

Electric shock may occur as a consequence of an electric current through the body. Treat as shock.

If the child is unconscious but breathing, place in the recovery position. If the child is unconscious and not breathing, give artificial respiration. External cardiac massage may also be necessary if the heart has stopped.

STINGS
Insect stings Bees, hornets, and wasps often leave a sting in the wound; they all inject a small amount of poison, which causes pain and swelling in the skin.

If possible, remove the sting with sterilized tweezers or the point of a needle, taking care not to squeeze the sting as this will cause more poison to enter the wound. Apply antihistamine cream immediately; if this is not available a solution of ammonia (one teaspoonful to a cup of water) or bicarbonate of soda (two teaspoonsful to a cup of warm water) may be used to relieve the pain. Soak a piece of cotton in the solution and bandage lightly in place.

If the sting is in the mouth, give a mouthwash solution of one teaspoonful of bicarbonate of soda to a glass of water. If the sting causes swelling in the mouth or the child has any difficulty breathing, place him in the recovery position and give him a piece of ice to suck. Obtain medical help promptly. If your child is especially sensitive, prophylactic immunizations may be indicated.

Jellyfish stings Apply antihistamine cream or calamine lotion

UNCONSCIOUSNESS
A child may become unconscious for a variety of reasons such as a head injury, asphyxia, epilepsy, shock, infantile convulsions, overwhelming infections, and poisoning.

Treatment If the child is breathing and has a pulse, put him in the recovery position. If the child is not breathing, give him artificial respiration.

If the child has no pulse this means the heart has stopped beating and circulation must be maintained by external cardiac massage. It is worth trying a short, sharp thump to the left of the lower part of the breastbone, as this sometimes restarts the heart. If not, start external cardiac massage.

To learn how to cope with this and other emergencies it is advisable for parents to attend a course in CPR (cardiopulmonary resuscitation).

WINDING
This is caused by a blow to the upper part of the abdomen. The child may faint or collapse as a result.

Treatment Place the child in the recovery position. Loosen tight clothing at the neck, waist, and chest. Gently massage the upper abdomen.

Home first aid kit
Assorted band-aids
Adhesive tape
Gauze bandage (2 and 3 in widths)
Triangular bandage (for slings)
Sterilized eye pad
Sterilized cotton balls
Scissors
Safety pins
Tweezers
Eyewash
Rubbing alcohol
Antiseptic ointment
Antihistamine ointment
Soluble aspirin
Baby aspirin
Paregoric
Indigestion tablets

8 Section Two

A TO Z

An alphabetical guide to child development and the ailments, diseases, and problems of pregnant mothers and of children from conception to adolescence.

Abdominal pain Abdominal pain in a child has many causes, ranging from acute *appendicitis* and *indigestion* and the recurrent pains induced by anxiety such as *"growing pains"* and cyclical *vomiting.* The urgency with which medical help should be sought varies with the severity of the pain, the speed of onset, and the associated symptoms.

In an otherwise healthy child abdominal pain is rarely due to *constipation* or to eating habits. Abdominal pain that alters neither the child's demeanor nor his appetite is unlikely to have a serious physical basis. A child who is vomiting and feverish is obviously ill, and, particularly if his belly is tender to the touch, needs urgent medical investigation. Occasionally a child may complain of acute, often colicky, bellyache, following, for example, eating large quantities of unripe fruit. If this does not pass off within a short time, or if the child also appears unwell, medical advice should be sought.
See also Colic, Gastroenteritis.

Abscess The body reacts to some invading germs by building a wall of tough fibrous material around the infected area. Large numbers of white blood cells then pass into the cavity to kill off the germs. A thick creamy fluid, pus, is formed from the dead white cells and germs. The pressure inside this abscess builds up until it either bursts or is lanced by a doctor. Once the pus has been let out, the acute inflammation subsides and finally heals over, leaving a scar. *See also* Boils.

Accidental poisoning *see* pages 202–3.

Accommodation *see* Assimilation and accommodation.

Achievement Children and adults vary in their need to achieve success. Both school and home environments influence strongly how hard a child works. If a child's achievement need is high he may do better at school than a child with higher intelligence who is not so strongly motivated.

It is possible, however, to have too high an achievement need. If a child aims too high, he will set himself targets that are impossible to reach. He will need only a few failures to attain these impossible standards to give up trying altogether. He will then appear shiftless, lazy, and ill-motivated, when his real trouble is the opposite.

Many great men in history have done outstandingly badly at school. But such opportunities for recovery are not guaranteed, and if you think that your child is not doing as well at school as he should, you should consult an educational psychologist.

Acne At *puberty,* in either sex, there is increased activity in the sebaceous glands, which produce the natural skin oils. As a result, the duct from the gland to the surface of the skin may become blocked, especially when the adolescent has a greasy skin.

The block causes oils to build up in the gland and forces the plug out of the mouth of the duct, forming a blackhead (comedo); alternatively it may so enlarge the gland that yellow pustules are formed. Germs that are normally harmlessly present in the gland may, in these circumstances, break down the oils into acids, which then leak out and irritate the surrounding skin. Acne eventually clears up after *adolescence,* but if it is severe it needs to be controlled if considerable permanent scarring, as well as misery and embarrassment, is to be avoided.

Treatment is aimed at cleaning the blocked duct and preventing the irritation. The child should wash his face two or three times a day. Use a sulfur-containing soap if your doctor thinks this is necessary. The blackheads should be removed and the pustules lanced; both these tasks are best done under medical supervision. Occasionally, a long course of antibiotics may help by killing off the germs.

If scarring does occur, the appearance of the face can usually be improved by plastic surgery, but this is not done until adolescence is ended and the acne has burned itself out.

Addiction Addiction, whether to so-called soft or hard drugs or to alcohol or tobacco, is a problem of only a small number of adolescents. Opinion is divided about whether soft drugs lead to hard, or whether drugs like marijuana cause permanent brain damage, but there is no doubt that whether or not a child develops a drug problem depends as much on his personality as on the drugs.

If a child has been brought up in a stable home background, and has been allowed to develop within a disciplined framework, where the socially acceptable drugs (tobacco and alcohol) are not abused, and where self-medication is rare, then he is less likely to resort to drugs than is a child who has no frame of reference, who is used to drunkenness as acceptable behavior, and whose family faces every problem with a pill.

By far the commonest form of drug problem in children and adolescents is alcoholism, and this is undoubtedly related to their family experience.

Adenoids The adenoids are situated at the back of the throat, above the palate and behind the nose. They are similar to the tonsils and have the same function. As a result of repeated minor infections they may become so large that they block the openings of the two fine tubes (the Eustachian tubes) that drain fluid from the middle ear. Fluid will then accumulate in the middle ear, and may interfere with its function so that the child becomes deaf. Removal of the adenoids (adenoidectomy) may then be necessary to reopen the drainage channels and restore hearing.

Adolescence This term originates from the Latin and means "to grow up" or to "grow into maturity." Adolescence is usually considered as a transitional stage between childhood and adulthood, during which the individual has to cope with marked changes both physically and emotionally. It is generally accepted that adolescence begins at eleven or twelve (usually with the onset of *puberty*) and continues until the late teens or early twenties. While adolescents may sometimes seem rebellious, moody, contradictory, or difficult to understand, it is important to remember that the breaking of childhood ties, the achievement of independence, and the physical changes associated with the arrival of sexual maturity impose considerable strains upon the young person. Thus behavior that may at first sight appear "out of character" will very often simply reflect this normal process of adjustment. *See also* Acne, Addiction, Alienation, Anorexia nervosa, Delinquency, Generation gap, Growing pains, Growth spurt, Identity crisis, Menarche, Menstruation, Nocturnal emissions, Peer group, Puberty, School phobia, Self-esteem, Suicide, Truancy.

Adoption It is a common belief, not only among parents but also among social workers and other professionals, that it is best for a child to be brought up by his natural parents. It is clear, however, that the quality of parenting is more important than blood ties.

Professor Rutter's studies on maternal separation show that separating a child from his mother in early life may not give rise to emotional or behavioral disorders in the child. Dr. Barbara Tizard from the University of London has followed up one group of children who were placed in institutions shortly after birth. Some of these children were later adopted, while others were returned to their natural mothers. Dr. Tizard's data indicated that the adopted children were happier than those who were returned to their natural parents.

On balance it is probably better for a child to be adopted than to remain in a bad "natural" home, but it may be preferable for a child to remain in a bad "natural" home than be placed in institutional care. Those children fare worst who suffer several changes during their childhood.

Aggression There are many types of aggressive behavior, not all of which involve physical attack. Aggression can equally well be expressed by destroying toys or possessions, by rejection, by criticism, by disruptive or antisocial acts, by *temper tantrums,* and so on. In children it is expressed in different ways at different ages, and behavior that may be appropriate for a three-year-old will seem very odd in someone of ten or eleven years of age. It is usually during the preschool or early school years that the child learns to manage his aggression, and it is at this time that he should be developing self-control and acquiring the ability to inhibit his angry or destructive feelings, or to express them through socially acceptable channels. Thus sport, competition, or rough-and-tumble play serve a most valuable function in allowing the child to express feelings within a structure where they cannot get too much out of hand. In this context research has shown that from a very early age boys express more physical aggression than girls, and it is probably for this reason that sport occupies such a central position in the lives of most schoolboys. Some children, especially those with a strong sense of jealousy or rivalry, do find it difficult to master their aggressive impulses, and these children may continue to bully or attack others. Frequently the close attention of an adult, and the proper provision of alternative rewards, will help such children develop self-control.

Alcohol *see* Addiction.

Alienation It is important to distinguish between alienation and the normal adolescent growth process. Almost all teenagers will at some time express criticism of their parents' views, will experience disillusionment with adult values and standards, and will feel the loss of the close childhood relationship they once had with their parents. While all these factors are undoubtedly present in the alienated young person, on their own they should not cause any anxiety. True alienation, however, will include withdrawal from personal contact on the part of the adolescent, an extreme hostility toward his or her parents, and serious communication difficulties. Research has shown that only a very small proportion (approximately five percent of teenagers) experiences severe alienation. Where it does occur it should be taken seriously.

Allergies *see* Asthma, Eczema, Hay fever.

Anemia (in childhood) A deficiency in either the red blood cells or in the hemoglobin, which carries oxygen around the body. The majority of children thought to be anemic usually just have naturally pale complexions. The only reliable way for a doctor to diagnose anemia is to measure the amount of pigment hemoglobin in the patient's blood. If anemia is present, however, it requires investigation, as it has many causes. Among these are poor diet, failure to absorb an adequate diet, *lead poisoning,* iron deficiency, internal bleeding, or a disorder of the bone marrow that prevents production of the red blood cells.

An anemic child will be pale, listless, and easily fatigued, and may become breathless on exertion. Such symptoms require investigation by a doctor. The treatment of anemia depends upon the cause. Medicine containing iron, which is a constituent of hemoglobin, usually helps, but not all anemia will respond to this treatment. *See also* Leukemia.

Anemia (in pregnancy) Providing the developing fetus with all the nourishment it requires takes precedence over the needs of the mother, so that her stores of, for example, iron and vitamins can become seriously depleted if precautions are not taken. Because of this a woman is prone to anemia during pregnancy, but she can easily avoid it by taking a small dose of iron and vitamins daily. Since no preparation of iron suits every woman, it is essential that you should tell your doctor if the form prescribed makes you feel ill.

Animal bites There is always the possibility that an animal bite is infected, so if the skin has been pierced it should be taken seriously.

Almost any warm-blooded animal can carry rabies, so, if there is the slightest suspicion of this, urgent medical attention may be lifesaving.

To be bitten by an animal is a very frightening experience for a child, and may produce severe shock which will need to be treated appropriately. *See* pages 202–3 for treatment.

Ankle swelling (in pregnancy) *see* Toxemia of pregnancy.

Anorexia nervosa This is a serious and comparatively rare condition characterized by a persistent refusal to eat and a marked loss of weight. Most commonly the disorder occurs in teenage girls; only about one in fifteen cases of anorexia is male. The disorder tends to start with a wish to lose weight with rigorous dieting and develops into virtual starvation. As her weight continues to drop the patient becomes emaciated, and may stop menstruating, but nevertheless may claim that she is well and is eating as much as she can. In some cases the patient may swing from periods of virtual starvation and weight loss to binges of overeating, producing gross obesity. Usually the anorexic patient has had a *normal development* before the onset of the disorder; she may well have been very hardworking and excelled academically; often she is physically active and athletic. It has been suggested by some authorities that the anorexic finds *adolescence* a very threatening stage of development and that her weight loss and disappearance of *menstruation* represent an escape from the demands of growing up, but this is not certain, and other people have suggested different causes, including physical, rather than psychological, ones. A variety of treatments has been used for this problem, including psychotherapy, family therapy, and *behavior therapy*. In severe cases the patient is usually hospitalized.

Parents who are concerned about this problem should consult any appropriate professional, including family doctor, pediatrician, or member of a child guidance clinic.

Aphasia This term refers to the loss of or reduced ability to speak, write, or to understand the meaning of words due to brain damage resulting from such varied factors as cerebral vascular accidents (strokes), tumors, penetrating wounds, and diseases that produce brain damage. The brain is divided into two hemispheres; normal adult language is controlled by the left hemisphere regardless of whether the individual is left- or right-handed. This dominance is not well established in young children and a newborn infant or an infant with damage to the left hemisphere develops language normally with the right hemisphere. As the child gets older the left hemisphere dominance becomes stronger and its ability to recover from injury to this hemisphere declines, thus a two- or three-year-old suffering from damage to the left hemisphere will lose his language to some degree, but within months the right hemisphere will take over the

language function and language development will be normal.

In *adolescence* the ability to recover from such injuries lessens as the brain becomes less plastic, and injury to the left hemisphere may result in loss of the ability to understand language or to use it.

Appendicitis The appendix is a short, blind-ended tube at the beginning of the large bowel. If for any reason it becomes blocked it may become inflamed, and the child is said to have appendicitis. Appendicitis is uncommon before the age of three, but can occur any time after that.

The child with appendicitis will complain of pain in the belly, often at first rather ill-defined around the umbilicus (belly button), but then moving to the right lower quarter. He will be generally unwell, will stop eating, and may have a slight fever. The tongue is often furred. Vomiting and occasionally *diarrhea* may occur, but if you are in any doubt about whether the child may have appendicitis call the doctor immediately.

The only effective treatment is to remove the appendix by an operation (appendectomy), after which the child will be in the hospital for four or five days. Recovery from the surgery is usually rapid and complete.

Artificial respiration *see* pages 202–3.

Assimilation and accommodation These are terms used in Jean Piaget's description of concept development in young children. Assimilation is the process of incorporating new ideas and perceptions by integrating them with existing schemes of thought. An analogy of this process is the absorption of various foods by the body to supplement existing tissues. Accommodation on the other hand involves the altering of existing schemes of thought to meet new demands from the outside world. The analogy here is the process of adaptation in the body when the baby is weaned from milk to solid foods.

Asthma Asthma is an allergic disorder that tends to run in families whose members may have a history of asthma, *eczema,* or *hay fever*, and sometimes *migraine*. The child himself often has had eczema as an infant, and may have hay fever.

In an asthma attack, the child's breathing becomes very noisy (wheezy) and labored, and he may seem to fight for breath. An attack may come on without any apparent cause or may be brought on by anxiety or excitement, by exercise, or by exposure to, for example, pollen or cats. A pattern can often be found: for example, attacks may come on in particular rooms in particular houses. It is likely in these cases that allergy to the house-dust mite is a factor. Where this is so, changing the environment, by using foam pillows, for example, covering the mattress in dustproof material, and vacuum-cleaning the room and bedclothes daily, may greatly diminish the severity and frequency of the attacks.

Medicines are now available that, if taken regularly, can sometimes minimize the attacks, and may prevent them entirely. If an attack starts, various drugs, taken by mouth or by

inhaler, are usually effective in stopping it.

Athlete's foot This condition is caused by a fungus which grows on the soft, warm, moist skin between the toes, causing painful sore areas on the skin. It is contracted by wearing the footwear of infected individuals or by walking barefoot at swimming pools and similar public places. If the diagnosis is confirmed by your doctor, then treatment consists of keeping the feet clean and drying the skin between the toes very thoroughly. He may prescribe an anti-fungal cream for local application. Any person who has this condition should not walk barefoot in the house or outside, and should have his own towel and washcloth.

Attachment The emotional bond or tie that develops between the young child and his parents. Typically the child begins to show signs of having developed this bond sometime during the second half of the first year. He will smile or call out when he sees his mother or father and may show signs of distress when they leave him. A child will vary considerably in the degree to which he shows signs of attachment. Some infants are clearly distressed when the mother leaves and may be very anxious in the presence of strangers, whereas others show little reaction to being left on their own. Attachment is regarded as a key developmental step because it is through his emotional dependence on his parent that the child comes to accept the rules and constraints that the parent imposes on him.

Autism The word autism is derived from the Greek "autos," meaning self, and the basic problem of an autistic child is his inability to relate to people from an early age; he is socially withdrawn and appears totally self-absorbed, though he may eventually cease to be withdrawn. He shows speech disorders, language may not develop at all in fifty percent of cases, or when it does it is frequently characterized by echolalia—the phrase or word just spoken to the child is repeated back, often in an identical tone. An autistic child insists on maintaining "sameness" and gets very distressed if his routine is disrupted in any way.

Research has shown that the primary handicap of an autistic child is not emotional; rather it is an inability to make sense of incoming information from his eyes and ears; thus visual avoidance is common, turning away the head or covering his eyes, and when he does look at an object or a person he looks for much less time than other children. The speech disorders can be explained by his inability to differentiate between sounds; and the resistance to change by the fact that understanding even one thing gives security.

There is some evidence to show that the electrical activity of the brain waves of an autistic child is similar to that usually associated with states of excitement, anxiety, or extreme alertness in a normal adult; so that despite his apparent withdrawal an autistic child is in a very excited state. Autism is rare, affecting about five children in 10,000. It affects more boys than girls and is commoner in higher

socio-economic families. There is no higher incidence of mental illness in autistics' families than in the general population, and siblings are likely to be normal.

Autistics have often suffered birth complications. Some have other handicaps, sometimes severe. An autistic's intellectual function is naturally impaired, but *IQ* scores vary from severely subnormal to above average. *See also* Rocking.

Bacteria Bacteria are minute single-celled organisms that are widespread throughout nature. Even within the human body, most bacteria, such as those on the skin and in the mouth, are harmless; some are beneficial, such as those in the gut; but some cause disease. It is against bacterial diseases such as pneumonia and meningitis that antibiotics are most effective.

Bed-wetting All babies are bed wetters. Some develop control of their bladders earlier than others—girls usually earlier than boys.

A child who has never been dry from babyhood and remains wet into early childhood even up into the teenage years may be merely a child with delayed maturation. This is a condition which quite often runs in families. A child who, however, having gained control of his bladder at night subsequently becomes wet presents a different problem. This may occur following some emotional upset such as starting school, a hospital admission, or the birth of a baby, or may have a physical basis such as a *urinary infection*.

Treatment should at first be simple. The last drink at night should be given well before bedtime, and the child should be awakened to empty the bladder when the parents go to bed. This can be done in conjunction with a reward system, such as a chart on which each dry night is rewarded with a star, but wet nights are ignored.

If this fails, older children may respond to conditioning with an enuresis alarm. A specially prepared foil sheet, which completes an electric circuit when wet, is placed on the child's mattress. When he wets, a bell rings and wakes him; he turns it off and then goes to the bathroom. Eventually, he will wake before wetting in order to empty his bladder. These alarms are usually obtainable from a doctor or child guidance clinic. If these simple measures fail, then drug treatment under the supervision of a doctor is sometimes helpful.

Behavior problems In his second, third, and fourth years, a child is establishing a degree of independence from his parents, and so he will tend to be very negative and disobedient and will throw *temper tantrums* when frustrated, which may lead on to *breath-holding attacks*.

During this period, food refusal, refusal to be helped at the table, temper tantrums when put into or out of the bath, and misbehavior at bedtime are common.

If parents can accept these things as a normal part of development, and treat them accordingly, ignoring the "bad" behavior as much as possible and rewarding the desired behavior by attention, then the phase will pass.

If, however, behavior problems become a cause for battle between parent and child, with all the attention, albeit punitive, focused on the "bad" behavior, then this will become reinforced and the problem behavior will be extended throughout childhood. Once established, food refusal, sleep disorders, soiling, and so on are difficult to eradicate, but usually respond to treatment that reinforces the good and ignores the bad.

Behavior problems are treated separately by psychologists. They are not due to defects in the child's personality or character.

Behavior therapy Behavior therapy is an approach to psychological problems that focuses on the patient's behavior rather than on possible origins of the problem. The behavioral approach accepts the premise that many psychological difficulties are conditioned patterns of behavior that have no deep hidden motivation. The treatment procedures are derived from principles of experimental psychology and include techniques to help the patient reduce high levels of anxiety and to teach him more adaptive ways of dealing with the situations he finds distressing. Behavior therapy has been used successfully to treat phobias, obsessions, nervous habits, stammering, and marital and sexual difficulties and is being applied increasingly in schools and in homes to help teachers and parents handle disruptive attention-seeking behavior in children. *See also* Hyperactivity, Psychologist.

Birthmarks Almost everyone has at least one birthmark on his skin somewhere. They take many forms: raised or flat; small or large; red, white, brown, or black. Most are of no importance whatsoever, and may fade gradually, but some, such as the *port-wine stain,* because of their position and permanence, may be very disfiguring. The skillful use of cosmetics can usually greatly improve their appearance.

The old wives' tale that birthmarks are related to experiences during pregnancy is quite without foundation. *See also* Strawberry nevus.

Blackhead *see* Acne.

Bleeding, accidental *see* pages 202–3.

Bleeding (in pregnancy) Loss of blood from the womb during pregnancy is always serious. In the early months it may indicate the onset of a threatened *miscarriage,* and in the later months the onset of premature labor or the presence of a *placenta previa.*

A woman who bleeds during pregnancy should go to bed and seek medical help immediately. Do not go to the hospital; ask the doctor to come to you.

Blindness Very few people are so blind that they have no vision at all unless for some reason both eyes have had to be removed. Many people, however, who may be able to differentiate light from dark, or to avoid large obstacles, are not able to learn or perform in a job. Such people are properly described as blind, and they need to learn techniques such as Braille, that do not depend on vision. Children's vision should be checked periodically.

Blocked tear duct A gland (the lacrimal gland) deep in the eye socket produces a continuous flow of tears that keeps the surface of the eyeball (the conjunctiva) moist and healthy. A fine tube, the tear duct, drains the surplus tears into the nose. If the tube becomes blocked, the tears overflow and run down the cheek. If the block continues, the tube may become infected, and the child develops a sticky eye.

Although the blockage may right itself, or can be cleaned by simple methods, it is sometimes necessary for the surgeon to pass a fine wire, under general anesthetic, down the tube to unblock it. Any child with a sticky or persistently watery eye should be seen by a doctor.

Boils Boils are small abscesses that form around hair roots when these become infected with a particular germ, the staphylococcus. They may burst of their own accord onto the surface of the skin, or may need to be lanced. Squeezing them only spreads the infection. It is very dangerous to squeeze boils on the face as the infection may spread through channels in the bone and cause the blood vessels draining the brain to clot, which can be fatal. Such a boil is best treated by a doctor.

Bottom shuffling About ten percent of normal children never crawl; they move about in a sitting position, "shuffling" on their bottoms. Although, on average, they start to walk two to three months later than crawlers, they catch up in their third year and eventually there is no difference between them.

Bowlegs All babies have slight bowing in their legs. This is quite normal, requires no treatment, and straightens with growth.

Very occasionally excessive bowing is due to some disease such as *rickets,* which does need treatment. If in doubt, it is worth seeking a medical opinion.

Brain damage A blanket term to describe what is presumed to have happened to a child who shows evidence that his brain is not functioning properly; for example, a child who has *cerebral palsy,* or is mentally retarded. It is not always possible to demonstrate actual damage to the brain itself in these children. *See also* Aphasia, Hydrocephaly, Microcephaly.

Breath-holding attacks It is common for a child in his second and third years to respond to frustration with a tantrum, caused either by being unable to do something for himself or by being prevented from doing it by an adult. During the course of a tantrum a child may take in such a deep breath that he is unable to release it, or may on breathing out, be unable to take a breath in. He may even hold his breath until he loses consciousness, when normal breathing resumes, and the child recovers. Occasionally the child needs to be induced to start breathing again by a slight shock, for example a loud noise or a light slap on the cheek.

It is important to realize that these attacks are not epileptic *fits* or *convulsions,* and cause no lasting damage.

Breathing difficulties *see* Asthma, Breath-holding attacks, Bronchitis, Croup, Whooping cough.

Breech Some babies are born buttocks (or breech) first. This is known as a breech delivery.

Broken bones *see* pages 202–3.

Bronchitis Bronchitis in a child occurs only in association with other infections of the respiratory tract, and is almost always due to a virus.

The child with an *upper respiratory tract infection* gradually develops a dry, hacking cough and complains of discomfort in the chest, often behind the breastbone. Moderate fever (102°F) and considerable malaise are common.

Treat the child by making sure that he is kept as comfortable as possible and that he drinks enough. Expectorants are ineffective, and cough suppressants may, by preventing the clearance of the breathing passage, increase the infection. Antibiotics are not usually helpful.

The illness usually lasts for about a week to ten days, and then clears up spontaneously. Repeated attacks of bronchitis merit further investigation.

Burns *see* pages 202–3.

Caesarean section If for some reason it is not possible for a baby to be delivered normally through the vagina, it is possible to perform an abdominal operation, whereby a cut is made in the wall of the womb and the baby is delivered through it. In some instances it is known in advance that this will be necessary; in others it is an emergency procedure when normal labor has proved unsuccessful. A Caesarean is now a very safe procedure that can be performed under either local or general anesthetic. It is known as Caesarean section because, traditionally, Julius Caesar was born in this way after his mother's death.

The most common cut today is the "bikini" cut, along the pubic hairline, which is neat and unobtrusive. There is no reason why a mother who has had a Caesarean should not breast-feed, and, depending on the circumstances that necessitated the Caesarean, she may be able to have a normal delivery for any future child. *See also* Placenta previa.

Caries If food matter, particularly sugars and starches, is left in contact with the teeth, the germs normally present in the mouth break it down into acid. This wears away the enamel, leaving holes that may penetrate down to the pulp in the center of the tooth.

The best way to prevent caries is to clean the teeth thoroughly after every meal and snack, and to avoid eating between meals. Chewing hard candies and toffees, allowing children frequent drinks of sweetened fruit juices or, worse, pacifiers containing a syrup or sweet drink are particularly damaging. Your dentist, or his hygienist if he has one, will show you the correct way to clean teeth effectively. It is not simply a matter of brushing them quickly once or twice a day.

People who come from areas of the world where the water contains a high proportion of fluoride are least prone to caries, so some local authorities are adding fluoride to their water supplies as a preventive measure. Fluoride tablets are also available, and can be helpful if taken from an early age.

It is important that children's teeth be inspected at six-monthly intervals by a dentist, so that any caries can be dealt with early.

Cataract In some children, the lens, which is situated in the eye behind the pupil, is opaque instead of being clear.

This condition, known as cataract, may be present at birth or soon after, having arisen during the pregnancy as a result of, for example, a tendency in the family or an infection with *German measles* in the first three months. It may arise after birth as a result of injury to or infection of the inner coats of the eye.

Depending on how much it obstructs the passage of light into the eye, a cataract may not affect sight at all, or may produce varying degrees of impairment of vision up to the point where the lens has to be removed by operation. A child who has had the lenses removed usually has to wear either very thick glasses or contact lenses.

The condition is not common. It can occasionally be seen at birth, when the pupil appears white rather than black, but usually it is poor vision that brings it to the attention of the parents and the doctors.

Catarrh Many children have a more or less permanently blocked or runny nose, a cough due to nasal secretions running down the back of the throat, and intermittent *otitis media,* in the absence of obvious infection. Although the child usually eventually grows out of the tendency it can be distressing both to the child and his parents during childhood. Decongestants occasionally help. In some children large *adenoids* aggravate the condition. Although the child often has a cough there is usually no abnormality in the lungs.

Celiac disease A condition in which the lining of the gut is unusually sensitive to gluten (one of the proteins in wheat), which causes the surface cells to die, so preventing absorption of the food.

The result of this is that the child fails to thrive, is small, thin, and often potbellied. The stool is bulky, pale, and has a very offensive smell. The diagnosis can be made only by a biopsy, that is by removing and examining a small piece of the gut lining under a microscope.

Treatment consists of excluding wheat completely from the child's diet, using only gluten-free foods. These children must keep to a strict diet at all times. Relatives or friends who, in order to be "kind," feed them cake and cookies do untold damage to their health.

Cephalhematoma Many children are born with a soft swelling on the top of the head caused by bruising between two of the layers of the scalp. This probably occurs as the baby's head is pushing its way through the bony canal of the mother's pelvis during the last month or so of the pregnancy. This swelling, a cephalhematoma (head bruise), is entirely harmless, disappears of its own accord, and does *not* mean that the baby has a skull fracture or brain damage.

Cerebral palsy A condition in which the brain's control over muscles is disturbed, either because it has been damaged (for example, by *German measles* infection in early pregnancy, or by lack of oxygen during a difficult birth) or because, for some reason, it has not fully developed during pregnancy.

The effect is that either the muscles become very stiff (spastic) and very liable to go into spasm or they become somewhat floppy (hypotonic) and liable to cause the limb to writhe about uncontrollably whenever a movement is attempted (athetoid cerebral palsy). The latter type is particularly likely to follow severe *jaundice in the newborn* period.

Although cerebral palsy may be associated with *mental retardation,* this is not always the case; athetoids particularly are often of normal intelligence.

There is, unfortunately, no way in which the damaged brain can be replaced, but involving his parents in the child's management from the beginning, and helping them to learn how to help him, can often avoid many problems and lessen others.

As skills in managing pregnancy and caring for very small babies are improving, so the number of children who develop cerebral palsy is falling. *See also* Microcephaly.

Cheating Cheating and *lying* are very common in children. A number of studies have shown that, whenever a child thinks he will not be found out, he will cheat to obtain some goal. The same child will at other times behave perfectly well. Occasional cheating and lying, therefore, should certainly not be regarded as a problem. If they occur more persistently and with other antisocial behavior, such as *stealing* and noncompliance at home or at school, then professional help should be sought.

Chicken pox Chicken pox is a very infectious disease caused by a virus. It has an incubation period of two to three weeks, after which the child becomes generally unwell, feverish, and may lose his appetite and develop a fine pink rash. Within a day, he develops crops of raised red spots that rapidly turn into small blisters (vesicles). Over the course of two to three days, these become cloudy, burst, and form crusts. During the week to ten days that the illness lasts new crops of spots continue to appear, so that at any one time all stages of the rash may be seen. The rash is usually confined to the trunk and head with only a few spots on the limbs, and is extremely itchy. The child is infectious from the day before the appearance of the rash until all the spots have crusted over.

There is no specific treatment, but try to keep the child occupied, so that he scratches as little as possible. Reduce the itching by applying some soothing lotion such as calamine.

Anyone who has not already had the condition should be kept away as much as possible from the patient, but most of the family will catch it whatever precautions are taken. Second attacks are very rare.

Child abuse *see* Nonaccidental injury.

Chromosome abnormalities The code that governs all our inherited characteristics, normal and abnormal, is carried on the chromosomes, the thread-like structures present in every cell of our bodies. Every human cell contains twenty-three pairs of chromosomes. In twenty-two pairs the members of each pair are alike: one pair, the sex chromosomes, are alike in females and different in males. Abnormalities in the chromosomes result in *inherited abnormalities* in the child. Occasionally, these are so large that they can be seen by examining specially prepared cells under the microscope. All the chromosomes are numbered according to their size and shape, so that if an extra one is present it can be identified. *See also* Down's syndrome.

Circumcision The tip of the penis (the glans) is covered with very sensitive and delicate skin, which is protected by the foreskin (prepuce). In early life the foreskin is attached to the glans by a fine network of bands. At some point, usually before the child's fourth birthday, these break down naturally, and the foreskin becomes easily and painlessly movable over the glans.

Do not try to force back the foreskin of a little boy before it is free. If you do you will hurt him and may tear the bands. The subsequent scarring may obstruct the flow of urine. Very, very rarely the natural opening of the foreskin is so small that the child cannot pass urine through it. These are the only two medical reasons for circumcision, although the operation is commonly performed for religious and social reasons. There is no evidence that circumcision affects later sexual competence in any way. *See also* Meatal ulcer.

Cleft lip and palate When the baby's face is being formed during the early weeks of pregnancy, it starts as a central piece and two sidepieces, which join together and form the center of the face: the nose, the upper lip, the upper jaw, and the roof of the mouth (palate). Occasionally, for reasons that are not fully understood, the joining is not complete, so that a cleft remains. This may involve only one side or both, or only the lip, or the palate; alternatively, the cleft may extend right through lip, jaw, and palate.

The surgical treatment of these conditions is now so good that not only can the appearance be improved virtually to normal but the patient will usually be able to speak adequately. Depending on the severity of the cleft, repair may need one or more operations; these are usually completed in the first eighteen months of life.

Clubfoot Many children are born with what looks like a clubfoot, possibly due to the position of the foot during pregnancy. Gentle pressure on the sole, however, is enough to restore the normal position. Sometimes, a baby will have a true clubfoot, usually with the foot twisted downward and inward (equino-varus), but occasionally upward and outward (calcaneo-valgus). In these children, the foot cannot easily be pressed back into a normal position, due to an abnormality of either the bones or the muscles. This often responds, nevertheless, to fairly simple measures, such as plaster of Paris boots, but sometimes requires an operation. The eventual result is usually excellent.

Clumsy child Some children are "born clumsy." They tend to walk in a rather ungainly way, trip over their own feet, confuse left and right, and are late in developing a dominant hand. They may have difficulty in learning to write, and when they do their writing is very messy. Their spelling is often poor, and they may have difficulty with reading. In short, although there is no gross abnormality present, they have a poor appreciation of and control over the space around them. They often have fairly minor difficulties at the time of their birth.

With help from a skilled remedial teacher, *psychologist,* or occupational therapist, a great deal can be done to help such children overcome their difficulties.

Cold sore The "cold sore" virus (herpes simplex) is very widespread, and in most people the primary infection passes unnoticed. In some people, however, particularly young children, it may cause a very painful ulceration of the lips, mouth, and gums. Eating is difficult because of the pain, and in severe cases the child may have to have a tube passed through his nose into his stomach to get fluid and nourishment into him during the week or so of the illness. It is often necessary to admit the child to a hospital for this.

Once a person has been infected with herpes virus it remains passively in the body until some stress, such as an emotional upset or a cold, or sometimes exposure to the sun, reactivates it, when the familiar cold sore appears, usually around the lips or nostrils. This disappears without treatment in a few days, but may reappear at times of stress. There is no specific treatment other than to keep the area clean and dry.

Colic This condition affects young babies under the age of about four months, and for this reason is often referred to as "three-month colic." The baby appears to have spasms of pain, during which he draws up his legs and cries. His face may be pale, particularly around the mouth, and the abdomen is often distended.

Each attack may last minutes or hours, often occurs in the evening, and may be relieved by passing a stool or wind (flatus). If your doctor feels that your baby's symptoms are due to three-month colic, a mild sedative or muscle-relaxant is sometimes prescribed.

Color blindness This usually refers to an inability to distinguish between specific colors, rather than to an inability to distinguish color at all, which is very rare. The commonest form of color blindness, usually found in males, is the inability to differentiate between red and green.

It is very important that color vision is tested during routine school medical examinations in order that career advice can be given, because some jobs require perfect color discrimination.

Colostrum During the first one to two days after the birth of her baby, a mother produces, instead of milk, small quantities of a thin fluid called colostrum. This is very rich in antibodies and contributes greatly to the child's immunity to such infections as *gastroenteritis* and common childhood diseases. If, in the mistaken belief that it is inadequate for the baby's needs, cow's milk supplements are given, this protective effect is largely destroyed.

Concussion Concussion results from a blow on the head of sufficient severity to cause loss of consciousness. This may be just momentary, and may show itself as an inability to remember the precise point of impact, or as a delay between the child falling and beginning to cry. There is also often a loss of memory of events that occurred just before the blow (retrograde amnesia).

A child with a concussion should be kept calm and quiet and should be seen by a doctor as soon as possible so that any more serious damage, such as a fractured skull or bleeding within the skull, can be dealt with. Such complications are rare but dangerous.

Congenital abnormalities Congenital means present at birth. Such abnormalities may be inherited from the parents (for example, *Down's syndrome*), the result of an adverse environment (for example, *German measles* infection in early pregnancy), or a mixture of both (for example, *spina bifida*). *See also* Cerebral palsy, Cleft lip and palate, Clubfoot, Cretinism, Cystic fibrosis, Dislocated hip, Hernia, Hole in the heart, Hydrocephaly, Microcephaly, Phenylketonurea, Spasticity, Tongue-tie, Undescended testicles.

Conjunctivitis The conjunctiva is the thin membrane that covers the front of the eyeball, and is folded over at top and bottom onto the underside of the eyelids. Conjunctivitis is the inflammation or infection of this membrane, and some forms are highly contagious. The eye becomes bloodshot, and may be painful or irritable. There may be a sticky yellow discharge from the eye, particularly if the tear duct is blocked.

Since there are many causes of conjunctivitis, some serious and some not, and some contagious, it is important that the child is examined by a doctor so that the correct treatment can be given. *See also* Measles.

Conscience Conscience is that aspect of the personality that has to do with moral values. It is generally accepted that the most powerful influences upon the child's conscience are the moral attitudes and beliefs of the parents. These beliefs are not necessarily taught directly to the child, but are picked up almost unconsciously as a result of day-to-day experience in the home.

Conscience is also associated with the type of discipline used by the parents. Children with the most highly developed conscience tend to be those growing up in a home where discipline is firm but not excessively severe, where parents are consistent in the rules they impose, and where the use of physical punishment is kept to a minimum. Children progress through various stages in the development of their ideas about what is right and wrong. A young child will tend to make judgments according to the amount of damage done (i.e., to break six cups is worse than to break one cup, no matter what the circumstances) and older children often go through a phase of making judgments according to whether they will be punished or not (i.e., there is nothing wrong with stealing from a supermarket so long as you are sure not to be caught). Gradually a child progresses to a stage where he can make judgments according to the intention of the act and according to a set of principles generally accepted in society. *See also* Psychoanalysis.

Constipation A child who eats a normal balanced diet, containing plenty of vegetables and fruit, will pass a normal soft stool regularly. Most people have a bowel movement every day, but it is not unusual for the rhythm to be once every other day, or even every third day.

Constipation is the irregular, infrequent passage of very hard stools, which are sometimes so hard that they graze the bowel wall while being passed, and so become streaked with blood.

Moderate constipation usually responds to an increase of fiber, root vegetables, and fruit in the diet. If this does not restore the rhythm to normal, then treatment under medical supervision is desirable. The indiscriminate use of proprietary laxatives is potentially dangerous, and they should not be given to a child unless your doctor advises it.

Convulsions *see* Fits.

Cortisone therapy Cortisone is one of a family of drugs (the steroids) that are either identical with or very similar to the hormones produced in the body by the adrenal gland. These hormones, among other things, help to regulate the body's response to physical or emotional stress, and if for some reason they are lacking, the appropriate steroid can be given instead.

The main use of the steroids, however, is to lessen the effects of inflammation. Given in high doses they suppress the adrenal so that it does not produce the natural hormone. This is why it is important that anyone who has ever had steroids must tell his dentist and doctors so that they can compensate for the inactive gland if necessary.

Steroids are often used in the treatment of ulcerative colitis, nephrosis, adrenal insufficiency, some forms of arthritis, and inflammatory disease states. Prolonged use can produce a "Buffalo" limp, weight gain, swelling, and mental derangements, so they must be prescribed and carefully monitored by a physician.

Cough *see* Asthma, Bronchitis, Croup, Cystic fibrosis, Measles, Pneumonia, Whooping cough.

Cradle cap Cradle cap consists of a layer of scales over the scalp, firmly stuck to the underlying skin. It commonly occurs over the soft spot on the top of the head (the fontanel), possibly because mothers are often afraid to wash this area.

Flakes shed from the affected scalp may cause irritation of the skin of the eyebrows, eyelids, and the creases behind the ears.

The cradle cap should be treated by a daily routine of rubbing in an oil such as olive oil at night, then shampooing the hair in the morning until the cap has gone. (The fontanel is covered with a tough membrane and can safely be treated as firmly as the rest of the scalp.)

Creativity The capacity to think in an unconventional way, to make original use of materials such as paint, clay, etc., to use words imaginatively, or to see unusual or novel solutions to problems. Creativity is considered by *psychologists* to be one aspect of personality. Although it is linked with intelligence, studies show that, while creative children usually do well in intelligence tests, not all children who do well in intelligence tests are necessarily creative.

There is no doubt that a lot can be done by parents and teachers to encourage creative play and activities in all children. Creativity is extremely difficult to define or assess, for there are no clear criteria against which to judge painting, poetry, etc. As far as children are concerned anything that involves the imaginative use of materials, whatever the outcome, is undoubtedly to be encouraged.

Cretinism This is a condition of babies caused by the baby's thyroid gland failing to produce its hormone, which is essential for the processes of the body to be maintained at the correct rate. The baby with cretinism (or hypothyroidism) is characteristically fat, sluggish, coarse-featured, and slow generally. The diagnosis is not usually in doubt, and can sometimes be made within the first few days of life. Screening tests are given at birth in many hospitals. If untreated, the condition progresses to irreversible mental retardation. Carefully monitored doses of the missing hormone are given by mouth to correct the condition. The need for treatment is usually lifelong and should be under the supervision of a doctor.

Crib death Sudden Infant Death Syndrome (SIDS) is an elusive and frightening disease which strikes at least 10,000 infants a year: a seemingly well child goes to bed and is found dead in his crib in the morning. It has been the subject of a good deal of concern and research during the past decade, and although definite conclusions as to cause have not yet been reached, progress is being made.

The name SIDS is given to what are in fact a number of related, but different diseases, and as more work is done in this field, their complexity becomes more evident. Although various theories as to cause have been put forth, many of them have been disproven, and to date none has been substantiated.

The disease has undoubtedly existed for centuries, but only recently has it commanded the attention it deserves. Research grants have been given by the federal government to many task forces and research projects that have SIDS under study, and the Sudden Death Syndrome Foundation and many local organizations provide information and counseling to bereaved parents and to others who are concerned.

Although SIDS strikes babies of all economic, social, and racial groups, its victims for the most part are premature or of low birth weight, and are often children of very young mothers.

Parents can be reassured that SIDS is now capturing the concern and attention of the medical profession and they can be hopeful that, like diphtheria, polio and tuberculosis, it will one day be preventable and more clearly understood.

Cross-laterality Most people have a preferred or dominant hand, foot, and eye when performing actions requiring only one of the pair, such as writing, kicking a ball, or looking through a telescope. Usually the dominance is all on one side, so that, for example, a right-handed person will also be right-footed and right-eyed. In a proportion of normal people, however, the dominant eye is on the opposite side to the dominant hand, and they are then said to be cross lateral. There is no evidence that this has any significance whatsoever. The proportion of children with reading and writing difficulties who are cross lateral is the same as in children without such difficulties, so that this is unlikely to be the cause of their problems. *See also* Handedness.

Croup The young child's voice box (larynx) is very narrow, so that the slight swelling associated with infection can cause it to close sufficiently to make breathing difficult. This is what happens in croup, which is almost always due to a virus infection of the larynx. The croup itself, the whooping noise accompanying breathing, is caused by the air being forced through the narrow tube.

A child with suspected croup should always be taken to the doctor, who will supervise treatment. This is necessary because, although a hospital admission is not always necessary, some forms of croup can cause the airway to close off completely. If the croupy child becomes increasingly distressed by breathing, is frightened, and goes a pale or dusky grayish color, then urgent medical attention is necessary.

Cuts *see* pages 202–3.

Cystic fibrosis (CCF) This is an inherited disorder that appears only if the child inherits the trait from both parents.

There are three main features: the pancreas, the main digestive gland, fails to produce its juices, so that the food cannot be digested and is therefore not absorbed; the mucus-producing glands in the lining of the main air passages do not function properly, so that the child gets frequent and persistent chest infections; and the sweat glands produce very salty sweat.

The child with cystic fibrosis fails to thrive, usually has a constant cough, and passes bulky, offensive stools containing the undigested food.

The disease may affect a number of children in a family. It can appear at birth as an intestinal obstruction or can manifest itself later in life. It is the most common fatal disease of childhood. Present treatment has extended the life of a child with cystic fibrosis to an average of nineteen years.

Day care The provision of facilities for the care of young children during a full weekday, thus enabling mothers to go out to work. The actual administrative structure of such facilities varies, but usually day-care staff have a strong background in pediatrics and child health, as well as some knowledge of child psychology. In most countries, especially in Britain and the United States, day-care facilities are grossly inadequate, especially in the inner city areas, where they are most needed, and this has led to an increase in the number of untrained child-care workers.

Deafness It is a sad statistic that almost half the children found to be deaf do not have their hearing difficulty discovered until they are five or six, or even older. The deaf child misses out on the experience of speech and music, and noises in the environment that help him to orientate himself.

He is also deprived of much social contact and comfort, so he may become a withdrawn, speech-delayed child with *behavior problems*. As many causes of deafness can be prevented or treated, and those that are not treatable can be compensated for, delay in diagnosis imposes an unnecessary handicap on the child.

If your child does not appear to respond consistently to the spoken voice, is delayed in speech, does not respond to music, or does not babble tunefully, he may be deaf.

If you think your child is deaf, do not give in until a doctor has done something about it, or has convincingly demonstrated to you that the child can hear. *See also* Hearing tests.

Delayed speech In order to learn to speak a child must be spoken to, be able to hear what is said, understand what he hears, and be able to relate what he understands to previous experience. To speak himself he must be able to draw on his past learning, formulate a message from the brain to the muscles of lip, tongue, cheek, palate, voice box, and chest, and have muscles able to respond to the message. Above all he must want to speak. Delay in speaking may be due to a block anywhere in the above chain, and may need the combined skills of physicians, speech therapists, and *psychologists* to sort it out. Continuous background noise from, for example, a record player or a television is a potent cause of delayed speech in children, since it usually destroys the first link in the above chain.

Most children have two or three words with meaning (mama, dada) at a year, and are forming two- or three-word phrases at two years. If a child is not doing this, or appears not to speak as well as other children of his own age, he is nevertheless probably normal, but it is worth seeking a doctor's advice. Boys are usually slightly slower in developing speech than girls.

Delinquency This term is used to describe illegal acts performed by a child or adolescent under the age of eighteen. Delinquency is extremely difficult to quantify, because all the official figures reflect simply the numbers of individuals appearing in court. However, it is generally accepted that the incidence of delinquency has increased greatly in the last ten to fifteen years. Most common forms of delinquency are theft and damage to property. It is important to distinguish between those young people (the majority) who commit one or two delinquent acts and then settle down, perhaps after a period of probation or a suspended sentence, and those (the minority) who become persistent offenders. Among this latter group delinquent behavior is strongly associated with family background, and many studies have shown that it is possible to predict with a fair degree of accuracy from a relatively early age those children who will later become "hard-core" delinquents.

Dependency Dependency is the wish to be nurtured, comforted, and protected by others, or to be emotionally close to or accepted by other people.

Situations that elicit dependent behavior, as well as the targets of the behavior, change with age, so that a two-year-old expresses dependency by direct bids for affection, for example by clinging, touching, and crying; whereas an older child expresses his dependency by seeking attention and approval. Anxiety-producing situations, such as being left alone in a strange place or with a strange person, tend to increase dependency behavior, especially in younger children. Dependent behavior is an expression of real need, and is not under voluntary control. Many children, especially boys, are made more anxious by their own dependent behavior, which is not acceptable to them.

Girls have always been more dependent than boys, perhaps because it is a traditional form of feminine behavior. In many respects they are encouraged to be dependent in ways that would be socially unacceptable for boys.

Diabetes Diabetes mellitus (or sugar diabetes) results from failure of the pancreas to produce the hormone insulin, which is normally responsible for aiding the passage of glucose from the blood into the cells, and therefore controlling the amount of glucose in the blood. A person may have a tendency to diabetes which may be sufficiently well compensated not to cause him any trouble until an additional stress is added. This may be a relatively minor infection or even occasionally emotional stress. This can then bring the diabetic tendency out of balance so that the person becomes diabetic.

Babies born to women who either have diabetes or whose diabetic tendency is brought out by pregnancy tend to be very large and rather "flabby," but behave as if they are premature, being very prone to breathing difficulties in the first few days after birth. It is very important, therefore, that they are delivered in a hospital, where they can receive all necessary medical care.

Diabetes is relatively rare in childhood, occuring in approximately 1 in 2500 births, but it is nevertheless important that the diagnosis is not delayed and the disease is brought quickly under control.

The uncontrolled diabetic child may be very thirsty, lose weight, and be constantly hungry. He may also pass a lot of urine and be prone to minor infections such as boils. He may be listless, may even lapse into a coma, and his breath and urine may have a smell of acetone.

A child with any of the above symptoms needs urgent medical care. If diabetes is confirmed, treatment will need to be by injections of insulin. Most diabetic children rapidly adjust to this and become expert in giving themselves the injections.

Diaper rash The gut contains a large number of bacteria that help to complete the digestion of the food and then pass out in the stool. If these bacteria remain in contact with warm urine for any length of time, they produce a solution of ammonia that burns the skin. This is particularly likely to occur if the urine is held in the diaper for a long time by plastic pants.

Commonly, the burned area becomes infected by *thrush* (monilia). The treatment is to remove the cause. The child should remain in a soiled or wet diaper for as short a time as possible, should be washed and carefully dried at each diaper change, and left without a diaper as much as possible. A barrier cream sometimes helps, and if thrush is present your doctor may prescribe a special cream for it.

Diarrhea Diarrhea is the passage of frequent watery stools, which are often a symptom of infection but may be due to other causes as well. Some people, however, develop diarrhea as a response to emotional stress in the absence of infection.

A child with diarrhea, particularly a young child, should be seen by a doctor, since he rapidly loses fluid by this means and can become very ill within a short time. *See also* Celiac disease, Cystic fibrosis, Gastroenteritis.

Diphtheria An illness caused by a bacterium that commonly lives, quite harmlessly, in the nose and throat of many people. In some, however, particularly those not protected by *immunization*, it can cause a crippling and deadly disease. This usually starts in the nose or throat, where a thick yellow membrane is formed. This may completely block the airways so that the child chokes to death. At the same time the germ produces a poison (toxin) that is carried throughout the body by the bloodstream, causing widespread damage, the most serious of which is to the heart, which may fail completely as a result so that the patient dies. Immunization is entirely safe and gives excellent protection.

Dislocated hip In some children at birth, the top or head of the thighbone (femur) does not fit snugly into the hip joint cavity, which is often shallow. If the baby is checked for this condition in the newborn period it usually can be easily detected. Simple treatment, often no more than keeping the legs apart by wearing two diapers instead of one, is usually effective, although some children require a plaster cast to keep the hip in position. If it is discovered late, particularly if the child has started to walk, an operation may be necessary to correct the deformity.

Distress and anxiety see Bed-wetting, Diarrhea, Elective mutism, Failure to thrive, Head banging, Nightmares, Rocking, Separation anxiety, Sleeping difficulties, Sleepwalking, Soiling.

Down's syndrome Some children are born with extra chromosomes. If this is number 21 (trisomy 21), the child will have Down's syndrome, sometimes called mongolism. These children are usually born to mothers in their forties, although they are sometimes born to younger women.

The appearance of a child with Down's syndrome is so characteristic that a group seen together all look like brothers and sisters. Their faces are round, with broad flat noses and with folds in the corners of the eyes. Their tongues tend to be large. They are rather short for their age, and tend to have very lax muscles. There is always some degree of *mental retardation,* which may be severe. Such children have a tendency to other problems, such as heart disease, myopia, and *deafness.*

Down's syndrome children are often happy, pleasant children, and the old wives' tales suggesting that they are unusually aggressive or, later on, unusually active sexually, are without foundation.

Dumbness There is no such thing as dumbness in itself. If a child fails to speak it may be due to deafness or to a specific problem of language, to a general retardation, or to some other cause. Failure to speak needs evaluation by a doctor or *psychologist.*

Dyslexia or specific reading disability is a condition thought to be caused by a flaw in a child's perception, which prevents him from recognizing letters or words. The causes are under question. The condition may be due to minimal brain damage, or to some minor inborn (though not necessarily inherited) brain malfunction. Dyslexia occurs in approximately ten percent of the population. With proper diagnosis and the guidance and help of professionals, a dyslectic child can usually be taught to read successfully. The emotional "lift" he will get as he gains a feeling of success and his reading problems diminish will not only accelerate his progress but will positively affect his total sense of confidence and well-being.

Ear The ear has three compartments. The outer (external) ear consists of the funnel on the side of the head, the pinna which traps the sound, and the passage (the meatus) that channels it down to the eardrum. The middle ear, behind the drum, contains a chain of three bones (the hammer, anvil, and stirrup bones) that picks up the vibrations of the drum as the sound wave hits it, and carries them to the inner ear (the cochlea). In the inner ear they are converted into nerve impulses that pass back to the brain, which interprets them as particular sounds.

Earache The most important cause of earache is *otitis media,* and it is essential that a child who complains of pain in the ear is examined by a doctor so that this condition is not missed.

Otitis externa (inflammation of the outer ear), *boils,* and *foreign bodies* in the outer ear will also cause earache.

If the Eustachian tubes are blocked because of, for example large *adenoids* or *catarrh,* the middle ear cannot adapt easily to changes in the atmospheric pressure, and painful distortion of the eardrum may occur.

Pain described by a child as earache may in fact have nothing to do with the ears, but may arise, for example, from a nearby bad tooth or an infection of nearby skin.

Eczema Eczema is one of the allergic disorders like *hay fever* and *asthma* that tend to run in families. It usually starts in early childhood, and many children grow out of the tendency after a few years, although they may develop one of the other allergic conditions later.

The child with eczema develops raised red weeping areas on the skin, particularly in the joint creases (flexures). Since these itch they often become infected as the child scratches.

Treatment requires that the skin is kept clean, and the affected areas are usually treated with special creams. It is sometimes helpful for the baby to wear "scratch mittens" to prevent him making the irritation worse.

EEG Throughout life, there is continuous electrical activity in the brain, resulting in frequent, minute changes in voltage that can be detected by small metal plates (electrodes) placed on the scalp. These changes are then amplified and turned into a trace drawn by a pen on paper, or electro-encephalogram (EEG). The main value of the EEG is in sorting out and assessing treatment in *epilepsy,* but it also helps in the elucidation of other brain disorders.

Elective mutism Language development is normal, but the child only speaks in some situations, for example in the home, but never speaks in other situations, for example at school. This is usually associated with emotional conflict and the child may be rigid, unable to eat or use the bathroom in the "nonspeaking" situation. This disorder is rare, though some children may be shy in strange situations and not talk for some time.

Electric shock Before touching a child who has sustained an electric shock, make sure that he is not still connected to the electrical supply because, if he is, you will receive a shock from him and may end up in as much need of help.

Cut off the electricity supply if possible. If you cannot, dislodge the child from it with a dry stick or some such object, or stand on a rubber mat. *See pages 202–3 for treatment.*

Epilepsy Although *fits* can have many causes, for example, as a result of an injury to the brain, some people have an ill-understood tendency to have a fit in the absence of these known causes, and they are said to be epileptic. Epilepsy may be detected by an *EEG* test, although not always. The fits vary greatly, and may or may not be associated with jerking of the limbs.

Usually epileptics are normal in all other respects, and within certain commonsense limits should lead a normal life. They obviously should not be allowed to get into situations where a fit would make them dangerous to themselves or others, but there is no reason why, for example, they should not swim if someone is in the water with them.

Most epileptic fits can be controlled by drug therapy.

Extraversion *see* Introversion.

Eye trouble *see* Blocked tear duct, Cataract, Color blindness, Conjunctivitis, Lazy eye, Squint, Sticky eye, Vision testing.

Failure to thrive Some children, despite apparently adequate nutrition, fail to thrive. They don't grow taller, don't put on weight, and are often apathetic and listless.

In order to thrive a child not only requires adequate food but he also needs a stimulating, caring environment.

When a child who has failed to thrive is taken into a hospital for investigation, doctors may find a physical reason why he has been unable to absorb or utilize the food given to him. He may have cystic fibrosis, celiac disease, a congenital heart condition, or an endocrine disturbance. To treat such a child, help must be given to the whole family, and it will include health education and social work support for the parents as well as attention to the housing and financial state of the family. With such help, which needs to continue even after the initial crisis seems to have been resolved, most children can be left with their parents, and do well. Occasionally the family is so damaged that the child is better off in another setting. *See also* Maternal deprivation, Nonaccidental injury.

Fears Almost all children develop fears of one sort or another at some time during their early years. Especially during the preschool period it is very common for children to express irrational fears, of dogs, cats, elevators, the moon, fluff in the bath, a particular toy, etc. Almost all of these will eventually disappear, but they should be handled sympathetically. Do not force the child to "overcome" the fear, but simply acknowledge his anxiety and make allowances for it. Some children, however, will continue to have fears, one of the most common being of the dark. It is usually possible to help the child by, for example, providing a night-light just outside his door. If the fear seriously interferes with the child's normal life, professional advice should be sought.

Febrile convulsions *see* Fever fits.

Feeding problems Feeding problems have two types of cause, physical and behavioral. An example of a physical cause is difficulty in controlling the muscles of the mouth, tongue, and throat. Such problems may occur in, for example, a child with *cerebral palsy,* who has difficulty holding the food or drink in his mouth, chewing, and swallowing it. Speech therapists and doctors can often help the parents considerably by showing them techniques to overcome these problems.

Behavioral feeding problems usually occur in otherwise healthy children. During the child's second and third years he is not only learning to feed himself (often very messily)

but is also developing independence from his mother, expressed as refusal to conform with her wishes. At the meal table these two come together, and he may refuse to eat certain foods or to use a spoon. He may also throw his food.

If this is recognized as the entirely normal phase of development that it is, refused food being removed and unacceptable behavior either checked calmly or ignored, then the child will respond to the attention he receives and the pleasure shown when his behavior is acceptable.

If, however, the table becomes a battlefield between mother and child, then the unacceptable behavior will be reinforced, and food fads and feeding difficulties will become entrenched and very difficult to alter.

Fever The rise in temperature that occurs during fever is part of the body's defense mechanism, and except in a young child, when a rapid rise may cause *fever fits,* is usually beneficial.

Fever fits (convulsions) Between the ages of about six months and five years a child's brain is particularly susceptible to irritation, and he may have a fit in which his whole body twitches and shakes for two to three minutes, during which time the child is unconscious. After the fit the child may sleep for several hours.

The most common cause of a fever fit is a rapidly rising temperature such as occurs at the beginning of the *measles* rash or with *otitis media.*

Although a child in a minor fit is a very frightening sight, it is essential that the adult remains calm. See that the child is in a safe position, where he can neither fall nor hurt himself, and stimulate him as little as possible; keep quiet, and do not touch him more than is absolutely necessary for his safety while he is convulsing. Never try to put anything between his teeth to stop him biting his tongue. Once the fit is over, keep him as cool as possible, if necessary sponging him with tepid water.

If, at the beginning of an illness, precautions are taken to keep the child cool, fever fits can often be prevented.

Nine out of ten children who have fever fits grow out of them by the age of five or six.

Fits Throughout life, the brain is in a constant state of activity, which shows itself as repeated bursts of electric discharge. If for some reason this activity becomes greatly increased, either generally throughout the brain or in one particular part of it, then a fit may occur.

Fits take many forms, from general jerking of the whole body, lasting several minutes, to brief periods of blankness, without any movement, lasting less than a second. Some have no apparent cause; others, such as *fever fits,* have a definite cause. *See* pages 202–3 for treatment.

Flatfeet All babies are flat-footed. By continually exercising the feet while learning to walk and run, the arch develops naturally. There is no evidence that special exercises (physiotherapy) or special footwear are either useful or necessary.

Flu (influenza) A virus infection that

tends to occur in epidemics every two years or so, and is highly contagious, striking the whole family at times. There are various types or strains of the virus and immunity to one does not give immunity to the others. Therefore *immunization* is only effective once the strain causing a particular epidemic has been isolated and identified. The illness resembles an *upper respiratory tract infection,* and often the child is not particularly ill. In other instances he feels very lethargic and suffers considerable muscular aching. Occasionally a bacterial pneumonia, which may be difficult to treat, complicates influenza. Apart from dealing with such specific complications there is no treatment for the disease other than rest. People at special risk, such as doctors, nurses, and children with a long-standing illness, should be immunized.

Fluoride *see* Caries.

Foreign bodies Young children are prone to put small objects, such as beads, berries, and the like, into their ears, nose, rectum, or vagina, and they are a common cause of chronic discharge from these organs. If you can see and remove the object easily, then do so, but if there is any difficulty at all, the child should be taken to a doctor, because unskilled attempts to remove the object may lodge it more firmly in place.

Objects stuck in the throat can be dislodged by holding the child face downward and patting his back. If this fails, then again medical help may be needed.

The trick of throwing small objects in the air and catching them in the mouth is particularly likely to result in them becoming inhaled into the lungs. *Peanuts* should never be given to a small child. *See* pages 202–3.

Fractures If you suspect that a child has broken a bone, then urgent medical attention is necessary.

If a bone is broken, the area around the break will be painful and tender to the touch. There is likely to be bleeding into the tissues with resulting swelling and bruising, and if the break is complete the limb may be bent at an odd angle. The skin around a fracture may be intact (a simple fracture) or broken (a compound fracture). If the skin is broken, the wound is more likely to become infected.

A child's bones are softer than an adult's and are therefore more able to bend. The resulting fracture, called a "greenstick fracture," is more a split along one side than a complete break, rather as a new green twig breaks if an attempt is made to snap it. Treatment is essentially the same as in the first instance.

In general, fractures in children heal well without deformity. *See also* pages 202–3.

Freckles Freckles are a variety of *mole;* usually flat, and about 1–2 mm in diameter, occurring on the face, arms, back, and legs. They may develop during childhood or later. They are not caused by sunlight, although tanning can make pale freckles more apparent. Their only significance is their effect on the appearance of the face.

Freud, Sigmund *see* Psychoanalysis.

Gastroenteritis A disease caused by infection of the gut by a virus or bacterium. The main symptoms of the illness are profuse *vomiting* and *diarrhea.* As a result, the child loses a lot of fluid and becomes rapidly dehydrated. The dehydrated child is listless and irritable and usually feels dry and hot to the touch; his eyes sink into their sockets and his skin loses its suppleness, so that if picked up gently between finger and thumb, it does not spring back into place when released.

A child with gastroenteritis should always be under medical care. So if you suspect your child may be suffering from it, always call your doctor. In mild attacks a child may recover on a diet of clear fluids for a day and then gradually be introduced to diluted milk. More serious attacks may warrant hospital treatment to give the gut a complete rest, the child receiving fluid and nourishment intravenously instead.

Generation gap This concept has been taken to mean a major divergence of opinion, attitude, and belief between parents and teenagers. In particular, it has been thought to apply to sexual and political attitudes. The term "generation gap" is one frequently used in the press and on television, but is one which has been shown by research to have relatively little basis in reality. While adolescents and parents undoubtedly disagree over day-to-day issues, such as what time to be home at night, all the evidence indicates that on major questions the generations are comparatively closely in agreement. Evidence also shows that by and large adolescents look up to their parents, and respect their views. It seems most likely that the "generation gap" is true only of a small but vocal minority.

Genetic counseling As more and more is learned about the causes of disease it is becoming clear that many diseases have an inherited component to them. This varies from the very strong inherited component in, for example, *muscular dystrophy* or *hemophilia* to the less clear-cut but nevertheless definite inherited characteristics of, for example, *spina bifida.* It is possible to advise parents who have given birth to a child with one of these conditions of the likelihood of it recurring in subsequent pregnancies. Adults with a family history of a condition can be told the likelihood of the condition occurring at all in their children. This genetic counseling is of great value in assisting couples to plan their families, although advice for or against pregnancy is never offered.

German measles (in childhood) German measles (rubella) is a very mild viral illness that has so much in common with other mild infections that except in epidemics it is impossible to diagnose definitely without a blood test. Two-thirds of children who catch German measles show no symptoms of it, but nevertheless develop immunity to further attacks. This means that there is no way of knowing for sure whether, for example, a pregnant woman has had the disease in childhood without giving her a blood test.

After an incubation period of two to

three weeks, the child may be snuffy for a day and then develop tender *swollen glands*, about the size of peas, in the back of the neck and behind the ears. Two to three days later a red slightly raised rash appears on the face at first, which then spreads to the trunk, and rapidly fades. The child is usually not particularly ill, and it is rare for the temperature to rise above 101°F. *Immunization* is safe and gives good protection.

German measles (in pregnancy) If a woman contracts German measles (rubella) during pregnancy, the infection can pass to the unborn child. If this occurs early in the pregnancy, the child may be born with severe *deafness, mental retardation, spasticity*, impaired sight, heart, bone, or liver disease.

If the woman has been protected by a previous attack of German measles or by immunization, such damage does not occur, whether or not she is in contact with the disease in pregnancy. *See also* Cataract, Cystic fibrosis, Hole in the heart.

Glandular fever (infectious mononucleosis) This disease, which is more common in adolescence than in childhood, is thought to be due to a virus and takes many forms. The average incubation period is about ten days, but may be as long as six weeks. It may come on suddenly or slowly. Common forms that it may take are: a mild to severe sore throat; tender enlarged glands in the neck, armpits, and groins; a general feeling of being unwell and lethargic; a skin rash over the body. These symptoms may occur separately or in combination with each other.

Once the initial illness is over, full recovery may take some time, during which the patient is very easily tired and becomes lethargic, and prone to depression.

There is no specific treatment; the child should be kept comfortable and symptoms treated as they arise.

The illness can be diagnosed by blood tests.

Glue ears If a child has repeated attacks of *otitis media* that are not adequately treated, a glue-like fluid accumulates in the middle ear. This prevents the eardrum from vibrating properly, and interferes with the free movement of the chain of small bones in the ear. The child therefore becomes deaf.

In order to restore hearing, it may be necessary to drain the fluid out through an artificial hole in the eardrum by means of a small plastic tube (grommet).

Gonorrhea see Venereal diseases.

Growing pains Growth is not painful! Some children, however, do complain of recurrent pain in the limbs, in the absence of any demonstrable physical cause. They are often "highly strung" individuals, prone to other psychosomatic disorders such as recurrent stomachache, recurrent *vomiting*, and so on. They may have an allergic tendency, their *eczema* or *asthma* being particularly provoked by anxiety.

If this tendency is accepted as part of the child's personality, and he is helped to live with it, then its effect on his life will be diminished.

If, however, it provokes great anxiety in the parents, or an intensive search for a nonexistent physical cause, or if it is allowed to disrupt day-to-day activities, then the effects can be crippling.

Growth hormone deficiency Some very *short children* have failed to grow because, for some reason, the pituitary gland has failed to produce the hormone that stimulates growth.

If the height of these children is measured several times over a period of one or two years it will be found that not only are they short but the rate at which their height increases is very slow.

The pediatrician can then measure the amount of growth hormone in the blood, and if it is low or absent a course of injections and growth hormone will restore the normal rate of growth.

Unfortunately, at present, the only source of growth hormone is from the pituitary glands donated by people who die, so that the supply is limited. It is important to remember, however, that the majority of short children are perfectly normal and are not suffering from this problem.

Growth spurt During *puberty* the rate of physical growth increases so that the child becomes rapidly taller and heavier. This period is familiar to all parents as a time when clothes have to be replaced frequently.

In girls the spurt occurs early and is usually almost complete at the *menarche*, after which there is very little increase in height.

In boys the spurt occurs later, and the bodily changes of puberty, enlargement of the penis and scrotum and growth of body hair, are usually well under way before the onset of the spurt. Boys who go through puberty early will become temporarily very much taller and bigger than their contemporaries. Parents should make sure their child realizes that the differences are temporary, and that they will even out by the end of *adolescence*.

Guthrie test This is one method of screening babies of one to two weeks old for a rare condition, *phenylketonuria*. The test is simple, a spot of blood from the baby's heel is put onto blotting paper, and then tested to see whether it will nourish a particular germ in the laboratory (suggesting the presence of the disease if it does). The test is an effective way of screening large populations.

Handedness Most children begin to show a preference for using one hand rather than the other soon after their first birthday, and usually by the age of three this has developed into definite dominance; the child is either right- or left-handed. In some otherwise perfectly normal children the development of dominance may be delayed beyond this, and some use either hand equally well, remaining ambidextrous all their lives. *See also* Cross-laterality, Left-handedness.

Hay fever Hay fever is one of the group of allergic disorders that tends to run in families. It usually starts in late childhood or early *adolescence,* and the patient has often had *eczema* as a

baby and/or *asthma* as a young child. Attacks may be seasonal, usually reaching a peak in late spring and early summer, or may occur at any time during the year. They vary in severity from being a trivial nuisance to interfering substantially in the life of the patient.

During an attack a clear watery fluid streams continuously from the nose, and the patient sneezes frequently. His eyes may also be affected by irritation and continual watering.

There are now many medicines available either to treat the established attack or to prevent its onset, so that the condition can be controlled in most patients. If there is a definite cause for the attacks, contact with grass pollen for example, then a course of desensitizing injections may be helpful.

Head banging Some small children often bang their heads gently against their pillows before going to sleep; it seems to be a comforting sensation. However, repeated head banging against hard surfaces, such as floors, furniture, and walls, especially if this is not happening during a *temper tantrum*, is a sign of serious disturbance and distress, and professional help and advice should be sought.

Hearing This sense plays the major part in developing communication between people, as it enables us not only to receive the speech of others but also to monitor and perfect our own speech. It also plays a large role in helping us to learn about our environment and to orientate ourselves in space.

The ability to discriminate between sounds develops slowly. It is a gradual progression beginning with the mother's voice being recognized from all other sounds, moving on to the differences between voices of near relatives; familiar noises in the environment; and eventually ending with the complexity of different languages, different birdcalls, music, and in some even perfect pitch.

Similarly, response to sound becomes more subtle with age. The young baby awakened by his mother's voice will respond with a mass movement of his whole body and limbs, the older child with a smile.

Hearing tests Because of the importance of hearing in learning, and the disadvantages of undiagnosed *deafness*, it is very important that all children are checked periodically to make sure their hearing is normal.

No child is too young to have his hearing tested; if you hum softly to a newborn baby, he will stop fussing and be still for a few seconds if he can hear you. It is essential not only that the test is appropriate to the age and development of the child but that the response expected is also appropriate. For example, a three-month-old will quieten to a familiar soft noise close to and level with his ear; a six-month-old will turn his head to the same noise; a three-year-old will be able to perform some task such as putting a bead in a box each time he hears a soft buzzer; a six-year-old will tell you when he hears it.

Hemophilia This is an inherited disorder carried in the mother's chromosomes without affecting her, but which she passes on to half her

sons, who will show the symptoms of the disease. Half her daughters will carry the trait, as she does, without themselves having symptoms. Now that families are usually small, the proportions are approximate in any one family.

Boys with hemophilia are lacking in one of the factors necessary for blood to clot, so that once bleeding has started, often from a trivial wound, it does not stop. They are also prone to bleed from tooth sockets, into joints, and so on even if there is no obvious injury.

The missing factor can, fortunately, be purified from donor blood and can be given to the boys to control bleeding, either accidental or caused during surgery. There may still be a need for certain limitations on their life-style to minimize possible injury.

At present, however, many patients with hemophilia can lead a normal life and participate in sports, due to the availability of the missing protein in their blood which can be given on a regular prophylactic basis.

Hernia A hernia is the protrusion of some internal organ such as the gut through an opening in the wall of the cavity that should normally contain it.

HIATUS HERNIA is the protrusion of the upper part of the stomach through the diaphragm into the chest. The result of this is that the valve-like action of the diaphragm, which normally prevents food from passing back from the stomach into the gullet (esophagus), is lost, so that the child vomits. Although hiatus hernia is often detected during the first year of life, it may not be diagnosed until late childhood or even adulthood.

Hiatus hernia usually improves through nursing the child upright in a special chair and thickening the feedings, but occasionally an operation is necessary to keep the stomach in the abdomen.

UMBILICAL HERNIA The umbilicus, or belly button, represents the remains of the opening through which nourishment passed to the baby from the *placenta*. The hole may take some years to close completely, so that a hernia through it is common. Although it may look alarmingly distended when the child is crying, it is never painful, never bursts, never gets stuck, and almost always eventually closes on its own without treatment. Old-fashioned treatments are uncomfortable and may irritate the skin.

INGUINAL HERNIA This type of hernia can occur in either sex, but it is more common in boys, since the gut can pass more easily through the hole normally present through which the testes pass down into the scrotum (the bag hanging on either side of the penis). In the early stages the gut passes freely in and out, and the distended scrotum can be emptied by pushing the gut back into the abdomen. Commonly, however, there comes a time when the gut cannot be easily pushed back, and it is then in danger of dying because its blood supply may be cut off. An inguinal hernia should be operated on before it reaches this stage, since the operation is simple while the hole is still freely open. Any child, therefore, who is thought to have an inguinal hernia should be examined by a doctor, so that it can be treated early.

Hole in the heart This is the lay term used to cover all forms of congenital heart disease. Very early in pregnancy the baby's heart starts to develop from a simple tube, which becomes folded and divided until the mature heart is formed. This should have two pairs of separate chambers, each member of a pair being connected to the other by valved openings, and to the rest of the body by veins and arteries. There are many opportunities for defects to develop in this process either by chance or, for example, as a result of *German measles* infection in the early months. The different parts may become connected up wrong; openings that should have closed remain open, or those that should have opened remain closed. Despite the complexity of the process, congenital heart disease is rare, and many forms of it can now be treated successfully by surgery.

Homosexuality This means adult sexual relations with members of the same sex. It is not at all uncommon for parents to worry that their children will grow up to be homosexuals. In particular when boys become involved with what are traditionally considered feminine activities, such as cooking, dressmaking, and wearing jewelry, parents are likely to fear the worst. It is important to bear in mind that such interests in childhood bear virtually no relation to adult sexual adjustment. There is no obvious or easy answer to the question "why do people become homosexual?" It is almost certain that there are a number of different reasons, any combination of which might be relevant to one particular individual. Homosexuality is, however, highly unlikely to be the result of one particular experience in childhood, such as seduction by an older adult. It is much more likely to result from constitutional factors and/or circumstances in the family. Parents should certainly not worry about this before the child reaches adolescence. In *adolescence* itself transient homosexual experiences are common, especially in single-sex boarding schools, and again bear no relation to adult sexual behavior. Individuals who become homosexual in adulthood rarely become sure of their feelings until at least late adolescence.

Hormone A chemical produced by one of the specialized glands of the body (the endocrine glands), which then passes into the blood and influences the growth and function of other parts of the body. For example, growth hormone, produced in the pituitary gland deep within the skull, controls the rate at which a child grows.

Hydrocephaly (water on the brain) The brain is continuously bathed in a fluid that is produced in cavities inside it (the ventricles). The fluid passes out through small holes to the surface, where it is absorbed back into the bloodstream. If for some reason the balance is disturbed so that more fluid is produced than is absorbed, then it accumulates inside the ventricles, causing them to enlarge.

If this happens during infancy, before the skull bones have fused together, the head can enlarge by a considerable amount, but the brain is usually damaged by the pressure. Fortunately this can now be largely prevented by controlling the amount of fluid in the brain by means of artificial one-way valves, if necessary. *See also* Spina bifida.

Hyperactivity Very many healthy normal children are very active, restless, and easily bored, yet they are clearly interested in certain activities or games that may keep them occupied for a short while. Hyperactivity refers to a psychiatric condition in which a child is extremely overactive; he is unable to sit still for even a few minutes, requires very little sleep, shows little interest in any activity, and can usually be easily distracted by even the slightest noise. Normally this condition is present from an early age and seriously affects the child's performance at school. Hyperactivity is more common in boys than in girls, is often associated with slower-than-average development, and may be related to some form of brain damage. These children require psychiatric attention. Often the problem can be helped with drugs or by *behavior therapy* that attempts to give the parents some control over the child's behavior.

Hysteria The mind and body are so intimately linked that it is not surprising that situations that cause worry and anxiety can lead to physical symptoms in the absence of actual physical disorder. The symptom produced, the hysterical symptom, usually makes it impossible for the patient to take part in the situation that has caused the anxiety. For example, a child who is having learning difficulties at school, or who is unable to satisfy the expectations of his teachers or parents, may develop hysterical blindness.

It is of course essential to be absolutely sure that the symptom does not have a physical cause. Both doctor and parents should be aware of the cause of anxiety, because only by dealing with this can they help the child to overcome the hysteria, and thus cure the symptoms.

Identification A term used to describe the process by which a child incorporates the values and attitudes of his parents. It is used in particular to apply to the development of conscience and attitudes concerning sex roles. Recent research has shown that the more positive the relationship between parent and child, the greater the degree of identification. *See also* Psychoanalysis.

Identity crisis The writer Erik Erikson has suggested that adolescents, especially those between the ages of sixteen and twenty, are likely to have a period of acute difficulty relating to questions such as "Who am I?" and "Who will I become?" Erikson believes that the crisis occurs as a result of the necessity at this stage to take major life decisions in jobs, relationships, beliefs, etc. Although research shows that this might occur in some young people, it seems probable that they will be in the

minority. The biggest change in young people's self-concept is likely to occur much earlier, say between eleven and thirteen, as a result of *puberty*.

Immunization When the body is invaded by an organism it reacts by producing antibodies, which fight off the disease. Immunization is the process of giving a child a minute dose of the responsible germ or one related to it, or of the poison (toxin) that it produces. This causes his body to produce the antibodies, but the dose is not enough to cause the disease itself. The potential for producing the antibodies remains in his bloodstream and protects him against any new infection for a period afterward.

It is recommended that a child should be immunized against *diphtheria, tetanus, whooping cough, polio* (poliomyelitis), *measles,* tuberculosis, and *German measles* (rubella), and your doctor will schedule your child's shots.

Immunization against diphtheria, tetanus, and polio is harmless, and gives long-lasting protection against organisms which are still widespread in the environment and which are crippling killers. This is particularly so if the immunization is boosted at three-to five-year intervals.

Measles immunization usually causes no upset at all, but may produce a very mild measles-like illness. It gives good protection against a disease which is often severe, and which may cause permanent damage to brain, ears, and lungs.

Immunization against tuberculosis is usually offered to children of about eleven to twelve years who have been shown, by a skin test, to be susceptible to the disease. If there is a family history of TB, BCG vaccine may be offered in the newborn period.

German measles immunization is usually offered to prepubertal girls, regardless of whether or not they have a history of the illness. German measles is a mild illness unless it is caught during early pregnancy, when it can cause devastating handicap to the unborn child. Immunization is also offered to women of childbearing age who have been shown by a blood test to be susceptible to the disease.

Smallpox vaccination is no longer recommended unless there is an outbreak of the disease or the child is traveling to an area where the disease still occurs. It is dangerous to give smallpox vaccination to a child subject to *eczema,* or to allow such a child to come into contact with a recently vaccinated person, as a generalized skin infection may ensue.

Finally, there is the question of whooping cough (pertussis) immunization. The disease itself can be severe, especially in the first year of life, and is always distressing. Immunization does not afford complete protection, and, unfortunately, in a small number of children it may cause brain damage. Certain children are more likely to react than others. Those who have a brain disorder (such as *cerebral palsy* or *hydrocephaly*), who have had *fits* or *convulsions* of any sort at any time, or who have had a reaction to a previous immunization should not be immunized against whooping cough.

Impetigo An infection of the skin,

usually by the germ known as the staphylococcus. It enters the skin through small cuts or grazes, causing widespread weeping sores that crust over. It is extremely contagious, spreading easily from child to child, and so needs urgent treatment from a doctor. He will usually recommend scrupulous cleanliness and will often prescribe an antibiotic cream. In some cases, antibiotics by mouth are necessary.

Incubation period After coming into contact with an infectious disease, there is a time lag, usually of several days, known as the incubation period, before the symptoms of the disease appear.

Induction of labor If it becomes clear that the baby's well-being will be at risk if the pregnancy is allowed to continue, and if he is mature enough to survive independently, then labor can be started (induced) by several means.

Usually, the bag of water surrounding the baby is broken deliberately, and injections of certain hormones are given to encourage the womb to contract. Once labor has been started by this means, it usually then proceeds normally.

In recent years it has become fashionable to induce labor at the calculated full term, even if the baby is apparently doing well, in order that the labor can be conducted when most facilities are available. This has been done although there have recently been suggestions that an induced labor is more painful, more likely to need the aid of forceps, and more likely to produce a distressed baby.

Infectious diseases see Chicken pox, Diphtheria, Flu, German measles, Measles, Mumps, Polio, Scarlet fever, Whooping cough.

Influenza see Flu.

Inherited abnormality An abnormality that is passed down from one or both parents. One or both of them may show the same abnormality, for example, some forms of *cataract* ; both parents may carry the tendency without showing the abnormality themselves, for example *cystic fibrosis* ; or it may be carried by the mother and only passed on to the sons, for example *hemophilia*.

The abnormalities may be congenital, or they may appear later in life, for example *muscular dystrophy*.

Insect stings and bites *see* pages 202–3.

Introversion Introversion-extraversion is a personality dimension that has been given prominence by Professor Eysenck of the University of London. People who are high on extraversion tend to be sociable, have many friends, and need people to talk to; they crave excitement, take chances, and are impulsive. Introverts tend to be quiet, retiring, have fewer friends, and mistrust impulsiveness or emotional expressiveness.

IQ is a measure of intellectual performance that is derived from comparing a person's score on an intelligence test with the scores obtained by a large number of similar people. An IQ in excess of 100 indicates that the person's intellectual performance is greater than the average for people of his age, whereas an IQ below 100 indicates that the score is lower than average. An intelligence test should only be given by a qualified person (for example, a *psychologist*) and the scores should not be seen as absolute; an adult's score may vary by five to ten points on two occasions and a child's IQ may change considerably as he grows older. Although intelligence is obviously important in determining how well a child does at school, it is by no means the only determining factor; his interest in his schoolwork and the encouragement he receives at school and at home play a very important role. The results of an intelligence test are particularly useful when a child is performing poorly at school. Often the results suggest that the child may benefit from a different type of teaching environment or that his performance is being hampered by emotional difficulties that may require separate attention.

Jaundice (in childhood) Yellow discoloration of the skin because of an excessive amount of the dye bilirubin in the tissues is an indication that either there is some disorder or infection of the liver or that for some reason the red cells of the blood are being broken down in greater numbers than usual. Either way, the child should be seen urgently by a doctor.

Jaundice in the newborn (neonatal jaundice) When a baby is born, his system has to take over, at very short notice, all the work of absorbing oxygen and nourishment, and getting rid of waste products, which had previously been done by his mother via the *placenta*.

The liver is the organ mainly concerned with breaking down waste products, so that they may be more easily disposed of. At birth the liver is immature, and may take two or three days before it can cope sufficiently. This delay may be increased if the baby is born prematurely. One of the waste products that builds up during this period is bilirubin, a dye that is released during the natural breakdown of red blood cells and which causes the yellow coloration of the skin in jaundice. In most babies, the liver takes over and eliminates the bilirubin before it reaches dangerous levels, and this can also be helped by photo-therapy. In some babies, however, if there is an increased breakdown of blood cells because of, for example, infection or blood group problems, it may be necessary to exchange the baby's blood for nonjaundiced donor blood. Excessive jaundice in the newborn can cause damage to parts of the brain, leading to *cerebral palsy* and fits.

Jealousy Jealousy is a normal emotion in situations where children have been displaced in their parents' affection, where they have had to make way for the arrival of a new sibling or where they have lost possessions or status to another child. Adults who are understanding can almost always compensate children in such circumstances. For example, after the birth of a new baby an older child can be given new privileges, and parents can make sure that this child has a "special time" of his own when he can

have the undivided attention of mother or father. Plans such as this can usually prevent the development of unmanageable jealousy. Remember that it is very much easier to prevent something arising in the first place than it is to stop it once it has got under way.

Knock-knees Many children have an inward curvature of the legs at the knees, often to such an extent that their knees sometimes knock together when they walk. This will disappear with growth and requires no treatment.

Laxatives Laxatives are very occasionally necessary for the treatment of true *constipation*. The regular use of these drugs to "keep the bowel regular," "to clean out the system," or for any other similar nonsensical reason is both unnecessary and potentially dangerous.

Lazy eye If a young child *squints* continuously, the confusion of seeing different images with each eye may be resolved by unconsciously suppressing the image from one eye, which then becomes "lazy," and may suffer a permanent loss of vision. To prevent this, a patch is worn over the good eye to force the lazy eye to work. It is essential that this treatment is only carried out under the supervision of an eye specialist.

Lead poisoning Lead is a poison which, if absorbed into the blood-stream, causes widespread problems in many organs. Its effect on the brain may range from irritability and hyperactivity to *convulsions,* coma, and death. It can cause profound *anemia,* and is deposited in bone.

The two main sources of lead poisoning in children are exhaust fumes of vehicles using lead-containing fuels and eating flakes of lead-containing paint. These paints are particularly found in old buildings, and attention to the interior and exterior paintwork of such buildings is mandatory if children are in the neighborhood. Be very careful with secondhand or handed-down toys that may once have been treated with lead paint.

Children with lead poisoning can be treated by giving them chemicals that combine with the lead and carry it out of the body in the urine. This treatment must of course be under the supervision of a doctor.

Left-handedness It is perfectly normal to be left-handed, and most left-handers develop tricks for over-coming the difficulties of living in a right-handed world. Difficulties arise only when an attempt is made to force a natural left-hander to become right-handed, causing confusion of left and right, poor performance with either hand, and possibly contributing to later learning problems. The problems of a left-hander are lessened if he is given implements designed for left-handers. Left-handedness often runs in families.

Leukemia A condition in which the bone marrow, instead of producing normal red and white blood cells, produces large numbers of an abnormal blood cell, which are not

able to take on the function of the normal cells they displace. The child therefore becomes anemic, unable to resist or fight infection, and tends to bruise and bleed easily.

Although this is an extremely serious disease that has by no means been conquered yet, treatment is improving all the time, and the marrow can usually be made to return to normal, sometimes for as long as five or ten years, with an occasional complete recovery.

Lice *see* Nits.

Lisp A speech defect caused by protruding the tongue through the teeth when attempting to pronounce "s," so that it becomes "th."

If this persists after the permanent (second) front teeth have grown, then the child should be examined by a speech therapist in case treatment is necessary.

Lockjaw *see* Tetanus.

Lying When a child tells a lie it is important to distinguish between a number of different types of behavior. In the first place it is quite common for younger children, particularly during the preschool years, to indulge in vivid storytelling where their own feats and activities are concerned. It will often seem that this involves a failure to distinguish between fantasy and reality, and parents should not worry about it. As the child grows older this stage will disappear.

Secondly, all older children tell some lies, but then so do adults. Trying to avoid blame, to deny wrongdoing, or to protect the feelings of others (so-called white lies) are distortions of truth we all become involved in at some time or other.

However, the third type of lying, often called pathological lying, is very different in its extent and implications. Such a term can only be applied to older children, and refers to a process whereby the individual gradually gets more and more entangled in a web of untruth. These children are not hard to spot. They will almost certainly be exhibiting other problems, and are distinguished by a painful inability to tell the truth, even about the simplest matters. Such behavior is almost always the result of the child's attempts to deal with overwhelming anxieties of some sort, and in these cases professional help should be sought.

Maternal deprivation In the past much emphasis has been placed on the importance of the mother/child relationship in the first five years of the child's life. Mothers were advised against working, putting their children in day nurseries, or leaving their child at all in the care of others; it was thought that any of the foregoing led to emotional disturbance and subsequent delinquency.

Recent research has shown that who looks after a child is unimportant: it does not have to be a blood-relation for instance. What is important is the quality of the care received by the child; this should be warm, under-standing, and consistent. A child may be deprived of this warmth, understanding, and consistency in his home because of family arguments, tension, and disharmony perhaps

preceding a divorce; and it is being in this situation that can be subsequently harmful, resulting in the child's social withdrawal, possible delayed intellectual development, and distorted emotional development.

In such situations good, stable care of the child outside the home is infinitely preferable.

Measles A highly infectious viral illness caught by inhaling the virus that has been breathed out into the air surrounding an infected person. About ninety percent of children who have neither had measles nor been immunized against it will catch it if they come into contact with an infected person. The incubation period is nine to ten days, and the patient is infectious from the beginning of symptoms until about five days after the appearance of the rash.

Measles is often not diagnosed during the initial stage (the prodromal phase) because the symptoms are so general. The child becomes rather unwell with a slight fever, a runny nose, and a cough. He also usually has *conjunctivitis,* and will object to bright lights. Raised red spots appear on the lining of the mouth, and after two or three days some of these, particularly in the cheek opposite the back teeth, develop small white centers rather like a grain of salt. These Koplik spots are seen only in measles.

About five days after the start of the prodromal phase, the temperature suddenly rises to 102–104°F, and the typical red, slightly raised rash of measles appears, at first on the face and neck, and then spreading over the course of five or six days to the body and then the limbs. As it reaches the feet, the rash begins to fade, again from the head downward, leaving a brown discoloration that fades in about a fortnight.

During the prodromal phase, the child is usually not particularly ill, although the cough may be trouble-some. During the first few days of the rash, however, he may be quite ill, and may want to stay in bed in a quiet room. It is important that he is given plenty to drink, but it does not matter if he does not feel like eating over this short period. He should be kept cool, and if necessary sponged down with tepid water (particularly if he is subject to *fever fits*). After two or three days, during which he may be quite ill, the child usually recovers rapidly over the next twenty-four hours.

The most serious, and the commonest, complications of measles are *pneumonia* and *otitis media*.

Immunization is safe and gives good protection.

Meatal ulcer If the tip of the penis has lost its protective foreskin by circumcision, an ulcer may develop around the urinary opening (the meatus) which may completely obstruct the flow of urine. This is rare but particularly likely to happen to babies still in wet diapers.

Menarche This term refers to the appearance of the first menstrual period in a girl at *puberty*. This normally occurs between the ages of nine and sixteen, and while its appearance outside this age range may still be normal, it is worth having this checked by a doctor. Once menarche has occurred, the girl does not usually grow very much taller.

Meningitis The brain and spinal cord are entirely covered by a fine sheet of tissue, the meninges. Meningitis is the infection of this layer by a virus or bacterium.

The child with meningitis generally looks ill, may complain of a headache, and may vomit. He may be intolerant of bright light (photophobic). His neck will be stiff and he may resent movement. Meningitis may follow closely on another infection such as *otitis media ;* or it may occur alone.

It is a serious illness, which usually responds well to treatment, but can cause permanent disability or death if left untreated. Urgent medical attention is essential for a child thought to have meningitis.

Menstruation For a young girl to find, suddenly, and for no apparent reason, that she is bleeding is very frightening, and may color her whole attitude to menstruation (periods) for the rest of her life. It is absolutely essential therefore that the process is explained to her well before its onset.

She must know that this is something that happens to all girls, and means that she is growing into a young woman, whose body is gradually preparing itself for the time when she may bear children of her own. She should be shown ways of coping with the bleeding by pads or tampons. If the whole exercise is conducted calmly and in a matter-of-fact way, she will be less likely to experience discomfort, though some girls do experience cramps, headache, and lassitude. It is important not to convey the notion, however, that periods are normally a time of trouble and distress.

General cleanliness during a menstrual period should be encouraged. Bathing and swimming are in no way dangerous.

Mental retardation There is a wide range of intellectual ability among normal children, from extremely bright to dull but competent. There is, however, a small group of children whose intellect is such that they are unable to cope adequately with the normal requirements of everyday life, and who can be said to be mentally retarded.

Such retardation may occur in an otherwise fit child, or may be associated with physical abnormalities. Sometimes the cause of the retardation is known, for example in *Down's syndrome,* but usually it is quite obscure.

Much can be done by teaching these children skills appropriate to their intellectual abilities, to enable them to achieve their potential. Some are able to live a more or less independent life with a minimum of supervision, but most require fully supervised care. *See also* Cretinism, German measles (in pregnancy), Hydrocephaly, Microcephaly.

Microcephaly As the brain grows in size, so the skull enlarges to accommodate it. If the brain is so grossly malformed or damaged that it fails to grow, then the skull and hence the head will remain small. Because the brain in children suffering from this condition is not properly grown, they are almost always mentally

retarded, and often have *cerebral palsy.* They are said to be microcephalic (small-headed).

Migraine Migraine is rare in children, but does occur. There is often a personal or family history of one of the allergic disorders such as *asthma* or *hay fever.*

The main feature of migraine is the headache, which may or may not be confined to one side of the head.

Often the patient has warning before an attack, in the form of flashing lights or other visual disturbances. *Abdominal pain* and *vomiting* are common, and may occur without the headache.

Treatment depends on the degree of disruption the attacks cause to the patient's life. Mild attacks can often be ignored ; some only respond to a complete rest in a darkened room, others to a mild analgesic.

Medicines are available which can prevent attacks or minimize their seriousness.

Miscarriage Some pregnancies do not continue long enough for the unborn child to mature sufficiently to be capable of an independent existence outside the womb. The fetus and the *placenta* then pass out from the womb, usually with some bleeding, resembling a heavy period. The reason for this is often unknown, but sometimes the baby has many abnormalities incompatible with continued life, or it may be that the hormones circulating in the mother's body are insufficient to maintain the pregnancy.

Except for the recognition that sexual intercourse is unwise during the first three months of pregnancy if there have been previous miscarriages, particularly around the time when the period would have been due, it is unlikely that any unwitting action by the mother will cause her to miscarry.

Mongolism see Down's syndrome.

Mononucleosis, infectious see Glandular fever.

Morning sickness It is common, in the early months of pregnancy, for women to feel nauseated, or even to vomit a little. This usually occurs in the morning, but can crop up at any time of the day. It can often be prevented by a light snack, such as a cup of tea and a cracker, before getting up. It is very important that no drugs are taken to combat it without the advice of a doctor, because some antivomiting drugs, although perfectly safe for adults, may harm the developing fetus.

In a few cases, *vomiting* becomes so severe that it interferes with the mother's nutrition, and also that of her baby. This requires treatment, usually in a hospital, under close medical supervision.

Mumps A common virus infection spread by droplets of saliva in the air and by contact with materials such as clothing which have been contaminated by infected saliva. The virus usually enters the body through the lining (mucous membrane) of the mouth, nose, or throat, and is then spread throughout the body by the bloodstream. The incubation period is two to three weeks.

By far the commonest form of mumps is swelling of one or both

parotid glands (the saliva-producing glands in the cheek), but the other salivary glands in the floor of the mouth and under the jawbone may also be affected, either on their own or in addition to the parotids. Rarely, other glands in the body are affected.

Sometimes there is a short period (about a day) during which the child is unwell and snuffly. The child may have a slight *fever.* The swelling of the glands is often the first sign of the disease. If both parotids are involved, one often swells two to three days before the other. The swollen glands are often tender, and attempts to eat or drink acidic foods such as fruit juices may make them painful.

The swelling usually subsides over the course of a week to ten days. The length of time during which the child is infectious varies, but is usually a day or two before the swelling appears and lasts for four or five days afterward. Only about a quarter of the people who catch mumps show symptoms ; the rest develop immunity to further attacks without themselves being ill.

If a boy catches mumps after *puberty,* the testicles may be affected and become swollen and painful. This, however, does not affect fertility.

There is no specific treatment for mumps. The child should be given plenty to drink, and initially at least will probably prefer bland foods. The American Academy of Pediatrics suggests that children be immunized against mumps at 15 months.

Muscular dystrophy This is an inherited disorder that is carried in the chromosomes of the mother without affecting her, but which will affect about half her sons.

The affected boy is usually normal at birth, but in later childhood his muscles gradually begin to lose their function, usually starting with the muscles that control the hip and shoulder joints. Movements become progressively weaker, until he becomes dependent on a wheelchair. He usually develops curvature of the spine because of the weak back muscles. These boys tend to die in their late teens or early twenties.

Although there is no cure for this condition, much can be done to lessen the emotional and physical stress on the child and his family.

Nail-biting results from tension and is common among high-strung children. It is not something to be taken too seriously in a well-adjusted and happy child. Nail-biting cannot be cured by nagging or punishment because the nail-biter is usually unaware of what he is doing. Bitter aloes on the nails are rarely effective. Instead try to find and remove the causes of anxiety. Ask yourself if you are asking too much of your child at school, if you are being too strict, or if the influence of a particular program on television is the cause. Ask his teacher if he is happy at school. Among older children an appeal to their vanity may be effective.

Nightmares Nightmares are quite common in children of all ages, but particularly between the ages of four to six and later around ten to twelve. Occasional nightmares need not alarm

the parents, but if they are more frequent, or more severe, they may cause the child considerable anxiety and lead to additional problems such as unwillingness to go to bed or to repeated attempts to sleep with his parents. Nightmares frequently occur following a stressful or disruptive episode in the child's life such as moving or changing schools, and often recur during illness. Many parents consult their doctor if their child is having frequent nightmares. In severe cases child psychotherapy will elicit the child's underlying anxieties.

Nits These are the eggs of the head louse (pediculus), which infests the hair of the scalp. The louse lives on blood that it sucks up from the skin of the scalp. The bites are very itchy, and scratching them may spread infection all over the scalp. The eggs that the lice lay become glued onto the hair and remain there until they develop into mature lice over a period of two to three weeks. The lice are spread from person to person by direct contact with infested hair, so if one person in your family is affected, every other member must be examined.

The infestation is most effectively treated by combing the lice and nits out of the hair with a fine-toothed comb after they have been loosened by a special shampoo obtainable from a drugstore.

Not only dirty, "unhygienic" people suffer from lice ; anyone can catch them. There is nothing to be ashamed of, and treatment is simple and effective, although it may need to be repeated if the original patient is not treated.

Nocturnal emissions At the beginning of *puberty* when the boy's testicles begin to produce semen, it is very common for it to pass out of the penis in an involuntary emission. This is particularly likely to happen during sleep. It is an entirely normal, almost universal occurrence and has no significance whatsoever other than signifying the child has reached puberty.

Nonaccidental injury One of the most distressing problems in pediatrics is the care of children whose disabilities are the direct result of the deliberate actions of their parents or other guardians. The forms that this problem takes vary from the child who fails to thrive because of neglect and emotional deprivation to the one with multiple fractures caused by direct physical violence. The latter is now one of the commoner causes of death in childhood.

The parents of the injured child were often emotionally deprived in childhood, and many were battered. Opportunities for bonding between mother and child have often been limited by illness of one or the other, particularly if this has caused separation in the first few days after birth. Children who are unable to respond to their parents' needs because of mental or physical handicap may also be subjected to abuse.

Much can be done to prevent this problem by, for example, more enlightened policies in maternity wards : allowing immediate contact between mother and baby at birth ; rooming in (allowing the baby to be cared for in the same room as the mother); and letting mothers handle their sick infants in special-care nurseries. A more sympathetic, supportive management of families with handicapped children would also help. It is necessary that parents who know they need assistance should be able to get it, immediately and easily. Once the problem is recognized, it can often be reversed by intense supportive work with the parents by, for example, social workers. Occasionally, however, the family environment is so damaged that the child has to be taken away, either temporarily or permanently. *See also* Maternal deprivation.

Normal development Normal, healthy children vary widely in their physical and intellectual development. When deciding whether or not a given characteristic in a particular child, such as height, weight, and reading ability, is within the normal range, it is necessary to take into account not only his age but also the family characteristics; a short child with short parents is less likely to be abnormal than a short child born to six-footers.

In deciding whether a child is outside the normal range of development, doctors use charts and tables based on the measurement of hundreds, often thousands, of children. It is very important that these are relevant to the child in question; for example, tables based on measuring girls may not apply to boys, those based on children born in London may not apply to children born in Texas.

The rate at which a child develops over a period is of far greater interest and importance than his actual development on a single occasion; if this proceeds in parallel with his peers, he is less likely to be abnormal than if the rate becomes slower and slower as time goes on. *See also* Deafness, Hearing, Short children, Tall children, Thin children, Walking.

Nosebleeds Most nosebleeds stop of their own accord, but if not then refer to pages 202–3 for treatment.

Frequent nosebleeds may be caused by the breaking of a small vein on the surface of the nasal lining, and this may require treatment from a doctor. If much blood has run down the back of the nose and been swallowed, it may be vomited later, or it may pass through the gut and be excreted as a black tarlike stool two to three days later.

Obesity This is the commonest form of malnourishment in children in developed countries, and is caused by eating too much of the wrong sort of foods. The body requires food to provide energy, but if it consumes more than it needs, the body converts it into fat. Therefore proteins (meat, fish, eggs, etc.), fats, and carbohydrates (sugars and starches), which all provide energy, are all potentially fattening. There is no such thing as a slimming food! However, because protein is expensive, and a lot of fat is difficult to stomach, carbohydrate is the food mainly responsible for obesity, particularly in children who are allowed unlimited access to candy, cookies, and cakes between meals.

The best treatment is prevention, by instilling in the child regular habits of eating a balanced diet at mealtimes with no intervening snacks. If, however, your child does become fat, you can solve the problem only by making him stick to a balanced diet of restricted amounts of food at all times, including vacations and holidays. A diet like this is best carried out under the supervision of your doctor or a dietitian, but your complete co-operation as parents is essential.

Uncontrolled obesity can decrease a person's life span by up to thirty years or more, and contributes to heart, lung, and joint diseases. It makes any necessary operations much more difficult, and may interfere with recovery from them. An obese person is also much more accident-prone than a thin one. It is therefore irresponsible not to do everything possible to control or, better, prevent obesity in children.

Oedipal conflict *see* Psychoanalysis.

Otitis externa This is an infection or inflammation of the skin of the outer *ear*. It is usually very itchy, and may be painful. Treatment with local ointments or lotions is sometimes needed, and this should be supervised by your doctor.

Otitis media This condition, infection of the middle *ear,* occurs either as part of a general *upper respiratory tract infection* or as the result of stagnation of fluid within the ear. This is caused by a blockage of the Eustachian tubes, which normally drain fluid away from the ears and regulate the ear pressure to that of the atmosphere.

A child with otitis media will be generally unwell and usually have a high *fever,* and may vomit. He may or may not complain of *earache,* but may indicate this by holding his ear.

If this condition is not treated promptly, pressure may build up in the middle ear with increasing pain until the eardrum bursts, so always call the doctor if in doubt.

It is essential that all attacks of otitis media are treated adequately, and in particular that the full course of antibiotics is given exactly as instructed, and not stopped after a few days if the child seems better, because repeated attacks of inadequately treated otitis media can be damaging. *See also* Catarrh, Deafness, Glue ears, Meningitis.

Partial sight Many visually handi-capped people have sufficient vision for learning or working, provided they can use special aids such as large print or magnifying glasses. Such partially sighted children can often cope in an ordinary school with sympathetic help. *See also* Blindness.

Peanuts Peanut oil is an irritant, which, if inhaled into the lungs, causes a dangerous and extensive inflammatory reaction. If, therefore, a child chokes while eating peanuts it should be assumed that he has inhaled some peanut oil. This should be regarded as an emergency and he should be taken immediately to an emergency room.

Although it would be unreasonable to forbid children to eat peanuts, except when they are very young, the habit of tossing peanuts in the air and catching them in the mouth is particularly liable to result in inhalation and should be discouraged. It is as well to avoid cooking children's food in peanut oil.

Peer group This term is used to refer to the child's contemporaries—those of the same age with whom he associates either at school or in social activities at home. It is usually assumed that the peer group has a very powerful influence upon the development of the child. There are three reasons for this. First, the peer group provides social experience outside the home and acts as an introduction to the world at large. Second, it contains a range of individuals from which the child may choose his or her own close friends, and, third, it represents a set of values that are not always in accord with those held by the parents, thus allowing the child to compare different points of view. While it is sometimes believed that the peer group acts in opposition to the parents, especially during *adolescence,* research does not support this view. By and large teenagers appear to choose friends whose values are in agreement with those of their parents, and where this does not happen it is usually because the parents have opted out.

Pets Pets are a great asset to the development of the growing child as they encourage responsibility and a sense of caring for others. They are, however, also a potential source of danger, because they may harbor disease-producing creatures, ranging from the relatively harmless pin-worm to germs and parasites, such as toxocara, which is capable of causing *blindness.*

To minimize the hazards, pets should be examined by a veterinarian and given any necessary treatment and immunizations at regular intervals. A sick animal in contact with children must be treated promptly. Animals should never be allowed to lick children's faces, and the "swapping" of food should be firmly discouraged at once.

Phenylketonuria (PKU) A condition affecting about one in 10,000 babies, in which the child is unable to break down certain constituents of the proteins in the diet. This causes them to build up to toxic levels in the blood and brain, and results in *fits* and severe *mental retardation.* It can be treated effectively by a controlled diet and is easily detected by the Guthrie test, which is performed in the nurseries of most hospitals in the USA.

Phototherapy Following the chance observation that exposure to sunlight caused the jaundice to fade from blood samples left on a laboratory window-sill, treatment with light (photo-therapy) is now used extensively in hospitals to lessen *jaundice in the newborn.*

Pigeon toes This condition may be due to several causes, but it always improves with the child's growth and does not need treatment. Pigeon toes are caused by: inward turning of the front half of the feet (this is so common that it must be regarded as normal—indeed most infant shoes are made to hold the foot in this position); inward rotation of the shinbone; or inward rotation of the thighbone, which may not completely straighten with growth, but its persistence into adulthood does not cause trouble. Several world-class athletes have this condition.

PKU *see* Phenylketonuria (PKU).

Placenta An organ developed from part of the fertilized egg, and therefore part of the developing baby, which becomes very closely and firmly stuck to the wall of the womb. It is very richly supplied with blood, and through it nourishment passes from the mother to the baby and waste products from the baby to the mother.

If for any reason *(smoking, toxemia)* the placenta becomes inefficient, then the baby is malnourished.

After the birth of the baby, the placenta is expelled as the afterbirth. Occasionally the placenta is "retained" in the womb after the birth of the baby. It may then have to be removed by the obstetrician.

Placenta previa If the *placenta* attaches itself to the womb in such a position that it covers the exit from the womb, then as this hole begins to enlarge, in the latter part of the pregnancy, part of the placenta may separate, and the woman will bleed. If this occurs, she should seek immediate advice from her doctor.

With the placenta in this position it is impossible for the baby to be delivered normally through the vagina, so that a *Caesarean section* becomes essential.

If a woman has had one placenta previa, there is no reason to suppose that it will recur in subsequent pregnancies.

Pneumonia Pneumonia is caused by infection of the lungs by *bacteria* or *viruses.* The child with pneumonia will be ill and feverish, often with a high *fever* up to 103–104°F. The diagnosis is usually confirmed by an X ray of the chest. He may be irrational at the height of the fever, and will have a cough that may be dry or may produce sputum.

In the early stages the child will probably wish to be quiet, in bed. He should be kept cool (sponging with tepid water may help) and be given plenty to drink; he will probably not eat much at this stage.

Treatment should always be under the supervision of a doctor, and may require admission to a hospital. Exercises (physiotherapy) may be given to drain fluid from the lungs, and, in bacterial pneumonia, antibiotics may be necessary.

With proper treatment complete recovery is the rule.

Polio (poliomyelitis) A *virus* infection that, so far as is known, only attacks man. In the days before *immunization* was possible, it used to occur in epidemics in the summer and early autumn. The old name of infantile paralysis is a misnomer, as people of any age can be affected.

The severity of the illness varies. Most people infected show no sign of any illness at all, or else have a mild *upper respiratory tract infection.* At the other end of the scale, infection can result in rapidly increasing total paralysis and death.

Immunization against the disease is safe and gives excellent protection. In the past Salk injections were used. These are not very effective and any adult who was immunized by injection against polio would be advised to have a re-immunization with the Sabin oral vaccine.

Port-wine stains Areas of skin that have a deep red or purple coloring and are usually flat. However, some port-wine stains may have a nubbly surface. This is the least common but most serious type of *birthmark*, as it can be disfiguring and it does not fade away.

Preeclamptic toxemia *see* Toxemia of pregnancy.

Pregnancy, complications of *see* Bleeding (in pregnancy), German measles (in pregnancy), Miscarriage, Placenta previa, Rhesus factor, Small-for-dates, Smoking (in pregnancy), Stillbirth, Toxemia of pregnancy.

Pregnancy, normal Pregnancy is a normal event, and there is no reason why a woman should not be perfectly healthy throughout. On average, pregnancy lasts for forty weeks from the first day of the last menstrual period (LMP), so the expected date of delivery (EDD) can be easily calculated.

During the pregnancy the mother's gain in weight will be the combination of the weight of the baby, the fluid in which he is cushioned, the enlarging womb, and the extra volume of blood that is produced—in all usually about 20–25 lb/10–12 kg.

The nipples darken in color and the breasts increase in size and become firmer. In the latter half of pregnancy, small amounts of *colostrum* may leak from the nipples. In some women the skin of the forehead, cheeks, and nose becomes darker—the so-called mask of pregnancy.

The pressure of the growing womb on the bladder makes it necessary to pass urine more frequently. As the womb grows up out of the pelvis, the woman's girth increases.

Because of the demands that the baby makes on the mother's body, it is usually necessary to take extra iron and vitamins throughout pregnancy. It is not, however, necessary to "eat for two," since this only leads to *obesity,* which is difficult to get rid of after the pregnancy. Regular visits to the doctor throughout the pregnancy, and strict adherence to the advice given, are the best ways for both mother and baby to remain healthy. *See also* Colostrum, Induced labor, Morning sickness, Placenta, Quickening.

Psychiatrist A medical doctor who specializes in the diagnosis and treatment of mental disorders. Patients are usually treated by medication or psychotherapy. Psychiatrists usually work in private offices or in hospitals or mental health clinics.

Psychoanalysis One of the most influential theories of personality development is that of Sigmund Freud. From the reports of patients undergoing psychoanalysis, Freud speculated that the young child passes through three stages of development during which environmental events can exert an enduring effect on his later personality. These stages—the oral, anal, and genital—correspond with the areas of his body with which the child is particularly concerned at that period in his life.

During the oral stage, the child's primary source of gratification and interest is centered on his mouth. His experiences at his mother's breast are considered to be of fundamental importance for his later personality. His feelings of security and dependency are considered to be related to his experiences in this early period of his life, and how early and suddenly weaning takes place is thought to be crucial.

Later, the child's interest moves from his mouth to his anus as he learns that he can control his bowel movements. Despite his mother's efforts, he can defiantly retain his feces if he wishes. It is considered that personality traits such as obstinacy, meanness, and obsessiveness may relate to experiences during the anal stage. Consequently, the manner in which the child was toilet trained is of considerable interest to psychoanalysts.

During the final stage the child's genitals become his focus of interest. Both boys and girls discover that they can be the source of pleasurable sensations. Freud argued that during this stage a boy develops very possessive sexual feelings toward his mother and sees his father as his rival. His jealousy of his father, combined with his fear of his father's considerably greater strength and power, produces the *Oedipal conflict.* Freud argues that the child may resolve this conflict and cope with the anxieties it creates by identifying with his father and by accepting for himself his father's attitudes and values. Through this process the child's conscience or superego develops.

If a child experiences a traumatic event during these vulnerable early years, the anxiety created may be stored up in the child's unconscious mind to appear as a symptom in later life.

Although it is now many years since Freud's theories appeared, his work is still the center of considerable controversy. His ideas are very difficult to examine experimentally. Psychoanalysis, the attempt to give the patient insight into the early origins of his emotional problems, is a very time-consuming and costly treatment, and its efficacy has not been clearly established. Nevertheless many present-day theories of psychopathology and treatments are founded on Freud's views.

Psychologist A psychologist has an academic training in the science of human and animal behavior. He may work in a private office, or in hospitals, schools, industry, or other agencies of the community assessing intelligence and personality, providing various forms of treatment, particularly psychotherapy, and advising on the most efficient ways of running organizations.

As a scientist he is concerned with research into human behavior.

Puberty This term refers to the attainment of sexual maturity. In girls this is signaled by the occurrence of the first period; in boys it may be the first *nocturnal emission,* the breaking of the voice, or the appearance of pubic hair. In general girls reach puberty between one and two years earlier than boys: girls between twelve and thirteen, boys between thirteen and fourteen. Parents should bear in mind that there is enormous individual variation, and perfectly normal children may reach puberty either well before or well after the mean age. Research shows that neither early nor late arrival of puberty has any effect on later physical or sexual development. The occurrence of puberty is usually associated with the adolescent *growth spurt,* which involves a rapid increase in height and weight as well as far-reaching changes in other bodily functions. It should be noted that the bodily changes associated with puberty have marked psychological effects, and that a considerable degree of emotional adaptation is required on the part of the teenager to this physiological process. *See also* Adolescence, Growth spurt, Menarche, Menstruation.

Punishment Many studies with children have clearly demonstrated that the most effective form of punishment is the temporary withdrawal of parental love and affection. Slapping, hitting, or any form of physical violence is likely to teach your child that these are acceptable forms of human behavior, and to encourage him to be violent in return. In the long run physical punishment is not likely to do very much to prevent the activities for which the child is being punished. However, there are undoubtedly circumstances where a slap or sharp tap is appropriate, especially where the child has been deliberately provocative. In such circumstances it is right that the child knows how angry you have become. Nonetheless it is disastrous to use such punishment too often.

Quarantine The isolation of patients with infectious diseases to prevent spread of the infection. Only patients suffering from dangerous (and usually rare) infections such as smallpox are now quarantined. There is no evidence that it helps at all where simple infections such as *chicken pox* are concerned.

Quickening The developing baby begins to move very early in the pregnancy, but at first the movements are so feeble that the mother cannot feel them. A woman bearing her first baby will usually become aware of the baby "kicking" (quickening) at about the twentieth week of the pregnancy. A woman who has already had a baby, and therefore knows what to expect, will often be aware of this three or four weeks earlier.

Rabies A *virus* infection that can affect most mammals including man, and is spread by contact with infected saliva. Therefore *animal bites* are particularly dangerous. Every effort must be made to capture the animal so he can be observed under suitable conditions. Bites on the face and neck are particularly dangerous and have a rapid course.

All animal bites need medical attention. A bite from an animal that is obviously unwell, or that has undergone a recent change in character, becoming more docile and listless, or more aggressive, is particularly dangerous.

If uncontrolled, the virus causes severe brain damage, with paralysis, muscle spasms, and eventually death.

Treatment is needed very urgently, and takes the form of repeated immunizations in an attempt to build up the body's defenses during the incubation period. *See also* pages 202–3.

Rashes Many conditions in childhood, particularly the common infectious fevers, such as *measles* and *German measles,* are accompanied by a rash. Although it is possible as a generalization to describe the rash typical of, say, measles, in practice rashes do not always conform to type, and it is often difficult or impossible to make a correct diagnosis from the rash alone. If a child with a rash is otherwise unwell, or if you are unsure of the significance of the rash, it is wise to have him seen by a doctor. The rash itself rarely causes trouble. *See also* Chicken pox, Diaper rash, Eczema, Glandular fever, Scarlet fever.

Rh factor Most men and women in Europe and America are Rh positive, that is, the Rh factor in their blood is positive.

An Rh negative woman who marries an Rh positive man is likely to have Rh positive children. During the pregnancy small quantities of blood leak backward and forward across the *placenta,* and blood from the baby, leaking into the mother if she is Rh negative will cause her to form antibodies to destroy this Rh positive blood. The first baby is unlikely to be harmed as the amount of antibody produced is slight, but it will sensitize the mother to future pregnancies with Rh positive babies. Therefore in subsequent pregnancies she will be more prone to produce a greater number of antibodies, which may then pass back through the placenta and attack the baby's blood, causing him to become anemic.

After birth the rapid breakdown of the baby's blood continues and, coupled with the immaturity of the liver, causes *jaundice* to spread rapidly. To counter this, a mildly affected baby may be induced early and the *anemia* treated by a transfusion of blood of the same type as the baby's. If the jaundice is spreading very rapidly it may be necessary to exchange the baby's blood for Rh negative blood, which will not be broken down by the antibodies that the baby has received from the mother during pregnancy. It is possible to give severely affected babies a transfusion through the wall of the womb before birth.

An Rh negative mother can now be prevented from becoming sensitized to her first Rh positive baby by injecting her with antibodies that will destroy the Rh positive blood that she has received from her baby. Thus, she will not produce antibodies during this and the subsequent pregnancy.

Rickets The strength and rigidity of bone depends on the amount of calcium in it. One of the factors that help us to absorb the calcium in our principal diet, and to use it efficiently in forming bone, is vitamin D. There are two sources of this vitamin, our diet and the effect of sunlight on the skin. In temperate climates this latter source is quite inadequate for the body's needs (particularly among dark-skinned people, who gain even less benefit from the sun than pale-skinned inhabitants). Therefore almost all of the vitamin comes from food. In babies under a year old supplements in the form of vitamin drops will be needed.

Because the bones of sufferers from rickets are deficient in calcium, they are soft and easily deformed. The legs become bowed, the ends of the long bones of the limbs become splayed out and swollen. A typical "rickety rosary" may develop on the chest wall as the front ends of the ribs swell.

Treatment is to give vitamin D. It is essential to follow your doctor's instructions precisely, because too much vitamin D can cause serious, occasionally fatal, illness. The idea that if a little is good a lot must be better is a fallacy.

Rocking Many children and adults rock gently backward and forward when under stress or tension as a comfort. Persistent rocking in a stereotyped fashion, especially if the child appears to be withdrawn from his surroundings, is often a sign of depression, distress, or serious disturbance (for example, *autism* and subnormality) and professional help is needed.

Rubella *see* German measles.

Scarlet fever (scarletina) Some types of streptococcus, the germ frequently responsible for sore throats, occasionally cause *scarlet fever*; the child will come out in a generalized red scaly rash. This used to be a very serious condition: children were often very ill, and sometimes died. Nowadays, however, the germ seems to be much weaker than it was, and is in any case readily killed by penicillin, so that it is no more serious than any other sore throat.

School phobia The school phobic, like the truant, is not attending school. School phobia is usually distinguished from *truancy*, however, on the grounds that the parents of a school phobic know that he is staying away from school while the truant's parents may not. There may be numerous reasons why a child resists going to school. He may be afraid of bullies or of insensitive teachers, or may be so dependent on his mother that he cannot separate from her. A child may also be kept from school by a mother who is so emotionally insecure that she cannot bear to be on her own; many agoraphobic women keep their children out of school to do shopping or to keep them company. In these cases treatment must involve helping the mother resolve her emotional difficulties. In the majority of cases, however, the mother is keen for her child to return to school, but cannot bear to put him through the distress of forcing him to go back. If the problem is due mainly to school factors (for example, avoidance of physical education), then a discussion between the parent and principal may well solve the problem. In other cases the child may require help from a child guidance clinic, which sees a very large number of school phobic children.

Self-esteem The way in which the individual evaluates himself or herself.

To put it another way, self-esteem relates to the extent of positive or negative feeling a person has about himself: whether he thinks of himself as good, having some worth or having something to be proud of or, alternatively, whether he feels shame, guilt, or some other negative emotion when comparing himself with other people. Most individuals, of course, fall somewhere between these two extremes.

Research has shown that self-esteem in children is closely related to the self-esteem of their parents, so that if a mother thinks very little of herself, then her child may grow up with low self-esteem. Also the more interested and involved parents are in their children, the higher the children's self-esteem is likely to be. Children who have very low self-esteem are likely to be depressed, to be unrealistic about their abilities and future careers, to do badly at school, to have fewer friends, and to be less involved in social activities than their contemporaries.

Separation anxiety For the first six months a baby does not distinguish his mother/guardian from other people; when he has enough understanding to do this he will start to show signs of fear or distress when strange people approach him. Having recognized his mother as a separate and distinct person, he becomes very anxious and upset if she leaves him, albeit only for a few minutes to go into another room, and he will show more distress if she leaves him in a strange place, where he feels more insecure. With time, as his understanding increases, he learns that when she goes away she has not disappeared for ever and that she will return to him; also as he becomes more mobile and is able to follow her when she leaves the room his anxiety will diminish. All children show this anxiety when separated from their mother/guardian between nine months and two years of age, and the anxiety slowly disappears as their understanding develops and their mobility increases. *See also* Attachment.

Sex role Behavior specifically associated with masculinity and femininity as distinct from maleness and femaleness. The child's discovery of his or her sex is an important milestone in the development of the self-concept. From a very early age a child becomes aware of whether he is male or female, and learns that some activities are expected of boys, while others are more appropriate for girls. This learning (of which most of us are unaware) will determine behavior, and will be continually reinforced not only by the expectations of the adults with whom the child is in contact, but by the values of society manifested on television, in children's books, in the theater, and so on.

Sex-role conflict Sex roles are not necessarily straightforward, and there are situations in which the individual is caught between two opposing elements of his or her sex role. A primary example of this is the working mother, who may at one moment be encouraged by society to contribute her knowledge, labor, or professional expertise at work, but at the next

moment made to feel guilty because she is not truly fulfilling her maternal role in the home. Another similar example may be found in the attitude of schools toward academically bright teenage girls, who are on the one hand expected to perform as well as boys in school, but even today are not always provided with the same encouragement and support in planning for future careers.

Sex-role stereotype This is the term used to describe the essential attributes of a particular sex role. Thus, for example, advertisements that portray women happily scrubbing away in the kitchen, or men chopping wood in the forest, are portraying stereotyped sex roles. These stereotypes are widespread in our society, and extend right through childhood. Boys and girls will, from a very early age, be given different sorts of toys, thus reinforcing sex-role stereotypes. It is of interest to note, however, that it is easier and more acceptable for girls to engage in masculine activities, thus defying the stereotype, than it is for boys to do the same by taking part in feminine activities.

Shock *see* pages 202–3.

Short children In order to decide whether a child is too short for his age, several factors have to be taken into consideration. How does his height compare with that of other children of the same age? How does his height compare with that of other members of his family, or other members of the same ethnic group? Is he growing? When all these factors are considered, most such children are found to be within the short end of the normal range of development, and their parents can be reassured that they are healthy.

Children who go through *puberty* late may become temporarily shorter than their friends, but they catch up.

If when all these factors have been taken into account the child is still found to be abnormally short, then investigations to find the cause for this need to be done by a doctor. *See also* Growth hormone deficiency, Growth spurt.

Sibling rivalry Sibling rivalry refers to the jealousy that brothers and sisters may feel for one another. A child may feel particularly jealous of a brother or sister who clearly enjoys a greater amount of parental affection than he does. But even in families where parents try to treat their children equally, feelings of jealousy inevitably occur. These feelings may be particularly evident in a first-born child following the birth of a new baby, as this will involve a reduction in the attention he receives from his parents. Children aged between two and five years are more susceptible to feelings of rivalry, because at this age a child is very dependent on his parents and has few interests or friends outside the family. To a large extent a parent can reduce sibling rivalry at any age by giving the child responsibilities of his own, by ensuring that he does not lose out on parental attention, and by avoiding comparisons between the children.

Skin disorders *see* Abscess, Acne, Allergy, Athlete's foot, Birthmarks,

Boils, Cradle cap, Eczema, Impetigo, Nits, Rashes, Verruca, Warts.

Sleeping difficulties Individual children need varying amounts of sleep; some very active lively children appear to need very little sleep and provided they are alert and well during the day there is no cause for anxiety, even though this may be a strain for parents who do need their sleep. Children who wake repeatedly in the night wanting to be taken into their parents' beds are showing signs of distress and anxiety; they are frequently frightened of missing something and this is often, although not always, associated with family arguments and tension. The temptation to take the child into the parents' bed should be resisted as once the habit of sleeping with his parents is acquired it is extremely difficult to break. Rather, the parents should look for the cause of the child's anxiety, with professional help if necessary, and seek to eliminate it.

The calmer and more peaceful the hours around bedtime can be, the more likely it is that the child will sleep through the night. If the sleeping problems are acute, sleeping drugs can be prescribed for children, but this remedy is probably more beneficial for the parents in giving them a good night's sleep than for the child, who needs help with the fears and anxieties that are causing disrupted sleep patterns. *See also* Hyperactivity, Sleepwalking.

Sleepwalking Sleepwalking occurs more frequently among children than among adults. The child's eyes are open and he seems to be aware of his surroundings, but it is obvious that he is not really awake and alert, and having been returned to bed, he will probably have only a dim recollection, if any, of the event next morning. Like *nightmares*, sleepwalking is a sign of distress or anxiety and discussing a child's fears and worries with him during the day will help to alleviate his anxiety. Contrary to what has often been thought, it does no harm to the child to wake him up when he is sleepwalking, though the least distress will be caused if he is just guided gently back to bed.

Small-for-dates If during the latter half of pregnancy the *placenta* becomes inefficient (which can happen for several reasons), the baby will be malnourished and will not grow as fast as a baby with an adequate placenta. For this reason some babies are born with a low birth weight and with very little food reserves stored either in the liver or as fat. This means that when they have to cope with the stresses of independent life outside the womb, they have difficulty in maintaining an adequate level of sugar in their blood. (This is known as hypoglycemia.) They have a tendency to stop breathing for short periods (apneic attacks), and occasionally have *convulsions*. Treatment consists of giving glucose, usually by injection. *See also* Smoking (in pregnancy), Toxemia of pregnancy.

Smoking Smoking is probably the major single cause of self-inflicted injury and illness in developed countries. The two factors that determine the severity of later disease are not only the amount smoked but also the length of time the patient has been smoking, and it is this which makes heavy smoking in *adolescence,* or even childhood, particularly worrying.

There is very little that parents and teachers can do to offset the massive advertising campaigns and the influence of popular culture that encourage a child to believe that smoking is not only acceptable but desirable. There is evidence, however, that children of nonsmoking parents are less likely to smoke than children of smokers. All parents can try to influence the later health of their children and improve their own health by not smoking themselves.

Smoking (in pregnancy) In order to grow satisfactorily while in the womb, a baby must be well nourished. The only source of nourishment is the *placenta.* There is no doubt that smoking damages the placenta and makes it less efficient. Women who smoke during pregnancy have more *miscarriages,* more *stillbirths,* and more "*small-for-dates*" babies than do non-smokers. No woman who has any concern for the welfare of her unborn child should smoke when pregnant.

Soiling (encopresis) Passing stools at inappropriate times, or in inappropriate places, beyond infancy, is always a sign of emotional disturbance, and requires careful evaluation by a pediatrician or child psychiatrist.

It is easy for the unwary mother, however, to mistake a leakage of mucus, induced by hard constipated stools irritating the bowel, for encopresis. The passage of mucus will usually respond to treatment of the *constipation.*

Sore throat Most sore throats are due to *virus* infections, are short-lived, and get better of their own accord without treatment. It is important that the child has plenty to drink; warm fluids, such as hot milk and honey, often soothe the pain. Very occasionally aspirin or tylenol may be needed. *See also* Diphtheria, Glandular fever, Mumps, Scarlet fever, Swollen glands, Tonsillitis.

Spasticity *see* Cerebral palsy.

Speech defects *see* Aphasia, Autism, Lisp, Stuttering.

Spina bifida A congenital disorder in which part of the spinal cord is poorly formed and the bony spinal column and overlying skin have failed to close around it.

This disorder can occur anywhere along the spine, but is usually confined to the small of the back. Because the spinal cord is badly formed, the nerves to and from the parts of the body below the defect are deficient, so that muscles are paralyzed, and there is no sensation in the skin.

As a result, the bladder and bowels may be uncontrollable. Mobility may be affected; at worst the child may be totally dependent on a wheelchair. Apparently trivial blisters or sores may not heal.

Eight out of ten children with spina bifida develop *hydrocephaly,* which can usually be treated effectively.

These children vary in intelligence; most are within the normal range, some are of high intelligence and some are mentally retarded.

The cause of the condition is not fully known, but it must be a combination of inherited factors from both parents and an environmental factor.

Squint Each eyeball is moved by six small muscles, which are usually perfectly balanced so that the eyes move in unison. Occasionally this balance is not perfect, and the two eyes look in different directions.

Any squinting child, however young, should be seen by a doctor or an ophthalmologist (eye specialist) to assess whether or not treatment is necessary, as the squint may be due to some other eye disease.

Many children show an occasional squint, particularly when they are tired or unwell. This condition will usually correct itself without treatment. For a constant squint treatment may be necessary, and may be by operation, by exercises, or by wearing a patch over one eye to strengthen the other. If treatment is left too long the sight of one eye may become permanently impaired. *See also* Lazy eye.

Stealing Stealing is a complex form of behavior, which can range from the trivial to the very serious and which can have a multitude of causes. Almost all children steal at one time or another, and usually firm handling without excessive *punishment* will be sufficient to deal with the situation. Making the child return the stolen object, even if this has to be done anonymously, is usually a sensible way to help the child acknowledge what has happened. There are, however, children who continue to steal, and for them a closer investigation into the causes of the behavior will be essential. Few in this group steal for the economic or financial gain involved; they are more likely to be stealing for symbolic gain—that is, for love, affection, or security. Such children will almost certainly need professional help.

Sticky eye If a child's eye discharges a sticky yellow fluid, this indicates that he has *conjunctivitis,* possibly with a *blocked tear duct.* This requires treatment from a doctor.

Stillbirth A child who is born dead after the twenty-eighth week of pregnancy is said to be stillborn.

Stomachache *see* Abdominal pain.

Strawberry nevus Some babies are born with one or more raised red *birthmarks,* which may at first be so small as to be barely visible, but which grow gradually. Later they develop pale areas on the surface, and then disappear completely without scarring, usually by the time the child is about five years old. Very occasionally, if they are large and on the face, they can be removed, but even these, if left alone, will eventually disappear.

Stuttering A disorder of speech characterized by hesitancy, difficulty in finding words, and pauses filled with compulsive repetition of initial sounds and syllables—the syndrome commonly called "stammering." It is thought that developmental stuttering in young children is a disorder in language learning that coincides with a disruption in the relationship between

the mother and child. When a child is learning to talk he develops expectations about his parents' responses. If these responses are disrupted frequently, or suddenly withdrawn, he may react with frustration and confusion and show signs of obvious difficulty in social speech. Stuttering can often be helped by speech therapy.

Sty A *boil* occurring around an eyelash.

Suicide Suicide is rare in children, and infrequent among young adolescents, rising to seven per 100,000 in the age range fifteen to nineteen years. Suicide is the fifth leading cause of death in this age group, following accidents, cancer, cardiovascular disease, and murder, in that order.

About six times as many girls attempt suicide as boys, but a boy is three times more likely than a girl to be successful. Of all attempts only one in 100 is successful. There are also differences in the methods used: females favor passive measures such as drug taking and poisons; males choose a more active way such as shooting and hanging. For both sexes, however, the use of firearms has proved the most successful way to commit suicide, and poisons the least so.

There is evidence that not all suicides are reported in cases of children and adolescents, perhaps because of the social stigma and distress they cause to relatives; also that many suicides disguised as accidents may go undetected.

If a young person makes a suicide attempt, however trivial, it is essential for the individual to be offered some form of help immediately afterward. In some circumstances attempted suicides appear to be devices just for getting attention. If this is so, attention must be provided if the problem is not to escalate. An attempted suicide should always be taken seriously.

Sunburn The normal response of the skin to sunlight is to produce the black pigment melanin, so that the skin becomes suntanned.

If, however, the skin is exposed to sunlight for too long or it is too intense, and the protective pigment has not yet formed, then a burn will occur.

To prevent sunburn, the skin should, at first, be exposed only for short periods and a sun-screen lotion should be used. If reddening, itching, or peeling occurs, the skin should then be covered by loose, clean clothing. *See pages 202–3 for treatment.*

Swollen glands When any part of the body is diseased the infection tends to spread. The lymph glands, part of the body's defense system, may then become activated, swell up, and become tender. They are particularly noticeable near the surface of the body. So, for example, *tonsillitis* is often accompanied by swelling of the glands in the throat, *German measles* by swelling of those in the back of the neck, and any infected cut on the limbs by swollen glands in either the armpit or groin.

Syphilis *see* Venereal diseases.

Tall children Most tall children are found to be within the range of *normal development,* and their parents can be confident that nothing is wrong. Even exceptionally tall children are usually entirely normal, but very occasionally they have a hormonal or other abnormality, so that it is wise to obtain a medical opinion.

Teething Teething is a natural process that most doctors would say produces nothing but teeth. Although some children do become unusually irritable and produce a lot of saliva, and may develop a cough and experience some looseness of the bowels, it is probable that this is due to a coincident infection and not to the teething itself.

It is very important not to attribute to teething symptoms that are due to some other coincident illness, which may require treatment. A teething child, however, particularly when cutting back teeth may become irritable. It may then be necessary to give him a mild painkiller such as children's aspirin or tylenol.

Temperament Temperament refers to one of the earliest signs of personality differences between very young infants. As every mother knows, babies vary from the first day in how active, cuddly, or grouchy they are. Some infants rapidly develop regular patterns of sleeping and feeding, whereas others do not. Some cry and fret at minor irritations; others tolerate discomfort without complaint. Some infants are active and restless, thrashing about even while asleep, and others are quiet and passive. Direct observations of three-week-old babies have shown that babies vary enormously in how much they sleep: some slept for twenty-five percent of the observation time, others for seventy-five percent of the time. These behaviors have been measured by child psychologists and have been found to be relatively stable in the young child. These temperamental differences modify the way in which a mother responds to her child. If a child is so irritable that he will not be comforted when his mother picks him up and cuddles him, then it is likely that she will stop trying to comfort him and her contact with her baby may diminish. Several studies suggest that a child who is extreme in temperament, i.e., is very active, needs little sleep, cries and frets at the slightest provocation, tends to have a greater chance of developing *behavioral problems* in early life than a child who is less extreme in temperament.

Temper tantrums Most young children have temper tantrums, particularly in the preschool years. They are caused by frustrations or by a failure to understand the demands of a situation. They are best handled by putting the child somewhere safe, where he cannot do himself or anything else any harm, and leaving him till he calms down. As he gets older and develops more appropriate ways of dealing with his frustrations his temper tantrums will diminish. In some cases the tantrum may be so distressing to the mother that she will do almost anything to quiet him down. This can lead the child to use the temper tantrum as a means of manipulating the parent. If the temper tantrums become frequent, firm consistent handling is needed by the parents and in severe cases professional advice should be sought. *See also* Breath-holding attacks.

Tetanus Tetanus is a crippling, often fatal, disease caused by a bacterium widely distributed in soil, dust, dirt, and so on. In humans it thrives best away from the air in a puncture wound such as might be caused by a dog bite or stepping on a rusty nail. Deep in the wound the germ produces a poison (toxin) that is carried around the body by the blood and that causes a painful spasm of the muscles. This spasm is commonly first noticeable in the jaw muscles, hence the popular name "lockjaw" for this condition. In advanced cases, drugs have to be given to paralyze the muscles completely, and the patient is put on an artificial respirator, in the hope of eventual recovery.

Immunization is harmless, and gives excellent protection. If a child (or adult) receives a wound likely to be infected, he should be taken to a doctor so that the wound can be thoroughly cleaned, and he can receive a booster immunization if necessary.

Thin children Most children thought by their parents to be too thin are in fact perfectly healthy and normally proportioned. A few, however, are found to have weights well outside the range that would be expected of someone of their age and height, and these children need further medical investigation to clarify the cause of their *failure to thrive.*

Thrush (monilia) This is an infection either of the skin or of the lining of the mouth and throat caused by a mold (fungus) called monilia (or candida). It is particularly likely to occur in babies with a severe *diaper rash,* which may then become very red and weeping, or else in the mouth, where it shows itself as white patches on the tongue, the roof of the mouth, and the inside of the cheeks.

Treatment, which should be under medical supervision, is by a special type of anti-fungal medicine.

Thumb-sucking Thumb-sucking occurs so commonly—about forty percent of children between two and seven years suck their thumbs habitually—that if there are no other symptoms of anxiety parents need not be concerned.

Thumb-sucking develops as a substitute for nipple or bottle sucking; it seems to reduce hunger contractions, and it is a natural result of the sheer frequency of contact between an infant's fingers and his mouth. Most fears about the effects of thumb-sucking are old wives' tales. One possible exception is that excessive thumb-sucking may produce malformation of the teeth; advice from the dentist should reassure parents about this.

Parents may object to thumb-sucking so much that they try to stop it by nagging, teasing, or the application of a bitter-tasting substance to the thumbs. It is not important enough to resort to these drastic methods, especially as they are often applied at the cost of good parent–child relationships. Rather than punishing

the habit, diversion is more likely to be effective: a child given an errand or a task to do that occupies his hands in a pleasant and interesting way will forget about sucking his thumb.

Chronic thumb-sucking—where it is virtually perpetual and preferred to other activities—may well be a warning signal of underlying anxiety or frustration, and in such cases parents should try to find the basis of the disturbance, possibly with professional help, rather than attack merely the symptom itself.

Toilet training All societies demand that their children learn to control their bladder and bowel functions. In Western societies, bowel control usually occurs sometime during the second year. Bladder control is usually established between the ages of two and three, but there is considerable variation to this. Children generally learn to be dry during the day before they can retain bladder control at night. At two and a half about sixty percent of children are dry during the day; about fifty-seven percent are dry at night; and forty-one percent are dry both day and night. But by the age of seven one child in five still wets the bed occasionally and at age ten about one in fourteen does so. Frequent lapses may occur before the child is satisfactorily toilet trained. Some mothers believe that it is better to initiate toilet training when the child is very young. Generally this makes the task a great deal more difficult for both mother and child. One study showed that if a mother begins toilet training before the child is five months old nearly ten months are required for success, but if the mother begins when the child is twenty months old, only five months are required.

Encopresis and enuresis are the terms used to refer to a failure to develop bowel and bladder control. Encopresis (involuntary defecation) is much less common than enuresis; about one child in sixty-five still soils himself by the age of seven to eight. It is more common in boys than in girls and may develop after a period of bowel control; in some cases it is associated with prolonged *constipation.* Clearly both enuresis and encopresis are particularly obvious and distressing conditions that may lead to the child developing other emotional difficulties if they are not treated. *See also* Bed-wetting, Psychoanalysis, Soiling.

Tongue-tie The fold that joins the tongue to the floor of the mouth commonly extends to the tip of the tongue in a young baby. Usually, as the tongue grows the fold moves back from the tip. Even if this is delayed it rarely, if ever, interferes with speech or feeding, and will almost always right itself without an operation.

Tonsillectomy is the name given to the operation of removing the tonsils. Since the tonsils are performing a useful protective function, the decision to remove them is not an easy one. If, however, the child is getting so many attacks of tonsillitis that he is, for example, losing a considerable amount of schooling, then the tonsils have obviously ceased to function efficiently, and should probably be removed. If your doctor thinks your

child may need this operation, he will refer him to an ear, nose, and throat (ENT) specialist for consultation.

Tonsillitis The tonsils are two small spongy masses that lie on either side at the back of the throat. They act as traps for germs entering the throat, and so perform a very useful function. Their size varies, and tends to decrease with age. They may be so small as to be barely noticeable, or they may fill the whole of the back of the throat. Even if they appear to meet in the midline, they very rarely interfere with speech, breathing, or feeding. They usually perform their function of trapping germs without upset to the child. Occasionally, however, they become inflamed—the condition known as tonsillitis. The child becomes unwell with a high *fever,* and may have a cough. The tonsils become red and enlarged, and the glands in the neck just below the angle of the jaw, which drain the infection from the tonsils, become swollen and tender.

Tonsillitis can result from an infection with *viruses* or *bacteria* such as the streptococcus. Only the latter type of infection will respond to antibiotics and, before prescribing treatment, your doctor may want to take a specimen from the surface of the tonsils with a cotton swab.

All children with tonsillitis should be kept cool, and given plenty of fluids. It is much more important that they drink plenty than that they eat during the few days of the illness. Aspirin or tylenol may help to relieve the sore throat.

Toxemia of pregnancy (pre-eclamptic toxemia, PET) During the course of pregnancy, some women have a tendency to accumulate water in excess of their needs. This shows itself as swelling of the ankles, and often of the hands and face (edema). Blood pressure may rise, and the kidneys may become less efficient at retaining the protein from the blood that flows through them. The precise cause of this condition is not known, but there is a tendency for it to run in families.

It is very important that this condition is treated promptly, because if unchecked it can cause parts of the *placenta* to die, and therefore it interferes with the nourishment of the unborn child. If quite uncontrolled, the woman may have *convulsions.* Thus it is important to have regular prenatal checkups so that any sign of toxemia will be spotted and treated immediately.

Treatment, which must always be supervised by a doctor, consists of rest, assisted if necessary by sedatives, and changes in diet aimed at reducing the intake of salt.

Transitional object Many toddlers become very attached to one particular object such as a soft toy or a piece of cloth that they carry about with them, and that is an essential part of the tucking in ritual at night. This may be seen as a transition from total dependence on their mother to dependence on an external object. It is a normal and desirable step in the emotional development of the child, and he should not be discouraged from continuing this practice until he drops it of his own accord.

Travel sickness Some children find that traveling in cars, buses, planes, etc., makes them feel sick, or sometimes even causes them to vomit. You can reduce the likelihood of this happening by ensuring that there is good ventilation, and that the adults in the vehicle do not smoke. The child should be kept occupied with car games and puzzles, though reading will often increase the symptoms. Avoid large, rich meals before traveling and keep chocolate, sweet drinks, and so on to a minimum during a journey. Sucking glucose candy is sometimes helpful. If you spot the signs early enough, stop the car and get the child out into the air.

If these simple measures are not effective, then your doctor may prescribe some tablets to be taken before the start of the trip.

Truancy Consistent or regular non-attendance at school, normally without the parents being aware of the situation. It is rapidly becoming a chronic problem in some areas, especially in deprived inner cities. It seems likely to be caused by a whole variety of factors, but undoubtedly the most powerful will be the lack of meaning that school has, particularly for disaffected working-class teenagers. Other factors that play their part are large, overcrowded classes and the attitudes toward school of both parents and peers. In the past persistent truants have been referred to child guidance clinics, but the success rate with this type of problem has tended to be low. Today, however, many cities are setting up alternative types of schooling, where there is a less formal structure and closer interaction between adults and young people. While it is still too early to evaluate the success of such schemes, they do seem to meet some of the needs of children who play truant from conventional schools.

Twins Throughout a woman's reproductive life, an egg is released from her ovaries each month (unless this has been suppressed by a contraceptive pill). It travels down the Fallopian tube to the womb, where, if it has been fertilized by a sperm, it will attach itself and pregnancy will start; otherwise it will be discarded from the womb with the next period.

Each fertilized egg is a single cell, which starts dividing rapidly to form a mass of cells, and eventually grows into a recognizable baby. Sometimes at the very beginning of this dividing process the egg splits into two separate pieces and each develops into a baby, giving rise to *identical* twins. Because they have both grown from the same egg, fertilized by the same sperm, they have identical inherited characteristics and, as well as being the same sex, they will be physically very similar.

If the egg does not divide completely, the twins may develop joined at the point at which the egg failed to separate, producing so-called Siamese, or conjoined, twins.

Sometimes, two eggs are released in a single month, and if both are fertilized then nonidentical (or *fraternal*) twins develop. Since they grow from different eggs they will be no more alike than any other brothers or sisters, and may not even be of the same sex. The tendency to release more than one egg at ovulation runs in families, and so, therefore, do twins.

Occasionally more than two babies can develop in the same pregnancy if the egg divides into more than two pieces, or more than two eggs are released and fertilized simultaneously. This latter is particularly likely to happen if the woman is taking drugs to increase fertility, as it can be difficult to judge the precise dose of the drug that each individual needs to stimulate her ovaries into producing just one egg. However, as medical skill in this area is increasing this type of multiple birth is declining.

Types of delivery *see* Breech, Caesarean section, Vertex delivery.

Undescended testicles The testicles begin their life inside the abdomen, and then pass down into the scrotum (the sacs on either side of the penis) through holes in the belly wall just above each groin. These holes remain open during early childhood, and the testicles pass to and fro between the scrotum and the abdomen.

Occasionally, one or both testicles remain in the abdomen and never pass through the hole into the scrotum, or else get stuck at the opening. This may right itself in time, but if it does not it may be necessary to bring the testicles down into the scrotum by an operation (orchidopexy).

If you believe that your son's testicles have not descended, then you should consult your doctor, however young the child is. Although no treatment will be required until the child is probably six or seven years old, the doctor will want to keep an eye on the situation.

Upper respiratory tract infection
Although the respiratory tract is one continuous passage from the nose and mouth to the depth of the lungs, infections in children, particularly those caused by *viruses,* are often restricted to the upper part of the tract above the voice box (larynx). The child will complain of a sore throat, will have a blocked or runny nose, and may have a mild *otitis media. Fever* is usually slight, and the child is not usually particularly unwell although he may go off his food for a few days. The cough is caused by nasal secretions running down the back of the throat, and is often worse at night. Since these infections are usually caused by viruses, antibiotics are not helpful. Decongestants may relieve the night cough and it sometimes helps to prop the head of the bed up higher than the foot. The illness usually gets better of its own accord in a few days. *See also* Bronchitis, Polio.

Urinary infection A child with a urinary infection will usually complain of burning pain on passing urine, and will have to pass urine frequently and urgently. There may be an ache in the loin, the child is usually feverish, and the urine sometimes smells fishy. Although the symptoms are often characteristic, the diagnosis can only be made accurately by examining a fresh clean specimen of urine, and growing the germs from it.

It is a relatively common condition in girls because the tube that leads from the bladder to the exterior of the body (the urethra) is short and

straight, offering very little hindrance to the passage of germs, and it opens into a moist, warm, potentially infected space near the vagina and anus.

In boys this condition is uncommon because the urethra is long and curved, and opens at the tip of the penis, well away from the anus. If it occurs, your doctor will want to look for a possible abnormality in the kidney, the tube from the kidney to the bladder (the ureter), the bladder itself, or the urethra, because these are often the cause of the infection. He may refer your child to a specialist.

Treatment, with the appropriate antibiotic, must be under medical supervision, and it is essential that the full course of treatment is given, even if the child seems to have recovered halfway through, otherwise a relapse is likely.

Venereal diseases These are caused in the main by germs that, to pass from one individual to another, require close, moist contact and are therefore almost always contracted during sexual intercourse.

One of the more alarming results of the current tolerance of sexual promiscuity is a world-wide epidemic of gonorrhea (about one in five of the new cases occurring in teenagers) and to a lesser extent of syphilis.

Although treatment with antibiotics is available, and usually successful, these young patients often delay seeking medical help until irreparable damage has been done to their health.

Much can be done to remedy this situation by ensuring that adolescents understand the cause of VD, the significance of such symptoms as discharge from the vagina or penis, pain on passing urine, *rashes* or sores in the genital area, and know that they can seek help without disrupting their family relationships. *See also* Urinary infection.

Verruca A verruca is a *wart* most often occurring on the sole of the foot. Because of its position, it tends to be pushed into the sole, and is often painful. This type of wart usually requires treatment under medical supervision.

Verrucae are very infectious, so that anyone who has one should not walk barefoot (particularly in swimming areas) or wear other people's footwear.

Vertex delivery Most babies are born with the head bent forward and the chin on the chest, so that the crown of the head (the vertex) is the first part to appear. This is known as a vertex delivery.

Virus A very simple living organism that can only survive by entering the cells of another creature and taking over the resources of those cells. The damage done to the cells in the process shows itself as the symptoms and signs of virus diseases. Viral conditions are not susceptible to antibiotics.

Vision testing The ability to see is one of the most important means by which a child learns about his environment. It is therefore essential that his vision be as good as possible, and that any deficiencies that the child may have are corrected if possible and compensated for if not. Regular eye checkups are most important, and

should take into account not only how small an object the child can see (visual acuity) but also what use he makes of his vision and whether it is adequate for his stage of development. Vision that is adequate for the child whose experience is mainly with large toys at arm's length may not be adequate for the child trying to read.

Ideally, vision testing should be done at the same time as an assessment of the child's general development, so that the appropriate test of acuity (small candies, graded sizes of white balls, shape matching, letter naming, etc.) can be used. *See also* Cataract, Color blindness, Lazy eye, Partial sight, Squint.

Vomiting There are many reasons why children vomit. The cause may be any infection (whether of the gut or not), or such acute conditions in the abdomen as *appendicitis.* Vomiting can also occur without any physical abnormality, particularly in the "high-strung" child prone to *"growing pains," "stomachache,"* and other physical symptoms of anxiety and emotional stress.

In a young baby, vomiting is always to be taken seriously, and requires medical attention, because a baby very rapidly becomes dehydrated.

In the older child, the degree of urgency depends not only on the frequency and volume of the vomiting but also on the accompanying symptoms. A listless, ill child with *abdominal pain* who is vomiting obviously requires more urgent attention than the child who is a bit sickly on gym day at school.

To treat vomiting, drink clear glucose fluids, and avoid solid food and opaque milky drinks. If, with these measures, the vomiting is not coming under control within twenty-four hours then medical help should be sought.

Walking There is a wide variation in the age at which normal children walk without support. On average they pull themselves to standing, holding on to the furniture, at about eleven to twelve months, and walk freely at about thirteen to fourteen months. Some, however, walk at nine months, and others not until eighteen months. *Bottom shufflers* tend to walk two to three months later than crawlers.

A child who is not walking by eighteen months may, nevertheless, be perfectly normal, but it is worth having this checked by a doctor to make sure that there is no medical reason for it.

Warts A wart is a localized *virus* infection of the skin, which results in a round horny lump. All warts eventually go of their own accord, but cure may be hastened by various treatments. The simplest is to paint the wart with salicylic acid (a chemical similar to aspirin) in collodion, which is often effective after two to three months' treatment.

Warts are infectious, and often occur in crops that may require more radical treatment under medical supervision. *See also* Verruca.

Whooping cough (pertussis) This is an infectious disease, caused by *bacteria,* with an incubation period of one to two weeks.

The illness starts with a catarrhal phase, which is indistinguishable from

a simple *upper respiratory tract infection,* and which usually lasts for about two weeks. It is followed by the characteristic whooping phase. The child has paroxysms of coughing, during which he becomes very distressed, turning red or even blue in the face, and may vomit. He fights for breath, and produces a loud whooping on drawing in breath. The number of paroxysms per day may vary from two to three to an almost continuous series. This phase usually lasts two to three weeks, but may be prolonged. The child then recovers over a further two to three weeks.

This disease is always distressing, and in young children can be very serious. *Immunization* gives good protection, but has occasional serious side effects. The incidence of whooping cough is rising as the proportion of children immunized falls.

Worms The commonest type of worm found in children in temperate climates is the pinworm. This lives in the bowel, but crawls out of the anus at night to lay its eggs on the skin around the anus. This process is extremely irritating and often disturbs the child's sleep, causing him to scratch the area, thus getting the eggs on his fingers. From there they are transferred to his own or someone else's mouth, thereby starting the infective cycle all over again.

In order to eradicate a pinworm infection it is necessary to treat all close contacts, that is, family, friends, and domestic pets. Treatment is by medicine prescribed by a doctor.

Other rarer types of worm may be found in children, and are seen in the stool. These need expert identification and treatment, so that the child should be seen by a doctor.

Different aspects of the many subjects included in this A–Z are discussed in detail in chapters 1 to 7. The information can be located by referring to the index or to the detailed contents listing on pages 4–7.

INDEX

References to the A–Z of child development and the ailments, diseases, and problems of pregnant mothers and children from conception to adolescence, which appears on pages 204–20, are to the appropriate heading within the A–Z and not by page number.

ACKNOWLEDGMENTS

General Acknowledgments
A great many individuals, organizations, and institutions have given
invaluable help and advice during the preparation of this book.
The publishers wish to extend their thanks to them all, and in
particular to the following: Eric Albany, Organizer of the Nuffield
Mathematics (five to eleven years) project; E. E. M. Angell,
Assistant Principal Careers Officer, ILEA, London; Professor
A. E. Bender, Professor of Nutrition, Queen Elizabeth College,
London; Boots the Chemists, London; Bourne and
Hollingsworth Ltd, London; Dr. M. G. Brush; Dr. Fergus
Campbell; Joan E. Clarke; Dr. Graham Curtiss Jenkins; Sylvia
Dadd, Head Teacher, Nelson Infants School, Newham; Dr.
Katherina Dalton; Department of Education and Science;
Department of Health and Social Security; P. Douglass, Head
Teacher, Martin Infants School, London; Eileen Elias; ESA
Creative Learning; David P. Evans, American Embassy, London;
The Family Planning Association, London; The Flour Advisory
Bureau, London; James Galt and Co. Ltd, London; R. V.
George, Rank Audio Visual; Jennifer Gower, Speech Therapist,
West Middlesex Hospital, Isleworth; Althea Graham-Cameron,
Dinosaur Publications, Cambridge; Brian Haynes; J. Heath, Head
Teacher, Staples Road Infants School, Loughton; Julie Hoyle;
Independent Schools Information Service, London; The
Institute for the Study of Drug Dependence, London; Laffeaty's
Ltd, London; A. A. Lines, Director of Public Affairs, The
Kellogg Company of Great Britain Ltd, Manchester; Clifford
Longley; Rosemary Macy; Gordon Marlow, Principal of the
Middle School, American School, London; Sally Marlow,
American School, London; The Marriage Guidance Council,
London; Dr. Mildred Marshak; Professor Geoffrey Matthews;
John May; Dr. W. S. Mitchell; Winifred Moore, Head Teacher,
Hollingwood First School, Bradford; Elizabeth Morse, Research
Officer, British Nutrition Foundation, London; Elaine Moss,
Mothercare Ltd, London; Pamela Munford, Department of
Nutrition, Queen Elizabeth College, London; The National
Adoption Society, London; The National Childbirth Trust,
London; The National Children's Bureau, London; Elizabeth
Parsons; Ruth Petrie; Phillips and Tacey Ltd, Andover; Dr.
Deborah Rosenblatt; B. H. M. Rothwell; The Royal Society for
the Prevention of Accidents, Birmingham; Antoinette Satow, The
Family Planning Association; Dr. Marten Shipman; Dr. F. A.
Sneath; D. M. Spong, Deputy Head Teacher, Balfour County
Primary Infants School, Rochester; M. W. Spong, Head Teacher,
Borstal Manor County Primary Junior School, Rochester; Margot
Srebering, The American School, London; Staines Group,
London; R. Taylor, Head Teacher, Fairstead House Nursery
School, Newmarket; Tiger, Tiger, London; Linea Timson; Dr.
Nicholas Tucker; Beatrice Tudor-Hart, Head Teacher, Fortis
Green Nursery School, London; The Staff of the Westminster
Libraries; Dr. Margaret Wood, City University, London.

Additional editorial assistance:
Ruth Binney; Mellita Brownrigg; Marsha Lloyd; Christine
McLaughlin.

Additional design assistance:
Alison Blythe; Cathy Caufield; Pauline Faulks; Francis Morgan;
Mike Rose.

Picture research:
Sue Pinkus.

Artists:
Olivia Beasley; Marilyn Bruce; Patricia Casey; Chris Forsey;
Charles Picard; Mike Saunders; Alan Suttie.

Indexer:
Michael Gordon.

Photographers:
All photographs, except for those indicated below, are by Anthea
Sieveking. Additional material: Graham Bishop pp.46, 47; Martin
Bronkhorst p.122 center right; Mike Busselle p.85
bottom left, bottom right; Claude Edelmann (from *The First Days
of Life*, ed. France-Impressions, Paris) pp.18, 19; Christopher
Macy p.95 bottom left; PAF p.181; Frances Pinkus p.159; Kim
Sayer pp.69 top, 86–87; Dr. Landrum B. Shettles p.12.

Children's illustrations:
Brookfield School, London p.194; Luisa Jane Elliott p.128 bottom
right; Patrick Fraher p.128 center top; Philip Goodliffe p.145
bottom; Steven Niall Graham p.128 top right; Wiebke Grimm
p.128 bottom left; Andrew David Howels p.128 top left; Alexander
Macy p.116 top left; Amaryllis Macy p.116 center top; "Mariella,"
Martin Infants School, London p.117 top, second from left;
Natalie Needham p.128 center right; Elizabeth Norris p.117 top,
second from right, p.117 lower right; Casey-Joe Parsons p.116 top
right; Thad Parsons p.117 top right, p.117 bottom; Karl Reed
p.117 top left; Sarah Thurnell p.116 bottom right.

Sources of reference:
The publishers are grateful for kind permission to use material
from the following sources: p.30 graph based on data from
Community Health Services Statistics (Department of Health and
Social Security: 1976); p.54 graph (lower right) based on research
from Goldberg and Lewis, *Child : Care, Health and Development*
(Blackwell Scientific Publications Ltd: Oxford 1969); p.98 graph
based on data reproduced from *Which?* magazine by permission of
the publishers, Consumers' Association; p. 114 graph based on
research by Brindley, Clarke, Hutt and Robinson, reproduced
with permission from P. R. Michael and J. H. Crook (eds.),
Comparative Behaviour and Ecology in Primates (Copyright by
Academic Press Inc. (London) Ltd: 1973); p.135 graph from E.
Edward, *Information Transmission* (Chapman and Hall: London
1964); p.135 diagrams based on research by R. Sears, reproduced
with permission from F. A. Beach (ed.), *Sex and Behavior*
(Wiley & Sons Inc.: New York 1965); p.138 graphs based on
originals from G. Orent-Heiles and L. Hallman, *The Breakfast
Meal in Relation to Blood Sugar Values* (The United States
Department of Agriculture: Washington 1949); p.143 graphs
(upper and center left) based on information from the draft report
of the Schools Council project, Primary Mathematics Evaluation
Studies. The report will be published for the Council in 1979 by
Evans/Methuen Educational; p. 146 diagram (far left) based on
information from Philippe Muller, *The Tasks of Childhood*
(George Weidenfeld and Nicolson: London 1969); p.146 diagram

(lower right) based on research from P. E. Vernon, *Intelligence and
Cultural Environment* (Methuen: London 1969); p.147 graph
(upper right) based on research by Morma Kent and D. Russell
Davis (British Journal of Medical Psychology: 1957); p.147 graph
(center left) based on research from A. I. Gates, *Interest and
Ability in Reading* (Macmillan: New York 1930) © A. I. Gates
1930; p.147 graph (lower left) based on statistics from B. S.
Bloom, *Stability and Change in Human Characteristics* (Wiley and
Sons: Sussex 1964); p.147 graph (lower right) from G. G.
Thompson, *Child Development* (Houghton Mifflin: Boston 1952);
based on research by the Berkeley Growth Study; p.161 graph
based on original in H. L. Barnett and A. H. Einhorn (eds),
Pediatrics, 15th Edn. (Appleton-Century-Croft Division of
Prentice-Hall Inc: New York 1972); p.163 graph from original by
K. Dalton, *Schoolgirls' Behaviour and Menstruation* (British
Medical Journal: 1960); p.163 diagram based on original from K.
Dalton, *The Pre-Menstrual Syndrome and Progesterone Therapy*
(Heinemann Medical Books Ltd: London 1977); p.167 diagram
based on statistics from *The Sentence of the Court* (HMSO: 1964);
p.168 graph based on original from M. Powell, *Age and Sex
Differences in Degree of Conflict within Certain Areas of
Psychological Adjustment* (Psychological Monographs: 1955)
copyright © 1955 by The American Psychological Association.
Reprinted by permission; p.175 graph based on original from
W. P. Coloquoun and D. W. T. Corcoran, *The Effects of Time of
Day and Social Isolation on the Relationship between Temperament
and Performance* (British Journal of Social Clinical Psychology:
1964); p.175 graph based on original from Henry Maddox, *How to
Study* (Pan Books: London 1963); p.178 chart (center right) based
on research from Dr. D. Demos, *Psychological Determinants of
Career Choice for College Honors Students* (Gifted Child
Quarterly; 1965) reproduced with permission from The National
Association for Creative Children and Adults; p.178 chart (top
right) based on research from R. B. Cattell, T. Meeland, M. Day,
*Occupational Profiles of the Sixteen Personality Factor
Questionnaire* (Journal of Occupational Psychology: 1956); p.187
graph by Cole, from C. I. Sandstrom, *Psychology of Childhood and
Adolescence* (Pelican: London 1969) based on material by the
Gluecks, p.190 graph based on data from A. Scheinfeld, *Your
Heredity and Environment* (Lippincott: New York 1965 and Chatto
and Windus: London 1966); p.190 graph based on statistics from
United States Department of Health, Education, and Welfare
Public Service, *Vital Statistics of United States 1965 : Volume One
Natality* (US Government: 1967); p. 190 graph based on statistics
reprinted with permission of Macmillan Publishing Co. Inc. from
Genetics, copyright © 1968, 1976 by Monroe W. Strickberger;
p.194 graph based on research from R. B. Zajonc, *Science* (vol.192,
pp.227–36, 16 April 1976) copyright 1976 by the American
Association for the Advancement of Science; p. 196 diagram based
on statistics from R. and R. Rapoport and Z. Strelitz, *Fathers,
Mothers and Others* (Routledge and Kegan Paul: London 1977 and
Basic Books: New York 1977); p.197 diagram based on statistics
from *One-Parent Families* (HMSO: 1974).

Mitchell Beazley Publishers has made every effort to trace original
sources of all research cited in this book. Any source inadvertently
omitted and subsequently brought to the publishers' attention will
be acknowledged in all future editions of this book.